Gov. Buckingham pg. 95

Advertiser

D1545726

Hartford Courant
Hartford Evening Press
Bridgeport Republican
Sam Fiske / Dunn Brown

Connecticut

in the American Civil War

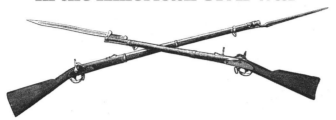

A

DRIFTLESS CONNECTICUT SERIES

BOOK

This book is a 2011 selection in the Driftless Connecticut Series, for an outstanding book in any field on a Connecticut topic or written by a Connecticut author.

Connecticut

in the American Civil War

Slavery, Sacrifice, and Survival

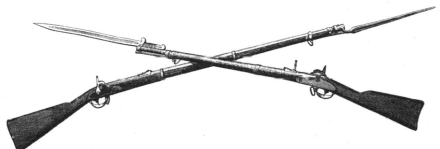

MATTHEW WARSHAUER

WESLEYAN UNIVERSITY PRESS *Middletown, Connecticut*

The Driftless Connecticut Series is funded by the
Beatrice Fox Auerbach Foundation Fund
at the Hartford Foundation for Public Giving.

Wesleyan University Press
Middletown CT 06459
www.wesleyan.edu/wespress
© 2011 Matthew Warshauer
All rights reserved
Manufactured in the United States of America

Wesleyan University Press is a member of the
Green Press Initiative. The paper used in this book
meets their minimum requirement for
recycled paper.

Library of Congress Cataloging-in-Publication Data
Warshauer, Matthew, 1965–
Connecticut in the American Civil War: slavery, sacrifice,
and survival / Matthew Warshauer. — 1st ed.
p.   cm. — (Garnet books)
Includes bibliographical references and index.
ISBN 978-0-8195-7138-0 (cloth : alk. paper)
1. Connecticut — History — Civil War, 1861–1865.
2. United States — History — Civil War, 1861–1865. I. Title.
E499.W37 2011
974.6'03 — dc22   2010040978

5 4 3 2 1

TO THE "CREW"

Jim Brown, Gregg Cerosky,

Kristin Duke, Jessica Jenkins,

Mark Shafer, and Mike Sturges

Contents

Acknowledgments / ix

Introduction / 1

CHAPTER ONE

Connecticut within the Nation, 1776–1860:

Slavery, Race, and Politics / 9

CHAPTER TWO

And the War Came, 1860–61 / 41

CHAPTER THREE

A Recognition of Death, 1862 / 71

CHAPTER FOUR

The Union Crucible, 1863 / 101

CHAPTER FIVE

Expensive Victory, 1864–65 / 139

CHAPTER SIX

Survival's Memory, 1865–1965 / 174

Epilogue / 219

Notes / 225

Further Reading and Research / 293

Index / 297

Acknowledgments

It is with true appreciation that I dedicate this book to the "Crew," a title used by the *Hartford Courant* in one of its articles about the wider Civil War project. Jim Brown, Gregg Cerosky, Kristin Duke, Jessica Jenkins, and Mike Sturges are graduate students at Central Connecticut State University; Mark Shafer is a graduate student at Trinity College. They spent countless hours researching nineteenth-century newspapers, soldiers' stories, regimental histories, and various other archival resources to help prepare this book for publication. They also read and commented on the manuscript, and offered important insights and suggestions for improvement. Each of them is a first-rate historian.

I am also indebted to a number of other people who read the manuscript. Sally Whipple, the education coordinator at Connecticut's Old State House and president of the Connecticut League of History Organizations, has been a steadfast friend and made wonderful suggestions that improved the book. Kathy Maher, executive director of the Barnum Museum, has only become a friend in the past year, but I feel as though I've known her forever. Sally and Kathy are DB I and DB II. Dean Nelson, the administrator of the Museum of Connecticut History, has been a remarkable resource on everything related to Connecticut and the Civil War. His constant refrain of "anything that is not the Civil War is an annoying distraction" has served me well. Dick Judd, president emeritus of Central Connecticut State University (CCSU), has been amazingly supportive of my work, read the entire manuscript, and is a real expert on the battle of Antietam. John Tully, my colleague in the History Department at CCSU, not only read the manuscript in a variety of incarnations but also listened to me pontificate on varying topics related to Connecticut and the Civil War. He's a true friend, and very patient. Eileen Hurst, the associate director of the university's Center for Social Research and Public Policy, also read the manuscript and always keeps me grounded at work. In a way, she's my therapist. Steve McGrath, another CCSU colleague, offered valuable insights. Special thanks also go to Peter Hinks. Peter is an excellent historian and pushed me to better understand the contributions of black abolitionists in Connecticut. Robert Pierce Forbes, an assistant professor at the University of Connecticut, Torrington, helped in this regard as well.

I am also hugely indebted to my friend Bill Hoelzel, who, though not a professional historian or teacher, asked incredible questions and offered wonderful feedback from the perspective of a really smart guy who came to the subject of the Civil War with a little background information and a variety of assumptions about what it all means. He pushed me to think this through and did some fantastic editing to boot. He and his children, Tanner and Merrill, have become a part of my family.

I also owe thanks to Leslie Gordon, a professor of history at the University of Akron, for helping me with material on the 16th Connecticut Regiment; Julie Frey, the curator of collections at the Litchfield Historical Society, for help on Josiah Beckwith and medical exemption certificates; and Paulette Kaufman, of the Madison Historical Society, for information on Sam Fiske.

Finally, my thanks would not be complete without acknowledging a debt that can never be repaid to my wife, Wanda. Not only is she the nicest person I know, but she actually, finally, and completely, read one of my books. Remarkable! Thanks also for providing me with three great kids: Emma, Samantha, and Jessica.

Connecticut

in the American Civil War

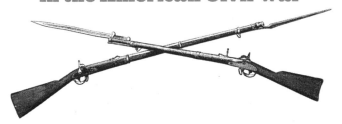

Introduction

On July 29, 1860, Milo A. Holcomb of Granby, Connecticut, wrote to Republican presidential nominee Abraham Lincoln: "I am not hostile to your election though You are represented to be an abolitionest and in sentiment I am a pro Slavery man. I would if I could have my way, authorize Slavery in New England and the importation of African servants." Holcomb went on to discuss Lincoln's famous House Divided Speech, in which he had stated that the nation could not continue half slave and half free. Clearly tired of the battle over slavery, Holcomb wrote: "The agitating question of slavery as it Exists in these U. S. has distracted the counsels of this nation long enough, you are reported to have said that the country could not remain a united people one half Bound the other free, that all must be alike and I agree with your reported sentiment." Holcomb's conclusion about the future of slavery, however, was not in accord with Lincoln's. For Holcomb, slavery was the future. Yet he was not opposed to allowing Lincoln to give abolition a shot: "I am willing You should try the experiment. I do not believe you can effect emancipation. If you can I have no obj[ection]. I only want all sections to be alike. I want the Experiment tried abolish Slavery if you can. If you find you cannot as I am sure you will do, then let us have the other as it will then be the last expedient."[1]

Holcomb's letter presents a problem for Connecticut. The state's residents after all, were the "good guys" in the Civil War. Along with the rest of the North, Connecticut staunchly opposed slavery and rallied to not only halt the westward spread of the "peculiar institution," but to defeat the Southern rebellion that had shaken the Union to its core. When considering Connecticut's connection to slavery and the Civil War, many immediately think of the *Amistad* case, the state heroine Prudence Crandall, the underground railroad, John Brown, and Harriet Beecher Stowe. These are certainly important and well-known events and people who, by today's standards, reveal the best in enlightened, antislavery thought. We conclude, therefore, that Connecticut was always generously disposed toward abolition, with its yearning for black freedom and civic equality. The result of such forward-looking racial attitudes resulted in the state's massive commitment to crushing the Southern rebellion.

The reality, however, is far from the constructed memory that flowed forth in the many years and decades after the Civil War. The simple truth is that in the "land of steady habits," one of the steadiest was a virulent racism. While New England was generally viewed as the national center of abolitionist thought, Connecticut stood apart. The famed abolitionist William Lloyd Garrison—outraged by attacks on Prudence Crandall's school for black girls and the decision by the town of Canterbury and the state to close the school—derisively referred to Connecticut as the "Georgia of New England."[2] More than one historian has noted that of the New England states, Connecticut was "the most inhospitable" to abolition.[3] It is not that abolition failed to have a foothold in Connecticut. Rather, support for abolition was not nearly as widespread as many today believe. Moreover, whatever the number of abolitionists, there were many more in the state who actively opposed the end of slavery and black equality. There existed within Connecticut a serious and formidable antagonism toward abolition and blacks. These attitudes can be seen throughout the antebellum period and well into the Civil War.

In 1833, the *Norwich Courier* announced that abolition was "an insane project—one which no man in full possession and exercise of his faculties can contemplate as being practicable, or at the present desirable."[4] In the same year, Prudence Crandall attempted to educate black girls, and if we remember her as a hero, we must also remember that she was heroic in the face of her own neighbors, who threatened her, vandalized the school by breaking windows and dumping manure down its well, and ultimately forced Crandall to flee the state. The state General Assembly sided with those opposed to a black school by passing legislation making it illegal to import blacks from outside the state, announcing: "We are under no obligation, moral or political, to incur the incalculable evils, of bringing into *our own State* colored emigrants from abroad."[5] One of Crandall's leading critics was Andrew Judson, a Democratic selectman in Canterbury who insisted: "Colored people never can rise from their menial condition in our country; they ought not to be permitted to rise here. They are an inferior race of beings, and never can or ought to be recognized as the equal of whites. Africa is the place for them. I am in favor of the Colonization scheme," in which free blacks were shipped back to their homeland.[6] The idea that free blacks should be shipped back to Africa, no matter how long they or their ancestors had been in America, was a popular solution to the race "problem."

One of the key aspects of freedom in America in general, and Connecticut in particular, was freedom without blacks. Colonization represented this idea, as did the desire to avoid the spread of blacks into the

West. Even as abolitionist and anti-Southern sentiments became more widespread during the 1840s and 1850s, expressed most visibly by opposition to slavery's westward movement, Connecticut's concern was far more motivated by "Free Soil" beliefs that free whites should inhabit these coveted lands than by a concern about the plight of slaves. As the Republican Party developed within the state and battled Democrats on the matter of slavery in the western territories, it clung to its notions of white supremacy, insisting that the lynchpin of "free" soil was that the land be untainted by slaves or even free blacks, who would compete with whites. The New Haven *Journal & Inquirer* announced of the new Republican Party: "It is not a negro party, but a *white man's party* — a FREE LABOR PARTY." Connecticut's Gideon Welles, who later became Abraham Lincoln's secretary of the Navy, insisted: "it is not the cause of the negro, but that of the . . . white man that is involved in this question." Thomas Day, the editor of the Hartford *Courant*, made the point even more starkly in an 1856 article titled "Sam and Sambo," declaring to his readers: "It is not because we feel any burning zeal in the black man's cause, that we resist the progress of Slavery in this country. We like the white man better than we do the black. We believe the Caucasian variety of the human species, superior to the Negro variety. . . . Color is not the trouble; thick lips and wooly hair are not the objections. It is, that the Caucasian variety is intrinsically a better breed, of better brain, better moral traits, better capacity in every way, than the Negro, or the Mongolian, or the Malay, or the Red American."[7]

The outbreak of the Civil War did little to change Connecticut's racial sensibilities. The war did not usher in any widespread acceptance of blacks. Few of the state's some 55,000 men who marched to war did so with the goal of black freedom, and though many in Connecticut came around to supporting Lincoln's 1863 Emancipation Proclamation, they did so primarily as a war measure that confiscated the South's main labor force. The supporters of emancipation never fully embraced abolition and its belief in racial equality. The attitudes of both Northern soldiers and those at home revealed a very clear difference between the two ideas. Nor did some within Connecticut believe that blacks should play any role whatsoever in the war against the South. William W. Eaton, who represented Hartford in the General Assembly and was one of Connecticut's leading Democratic spokesmen, blasted his colleagues in the legislature who had proposed creating a black regiment from the state. Eaton thundered: "It is the most disgraceful bill ever introduced into the Connecticut Legislature," insisting that "if it must pass it should be amended so as to include Camanchee and Ojibway Indians. . . . [I] would sooner let loose the wild Camanchees than the ferocious negro."[8]

Racism was so deeply entrenched that even as the Civil War came to an end and emancipation was enshrined within the protection of the Constitution through the Thirteenth Amendment, Connecticut was still unable to shed its steady animosity to black rights. In 1865 the General Assembly passed an amendment to the state constitution that removed the word "white" from the description of who could vote and authorized a general referendum among the state's residents to decide the matter. Voters readily demolished the amendment at the polls, revealing the unwillingness of Connecticut to accept any blacks as true members of the state or nation. The little Nutmeg State made an unabashedly clear statement to the other parts of the country that awaited the referendum's outcome. The *Hartford Times* gleefully announced the rejection of the amendment and the message its defeat sent regarding black rights in an article titled "A White Man's State in New England," concluding: "It is scarcely possible to overestimate the importance of this result, in its influence on the destiny of the nation." The *New York Times* had concurred with the meaning of the Connecticut vote before it had occurred, realizing that "the result of this vote will be awaited with considerable interest." After the referendum, the paper could come to only one, simple conclusion: "The decision is purely due to *prejudice* — to an unreasonable, unjust and cruel prejudice — against the negro."[9] Northerners realized that if Connecticut was unwilling to accord blacks such a basic right of citizenship, matters would probably be even worse in the defeated South.

This history of slavery and race as it relates to Connecticut and the Civil War is one that has been largely untold. The most recent book on the state's involvement in the war, John Niven's *Connecticut for the Union*, was published in 1965 during the centennial commemoration of the war.[10] It failed to even include "slavery" in the index and largely avoided any mention of problems within Connecticut related to race. The absence was conspicuous but not surprising, given the upheaval of the civil rights movement at the time of the book's publication, and the careful orchestration by centennial organizers to avoid any potential conflicts. Instead, the book focused on the sacrifices of both North and South and what Niven saw as the actions of Connecticut citizens in response to their call to duty in defense of the Union.

There is a remarkable story here, both nationally and within Connecticut. Many Americans today, even if they know little about the Civil War, recognize that it was a nation-altering event, the proportions of which the young republic had not yet experienced. The bloodshed was ghastly, the death tolls unimaginable. Some 620,000 Americans, both Northerners and Southerners, died in a conflict that lasted four horrific years. This is a large number to be sure, but as is the case with so many big figures, its impact can easily get lost in its sheer size. Historians often try to make it more comprehensible by noting that the Civil War alone had more casualties than every other American conflict combined: the American Revolution, both World Wars, the Vietnam War, and everything in between, as well as the current Iraq and Afghanistan wars. There are other ways to consider the loss of life. Imagine killing every man, woman, and child in Connecticut's six most populous cities today: Bridgeport, New Haven, Hartford, Stamford, Norwalk, and Danbury.[11] This is the level of desolation that occurred during the Civil War.

Out of these many dead, some 5,354 were among the 55,864 soldiers from Connecticut. Ten percent of the state's population served in the military. Again, as numbers go, this may seem like a rather minimal commitment to the war. Looked at in another way, however, the state's contribution becomes far more significant. It is not the percentage of the total population that mattered, but rather the percentage of men between the ages of fifteen and fifty, the most likely ages for service. In 1860, 118,041 men fell in this category, and 47 percent of them went to war.[12] The state's black residents also shouldered the burden of war. Although they numbered just 8,627, and only 2,206 of them were men between the ages of fifteen and fifty, some 78 percent of those men joined the 29th and 30th Connecticut Colored Regiments, which were authorized by the General Assembly in late 1863.[13] Overall, Connecticut sent a striking proportion of its male population to war. Every other father, brother, or son left home to serve. The impact was immense. Not only was it shouldered by soldiers, but every family and every community was affected. Every facet of the state's life was embroiled in the conflict.

Connecticut placed twenty-nine infantry regiments in the field and started the 30th Connecticut Colored Regiment, but that was combined with the 31st Colored Federal Unit. Connecticut also formed artillery and cavalry units. The state's soldiers fought in every major engagement of the war: from Bull Run to Antietam and Gettysburg, in Sherman's march on Atlanta and through the Carolinas, and at Petersburg and Richmond. Connecticut men bled and died in these engagements. In their letters home, they complained of army life, worried about their families, expressed their torment and frustration when battles went poorly, and questioned the war's meaning as they watched their comrades literally get blown to bits in front of them. They often wrote of the South's incredible beauty, lamenting its destruction by the cruel hand of war. Theirs are deeply personal stories. They extend from the battlefield to the home front and back again.

Just as the soldiers experienced the horrors of war, so too did those at home. Women made the war possible with their constant attention to the needs of the men in the field. A virtual river of supplies poured forth from Connecticut through the many soldiers' aid societies organized around the state. Women traveled to battlefields before the cannons had cooled to care for the sick and wounded. Regrettably, they attended funeral after funeral.

The state's industry also responded with alacrity. During the American Revolution, Connecticut won the nickname of the Provision State, and the Civil War reaffirmed that worthy title. Home to a vast array of fire-arms manufacturers — from Colt and Sharps to Eli Whitney and Henry — Connecticut supplied an incredible number of weapons. It was also home to the Hazard Gunpowder Company, Hotchkiss and Company (which produced the newest and deadliest artillery projectiles of the day), and myriad shipbuilding establishments in the Mystic region that contributed to the naval war. The state's textile industry produced uniforms, haver-sacks, and literally a ton of socks, while the brass foundries manufactured any number of items, including regimental insignia and percussion caps for rifles and pistols. The sheer number of state patents related to wartime production is astounding. Although a small state, Connecticut was instru-mental in the North's industrial ability to wage war.

The outpouring of support for the war, both in terms of people and materiel, made Connecticut a mighty contributor to the effort. Nonethe-less, it is a mistake to conclude that such dedication reflected any type of unified war sentiment. Nearly half of Connecticut's population was steadfastly opposed to fighting the South. The state descended into chaos at the outbreak of the conflict, splitting into warring Republican and Democratic factions that sometimes faced off violently. Throughout the war, the two parties maintained an intense opposition that put the state's commitment to the Union in jeopardy. The most momentous outgrowth of this division was the 1863 gubernatorial election, which pitted sitting Republican Governor William Buckingham against former Democratic governor and Mexican War hero Thomas Seymour. Had Buckingham lost this pivotal election, the state might well have ended its support for the Lincoln administration and the Union.

The divisions between Republicans and Democrats in Connecticut reflected the larger complexities that separated the North from the South.

These differences were at the heart of questions about why the war should or should not be fought, as well as the complicated arguments over federal power versus states' rights, the sanctity of the Union, and the place of slavery within America. For Thomas Seymour and many of his Democratic brethren, secession—the right of a state to leave the nation—was entirely legal, and the war had been precipitated not by the South, but by the agitation of abolitionists. These Democrats insisted that the North must recognize that it had a constitutional obligation to protect slavery. Even those Connecticut residents who disagreed with secession and supported the war effort readily agreed with some of Seymour's points. They were, after all, not fighting on behalf of black freedom. They were not abolitionists.

The primary issue that separated those who supported the war from those who did not was secession, along with its implication about the country's future as a nation. For supporters of the war, the sanctity of the Union surpassed all other considerations, including slavery. This is the reason why so many marched off to sacrifice their lives in such large numbers, to suffer the loss of limbs, the destruction of their families, and the misery that resulted for those they left at home. These men and those who supported them placed the life of the nation ahead of their own. One simply cannot underestimate the power of nationalism and the patriotic response to the call to duty when the nation is threatened. It goes beyond the complexities of policy, arguments over westward expansion, and issues of states' rights—though all of these are certainly intermixed with the larger issues of power and patriotism. As a nation we have heard this call to duty time and time again. Most recently it came in the aftermath of the September 11 terrorist attacks, when so many homes displayed the nation's flag and enlistment in the military rose dramatically. We see that basic element of service and sacrifice in a large portion of the Civil War generation, those who dedicated themselves to the Union's survival during its greatest trial.

Even when the war ended, the issue of sacrifice continued to resonate as survivors attempted to understand the conflict and come to grips with its incomprehensible death toll. Many came home physically or psychologically crippled, only to find a home front that was reeling from the same stresses they had experienced. To make sense of it all and to provide meaning for those who had fallen and those who had survived, cities and towns around Connecticut paid tribute through monuments that told the story of service and a cause bigger than any one individual. These monuments continue to stand as our most direct physical connection to the Civil

War. Whether they know it or not, Connecticut residents are confronted by these memorials on an almost daily basis. They dot town greens and parks and stand in the center of many of the state's cities.

These Civil War monuments also offer an additional reality and legacy of the war, one that brings us back to the issue of race and the war's causes. Of the more than 130 monuments spread throughout the state, only two include an image related to slavery or emancipation — the issue that so many modern Americans consider the motivating factor in the war. Just as those of the Civil War generation did not embrace abolition and march to battle in defense of black rights, so in the war's aftermath, they did not choose to remember the war in terms of those goals. Rather, they focused on service, sacrifice, and their own need to survive the war. Once again, black rights and their role in the Civil War were pushed to the side. It took almost 150 years before a tribute was erected in Connecticut specifically to black involvement in the war. In the fall of 2008, New Haven dedicated a monument to the 29th Colored Regiment. It is a stark reminder that the Civil War remains alive in our memories, and that race is unalterably interwoven in those memories.

A note: Some of the language of the day regarding race is offensive, but it is quoted to accurately convey the views of the time. Moreover, I use the term "black," as opposed to African American, because the latter is a more modern usage. I use the word "white" in describing people of European descent.

CHAPTER ONE

Connecticut within the Nation

1776-1860

Slavery, Race, and Politics

What was Connecticut's position on slavery and race? How did sectional politics between the North and South play out within the state? How do the answers to such questions explain the causes of the Civil War and Connecticut's involvement in it? The answers may not be what readers assume. Too often we wrongly conclude that the North had little connection to slavery, and those who gave the institution any thought were devout abolitionists, morally committed to its eradication. The truth is far different and more complicated. To better understand what happened in the state, one must view Connecticut's story within the wider context of slavery, race, and politics in the nation at large. Only then can the history of the war and how Connecticut fought it make sense.

When Thomas Jefferson wrote in the Declaration of Independence the now immortal words "all men are created equal," every one of the rebelling colonies possessed slaves. Connecticut allowed slavery for almost 200 years. By 1774, half of the colony's ministers, lawyers, and public officials owned slaves, along with one-third of its physicians. Some argue that large-scale plantations existed in the colony.[1] In 1776, there were just over 5,000 humans in bondage in Connecticut, the largest number of any New England colony. One in four estate inventories at the time included slaves.[2] So much for the idea of a historically free, white Connecticut.

Along with her New England neighbors, Connecticut contributed to the international slave trade, and its residents reaped fortunes in the West Indies' market that fueled a deadly sugar empire.[3] Even though the nation's Founders had built their economic success on the backs of enslaved

{ 9

Africans, they recognized the immorality and paradox of their actions. Yet they could not turn away from the profit. The single largest section of the Declaration of Independence that the Continental Congress deleted was a paragraph in which Jefferson blamed the king of England for polluting this "new" England with slavery.[4] Thus was born the idea of slavery as a "necessary evil." The Founders knew it was wrong and evil, but it was also a significant economic base for the new nation. They rationalized its continued existence as a necessity.

The Revolution, with its pronouncements of liberty and equality, caused many to continue their moral and philosophical misgivings about enslaving human beings. There was more than a little irony in fighting for freedom while slaves worked the fields. This is when the first abolition societies were established, and numerous states, both North and South, liberated some of their human captives. There were also economic considerations. The Revolution had disrupted the West Indies trade and caused enough of an economic readjustment that some questioned the feasibility and desirability of having slaves. The movement away from slavery had started. Vermont was the first state to outlaw slavery, upon entering the Union. Massachusetts, which was the first of the colonies to pass a law formally legalizing slavery, was also the first of the original colonies, through a court decision, to outlaw it in 1783.[5]

Contrary to what many might assume, Connecticut's involvement with slavery was long and hardly benevolent. Slaves arrived in the colony as early as 1639, with the largest increase in their population occurring between the early 1700s and 1774, just before the Revolution. This period corresponded with the greatest expansion of agricultural production and commerce. The colony often enacted harsh restrictions and punishments, such as a 1690 law that forbade any "negro" from wandering without a pass outside of the town where he lived and authorized any citizen to apprehend the fugitive.[6] A 1708 law restricted slaves' right to sell goods without their master's permission and imposed a punishment of thirty lashes for any black charged with disturbing the peace or attempting to strike a white person.[7] In 1717, New London, the largest slaveholding section of the colony, forbade free blacks or mulattoes from residing in town, buying land, or owning a business without consent from the town council. The law was retroactive, so blacks who had already established themselves were required to request permission to retain what was rightfully theirs.[8] In 1730, a new law imposed forty lashes on any black person who uttered or printed anything about a white person that could be considered libelous.[9] The General Assembly rejected emancipation bills on three occasions, in

1777, 1779, and 1780. Always at issue was the number of slaves residing in the state. Without slavery, how would the state control the black population? The legislature did decide, however, to curtail the growth of slavery and passed a law in 1774 that banned further importation of slaves.[10]

Finally, in 1784, the General Assembly approved a gradual emancipation plan freeing slaves born after the act became law, when they reached the age of twenty-five. Any slave born prior to the act would not be freed. The historian Joanne Pope Melish noted bluntly: "This act was utterly pragmatic; there was nothing idealistic or visionary about it." The larger bill had to do with slave codes and restricting social interaction between blacks and whites. As Melish described it, the statute "outlined a complicated system of seizures, fines, whippings, and other punishments for a legion of illegal activities: travel by slaves or free Negroes without a pass; vagrancy; unauthorized purchase or sale of any item; violating the nine o'clock curfew; and unauthorized entertaining of slaves."[11] The act also imposed a fine of 100 pounds for illegally importing slaves. Emancipation at the age of twenty-five was thrown in almost as an afterthought, in a single, short paragraph at the end of the statute. Another historian noted: "The law freed no slaves. It did promise eventual freedom to the future-born children of slaves. . . . The law reflected the legislature's intent to end the institution of slavery in the state in a way that respected property rights and preserved social order."[12]

Although the new law did not immediately end slavery in Connecticut, it marked progress on the issue. It was followed by the establishment of the state's first formal antislavery society, in August 1790, when a group of Congregational ministers created the Connecticut Society for the Promotion of Freedom and the Relief of Persons Unlawfully Holden in Bondage.[13] The organization met with limited success. In 1794, they convinced the General Assembly to consider a bill to end slavery immediately, on April 1, 1795. The legislators voted the measure down, and the society disbanded shortly thereafter. Yet the movement for black rights continued. In 1797, the General Assembly lowered the age of manumission to twenty-one, but only for those born after this new law. It was also at this time that many of the state's slave codes, which restricted the rights and movements of slaves, were repealed.[14]

The refusal to grant immediate abolition reflected at least two key problems: economic loss to slave owners, and white concerns over social control of blacks. Some slave owners avoided the first problem by selling their slaves to owners in the South, while others lied about their slaves' ages to ensure permanent enslavement or created indenture contracts that, in effect, replicated slavery. In 1792, the General Assembly specifically prohibited the out-of-state sale of slaves. Nonetheless, the practice continued, as did kidnapping.[15] The issue of controlling free blacks, or minimizing their influence on society, was one that became increasingly important as the black community expanded.

By 1800, Connecticut's slave population had dropped to 931, and the number of free blacks had risen to 5,300. This meant that many slaveholders had released their human chattels well before the possibility of freedom under the gradual emancipation act. The biggest wave of emancipation occurred during the revolutionary period, when many slaves were given freedom in return for joining the war against Britain.[16] This growing free black community continued to spark concern among whites. One solution to their concern about controlling the blacks was the 1818 state constitution, which denied blacks the right to vote by defining electors as "white."[17]

Obviously, the South did not have the same economic circumstances or attitude toward slavery as the North. With a far larger captive population and greater dependence on its labor, Southerners were not so quick to turn away from the peculiar institution, though they too experienced a wave of emancipation during the revolutionary period. This spirit did not last, and Southerners ensured that slavery would. The push and pull over the supposedly necessary evil continued.

In 1787, when the nation's Founders met in Philadelphia to draft the Constitution, Congress, operating under the ill-fated Articles of Confederation, passed the Northwest Ordinance. That law closed to slavery all the new territories carved out of the nation's western lands — what became the states of Illinois, Indiana, and Ohio. Yet during that same summer of 1787, Congress accepted the new Constitution, which protected slavery by including clauses granting the South extra representation in the House of Representatives (the three-fifths clause, which counted each black as three-fifths of a white person for purposes of the census, and thus representation in Congress), continuation of the international slave trade until 1808, and the promise that all states would return slaves who fled from their masters (later reinforced by the infamous fugitive slave laws of 1793 and 1850). Slavery was secure. Only three years later, in 1790, the Southwest Ordinance, which created the states of Tennessee and Kentucky opened these lands to slavery. This back and forth of limiting and expanding slavery at the time of the nation's birth revealed the inherent struggle over the necessary evil.[18]

Connecticut in the American Civil War

"The First Cotton-gin," wood engraving by William L. Sheppard, 1869.
Library of Congress, LC-USZ62-103801

It was also during this period that slavery received an immense economic boost, and the source had direct ties to Connecticut. Eli Whitney, a graduate of Yale College, traveled south to Georgia in 1792 to work as a private tutor. There he learned that cotton production required a great deal of time and labor to remove the seeds. In the following year, he invented the cotton gin, a machine that separated the seeds from the cotton fibers. What followed was an explosion in cotton production. Figures vary, but production jumped from about 150,000 pounds per year in 1793 to 6.5 million pounds in 1795, and it continued to multiply year after year. In 1800, U.S. cotton exports were $5 million and accounted for only 7 percent of the country's exports. By 1830, they had risen to $30 million and 41 percent, and in 1860 the numbers were a whopping $161 million and 57 percent. Much of that exporting was done by Northern firms, primarily in New York City, which bought the cotton from Southerners and sold it to textile mills in New England and Great Britain. Connecticut boasted a thriving textile industry, especially in Windham and surrounding areas.

There is no mystery why in 1858 South Carolina's Senator James Henry Hammond declared defiantly, "Cotton is King" and "no power on earth dares make war upon it."[19]

The rapid expansion of cotton production fueled a parallel explosion in the demand for slaves and new land. If the nation's Founders had really hoped slavery might somehow miraculously disappear over time, the cotton gin and the wealth that it brought ended such an unlikely notion. Cotton was a prince, soon to become king — and the economy of the entire nation, both North and South, had fallen under its rule.

———— • ————

From the early 1790s through 1815, the fledgling republic continued to grow. New states entered the Union, and the country's population roughly doubled. The United States attempted to increase its trade with the outside world, often having to navigate the rocky shoals of European conflict. During these years, the Napoleonic wars engulfed much of the Atlantic world, and though claiming to be a neutral in the conflict, America was nevertheless drawn into a second war with England because of British trade violations and illegal impressment (kidnapping and forced enlistment in the British navy) of American sailors. When the War of 1812 began in June of that year, Connecticut and New England staunchly opposed it and did everything they could to hamper war efforts: refusing to finance the war or allow militias to cross the Canadian border; maintaining an active, illegal trade with British troops; and, in the crowning offense, organizing the infamous 1814 Hartford Convention, in which New England states came together with the alleged aim of concluding a separate peace treaty with Britain and seceding from the Union.

The allegation was untrue, but it indicated the rather stark sectional divide that existed in the nation, as well as the belief that a state could secede. There were also serious questions about the rights of states versus the power of the federal government. Many states, Connecticut included, believed that the war was forced upon them by an expanding Republican Party in the South and West, while the Federalist minority, penned up in New England, declined in political importance.[20]

Slavery was not really a major political issue before or during the War of 1812, but New Englanders never lost an opportunity to argue that part of their political impotence was due to the Constitution's three-fifths clause, which, based on slave population, gave the South increased members in the House of Representatives. One historian noted: "Slave representation and the Hartford Convention became inextricably intertwined from the beginning." This did not have to do with abolition; it was purely about political power. Criticizing slavery was much more of a way for the North to bash Southern Republicans, who had always pointed a finger at "aristocratic" New England. Nonetheless, the Federalist willingness to criticize slavery and slave representation pioneered a sectional politics that opened the door for future antislavery, and anti-Southern, appeals.[21]

In the aftermath of the War of 1812, the entire nation flourished. The Napoleonic conflicts in Europe had ended, trade reopened, and the American economy boomed. An unparalleled nationalism emerged after the war. Americans had survived another war with the world's principal power. This period became known as the Era of Good Feelings, and even though Connecticut and New England had come out on the short end of the political stick—the Federalist Party had all but disintegrated— business was so good that few complained. The disappearance of Federalist opposition ushered in single-party rule in America, the only time in the nation's history when two-party competition ceased to exist. The end of the war and the following economic expansion also unleashed a wave of migration over the Appalachian Mountains. The thirst for property, much of it cotton land, continued. People moved westward to make their fortunes and futures.

<hr>

All of these factors led to the first post-Constitution conflict over slavery and revealed a source of disagreement that threatened the Union. When Missouri petitioned for statehood in 1818, it was only the second territory out of the Louisiana Purchase to do so. (Louisiana had come first, in 1812.) The roughly 60,000 residents of Missouri included about 10,000 slaves. The nation's first major internal battle erupted when New York Congressman James Tallmadge proposed an amendment to the Missouri statehood bill, calling for no further introduction of slaves into Missouri and gradual emancipation (at age twenty-five) of all slaves born there after statehood. Tallmadge was serving on a state commission charged with fulfilling New York's 1799 gradual emancipation plan. The Tallmadge amendment was a staunch test of whether slavery was really a necessary evil that would one day disappear, or whether it was a valuable economic institution linked to the nation's long-term future.[22]

For the next two years, Congress fought a battle royal, with Northerners and Southerners crossing swords over two essential issues: the future of slavery, and whether Congress had any constitutional authority to restrict it. The national legislature could accept or refuse a state's admission to the

Union, but could it dictate guidelines for admission? The final compromise said yes, but the issue resurfaced as a source of agitation in later years.

The South revealed its determination by hijacking Maine's request for statehood. If Missouri could not come in as a slave state, then Maine couldn't enter either. Ultimately, a compromise was reached in which the two states were paired, thus keeping sectional representation in the Senate — where each state had two votes — balanced. In the ensuing years, this deal became crucial to Southern power because even with the three-fifths clause, the Southern population and therefore its representation in Congress were far below those of the North. The other major part of the Missouri Compromise established 36° 30', a line drawn through the remainder of the Louisiana Purchase. Any area north of the line was to be free, but anything south of it was open to slavery. Missouri was the exception to the rule.[23]

<hr>

Little has been written about Connecticut and the Missouri Compromise.[24] The issue received scant newspaper coverage at the time, though the *Connecticut Courant*, sounding remarkably abolitionist, hit on the core issue, announcing "that the evils of slavery are to be forever hereafter experienced in this country" and insisting that the "Providence of God" would result in "fatal consequences." The *Hartford Daily Times* saw the matter pragmatically as "a choice of evils being presented," commenting that "the blacks were imposed on us without our consent and the management or disposal of them is a matter of most serious concern. . . . Their numerical force is justly feared in several of the states." One indication of hostility to the compromise was that Senator James Lanman of New London was apparently burned in effigy for supporting it, and Representatives Samuel Foote and James Stevens were not renominated as candidates for the House.[25]

Moreover, in May 1820, in his annual address to the legislature, Governor Oliver Wolcott commented on the Missouri question, noting that a "diversity of habits and principles" was developing in the nation: "I think it is evident that slavery is gradually forming those distinctions." Part of Wolcott's concern was that the continuance of slavery would influence the very nature of the republic. Even though he acknowledged that Southerners were firmly attached to liberty, and though he recognized that the continuance of the Union did not permit a change "in the adjusted relations of society" (those states that had slavery could keep it), he still announced: "I am compelled by a sense of duty, to declare it my opinion, that Congress

Connecticut in the American Civil War

is fully authorized to inhibit the further diffusion of slavery." Allowing the advance of slavery in the West would cause a "perpetual exclusion of the rights which appertain to the free agriculturalist of the United States."[26] Wolcott's speech was ahead of its time. He framed the issue in terms of the effects of slavery on white laborers and the competition between labor systems, not abolition or equal rights for blacks. In the 1840s and 1850s, this would become the core argument of the Free Soil movement.

Others took a different view of the matter. In December 1819, a group of Connecticut citizens had gathered at the State House in Hartford and declared: "The existence of slavery in this republic is an evil deeply to be lamented, and utterly repugnant to the principle of a republican Government." Quoting from the Declaration of Independence, they argued that Jefferson's famous preamble precluded the very idea that slavery would be allowed to spread, and they asserted that Congress "possesses the clear and indisputable right to prescribe the terms upon which any Territory may be admitted into the Union." The group followed with a memorial to Congress in which they lamented "the fate of thousands of our fellow-men, whose dearest rights have been so long sacrificed to the plea of necessity, or of interest," and insisted that efforts must be made "to prevent our vast portion of the western hemisphere from being any longer the disgraceful prison-house of the unfortunate sons of Africa."[27]

The results of the Missouri Compromise were significant. It established a deal between the North and South that, at least temporarily, settled the question of slavery's expansion westward. Yet the crisis also shocked both sections of the country — Thomas Jefferson called it "a fire bell in the night" that "awakened and filled me with terror" — and revealed poignantly the growing disagreements over slavery stemming from moral misgivings, competing labor systems, and sectional political power struggles.[28] It was a disagreement so momentous that it threatened the Union's very survival. Politicians concluded that slavery was so divisive, it should be consciously avoided as a topic of political discussion. Moreover, some concluded that the lack of a viable two-party system had allowed the Union to divide along purely sectional lines. One solution was the creation of national parties that crossed geographic borders and therefore made it far less likely that the country would splinter into North versus South. Thus was born the Second American Party System, in which Jacksonian Democrats battled Whigs over safer economic issues like banks, paper money, tariffs, and internal improvements.[29]

Politicians' efforts to avoid the politics of slavery did not stop the growing chasm developing over the peculiar institution. As the abolition movement continued to grow both nationally and in Connecticut, animosity over the slavery issue grew with it. Many whites struggled over what should be done with blacks once they were freed, and one conclusion was that they should simply leave. In 1816, the American Colonization Society was founded to achieve this purpose by helping to establish Liberia, a settlement in Africa to which free blacks could emigrate and thereby relieve the United States of its "problem." Many Connecticut residents viewed colonization as the best possible solution, and the Connecticut Colonization Society was established in 1820.[30] Others in the state were more sympathetic not only to slavery but to the South as well, reflecting the fact that slavery had not spread in Connecticut principally as a result of its climate. In 1828, Jonathon Mayhew Wainwright, a minister, reminded listeners at Christ Church in Hartford that "slavery once polluted the now free and untrammeled states of New England." "Had the banks of the Connecticut been rice meadows, its uplands the soil for cotton, and its summer climate fatal to all but the African race," he continued, "the African race would, in all probability, still be in bondage among us." He argued further: "And do we not at this very moment, manufacture and wear the cotton of their planting and gathering, and do we not eat of the rice and sugar which the toil of slaves has produced? Let us not then boast of our exemption from responsibility and from whatever may be the criminality of possessing a slave population."[31] An editorial in the *Norwich Courier* the following year concurred with Wainwright's sentiment: "We should reflect that it is but a few years since this curse was peculiar to the Southern States; and if slavery never existed to so great an extent in this and other New England States as in the South, or had been earlier abolished, it is owing more to the character of our climate, and soil, and productions, which render slave labor valueless, than to any superior virtue of our people."[32]

The 1830s placed this question of virtue in stark contrast. While a small but dedicated abolition movement developed throughout the North, an equal, if not larger, anti-abolition movement sprang to life. Abolitionists succeeded in encouraging Connecticut's General Assembly to enact a statute in 1830 making it illegal to "kidnap, or forcibly or fraudulently carry off or decoy out of this State any free person, or person entitled to freedom," and stipulated a prison sentence and a fine not exceeding $500 for violations. Yet at the same time, the growing number of free blacks in the state "aroused a popular aversion to blacks that significantly impeded the fledgling abolitionist movement," as one historian put it.[33] This ten-

*Amos G. Beman, from one of his scrapbooks.
Filled with newspaper clippings and other materials,
the scrapbooks are an invaluable source of black
abolitionist struggles against slavery and racism.
Yale Collection of American Literature,
Beinecke Rare Book and Manuscript Library,
Yale University*

sion over the status of blacks continued as both abolitionist sentiment and opposition to it grew.

Between 1833 and 1837, there were at least thirty-nine antislavery societies in the state, and in 1838 a state convention organized the Connecticut Anti-Slavery Society, though the total membership was under 2,000.[34] This rise in abolition corresponded with the thundering moral denunciations of slavery by William Lloyd Garrison and his Boston-based newspaper, *The Liberator*. Connecticut abolitionists such as Leonard Bacon and Simeon Jocelyn, both New Haven ministers, preached from their pulpits on the sins of slavery. They were joined by members of the growing free black community, who made a concerted effort to educate and inspire their people through the work of black churches. Ministers Amos G. Beman and James Pennington led this movement, initially focusing on temperance

Advertisement in William Lloyd Garrison's
The Liberator, *March 2, 1833.*

and education, then carefully turning these efforts into a formidable demonstration of the success of blacks despite the harsh realities of slavery and racism. The two ministers also were involved in the underground railroad, which helped slaves who had escaped from the South head farther North. Pennington himself had escaped from slavery.[35]

It was within the realm of education that Connecticut abolitionists, often encouraged and supported by those outside the state, focused their efforts. In 1831, Simeon Jocelyn attempted to form a "Negro College" in New Haven, insisting that "the literary and scientific character of New-Haven renders it a very desirable place for the location of the College."[36] The white residents of New Haven disagreed. Mayor Dennis Kimberly called a town meeting that passed resolutions promising to resist the plan. The New Haven *Palladium* announced with some astonishment: "We mean, without any jesting, to say that there has been an attempt, a serious attempt, to get up an institution in this place for the education of colored men . . . which if carried into execution would ruin the prosperity of the city." The paper added that "in connection with this establishment the immediate abolition of slavery in the United States is not only recommended and encouraged . . . but demanded, as a right."[37]

Certainly the most well-known attempt to form a black school was Prudence Crandall's ill-fated effort in 1833. Crandall had originally established a white female boarding school in Canterbury, Connecticut, and had inflamed the local population by admitting a black girl. When parents pulled their children from the school, Crandall opted to open an all-black female institution to educate girls from several states. A town committee interviewed Crandall twice and expressed concern not only over the fact that the students were "foreign" (not from Connecticut), but that Crandall was promoting abolition and intermarriage. Town leaders expressed concern over the number of free blacks in their midst, noting: "We might ask the citizens of *any town* in New England, wherever situated, would it be well for *that town* to admit the blacks from slave States, or other States, to

Connecticut in the American Civil War

"Colored Schools Broken Up, In the Free States,"
woodcut print, Anti-Slavery Almanac, *1839.*

an unlimited extent? Once open this door, and New England will become the Liberia of America!!"[38]

One of Crandall's leading critics was Andrew Judson, a Democratic town selectman who insisted: "Colored people never can rise from their menial condition in our country; they ought not to be permitted to rise here. They are an inferior race of beings, and never can or ought to be recognized as the equal of whites. Africa is the place for them. I am in favor of the Colonization scheme. Let the niggers and the descendants be sent back to their fatherland."[39] Judson and others petitioned the General Assembly, requesting that it "draft some law by which the introduction of foreign blacks, might be regulated in a proper degree, by the feelings and wishes of the inhabitants of the towns."[40] The Assembly obliged. Although commenting on "the unhappy class of beings, whose race had been degraded by unjust bondage," it determined that "*our* obligations as a *State*, acting in its sovereign capacity, are limited to the people of our *own* territory" and concluded: "We are under no obligation, moral or political, to incur the incalculable evils, of bringing into *our own State* colored emigrants from abroad." The Assembly then passed an act prohibiting the creation of a school for "colored persons who are not inhabitants of this State," unless written consent is granted by officials of the relevant town. The statute was greeted, as one historian wrote, with wild enthusiasm and by the "ring of the church bell and firing of the cannon thirteen times."[41]

Crandall actually defied the law, was tried for doing so twice, and was finally found guilty, though the decision was reversed on a technicality. Her school did not survive. Angry residents repeatedly vandalized the schoolhouse, attempted to set it on fire, and filled the well with manure, as noted in the introduction. Crandall had hoped the General Assembly would repeal its statute in 1834. Instead, it upheld the law and announced:

"Whether bond or free, the negro and 'his kind' have ever been blots on the fair face of civilized society, and corroding cancers to a free State." Crandall gave up and moved to Illinois.[42]

The hostility to the creation of a "Negro College" and Crandall's school revealed that abolitionists were not the majority in Connecticut, and that even attempts to educate blacks and thereby improve their lives were frowned upon by some residents of the state. The schools meant the importation of more blacks into a state where many whites already wanted the few blacks there to leave. The issue was fueled by widespread racism that grew with abolition itself. As Melish described it, "whites found any degree of success among blacks — any evidence of free people of color living like white people — to be as disruptive of the social order as the presence of indigent, dependent, transient, or publicly rowdy ones."[43]

Abolitionists did not give up. Garrison, who spent a good deal of time in Brooklyn, Connecticut, responded to a letter from his friend Amos A. Phelps shortly after the Crandall affair. Garrison wrote: "Connecticut has been let alone too long by us meddlesome and pestiferous abolitionists and I am rejoiced to learn that you have resolved to commence operations in this Georgia of New England — not having the fear of Canterbury before your eyes?" He advocated starting in the countryside, urging Phelps to "shun such places as New Haven, Hartford and Middletown — all the large cities and towns, until the country is revolutionized."[44]

———— · ————

The increase in abolitionist efforts was met with an equal, if not larger, increase in anti-abolitionist activities. Viewed by many as dangerous, these moral crusaders risked their very lives by openly attacking slavery and advocating immediate emancipation in the South. Such pronouncements were viewed as fanatical and a violation of the South's right to make her own determinations regarding "domestic institutions" — a code phrase for slavery. Certainly, part of the opposition to abolition was produced by a two-party political system that directed its members to avoid attacks on slavery. Compromise was the core of the party system, and most residents of Connecticut were convinced that compromise had formed the nation. In the spirit of that original agreement, abolitionists were a threat to the Union. It was therefore acceptable to assault them both verbally and physically. The historian Leonard Richards noted that from 1833 through 1837 — the very period when abolitionism expanded in the state — antislavery journals reported sixteen anti-abolition and antiblack mobs and some forty-six groups opposed to antislavery in Connecticut. He concluded that Connecticut had a much higher incidence of mob violence against abolitionists than other New England states.[45]

Indeed, the *Norwich Courier* announced in 1833 that abolition was "an insane project—one which no man in full possession and exercise of his faculties can contemplate as being practicable, or at the present desirable."[46] The New Haven *Palladium*, forgetting that slavery did still exist in the state, argued that "inasmuch as slavery does not exist in Connecticut," slavery was solely the concern of individual states, and the newspaper blasted abolition as "an unwarrantable and dangerous interference with the internal concerns of other States, and ought to be discouraged."[47] The *Courant* wrote: "The course pursued by this class of persons [abolitionists] is truly astonishing." Their conduct "betrays the greatest delusion and infatuation" and "the whole community is thrown into agitation; a spirit of distrust and alienation is awakened between the South and the North; and the Union itself threatened with destruction."[48] The New Haven *Herald* also reported that when a Reverend Rand of Boston came to the Baptist Church in New Haven to speak on behalf of the American Anti-Slavery Society, "he was loudly and violently interrupted," and the "violence increased whenever the subject of slavery was mentioned, until he found himself compelled to sit down." A portion of the rioters then proceeded to the home of Simeon Jocelyn, the church's pastor, and tore up the front fence, "assailed the windows and did other damage."[49] In Danbury, an antislavery lecturer was pelted with stones and had to be rescued by town constables. Middletown also experienced violent anti-abolition mobs. One historian noted that in 1834, abolition "proceedings were quickly and violently disrupted by a proslavery crowd that had gathered outside. Those abolitionists, both black and white, who were forced to flee for what seemed their very lives and unfortunately fell into the mob's hands were first insulted, threatened, jostled and then kicked through the city's streets. So vicious and daunting had been this attack, that it was three years before the Anti-Slavery Society assembled again only to fade quietly out of existence."[50]

A meeting of "the inhabitants of Farmington, who disapprove of Antislavery associations and the mode adopted by them of agitating the public mind on the great subject of domestic slavery" was called by 200 residents of the town. Not only did they resolve that slavery was a "domestic concern and cannot be abolished by Congress," they pointed out that Connecticut had gradually abolished slavery and announced with some astonishment, "this meeting cannot but deem it extraordinary, that any citizen or association of citizens of *Connecticut*, should demand, either from political or moral principles, that the other states, having a vast number of slaves, should *immediately* set them free."[51]

There are many examples of violence against abolitionists and blacks within the state. In 1834, a mob broke up a rally at the First Presbyterian Church in Norwich and threatened to tar and feather the pastor. In 1835, a series of violent attacks occurred in Hartford, and some homes of black residents were demolished. In 1838, Arthur Granger was dismissed as pastor of his church in Meriden after speaking against slavery. And in the same year, the city of Hartford broke a contract that allowed abolitionists to use City Hall. The list could go on.[52]

Nor were these the actions of only a few dedicated anti-abolitionists. In 1835, an anti-abolition meeting in New Haven appointed Democratic Governor Henry W. Edwards president and Noah Webster and Simeon Baldwin vice-presidents. Those present passed a series of resolutions insisting that Congress had no authority to abolish slavery: "We witness with mingled feelings of alarm and reprobation, the reckless course of some professed friends of the cause of freedom, whose efforts, under the *mask* of philanthropy, have infused gall and bitterness into our social system."[53] Such a message was a stark indication of the need in Jacksonian America to avoid any discussion of slavery. A few months later, Governor Edwards addressed the General Assembly, discussing the alarm created in the South by the mailing of abolitionist pamphlets from the North. Although he was uncertain "how far the citizens of this state are implicated in this complaint," he insisted that certain restraints were imposed at the nation's founding, and "slavery was one of those subjects with respect to which a compromise was made." Agreeing with the sentiment at the meeting over which he had presided, the governor declared: "The interference of slavery in the different States, was never conceded to the United States. Regulations on this subject were left to the control of the States individually."[54]

Even with this rampant hostility, the small number of committed abolitionists within the state continued to push for national emancipation and equal rights for blacks. They were led by a coalition of white and black leaders, such as Simeon Jocelyn and Amos Beman, and — as noted earlier — in 1838 they founded the Connecticut Anti-Slavery Society. Originally meeting at the City Hall in Hartford, they were forced to move to a local hotel after being threatened with violence. They persevered, founding their own newspaper, the *Charter Oak*, and they consistently questioned gubernatorial candidates on black civil rights — specifically on blacks' right to vote and the use of jury trials for alleged fugitive slaves. It was in this latter area that they met with the most success.[55]

In 1838, the General Assembly passed an act directly related to the Constitution's provision requiring states to aid in the capture of runaways. The new statute modified how Connecticut fulfilled its constitutional commitment by requiring slave owners to go through a detailed legal process and appear before a judge, rather than simply claim a slave and take him or her back to the South. Accused fugitives could request a jury trial and claim damages if they were determined to be free. The law also required slave owners to prepay all legal fees and imposed a $500 fine on any owner who attempted to take a fugitive without following the state's process.[56] Advocates of black rights had a success in this instance, but it was short-lived. In 1842, the U.S. Supreme Court ruled in *Prigg v. Pennsylvania* that states could not create such a process for recovering fugitive slaves because doing so interfered with federal law and was unconstitutional. Accordingly, in 1844, Connecticut repealed its 1838 act.[57]

Beman and his white compatriots were less successful when it came to changing minds about black voting rights. In 1839, after years of being pushed by abolitionists to give free blacks the right to vote, a committee of the General Assembly issued a decidedly harsh opinion on the matter: "The colored population is regarded as a distinct and inferior race, the proposition to admit them to a full participation of political power, can be regarded in no other light, than a proposition to promote by legislation, an equality in social condition, between the races. It is in fact a scheme to encourage the amalgamation of the two races, and a general admixture of blood." Throughout fifteen pages — which sound remarkably similar to the decision that the Supreme Court would reach in the *Dred Scott* case, when it declared that no black person, slave or free, was a citizen — the committee harped on one theme: "From this brief review of our legislation, it appears that the colored race have at no time since the first settlement of this State, been admitted to a participation in the political privileges of citizens." Rather remarkably, the report also insisted that Congress should not place any restrictions regarding slavery on any states seeking admission to the Union.[58]

About the same time, 1839–41, the famous *Amistad* case attracted much attention in the state and nation. The *Amistad* was a ship carrying kidnapped Africans who had managed to kill most of the crew; it had ended up in Long Island Sound. Apprehended by federal vessels, the captives were housed in New Haven while the case moved its way through the court system. At issue was the status of the ship and the so-called slaves, and whether they should be tried for murder. One author noted that the case aroused a humanitarian sentiment within the state and a larger recognition of the race problem, yet it did not erase antipathy for blacks.[59] Such a view is epitomized by an editorial in the *Courant* commenting on the District Court's ruling that the captured Africans were not slaves: "We are very much gratified at the decision. . . . The only point in the case, in which the community felt much interest, was the final disposition of the Africans." The editorial expressed hope that the case would be an admonition "to avoid bringing the miserable inhabitants of Africa within the reach of our laws and courts."[60]

If the mass of Connecticut residents reviled abolitionists and free blacks alike, issues like those presented in the *Amistad* case and the constant moral admonitions of the abolitionist minority did seem to make some changes in society. By 1840, there were only seventeen recorded slaves in the state. In 1844, Whig Governor Sherman Baldwin, who had served as a defense attorney for the Africans in the *Amistad* case, asked the General Assembly: "Is it not time that every vestige of a system founded in injustice and fraud, and incapable of being supported except by the provisions of positive law, should be effaced from our statute book?" It took another four years to accomplish the task, but in 1848, with only an estimated half-dozen slaves remaining in Connecticut, the General Assembly enacted a law that stated simply: "No person shall hereafter be holden in slavery in this state."[61] Slavery was no more in Connecticut.

The same could not be said for racism. Black abolitionists continued to press for voting rights, only to be denied again and again. In November 1841, Beman and other black leaders attended a meeting at Union Hall in Hartford at which they resolved: "Whereas the great body of colored people in this State are disfranchised, and deprived of an important right that is guaranteed to all men by the Supreme Ruler of the Universe. Therefore, Resolved, That it is the duty of every man to exert his influence and talents to bring about an equal participation in all the rights of man." Beman and several of his colleagues insisted that nature had endowed them with such rights and that the Declaration of Independence acknowledged this fact.[62] They urged their congregations to act, and in May 1843, the General Assembly received petitions from 115 black residents. The following year, blacks in Hartford sent some eighty additional petitions. All were held in committee and kept from being presented to the wider legislature.[63]

Similar petitions were finally moved out of committee, and in 1846 the General Assembly scheduled a statewide referendum for the following year on removing the word "white" from the constitution, thereby providing blacks with the vote. It was exactly what Beman and other abolitionist leaders, both black and white, had fought for, and they began a campaign to convince white voters to support the referendum. Beman, James Pennington, and Joseph Brown wrote a letter "To the Good People of the State of Connecticut," which appeared in the *Hartford Courant* (the *Hartford Times* refused to publish it). They argued that the remarkable progress made by the state's black residents justified their right to vote, insisting: "We have made this improvement, not *because* of this deprivation of our civil rights, but *in spite of it*, under the discouraging influences which always attend such a deprivation, and we have therefore shown ourselves worthy of the right to ask at your hands." They further noted that blacks paid taxes and had never asked to be relieved of that burden, and they concluded: "We only ask to be allowed to discharge the duties and exercise the rights of freemen. We appeal to the good citizens of this State, now to rise and do us justice—to blot out this unjust distinction from the fundamental law of the State, and no longer crush a people, who are making every effort in their power to do their part nobly in life's race."[64]

These heartfelt appeals did not compete with the racism still rampant in Connecticut society. The referendum failed by a vote of 19,148 to 5,353.[65] Perhaps more insulting was the General Assembly's action just a few years later, in 1851, when it passed a law exempting black property owners from paying taxes. The message was clear: the state's leaders would rather decline revenue than lift Connecticut's black residents to a position of equality by granting them the vote.[66] Still, Beman, Pennington, and others remained vigilant, and in 1854 they held a convention in Middletown at which Beman delivered the keynote address. He once again focused on the success of the free black community, and the *Hartford Republican* noted of the speech: "Such rich strains of eloquence as we never before heard from the lips of any man, white or colored, in this State."[67] The eloquence, however, was not enough. Although the matter made its way into the General Assembly in 1855 and even passed the Senate, it failed in two House votes. One of the most outspoken members of the House was Democrat Joseph Maddox, who had remarked that he "did not understand this sympathy for everything that is black, and opposition to everything white," and "denied that Negroes had been injured; their conditions had been ameliorated by bringing them from Africa here. God had set a seal of distinction upon the race, and had designed that they should be sent here in slavery." These comments outraged Beman, who sent a formal challenge for Maddox to debate the matter. Maddox never answered the challenge.[68] One biographer concluded: "Beman could well have felt that his seventeen years of labor in New Haven, along with the striking efforts of his father [Leverett Beman], Hosea Easton, and James Pennington, had had little effect on the rank-and-file racial prejudice in Connecticut."[69]

———•———

Despite the failure of abolitionists to secure voting rights for blacks, their concerted efforts had successfully brought slavery to the attention of Connecticut and the nation. The result was mixed. More people lamented the plight of blacks, but an equal or larger number expressed deep racial animosity. Some of this was fueled by the party system itself, which was soon to experience even greater agitation over the future of slavery. In fact, it became clear that the parties could no longer contain the problem. The initial source of this North-South division was the issue of westward expansion.

Historians have argued that the battle over Texas annexation and the resulting war with Mexico in the 1840s was the sectional turning point that caused the Democrat and Whig parties to disintegrate and the nation to spiral toward war.[70] The acquisition of new land (Texas, California, New Mexico, Arizona, and parts of Nevada and Utah) reopened discussions of slavery's movement west. This was an issue that had proved so divisive during the Missouri crisis that Congress had clamped the lid tightly down with the infamous compromise of 1820. When the issue arose again, both political parties attempted to avoid it, as they had throughout the 1830s.

The presumptive 1844 presidential nominees, Democrat Martin Van Buren and Whig Henry Clay, released public letters opposing the annexation of Texas. They realized the potential for division and the likelihood of war with Mexico, which still claimed ownership of Texas. The attempt to avoid annexation, and thereby avoid a discussion about slavery and the West, was lost to the fate of political maneuvering. Van Buren lost his bid for the Democratic presidential nomination and was replaced by the pro-annexation Tennessean James K. Polk. Northern members of the party were outraged, and they were further infuriated after Polk won the presidency and refused to appoint Van Buren's supporters to federal posts. Polk also failed to push hard in a boundary dispute with Great Britain over the Oregon Territory. Northerners had advocated "54° 40′ or fight," insisting that America's northern border should be above the forty-ninth parallel (the modern boundary between the United States and Canada). It appeared to many Northerners that the South was willing to wage a war with Mexico to expand slave territory in Texas, but not to fight England to

Slavery, Sectionalism, and the West

Texas Annexation and the Mexican War, 1845–48
*Adds new western territories and reignites arguments over the future
of slavery.*

Wilmot Proviso, 1846
*Proposes to make slavery illegal in any territory acquired during the
Mexican War.*

The Democratic Party Splits, 1846–49
*Martin Van Buren bolts the Democratic Party — rise of the Liberty
and Free Soil parties.*

Immigration and the Rise of Ethnocultural Politics, 1848–53
*The rise of the new Know Nothing Party in the early 1850s creates
problems for the traditional Democratic and Whig parties, which are
beginning to fall apart due to disagreements about slavery, economics,
and immigration.*

The Compromise of 1850
*An attempt to settle the rising sectional tensions following the Mexican
War fails, in part because of the new fugitive slave law.*

The Kansas-Nebraska Act, 1854
*Replacing the Missouri Compromise restrictions on slavery in the
Louisiana Purchase territories with popular sovereignty allows the
people in the territories to decide on the future of slavery there. Voting
becomes a mockery and violence quickly follows. Abolitionists make
"Bleeding Kansas" a rallying cry.*

The Rise of the Republican Party, early 1850s
*The new, anti-Southern Republican Party emerges out of the ruins of
the Democratic and Whig parties. It espouses free soil arguments about
white labor and argues that a "Slave Power" conspiracy threatens to
rob the North of its liberties.*

The Brooks/Sumner Beating, 1856
*Massachusetts Senator Charles Sumner is caned by South Carolina
Representative Preston Brooks, providing new evidence of the violent
and aggressive "Slave Power."*

The Dred Scott Decision, 1857
*The U.S. Supreme Court rules that Dred Scott is not a citizen and that
the Missouri Compromise was unconstitutional. Republicans charge
a grand conspiracy on the part of the "Slave Power."*

acquire nonslaveholding territory in the Northwest. These issues caused Northern Democrats, led by Van Buren, to bolt the party.[71]

Viewing the Southern wing of the party as in need of a wake-up call, David Wilmot, a Van Buren Democrat from Pennsylvania, proposed in 1846 the infamous Wilmot Proviso, which advocated excluding slavery from any territory acquired in the Mexican War. In doing so, he hurled a sectional bomb into Congress. The proviso never passed, but the very proposal was like whacking a hornet's nest with a stick.[72] Always sensitive about any discussion of slavery, Southerners were incensed over the attack on their much-vaunted rights. Most remarkable is that Van Buren had in large part made his national career by silencing slavery agitation within the two-party system. Yet when Southern Democrats refused to acknowledge the interests and needs of the party's Northern wing, all bets were off. Van Buren men, in the form of the Wilmot Proviso, shoved slavery in the face of their former Southern allies. Equally important is the fact that the catalyst was not motivated by abolition. It was about political power. Yet the shift unquestionably aided those opposed to the expansion of slavery, whether or not they were abolitionists. Van Buren even went so far as to ally himself for a time with the burgeoning Liberty and Free Soil parties and ran as their presidential candidate in 1848, though he later reunited with the Democrats.[73]

In Connecticut, opposition to slavery's expansion westward was immediate and broad-based. One historian noted: "Although unsympathetic to abolition, few Connecticut citizens wished to see slavery spread West, where they believed the free states had legitimate interests."[74] Those interests were the spread of a free labor system, unpolluted by slavery or the presence of blacks. This general opposition to slavery's extension aided the state's abolitionists, who in 1841 created a Connecticut Liberty Party. It also caused them to slowly meld their message with Free Soilers, who opposed slavery specifically because of its impact on free laboring whites. The basic idea was that black laborers would compete against white workers, depressing their wages and reducing their opportunities. This movement helped to increase antislavery attitudes among Connecticut residents who were traditionally racist and opposed to abolition. Nor did this shift in thought go unnoticed by blacks. Augustus Washington, a prominent Hartford daguerreotypist who ultimately moved to Liberia, commented: "Now that anti-slavery has become popular with many of the American people, it assumes another name, and is converted to political

Connecticut in the American Civil War

capital. Even Free-Soilism was not so much designed to make room for our liberties, as to preserve unimpaired the liberties of the whites."[75]

This new "political capital," the Free Soil movement, helped to draw support from both the Democratic and Whig parties. The discord in the Democratic Party, nationally and in Connecticut, is complex. Suffice it to say that some members of the party opted to bolt with Van Buren, while others stood by the traditional North-South Democratic alliance, and as a result, supported the annexation of Texas. Whigs, meanwhile, attempted to capitalize on the Democratic problems and become the party opposed to the extension of slavery. The Whig-supported *Hartford Daily Courant* announced resolutely: "We rely upon it, with confidence, that the people of Connecticut are opposed to the Annexation of Texas, to the United States. The general sentiment among them is against the extension or the perpetuation of the dominions of human bondage." The paper likened the battle to the Missouri crisis, though it insisted that the earlier conflict was "trifling in comparison." The *Courant* was clearly not advocating abolition. It recognized the nation's Founders' compromise over slavery: "The people of the North acknowledge, that they have no constitutional right to interfere with the domestic relations of South Carolina. Not so of Texas. That country is not within the compromise of the Constitution."[76] Most Whigs also supported the Wilmot Proviso, declaring it to be "a signal that the government is to be emancipated from the control of the slave states," in the words of the *Courant*, which defiantly announced: "They [the South] have even gone so far as to threaten the Dissolution of the Union — a threat which is so uniformly resorted to that it has begun to be considered too much a matter of course to be thought worthy of serious regard."[77] Traditional Democrats viewed the proviso differently, insisting, according to the *Hartford Times*, that "we are democrats of the constitutional faith — that constitution which recognizes slavery."[78] They painted Whigs as radical abolitionists bent on destroying the Union.

The battle over Texas, the Mexican War, and the Wilmot Proviso revealed significant cracks in the party system. These were further exacerbated by issues that had nothing to do with slavery. Democrats and Whigs had traditionally battled over economic issues that had seemed safer. But in the late 1840s and early 1850s, states went through a period of constitutional revision that settled many of the details related to such issues, and, combined with the vast amount of money supplied by the California gold rush that could now be invested, there were simply fewer economic issues to argue about. When the topics on which the parties had traditionally competed literally disappeared, the parties no longer seemed relevant to voters. The Democratic and Whig parties essentially began to disintegrate, while at the same time new issues arose that further eroded their power and relevance.[79]

Slavery was certainly one of these issues. The party system had managed to contain the problem for twenty years, but with the weakening of the parties and the increased agitation over Texas and the westward spread of slavery, the matter was not so easily avoided — especially when new politicians in the North specifically capitalized on anti-Southern sentiment and the threats of what they now called the "Slave Power." Another major issue was the rapid rise of anti-immigrant and anti-Catholic sentiment. The mid- to late 1840s was a period of extensive European immigration to the United States. German and Irish Catholics flooded into the nation, including Connecticut, and "native American" residents reacted with alarm at the dual threat of foreigners and popery. This problem had absolutely nothing to do with slavery, and its prominence demonstrates that Northerners were not fixated solely on the issue of slavery. Nativism also contributed to the breakdown of the Democratic and Whig parties. A brand-new party system was the result. By the early 1850s, the political landscape had been reshaped, and one of the new players was the anti-Southern Republican Party.[80]

Recognizing that the Democratic and Whig parties were severely affected by issues other than slavery helps us to understand the Civil War in three important ways. First, it rebuts the age-old claim that increased arguments over slavery alone destroyed the Whig and Democratic parties. Second, it explains why the war occurred when it did. If the parties had remained healthy throughout the 1850s, it is likely that they would have continued to consciously avoid divisions over slavery, at least for a time. It was only when the Whigs disintegrated completely, and the Democratic Party split into Northern and Southern wings, that war erupted. Third, the multiple reasons for the parties' destruction and the rapid rise of a competing anti-immigrant party, the Know Nothings, shows that other serious interests besides slavery were at play in Northern society. The war did not begin with a unified abolitionist North confronting Southern slaveholders.[81]

Historians agree that the rise of the Republican Party and Lincoln's election as president in 1860 were not inevitable outgrowths of antislavery agitation. They certainly were not the result of purely abolitionist sentiment. Far more resonant with Northerners, especially those in Connecticut, was the threat of the aggressive "Slave Power." The notion of power as a threat to liberty was one of the mainstream ideological legacies of the colonial and revolutionary periods. Republicans capitalized on that fact and utilized the language of republicanism—liberty versus power—to influence the public. Even in making such appeals, Republicans had to compete with Know Nothings for votes.

Voters viewed with alarm both slavery's westward expansion and the rising immigrant population. In many ways, immigration was a more immediate concern to Northerners because they faced the issue directly, on their own streets. Slavery was not yet so relevant to them. Slavery-related issues ebbed and flowed. Compromise over the matter had always been the solution, yet as Southerners appeared more and more aggressive, Northerners grew less tolerant and more defiant. The debate over annexing Texas alerted them that slavery was on the move again, and when the Treaty of Gaudalupe Hidalgo ended the Mexican War and provided the United States with vast amounts of new territory, new fears erupted over the spread of slavery. To settle this question—as well as arguments over slave trading in the nation's capital and the return of runaway slaves—Congress enacted the Compromise of 1850. The most salient parts brought California into the Union as a free state, organized into territories other parts of the land ceded by Mexico with no restrictions regarding slavery, and enacted a new fugitive slave law.[82]

It was this last act that most infuriated Northerners because it deputized every citizen to be slave catchers, decreeing that "all good citizens are hereby commanded to aid and assist."[83] It, more than any other single act leading to the Civil War, caused whites to express genuine sympathy for slaves. That sympathy was different from favoring outright abolition, but it nonetheless served abolitionists' purposes. An excellent example is Harriet Beecher Stowe's *Uncle Tom's Cabin*. The author was moved by the passage of the fugitive slave law to write the novel, which portrays the plight of the black family and the sins of slavery for which both Northerners and Southerners were culpable. Reverend Leonard Bacon of New Haven wrote of the book: "The tears which it has drawn from millions of eyes . . . and the deep and ineffaceable conviction of the wickedness of slavery, which it has stamped on millions of hearts" was testimony to "the sensibility of the public mind, on the question of slavery."[84]

Others in Connecticut were also moved. Judge Holbrook Curtis of Watertown put the matter simply: "Our people at the North will not all of them readily be made Slave Catchers." Throughout the state, protests erupted against the law, with many opposing it because it violated the ideals of the Declaration of Independence and because it required everyone to aid in the capture of fugitives.[85] A meeting in Middlefield adopted a resolution that declared: "This Fugitive Slave Law commands all good citizens to be slave-catchers; good citizens cannot be slave catchers any more than light can be darkness. You tell us, the Union will be endangered if we oppose this law. We reply, that greater things than the Union will be endangered, if we submit to it: Conscience, Humanity, Self-respect are greater than the Union, and these must be pursued at all hazards."[86]

Such sentiments were not universal or even mainstream. Both Whigs and Democrats supported the Compromise of 1850, thereby endorsing the legality and binding force of the new fugitive slave law. Democratic Governor Thomas Seymour insisted that the nation had been built on compromise. The historian Lawrence Bruser wrote that Democrats "stoutly defended the fugitive law as an integral part of the settlement." Even Whigs supported the measure. The *Courant*, though complaining about injustice, announced: "This act is now a LAW OF THE LAND, and as such, is to be respected accordingly."[87] At their state convention in November, Whigs rejoiced that "Connecticut took early measures to free herself from the evils of slavery within our borders," but passed a motion that said: "*Resolved*, that we will stand by the Constitution of our government and not countenance any attempt by violence to abrogate or nullify any provision legally enacted under that Constitution." Revealing the continued animosity toward abolitionists, the New Haven *Palladium* charged that "the fugitive slave law, itself, is a direct consequence of the efforts of abolition kidnappers to steal away the negroes from the service of their masters — it is the abolitionist who exposed the fugitive in free states to imminent danger of being returned to slavery."[88]

Connecticut residents may have been divided over the Compromise of 1850, but Whigs and Democrats were not yet ready to break with the South and in doing so endanger the Union. As always, they thought a better solution for the problem was colonization. In 1852 and 1853, the General Assembly supported Governor Seymour's belief that colonization "happily unites ... our obligations to the Union and to God," and appropriated funds to help the state's black residents who wanted to emigrate to Africa.[89]

The tipping point for Connecticut's patience with the South came with the passage of the Kansas-Nebraska Act of 1854, which organized those two territories directly adjacent to Missouri. Senator Stephen Douglas of Illinois had two goals in advocating the measure. The first was purely economic. Douglas wanted to ensure that the transcontinental railroad would run through the North, with Chicago as a major terminal. The second was to further reunite the Democratic Party along its traditional expansionist platform. The problem was the 1820 Missouri Compromise's exclusion of slavery from the region. Given the recent arguments over expansion, Douglas believed that Southerners would block the organization of the land into territories. His solution was to repeal the restriction in the Missouri Compromise and replace it with popular sovereignty, giving the residents the right to vote on the future of slavery. Douglas and other Democrats argued that popular sovereignty was the essence of democracy. Northern Democrats added that, because of the climate, slavery could never survive as far north as Kansas, and thus there was no need for concern. Southern Democrats supported the idea because it erased the offensive restrictions and allowed the possibility of slavery.[90]

The outcome of the Kansas issue was a distinct slide toward civil war. One of the early speakers on the measure was Senator Truman Smith, a Connecticut Whig. In an articulate and prescient speech, Smith warned: "I verily believe that this measure is contrary to the true interests of the South. What you want is peace. Often and often have you said, Let us alone—leave our institutions undisturbed. Your true position is a defensive one; but this is a measure of aggression on the North. You have commenced a war on northern feelings, northern sentiments, and what will be regarded as northern rights and interests; and you may depend upon it that war will be returned with relentless fury." After making such blunt, accurate statements, Smith also attempted to soothe his Southern listeners: "I have no prejudices against my southern brethren; slavery I consider rather the misfortune than the crime of the South. It is only when you become aggressive that I feel bound to resist you. Why should I have any prejudice? My honored father . . . was himself a slaveholder, and my earliest recollections are associated with what you call an institution." Balance and accord was Smith's message. He reviled extremists on both sides: "I hate a northern anti-slavery demagogue, and I hate a southern pro-slavery demagogue." He closed simply: "Sir, I have done; I wash my hands of all responsibility for the consequences of this measure."[91] He resigned from the Senate shortly thereafter.

In a speech filled with poignant statements, none rang more true than "it is only when you become aggressive that I feel bound to resist you." Until the Kansas-Nebraska Act, many in Connecticut were willing to patiently grant Southern rights, even those as obnoxious as the ones embodied in the fugitive slave laws. No more. The repeal of the Missouri Compromise was truly a line in the sand, one that revealed for many Northerners the dangerous, aggressive nature of the Slave Power. The *Courant* let loose a barrage of literary missiles. "Hurl Back the Invaders!" it blasted. "For thirty-four years, freedom has been in possession of Nebraska. It is de-voted to liberty, pledged by an inviolable compact—but now the cohorts of slavery, headed by a northern renegade [Douglas], and reinforced by a band of traitors and deserters from our own camp, HAVE DARED TO IN-VADE OUR FREE TERRITORY!" Other articles followed: "The whole nation is awake to the aggressions of the slave power. . . . There never has been in the free States a feeling like the present" and "the South have forced this issue upon us—forced it by their constant aggressions."[92]

Nor was abolition the issue. The New Haven *Palladium* insisted: "Op-position to the Nebraska fraud will embrace an immense body of men who are not actuated by sympathy for the slaves as much as they ought to be—by men who have some regard for the honor, independence and prosperity of *white men*." The Middletown *Constitution* announced: "The effect of this bill will be to create a feeling of most uncompromising hostil-ity to the institution of slavery. Much has heretofore been yielded to the South for the sake of harmony . . . hereafter southern slavery will be re-garded as a fair subject to talk and fight against." The *Norwich Examiner* stated plainly: "It is not a question of whether 3,000,000 of American negroes . . . shall continue in slavery. The question is this: 'Shall the slave power rule our national government, and corrupt the fifteen or sixteen millions . . . of freemen to obey its despotic behests?'"[93]

When the Kansas-Nebraska Act passed Congress with the help of Northern Democrats, retaliation against the party and the South was foremost on the minds of Connecticut residents. Connecticut Whigs, who had been so badly torn apart over the loss of economic issues and the rise of anti-immigration sentiment that in 1853 it had seemed the party was doomed, seized the compromise issue in 1854 and soared to victory, taking vast majorities in the state's House and Senate, as well as electing the new governor. The General Assembly promptly passed resolutions denouncing the act and shortly afterward formally censured Democratic Senator Isaac Toucey, who had voted in favor of the bill in Congress.[94] In denouncing Democrats, Whigs glided more closely and openly toward abolition than they had ever done before. In blasting Toucey, Francis Gillette, the Whig who had just been elected to the U.S. Senate, thanked God that Connecti-cut was finally washing her hands of blood and the "diabolical work of enslaving and imbruting man," and he thundered that it is time to "dis-card the vile and contemptible dogma that the Constitution of the United States is a shield of slavery."[95] This was shocking precisely because for so many years both parties had recognized that the Constitution protected the peculiar institution.

Gillette also attacked the new fugitive slave law, saying: "It was conceived in sin, shapen in iniquity, and baptized in blood." Do not, he exploded, "tell me that my constitutional oath imposes an obligation upon me to obey this infernal act — I spurn the deed — I scorn the behest — I defy the authority."[96] It is no wonder that in May 1854, the General Assembly passed "An Act for the Defense of Liberty in this State," often referred to as a personal liberty law, which essentially neutered the fugitive slave law by imposing a fine of $5,000 and five years in prison on anyone attempting to falsely claim a free person was a slave, and requiring slaveholders to present two credible witnesses to prove that an individual was an escaped slave.[97] The impetus for the law was clearly a mixture of abolitionism and revenge. The *Courant* announced: "The South have showed that past compromises have no value, by annulling that of 1820. We trust the North will not be slow to follow the example with reference to that most ignoble one, the Fugitive Slave Act of 1850."[98]

Although Whigs had a meteoric rise in Connecticut with the help of the Kansas-Nebraska Act, they fell just as quickly the following year. The disintegration of the party system had opened the door for new competitors, and the Know Nothing Party, devoted to anti-immigration and temperance, took complete control of the state in 1855, revealing that slavery was not the sole issue on the minds of Connecticut voters. Also competing was the fledgling Republican Party, which pulled voters from both the Whigs and those Van Buren Democrats who had not returned to the party after the Free Soilers bolted in the 1840s. In 1856, the Know Nothings were still the primary opposition party to the Democrats, but Republicans siphoned just enough votes to give the Democrats victory. If Republicans wanted to become the ascendant opposition party, they would have to organize more effectively and dilute the Know Nothing appeal.[99]

The Republicans succeeded in the 1858 election, defeating the Democrats by the largest margin of victory in twenty years, winning control of the General Assembly, and electing the first Republican governor, William Buckingham.[100] Their success was due to two principal issues. First was the continued aggression by the Slave Power. Popular sovereignty in Kansas quickly became a mockery of democracy, with Missouri slaveholders riding across the border and voting to make the region a slave territory. This fraud was exacerbated by Representative Preston Brooks's caning of Senator Charles Sumner, who had delivered a speech in the U.S. Senate entitled "The Crime Against Kansas," in which he castigated Brooks's uncle, Senator Andrew Butler. The beating was yet another example of the Slave Power's resort to aggression, and several Connecticut towns held indignation meetings.[101] Another primary example of Southern belligerence was the 1857 *Dred Scott* decision by the Supreme Court, in which Chief Justice Roger Taney declared that no black person was a citizen of the United States and, even more outrageous to Northerners, that the Missouri Compromise was unconstitutional. Congress had no authority to place restrictions on the spread of slavery, the Court announced.[102]

These examples of Slave Power aggression fit directly within the Republicans' second principal issue: divorcing themselves from being tainted as sympathetic to abolition by focusing more on the aggressive "Slave Power," as well as economic competition between free and slave labor. Though many in the Republican fold genuinely desired the ultimate extinction of slavery, they fully understood the negative reputation of abolition. Of course, Democrats portrayed their new opponents as abolitionists, labeling them "Black" Republicans. One Democrat charged: "It is not unjust or untrue to say that [R]epublicanism is unadulterated abolitionism. . . . It attempts to divide this country into two great geographical parties, and to array one against the other in bitter strife. It is violent, unrelenting, abusive in the last degree."[103] Such charges took on even more importance when John Brown, born in Torrington, Connecticut, attacked the federal arsenal at Harpers Ferry in October 1859, in the hopes of fomenting a massive slave insurrection. Democrats charged Black Republicanism was the cause. Republicans in Connecticut, as well as manufacturers who did business with the South, were quick to divorce themselves from Brown.[104]

Given Connecticut's traditional animosity toward abolitionists and blacks, Republicans in the state had to do far more than merely avoid sounding like abolitionists; they had to actively deny any motivations on behalf of black rights. Responding to Democratic barbs, the New Haven *Journal & Inquirer* announced that the Republicans were "not a negro party, but a *white man's party*—a FREE LABOR PARTY." A man named James Babcock insisted: "Those who persistently try to represent Republicans as fanatical negro worshippers are either stupidly blind or falsely malevolent." The *Courant* argued: "It is for the interests, the honor, and the prosperity of FREE LABOR that we struggle," adding in another article, "you know, in a Republic, that Labor, FREE LABOR, is the only true Democratic principle, and that all else is Aristocracy . . . Slave Labor, is the declared enemy of Free Institutions—of Republican principles."[105] LaFayette Foster, a Republican in the U.S. Senate, disavowed "any professions of extra philanthropy . . . in regard to the black race. . . . I speak for the white race . . . for their freedom of speech, for their freedom of the press, for all those rights."[106] Gideon Welles, who later became Lincoln's secretary of the Navy, insisted: "It is not the cause of the negro, but that of the . . . white man that is involved in this question."[107] Republicans also turned the attack on Democrats. For instance, the *Courant* argued that "the great Democratic Party of the country have become 'Nigger Extensionists,'" and that to allow slavery in the territories was "to wink at the pollution of that virgin soil by African Slavery." "Our aim," the paper said, "should be to Americanize this country . . . and keep the colored race within its present limits."[108]

In responding specifically to the *Dred Scott* decision, Republicans complained that the Supreme Court had asserted both that blacks could not be citizens and that the Missouri Compromise was unconstitutional. But their real focus was on the decision's impact on whites rather than the plight of Scott, the slave who had sued for his freedom. The *Courant* claimed that "the Decision of the majority of the Supreme Court is the most fatal blow ever struck at FREE LABOR. . . . The decision is the deadliest attack upon true Democracy ever made in our national history; for it establishes, as the law of the Republic, a system of Aristocracy, which utterly denies *all* rights to him who *works* for his daily bread."[109]

Pushing harder and harder to deny the charge of abolitionism and to attract wayward Know Nothings, Republicans at times went to extremes. In a remarkably racist article entitled "Sam and Sambo," the *Courant*'s editor, Thomas Day, pitted "Sam," the true, white American, against the black "Sambo" and demanded "the necessity of making a stand in favor of Freedom and the rights of the white man, to labor on his own farm, uncontaminated by the insulting contiguity of black slaves." "This is the white man's party," continued Day; "it is not because we feel any burning zeal in the black man's cause, that we resist the progress of Slavery in this country. We like the white man better than we do the black. We believe the Caucasian variety of the human species, superior to the Negro variety. . . . Color is not the trouble; thick lips and wooly hair are not the objections. It is, that the Caucasian variety is intrinsically a better breed, of better brain, better moral traits, better capacity in every way, than the Negro, or the Mongolian, or the Malay, or the Red American." Day concluded by insisting: "Republicans mean to preserve all this country that they can, from the pestilential presence of the black race. Some people think themselves witty and smart, in calling this cause the Black Republican cause; to our minds it is intrinsically aristocratic; it aims to save the country to the white man, and is aristocratic because it impliedly avows a preference of the white race, as settlers, over the black race. This cause has our heartiest sympathies."[110]

Day's article was extreme, but it reflected the wider Republican effort to attract voters based on the ideals of free labor and free white men. And again, it should be noted that there were some members of the party—those who had been the earliest proponents of the Liberty Party—who genuinely cared about the rights of blacks, both within and outside of Connecticut.[111] Such a message, however, would not carry the party to victory. Battling the South and winning control of the government of Connecticut required a strict focus on the Slave Power and the rights of white citizens. In this respect, the Republican Party was far more anti-Southern than antislavery. Abolition had never been popular in Connecticut. Thus the platform that won Republicans control of the state in 1858 announced that "the Slave Power" was the "most dangerous monopoly which had ever threatened our liberties," and that "Slavery and Freedom—slave labor and free labor—are irreconcilable antagonisms."[112] The same message allowed Republicans to maintain control of Connecticut in the following year, in the annual statewide election, and carry the state for Lincoln in 1860.

———————

The goal of this chapter has been to address the history of Connecticut's slave past in the light of America's struggle with slavery and race, and the sectional politics between the North and South that led to the Civil War. Too often modern Americans wrongly believe that Northern states had little connection to slavery. This is clearly not the case. Connecticut had a long history of slavery, and even after ultimately getting rid of the institution, its residents revealed little tolerance for or support of equal rights for blacks. True, there were dedicated, morally inspired abolitionists who fought for immediate abolition in the South and for black equality within Connecticut. There was also a formidable free black community that fought for its own rights and dignity. Yet most Connecticut residents were either ambivalent, or outright hostile, toward the blacks in their midst. When the nation began to slide further toward open rupture in the midst of the debate over the Kansas-Nebraska Act, the anti-Southern Republican Party did well primarily because it actively avoided any connection with abolitionism or black rights. Understanding this situation makes it difficult to argue that Connecticut went to war in 1861 to emancipate slaves and secure the future of its black residents.

CHAPTER TWO

And the War Came

1860-61

The Republican victory in Connecticut and Abraham Lincoln's election as president were not inevitable. Each was the result of carefully coordinated campaigns and the marshaling of voters into the anti-Southern, Republican camp. Nor was war certain. Some believed that talk of secession was merely a Southern bluff. South Carolina had made the same threat during the 1832–33 Nullification Crisis when the residents of that state refused to pay tariffs, announcing that they would secede if the federal government tried to force them. President Andrew Jackson stared down the "Nullies," as he called them, and the whole affair melted away. Still, the idea of secession as a state's right never disappeared. When Lincoln became president at the head of a decidedly sectional party, South Carolina once again led the way. This time, many of her sister states followed.

Yet even with this outcome, many Northerners assumed that if war came, it would be brief. The South, after all, had virtually no industry and a decidedly smaller population than the North. Moreover, slavery had corrupted the region's self-reliance. Sturdy Northerners — free labor — would force the South to capitulate in a matter of months. Such views shifted rather quickly. After taking a beating in the first major battle of the war, Bull Run (also known as Manassas), Northerners gave a collective gasp. The initial year of the war, 1861, was an unwelcome wake-up call. Residents of Connecticut learned quickly that war was hell; that the conflict would require incredible military, economic, and medical resources; and that those at home were as instrumental to the effort as men in the field were. Republicans realized the importance of maintaining political control within the state. Not all of their fellow citizens supported Northern "aggression" against the South. A significant Democratic peace movement sprang up in towns and cities across the state. Overall, however, Connecticut heeded the call for commitment to the Union and war against

Governor William A. Buckingham. Courtesy of the Museum of Connecticut History, Connecticut State Library

the South, though the first months of the war caused some to question what the aim of the conflict should be.

———•———

After Republicans took control of the state in 1858, with the election of Governor William A. Buckingham, they focused intently on maintaining that control all the way through the 1860 presidential contest. Connecticut held its state election on the first Monday of April, which made it one of the earliest of Northern states to vote and something of a bellwether for the November presidential contest. If Democrats could reassert control in Connecticut, they might turn the tide in New England and the North. Thus for Republicans, winning the state, and perhaps the nation, required keeping Buckingham in office. One could not happen without the other. All eyes were on Connecticut. The *New Haven Register* declared: "A nation is waiting in almost breathless suspense to hear the results."[1]

The 1860 gubernatorial contest was sure to be a close one. Democrats nominated Thomas H. Seymour, the popular former governor. Seymour had served as a major in the Mexican War and led a famous charge at the battle of Chepultepec, earning promotion to colonel for his heroism. He was Connecticut's governor from 1850 to 1853 and served as President Franklin Pierce's minister to Russia from 1853 to 1857.[2] Seymour had steadfastly argued throughout the 1850s that the North was constitutionally bound to support the compromises that had created the nation, including the acceptance of slavery. Democrats charged that a vote for Buckingham was tantamount to abolitionism and, further, would destroy the state's important commerce with the South. Republicans countered with their consistent free labor arguments, insisting that, "destitute of any great issue that will seize the attention of a young laboring man, they [Democrats] try to fill the ears with shouts of 'Chepultepec,' and call upon him to look rather at the past glories of the Mexican hero, than the present and future interests of himself, his friends, and his country. They think that the smoke of the gunpowder of a successful war, will call off the attention of the laboring man from the fact that he is shouting and voting, simply to assist our proud, overbearing, southern slaveowners, to carry their negroes into our free territories."[3]

Fearing Buckingham would lose to Seymour, the Republican Party went so far as to pull Abraham Lincoln from his travels in New York and New Hampshire so that the newly prominent Republican spokesman could attempt to work his common-talk magic on Connecticut. "You have a special call there, & a duty to perform," wrote James Briggs to Lincoln.[4]

*Governor Thomas H. Seymour. Courtesy of the Museum
of Connecticut History, Connecticut State Library*

Lincoln made five speeches in the state, in Hartford, New Haven, Meriden, Norwich, and Bridgeport. Each speech was essentially the same. His overarching theme was that a discussion of slavery could not be avoided: "Slavery is the great political question of the nation." Though he mentioned issues of free labor, Lincoln forthrightly denounced "slavery [as] a great moral, social and political evil, tolerable only because, and so far as its actual existence makes it necessary to tolerate it, and that beyond that, it ought to be treated as a wrong." He accepted that slavery could not be completely removed, first likening it to a rattlesnake that should be killed, unless the snake were in a bed with children, in which case going after the snake might threaten their safety. He also likened slavery to a wen or cyst that could not be surgically removed lest it kill the patient in the process. His solution was to contain slavery where it existed, and in doing so, make an agreement "as our fathers did; giving to the slaveholder the entire control where the system was established, while we possessed the power to restrain it from going outside those limits."[5]

Lincoln received a rousing reception from the state's Republicans, who packed meeting halls and organized torchlight processions. It was at one such parade that a new political assemblage was formed, the Wide Awakes, who dressed in military-like garb, with caps, capes and torches; marched in unison; and captured the imagination and admiration of the public. It was a smart, effective campaign strategy that caught on in other Northern states.[6] Lincoln was suitably impressed and recognized the state's importance, writing to Senator Lyman Trumbull: "They are having a desperate struggle in Connecticut; and it would both please, and help our friends there, if you could be with them in the last days of the fight. Having been there, I know they are proud of you as a son of their own soil, and would be moved to greater exertion by your presence among them. Can you not go? Telegraph them, and go right along. The fiendish attempt now being made upon Connecticut, must not be allowed to succeed."[7]

The Republican push worked, though barely. Buckingham won reelection by a mere 541 votes, receiving 44,458 to Seymour's 43,917, with some 10,000 more votes cast than in the previous year's election. Republicans insisted that, in reality, the victory should have been even larger, charging that Democrats had imported ineligible voters from New York, and that New York's mayor, Fernando Wood, had organized and paid for the fraud. James Babcock of New Haven wrote to Lincoln immediately after the election that "the Republicans have come out of their terrible conflict safely," adding that Lincoln's speeches had been instrumental to the success and his name was repeatedly mentioned as the party's next presidential nominee.[8]

Shortly after his reelection, Governor Buckingham delivered his annual message to the General Assembly, devoting the entirety of the last section to the troubles facing the nation. "The settlement of questions appertaining to the powers of the General Government over slavery," he began, "has hitherto baffled the efforts of our wisest patriots and ablest statesmen." Then, engaging in a brief exposition on the nation's foundations, the governor insisted that the Constitution was "scrupulously guarded from the use of the words 'slave,' or 'slavery,'" and that "testimony is abundant that this compact was made with the idea that slavery was an evil to be tolerated." "But now," he continued, "it is openly declared that slavery, as a system, is just and benevolent; that it is the normal condition of society. . . . Slavery thus becomes a national system, to be defended and protected by statute law." Buckingham expressed alarm that disunion was openly threatened in the halls of Congress: "It has been declared that the election of a President, representing opinions in opposition to the policy just referred to . . . will of itself be a sufficient cause for secession, or for a dissolution of the Union." He proclaimed that "it is hardly necessary to say that the freemen of Connecticut emphatically repudiate such dangerous and revolutionary sentiments, and all action so utterly inconsistent with the first principles of Constitutional liberty." He closed on a decidedly abolitionist note: Americans must "accomplish the mission which God designed this nation should fulfill—the establishment and extension of the blessings of freedom, civilization, and Christianity."[9]

Democrats, of course, ridiculed the governor's views on secession. The *Hartford Times* announced that if the South departed from the Union, "it will be useless to attempt any coercive measures to keep them. . . . We can never force sovereign States to remain in the Union when they desire to go out, without bringing upon our country the shocking evils of civil war."[10]

With the Connecticut gubernatorial election won in April 1860, Republicans looked forward to the presidential vote in November, hoping that they would finally wrest control of the federal government from the Slave Power. In May, Republicans nominated Lincoln as their presidential candidate and carefully prepared their free labor strategy to capture Northern votes. It was during the summer that Milo A. Holcomb of Granby sent his proslavery letter to Lincoln, cited in the introduction, insisting that slavery was the nation's future and asserting that "many Very many are in favor of having the system extended over New England." He also offered political analysis of the coming election, recognized the Democrats' difficulties, and predicted Lincoln's victory in Connecticut: "If . . . two Democratic, to wit, a Douglass [sic] & a Breckenridge [sic] ticket . . . be run in Conn of Course You will get the State If a united ticket in any Way wholy [sic] or partially favoring Douglass be attempted I will with hundreds of others oppose it it therefore matters not how I vote You can rely with certainty on the electoral Vote of Connecticut." Holcomb's implication was that Stephen A. Douglas—like Lincoln, from Illinois, and the probable Democratic nominee—was so unpalatable to many Northerners that he could not be elected president. Presumably, Holcomb would have been amenable to a Southern Democratic candidate, but he realized that such a nominee would split the nation's and the state's Democratic votes.[11]

This realization came from the fact that at the Democratic Party Convention held in Charleston, South Carolina, in late April, the party had divided over Douglas's nomination. Southerners insisted on a platform that explicitly protected slavery in the territories, but Douglas and his followers continued to advocate popular sovereignty, understanding that abandoning it, along with outright support of slavery in the West, was political suicide in the North. The problem for Douglas was that the *Dred Scott* decision had killed popular sovereignty by decreeing unconstitutional any federal restriction on the extension of slavery. Nonetheless, Douglas clung to his dead doctrine. When the party reconvened a little over a month later, in Baltimore, Southerners walked out of the convention, reassembled at a different location, and promptly nominated John C. Breckinridge of Kentucky. The remaining Northern Democrats nominated Douglas. The die was cast. Lincoln's victory was pretty much assured.[12]

Even had the Democrats been able to agree on a single ticket, their victory was unlikely. Although Lincoln received only 39 percent of the nation's popular vote, he won 173 electoral votes compared to the combined 130 votes won by his opponents. And as Americans witnessed in the 2000 election, electoral votes are the ones that count. In addition, in many states Lincoln received more votes than the other candidates combined. Nationally, the swing states of Ohio, Pennsylvania, and New York were key. Connecticut also went for Lincoln. He received 43,488 votes in the state, compared to Douglas's 15,431 and Breckinridge's 14,372. John Bell, running on a Constitutional Union ticket, won 1,528. Together, Lincoln's opponents received 31,331 votes, fewer than he won. True, the Democratic Party split clearly discouraged some Democrats from voting, given that in the April election, before the split, Seymour had received almost 44,000 votes for governor. Nationally, voter turnout in 1860 was 81.2 percent, up from 78.9 percent in 1856.[13]

Whether or not Lincoln's victory was assured by the Democratic split, his accession to the presidency promised repercussions in the South. Only days after his victory, South Carolina called for a convention that assembled on December 20, 1860, and voted 169 to zero in favor of secession. The convention's official resolution dissolved "the union now subsisting

Advertisement for Kibbe & Co., Hartford Daily Courant,
December 21, 1860.

---

between South Carolina and the other States."[14] The lead up to the convention had featured marching bands, fireworks, the waving of the state's palmetto flag, and with odes to Southern rights.

One might assume that secession unleashed panic in Connecticut, or at least fiery denunciations. Instead, the news was greeted with a mixture of hope, apathy, and amusement. One of the first items to appear in the *Courant* was an advertisement from Kibbe & Co. that actually poked fun at the idea of secession, as shown above.

Other news items discussed how mail would be delivered to South Carolina and reported charges that "Lincoln men in the North" were sending "foul rags" infected with smallpox to break up secession conventions. One article published only two days after secession proclaimed that "the people of the North are getting tired of being bullied, and badgered, and insulted with every mail that comes from the South." Overall, Connecticut revealed no great fear, and one article even argued that South Carolina's action "is a *verbal secession* merely; the Post Office and the Custom House business goes on as usual; and the solemn secession remains a *theory* merely. The fact is, that South Carolina has practically demonstrated that the Union cannot be dissolved by a single State; and yet everybody says, 'South Carolina has seceded!'"[15] Skepticism and apathy continued well into March, even as other Southern states seceded: Mississippi on January 9, Florida on the 10th, Alabama on the 11th, Georgia on the 19th, Louisiana on the 26th, and Texas on February 1.

Although Connecticut newspapers initially seemed indifferent to the crisis, Governor Buckingham reacted promptly, issuing a proclamation on December 21 in which he beseeched everyone to pray that God "will carry us through this crisis in such a manner as shall forever check the spirit of anarchy, bring peace to a distracted people, and preserve, strengthen, and perpetuate our national union."[16] He ordered the state's quartermaster general to purchase equipment, knapsacks, cartridge boxes, rifles, and bayonets for five thousand men. Fortunately, with Connecticut's excellent arms industry, the quartermaster did not have difficulty filling the order.[17] The Democratic press responded with characteristic viciousness and incredulity, announcing: "Gov. Buckingham has buckled on his spurs, and calls for a demonstration of the Connecticut Militia. . . . We trust he is not so far lost to common sense as to suppose the people of this state are disposed to draw the sword to compel seceding states to return to the Union!"[18]

Remarkably, during this period, Connecticut's weapons industry was still doing a brisk business with the South. On December 29, Eli Whitney's arms company shipped eight wagonloads of pistols and carbines to its New York agent for sale in the South. Colt and Sharps were both selling arms to Southerners, Sharps having sent 180 cases of carbines and 40,000 cartridges to Georgia. In 1859, Colt had actually contemplated building an armory in the South. Even as late as April 1861, the Confederate agent John Forsyth purchased 2,000 Colt pistols and 2,000 Sharps rifles. Between January and mid-April, the Hazard Powder Company— owned by Augustus Hazard, who had always been a stout Democratic defender of the South's control over its own domestic institutions—sold tons of powder to the South. On April 7 alone, he concluded a deal with Forsyth for the sale of 200 tons of cannon powder for $80,000. Horace Staples, the president of the Saugatuck Bank in Westport, Connecticut, wrote to Governor Buckingham on April 23, 1861, informing him, "It has been said N York City that Mr. Hazzard has been & still is supplying secessionists with powder & that Mr. Colts arms are still being forwarded to our enemies within the last week."[19]

Other Connecticut businessmen assiduously avoided sending any aid to the South. When Charles Henry Mallory, a shipbuilder in Mystic, received a letter in March from his cousin Stephen Mallory, the prospective Confederate secretary of the Navy, asking for "any light draft strong fast ship of this design (a screw ship) [a steam-powered vessel with a propeller, or screw] for sale," or "a first rate ship carpenter," Charles responded that he would remain "strictly legitimate and above board," hoping for a peaceable settlement as opposed to the horror of "a collision between the two sections of my beloved country."[20]

Also during this time, two interesting news items appeared. First, on January 22, the *Courant* ran a brief story introducing an issue that would be crucial in the coming months and years. The paper announced that Charles Morehead, a former governor of Kentucky, had written a letter to a gentleman in New Orleans, insisting that secession "would be a severer blow to Slavery than all the Abolitionists of the North could inflict in the next twenty years." The *Courant* concurred: "The dissolution of the Union—whether effected by separate secession or by co-operation—inflicts a death-blow upon Slavery. No future event is more certain than this."[21] The second item was more a college prank than an act of aggression. The *Courant* reported: "Somebody made some very large secession badges, and employed two or three dirty, colored persons to wear them on the green in New Haven for the gratification of the southerners in Yale College." These Yale students promptly retaliated by hoisting South Carolina's palmetto flag over Alumni Hall and barricading the doors. The paper noted "there was some profanity and touch work before the obnoxious banner was hauled down."[22] Two weeks earlier, also in New Haven, a large palmetto flag had been raised at Fort Hale, the abandoned defensive works at the mouth of the city's harbor.[23] Many residents of the state supported the South and states' right to secede.

Over the next few weeks, Connecticut continued to read in the *Courant* about the South's many problems concerning secession, and the paper's prediction that the matter would probably be solved without war.[24] Kentucky Senator John Jordan Crittenden had offered in December what became known as the Crittenden Compromise, a series of resolutions outlining settlements concerning slavery. Throughout February, numerous Connecticut towns sent petitions to their senators and representatives, either requesting that the compromises be "speedily adopted," or "opposing any compromise by which slavery may be extended." One memorandum called on "Congress to put down treason and rebellion."[25] A peace conference was convened in Washington and, though initially hesitant to send representatives to it, Governor Buckingham agreed to do so, giving them strict instructions "that no sanction be given to measures which shall bind the government to new guarantees for the protection of property in man — a principle subversive of the foundations of a free government."[26]

As March 4, 1861, the day of Lincoln's inauguration, drew near, reports were heard that South Carolina planned to attack Fort Sumter during the ceremony.[27] The attack never materialized, and Lincoln told the South in his inaugural address that no aggressive move would be made by the North, nor would slavery be touched where it existed, but that the Union was perpetual and no state could secede. The *Hartford Times* referred to the speech as "unmanly."[28] For the next several weeks, the new Lincoln administration attempted to negotiate for the resupply of Sumter, which was running low on food and medical supplies. The *Times* criticized Lincoln's actions as "coercion," insisting that "terrible work for this Republic is about to commence."[29] On April 12, while the fort was actually under attack, the *Courant* reported that just such an attack was expected the very next morning.[30]

And the war came. "The awful fact that CIVIL WAR has begun in bloody earnest seems to be only too well authenticated," announced the *Courant*. "Let it forever be remembered," it continued, "that the greatest crime since the crucifixion of our Saviour, was wantonly and willfully committed in behalf of American Slavery! . . . The loyal heart of the nation will pant for retribution, and every drop of blood shed at Sumter will be amply atoned for hereafter. . . . Men of Connecticut! To ARMS! You must be counted for or against the government." The Democratic newspapers also received the news as calamitous, with the *Hartford Times* announcing: "Friday, the 12th day of April, 1861, will be recorded as the Black Day in the history of our Republic . . . when the first clash of arms commenced between the two Governments into which our wretched country is now divided." The *Times* blamed Lincoln and the Republicans for the hostilities, insisting, "this horrible drama could have been stopped." The talk of war filled streets throughout Connecticut, and residents came together in spontaneous meetings to discuss the situation. Governor Buckingham immediately wrote to President Lincoln: "I beg leave to assure you that the Government and citizens of this state are loyal to the national union."[31]

Lincoln needed such loyalty, and the troops that came with it. Expecting an imminent attack on Washington, the president issued a call for 75,000 troops on April 15. With the General Assembly not in session, and

Broadside announcing "To Arms!" Courtesy of the Museum of Connecticut History, Connecticut State Library

the state's 1818 constitution reserving all control over the m
legislature, Governor Buckingham acted on his own authorit
for volunteers to meet the need. The response was immediat
whelming. Within four days the need was filled: the 1st Regir
Connecticut Volunteer Infantry (CVI), with 820 men committ
months of service, and armed with Springfield and new Sharps   . oil
April 20, the regiment left Hartford for New Haven, awaiting transport to
Washington. Commanding the unit was Colonel Daniel Tyler of Norwich.
The men were officially mustered into service on April 23 and departed
for the nation's capital aboard the steamship *Bienville* on May 10, amid
cheers and the waving of flags.

After the 1st Regiment was filled, it took only two more days to fill the
2nd with 793 men, also three-month volunteers; the 2nd was commanded
by the popular Colonel Alfred H. Terry of New Haven. These troops also
mustered in New Haven, supplied with Model 1855 percussion rifles
and Sharps rifles. They departed for Washington on board the *Cahawba*
on May 10, just after receiving their regimental colors, which had been
elaborately embroidered by the women of New Haven. The 3rd CVI was
formed a mere two weeks after the 1st and 2nd, made up of 781 recruits
serving for three months, and armed with Model 1842 smooth-bore flint-
lock muskets that had been altered to use percussion caps. Commanded
by Colonel John Arnold of New Haven, the men mustered in Hartford
on May 14 and encamped two miles from the State House. Ordered to
Washington on May 19, they were presented with their company colors
by Governor Buckingham and then departed for New Haven, where they
boarded the *Cahawba*. They met up with the 1st and 2nd Regiments outside Washington.[32]

In the midst of these harried preparations, Governor Buckingham was
faced with the issue of paying for everything that was happening so quickly.
On the morning of April 16, the governor, as a well-respected Norwich
businessman, used his own credit to borrow $50,000 from the Thames
Bank of Norwich. The very next day, the bank offered the governor a line
of credit worth $100,000. Nor was it alone. The Fairfield County Bank at
Norwalk offered $25,000; the Mechanics Bank of New Haven, another
$25,000; the Elm City Bank of New Haven, $50,000; Hartford banks
jointly, $500,000; and two private citizens, $50,000 and $10,000.[33]

When May arrived, the General Assembly gathered for its spring session
and listened to Governor Buckingham's annual message. He announced:
"The condition of our country is critical. . . . Seven thousand men in arms,
backed by nineteen batteries of artillery, have, in open day, with disloyal

arts and traitorous hands, struck at the national flag in the harbor of Charleston." And though he addressed the wider issues related to the conflict, the governor was resolute: "The sceptre of authority must be upheld, and allegiance secured. It is no time to make concession to rebels, or parley with men in arms . . . indifferent or disloyal we can not be. Fail or falter we shall not."[34] He made numerous recommendations for military preparedness. The Assembly listened and promptly passed legislation authorizing the raising of 10,000 volunteer soldiers; a monthly payment of $10 in additional compensation for each soldier; the organization of towns to help with enlistments and supplies; and the arming of troops and provision for their families. It also appropriated $2,000,000 for war expenditures.[35]

By this time, Virginia had seceded, and Arkansas, North Carolina, and Tennessee were about to take the same fateful step.[36] On May 3, President Lincoln called for another 42,000 volunteers, and Governor Buckingham quickly organized the many other companies that had been formed, as well as recruits who agreed to serve for three or four years. The new units included the 4th Regiment, which shortly thereafter became the 1st Heavy Artillery, and the 5th Regiment CVI. In all, Connecticut produced many more men than the federal government initially requested. Yet the alacrity and ardor of enlistments did not match the state's rather dismal state of preparedness for war and inefficient organization of the troops. It was no easy task to find enough equipment for so many men, encamp and feed them, and teach them to shoot and learn the discipline necessary for war. Soldiers in the encampments noted many problems: too much discipline; too little food, and what was provided was of poor quality; inferior cloth for uniforms (which gave "shoddy," then simply referring to a kind of cloth, the derogatory meaning we know today). Complaints swarmed, and the General Assembly organized a series of special committees to investigate the problems. The governor also had to deal with the politics of personality. Samuel Colt, the famed gun manufacturer, offered on April 25 to create an elite fighting unit in which each man would be over six feet tall and armed with a Colt breach-loading revolving rifle. On May 16, Colt was commissioned as colonel of the unit, but on June 20 his commission was revoked and the regiment of 700 men disbanded because of Colt's haughty demands and attempts at total control of the unit.[37]

———◆———

As those Connecticut residents unequivocally loyal to the Union prepared for war, a number of the state's Democrats continued to question the wisdom and rationale of an armed struggle. The *New Haven Register* insisted that the "Constitution recognized the right of slaveholding" and lamented "that the true policy of the 'friends of the Constitution and Union' should be to instigate a servile insurrection . . . a war of extermination, in which the 'olive branch' is unknown — a war of race against race — black against white." The paper also warned against enrolling any black soldiers, insisting, "public opinion here now is decidedly adverse to employing the services of negroes in the impending struggle."[38] The *Register* denounced the conflict as an abolitionist conspiracy, an "Abolition humbug," opining: "If Abolitionist anticipations are realized — what then? Sell them? Ough! Give them liberty — an injury to themselves and a burden to the community? Well, we don't know; but it is evident this subject is destined to give us a good deal of trouble for some time to come."[39]

At the same time that the *Register* was blasting the war, a white "peace flag" appeared in Ridgefield, where two men were shot while attempting to tear it down. Other peace flags were put up in Avon, New Milford, New Preston, West Hartford, and Windsor.[40] Upon hearing reports of these flags, Thomas Seymour, then serving in the General Assembly, announced that there existed "a growing sentiment among the people for a peaceful settlement — and honorable peace." He insisted that the South could not be forced back into the Union: "There seems to be a radical mistake on the part of many people. They appear to think the South can be conquered. Sir, this is impossible. You may destroy their habitations, devastate their fields and shed the blood of their people, but you cannot conquer them." Seymour also tried to substitute war resolutions for a "fair and honorable termination of the present troubles."[41]

Toward the end of June, tempers flared in Goshen, when Andrew Palmer raised a secession flag on several occasions. The *Litchfield Enquirer* reported that when he was asked to take it down by a committee of "prominent citizens," his remarks "were neither those of a gentleman nor a patriot."[42] By afternoon a crowd of hundreds assembled on the town green, and some 159 men armed with muskets and a cannon marched to Palmer's home, where they demanded the flag and threatened violence. Ultimately, one of Palmer's men was shot in the leg, the flag was "received with hisses and trampled in the dust," and the Stars and Stripes was nailed to the house. To other traitors in the area, the newspaper said: "BEWARE!" It proclaimed: "Those brave young men who have gone forth from us shall never be insulted by the traitor's standard, waving in sight of their own loved homes. Woe to the Traitor, Woe!"[43]

Such shows of Democratic opposition did little to reduce support for the Union. Towns and cities across the state continued to prepare for war. In

Stafford, for example, a committee of townspeople was organized to give $20 to each volunteer and provide assistance for local families with relatives in the armed forces. In Enfield and Waterbury, $10,000 was appropriated for similar purposes. In Woodbury, $5,000 in family aid was collected. Similar activity was reported in Coventry, Middletown, West Hartford, and other towns. Residents purchased equipment for soldiers and donated cloth for uniforms. Women across the state organized sewing groups. In Norwich, some 300 women assembled to sew uniforms and knapsacks, as well as company and regimental flags. They also collected medical supplies. By April 25, the women of East Hartford had made and rolled 6,000 yards of bandages and made 1,500 compresses. Meetings were held throughout the state, at which loyal citizens pledged themselves to support the coming struggle, delivered stirring speeches, and formed military companies.[44]

The patriotic ardor and preparation inspired some to continue poking fun at the South. Even after the attack on Fort Sumter, the *Litchfield Enquirer* published a poem entitled "Advice to South Carolina":

> Sister come my dear,
> I am sorry to hear
> That you are intending to leave us:
> They say it's a fact,
> That your trunk is all packed,
> And you hope by such conduct to grieve us.
>
> You have always been naughty,
> And willful and haughty,
> Like a spoiled minx as you are —
> So vain of your beauty
> Forgetful of duty,
> You owe to indulgent Papa.
>
> . . . Now be warned of your fate
> Before its [sic] too late
> Like a dear innocent lamb
> Come out of your pit
> And do not forget
> All the kindness of good Uncle Sam.[45]

The next month, the *Enquirer* made a much less light-hearted comment about the South's future: "We venture to predict that in three months at the farthest, the United States Government will have resumed undisputed sovereignty in all the present 'seceded' states, the Confederacy of thieves and rebels will finally be broken up, the chief rebels will be hung by due course of law, or be fugitives from justice, and the year of our lord 1861 will have seen the termination as the beginning of the rattlesnake rebellion against the most righteous government that exists upon the face of the earth."[46]

By mid-July, the *Enquirer* and most of Connecticut's residents had ample reason to doubt such predictions. On July 21, near Manassas, Virginia, Union forces under the command of Brigadier General Irvin McDowell and Confederate forces under the command of Brigadier General P. G. T. Beauregard met on the field of battle. Loyal civilians flocked to the hills overlooking the battlefield, bringing picnic lunches and expecting a complete route of the rebels. This was not to be.

McDowell's plan was to split his approximately 30,000 men into three columns, with the first two launching an attack at Bull Run, a river just north of Manassas, to force Beauregard's almost equal number of men (after reinforcements arrived) to respond, while the third Union column swung around to the rear, cutting the rail line to Richmond and endangering the Confederate flank. Connecticut had an important role to play in the battle. Colonel Daniel Tyler, commander of the 1st Regiment CVI, who had helped to train the new soldiers in New Haven with exacting discipline, was promoted to the rank of brigadier general and placed in command of a division. His mission was to distract the Confederates by having his troops make a very visible crossing of Bull Run at a stone bridge, so that the Union flanking forces could move undetected and surprise the enemy. When all the troops were in place, they would attack simultaneously and meet in the center.

It was a good plan, to be sure, but most certainly doomed from the start. It required far too much coordination for raw troops with limited training, and at least one historian has questioned Tyler's abilities as a field commander. He failed to get his troops organized promptly and thereby delayed the flanking column by some three hours. When he finally launched his crossing to mislead the enemy, it was less than effective and failed to hide the Union strategy. Some historians also argue that spies in Washington had informed Beauregard of McDowell's strategy. The Confederates had plenty of time to send in reinforcements. Still, the Union soldiers were not entirely ineffective. Both the 2nd and 3rd CVI Regiments engaged the enemy and, along with other units, pushed the enemy back for a time. The decisive failure in the battle occurred when two Union

"The First Battle of Bull Run, Va., Sunday afternoon, July 21, 1861,"
by J. Brown. Library of Congress, LC-USZ62-8376

artillery batteries mistakenly ceased firing and were subsequently wiped
out by Confederate infantry. Because the rebel soldiers, the 33rd Virginia,
wore blue uniforms, the Union batteries mistook them for Union reinforcements, which allowed them to move in and capture the artillery. At
that critical moment, General Beauregard called in reserve forces, and the
Confederates swept over the battlefield. Union soldiers fled in what some
observers described as a panic-stricken dash, throwing away their guns in
an attempt to escape the slaughter.

During this melee, the 2nd Connecticut, under the command of Colonel Alfred Terry, and the 2nd Maine guarded the Union retreat and faced
a Confederate cavalry charge of some 800 mounted men. The new Union
recruits, whose three-month enlistment was due to run out in a matter of
days, stood their ground and demolished the cavalry. Colonel Hiram Burnham of the 6th Maine said in his official report: "Our noble army is routed;
and the whole plain is covered with fugitives, nothing apparently left in
an organized state but the Connecticut Regiments. Marching across the
level, they reach the woods, when the enemy's cavalry come down. Facing
by the rear-rank the regiments repulse them by well-directed volleys."[47]

Connecticut in the American Civil War

Connecticut troops had been the first on the field of battle and were the last to depart. Even after all hostilities had ceased, they were charged with collecting the gear that so many others had thrown away in their hurry to escape the slaughter.

Although this one bright spot of the battle reflected well on some Union soldiers, losing the first engagement of the war spelled potential disaster for the Union. In all, some 625 Union soldiers were killed or mortally wounded at Bull Run, 950 others were wounded, and more than 1,200 were captured. Out of these, Connecticut lost four killed, twenty-two wounded, and thirty-seven captured. Confederate losses were 625 dead or mortally wounded, and 1,600 others wounded. Such numbers were a trifle in comparison to the bloodletting that was to come, but symbolically the outcome was horrible for the North.[48]

The Bull Run failure emboldened both the Democratic peace movement within Connecticut and the patriotic resistance to it. Stephen Raymond of Darien fired a cannon in celebration of the rebel victory, and he was quickly met by citizens who confiscated the cannon and threw it in a river. After cheering the Confederate victory, a man in Ridgefield was drenched at the town pump and forced to swear a patriotic oath under the American flag. A group of women in Danbury led a brass band down Main Street. Peace and Confederate flags appeared in Easton, Cornwall, Madison, New Britain, New London, North Guilford, Podunk, and Prospect, though they were all promptly torn down. A meeting at Cornwall Bridge passed resolutions calling for "peaceful separation" and declared that "the American Union is forever destroyed." Similar meetings occurred in Bloomfield, Canaan, Danbury, Monroe, New Fairfield, Redding, Saybrook, and Sharon. Fights broke out, weapons were brandished, and rocks thrown. The *Hartford Times* announced boldly: "We are opposed to this war. . . . It is crushing the life-blood of New England."[49] Nathan Morse, editor of the *Bridgeport Farmer and Advertiser*, displayed true venom, mocking the "grand army" that "ran back" from Bull Run, and jeering that "the heart of the Abolitionists heaved with sorrow at the blasted prospects of their fanaticism, and the diminished hope of a speedy gratification of their bloody will."[50]

As the heat of August descended upon Connecticut, tempers continued to flare and confrontations grew bolder. A. A. Pettingill, the editor of the *Bridgeport Republican*, wrote to Governor Buckingham: "I am becoming alarmed at the condition of things in this part of the State. Rebels — & very active ones — can be found without going south of the Mason & Dixon line.

In other words we have *open traitors* at home." Pettingill complained that the *Bridgeport Farmer* was partially responsible, and "the consequence is that we are now threatened with a *Peace party* & a formidable one. There are towns in this Co. in which these men now have a decided majority— towns in which a War Tax could not be collected without the aid of military force." He warned further: "There are secret organizations—one in this city—the members of which have *armed themselves for some purpose*— not a patriotic one."[51]

Pettingill added that "a Peace Meeting (so called) is held at *Stepney*, some nine miles from here, *this afternoon*. A flag is to be raised & word has been sent here that the thing is to be defended by armed men, 60 or 80 young men." Though he hoped that no violence would ensue, he recognized "this state of things cannot continue long without leading to *bloodshed*."[52] Union men, under the direction of P. T. Barnum, the flamboyant Bridgeport showman, paid for carriages to transport loyal men and returning soldiers to Stepney, where they tore down a peace banner, chased peace advocates into a nearby cornfield, and then regrouped and sang "The Star-Spangled Banner." When they returned to Bridgeport, the crowd swelled to several thousand and marched to the offices of Morse's *Farmer*, where they battered down the door and destroyed everything in sight. Morse escaped by fleeing across the rooftops.[53]

The disturbances of late summer were so widespread and so serious that Mark Howard, one of the leaders of the state's Republican Party, wrote to Secretary of the Navy Gideon Welles: "In no part of the free States is treason more malignant, defiant and insidious than in Conn., and Hartford is the seat of its influence. The feeling here is becoming intense on both sides—many of the traitors now go around armed, and the loyal portion of our community will have to do so, in self-defense. And but a spark is now necessary to kindle a flame that can only be extinguished in blood."[54] George A. Oviate, a Congregational minister from Somers, Connecticut, issued similar warnings to Governor Buckingham. "In Conn. there are many who favor the South, and such men, in the rural districts talk secession openly and do much in demoralizing the people," wrote Oviate. He insisted that the *Hartford Times* was largely responsible, noting: "Those who read this paper so exclusively are emboldened in their sympathy with the seceders. If this state of things continues, what is before us?" Oviate advocated shutting the *Times* down and implored the governor: "I hope in order to avoid bloodshed an [sic] Civil War, . . . [by] your Constitutional authority you would by Proclamation or otherwise would forbid the raising of peace Flags, and also peace gatherings in our area."[55]

Responding to just such concerns, Governor Buckingham issued a proclamation on September 1 in which he commented on "the public exhibition of *peace-flags* falsely so called." Although acknowledging that "the Constitution guarantees liberty of speech and that of the press," he insisted that "the very exercise of our government, the future prosperity of this entire nation, and the hopes of universal freedom, demand that these outrages be suppressed." He continued: "I call upon the officers of the law to be active, diligent, and fearless in arresting, and instituting legal proceedings for the punishment of, those who disturb the public peace, or those who are guilty of sedition and treason, and of those who are embraced in combinations to obstruct the execution of the laws."[56] U.S. Marshal David Carr subsequently announced that traitors would "be summarily dealt with."[57] Arrests ensued, and prisoners were transported to Fort Lafayette in New York.[58] Barnum wrote to Lincoln that these actions "have rendered secessionists so scarce, I cannot find one for exhibition in my museum."[59] The back of the peace movement was broken, at least temporarily.[60]

Bull Run was a humiliating disaster for the Union, but it steeled those in Connecticut for the real battles that were to come. The *Hartford Evening Press* announced: "We have had a little of the conceit taken out of us at Manasses [sic] . . . but failure only deepens our rage and strengthens our determination."[61] Horace Bushnell delivered a sermon in Hartford's North Church titled "Reverses Needed," in which he insisted that the North was being tested.[62] The *Courant* questioned how the war should be fought but had no doubts that it should go on: "This is not time for the North to talk about Peace with the South! Doubtless civil war is a terrible calamity; doubtless, we shall all realize it to be such, before we get through with it, and have as yet but sipped a foretaste of its horrors; but what then? . . . The naturally blatant South is in ecstacies [sic], over the retreat of our army from Bull Run! . . . After what has taken place, it is palpable to every man of common sense, that *this quarrel must be* FOUGHT OUT!"[63] The *Courant* followed with another article in October: "Since the Bull Run Panic, it is absolutely necessary for Northern military honor, that the disgraceful reminiscences of that mortifying day, should be wiped out. We have no alternative; we *must* fight, and fight bravely, and retrieve that day, or no Northern man can henceforth hold up his head."[64]

The realities of war were made even clearer when the troops who had enlisted for three months returned home. When the men of the 1st Regiment clambered off the *Elm City* steamship on the morning of July 28, the *Courant* reported: "The men presented the most dusty, tired and ragged aspect that we have ever witnessed in a large body of men. They went off with new and bright uniforms, wearing a martial and impos-ing aspect; they came back ragged and dirty."[65] Still, they were treated as returning heroes, marched to the State House, and formally thanked for their service by Governor Buckingham. Their patriotic fervor and dedica-tion to the Union had not diminished. Most of the men reenlisted in new regiments, and many ultimately became officers. The day after Bull Run, Lincoln issued a call for 500,000 three-year soldiers; only three days later, he signed a bill authorizing another 500,000. Connecticut responded to the call. Veterans traveled throughout the state encouraging enlistments, and in a little over a month, six new regiments were created — the 6th through the 12th CVI. Also formed were the 1st Regiment Connecticut Volunteer Cavalry, the 1st, 2nd, and 3rd Connecticut Volunteer Light Bat-teries Artillery, and the 1st Squadron Connecticut Volunteer Cavalry. In all, some 15,278 Connecticut men flocked to the Union standard. Their enlistments, for three years or more, revealed the North's acknowledg-ment of and commitment to an extended conflict.[66]

Those at home also dedicated themselves to the struggle. On the very day that Lincoln put forth the call for the first 75,000 troops, a Ladies' Aid Society, the first in the country, was formed in Bridgeport.[67] Similar societies sprang up all around the state, many of which were directed by prominent women whose husbands were serving in the army. Harriet Terry wrote to her husband, Alfred, who had been promoted to general: "What do they need to make them perfectly comfortable? Whatever it is they shall have it immediately if you will but let the New Haven *ladies* know through me. Our interest in these men is not to be shown in mere words."[68] The women of Connecticut raised money and collected items of every conceivable sort: sheets, pillows, pillowcases, and blankets; towels; handkerchiefs; shirts and socks; pins, needles, pincushions, and thread; bandages and compresses; dried fruit and jellies; and games, books, and magazines, to name but a few. All were sent in massive quantities. Ad-vertisements were placed in local papers requesting particular items, and instructions were given on how to knit socks to military specifications. On occasion, women added humor to their care packages. The *Litchfield En-quirer* informed readers of items sent to the Sanitary Commission, includ-ing a pair of ragged old socks marked "Jeff Davis," which they hoped would be excellent for "dancing on nothing," a clear reference to the Confederate president hanging from a tree.[69]

The *Courant* reported: "The ladies enter into 'the cause' heart and soul, and are working with a will to tender efficient aid to our sick, suffering and *fighting* soldiers."[70] A historian of Middletown wrote: "The work and powerful Aid of women in suppressing the Rebellion will not and cannot be fully written."[71] Similarly, a Civil War diarist noted in his journal: "I hope some future chronicler of the exertions of Connecticut in this war will award proper credit to the women whose industry and generosity in furnishing comforts to the soldiers have been unintermitting thus far since the very commencement of the war."[72] The soldiers recognized and valued the support of those at home. Late in 1861, Sophronia Barber of Canton received a letter from privates Henry Sexton, Isaac Tuller, and Martin Wadhams, also of Canton and stationed in Annapolis, Maryland: "We have this day been the recipients of some mittens and stockings which we are informed you helped to knit. We thank you kindly for them and as we are engaged in helping to maintain the government and wear these to keep our bodies warm." They told Barber: "You may be assured that our hearts will warm toward those who have remembered the Soldiers in their need." Within ten months, all three men were dead.[73]

The General Assembly also kept apace of war needs, enacting legislation for both financing and raising troops. In late June, the Assembly made provisions for the state to raise $2 million. It also replaced the $10 monthly payment to volunteers with a $300 annual payment and created a monthly payment of up to $10 to the families of volunteers: $6 per month for a volunteer's wife, and $2 per month for each of up to two children. This was the first time such payments were referred to as "bounties," intended to provide an incentive for enlisting. The same law authorized reimbursements to towns and committees that had provided uniforms for local soldiers.[74] In October — after President Lincoln called for 500,000 additional troops, of which Connecticut's quota was 12,000 — the General Assembly called a special session and lifted the cap of 10,000 troops it had established in May. The same law authorized the state treasurer to pay up to an additional $10 per month to the family of any soldier taken prisoner while serving the United States, for as long as the soldier remained imprisoned. In recognition of the fast pace of events and the potential for ongoing and increasing expenses, the law also appropriated another $2,000,000 and authorized the treasurer to issue bonds for up to that amount.[75]

The special October session also allowed the Republican-controlled Assembly to vent some of its anger toward Democrats: the Senate voted to remove from the walls of its chamber the portraits of former Democratic governors Isaac Toucey and Thomas Seymour because of their unpatriotic opposition to the war. The portraits were cut out of their frames, which were left empty on the wall for half a day before they too were removed.[76]

*Advertisement for Phelps & Crow, Hartford Daily Courant,
October 3, 1861.*

Connecticut industry also met the call. On July 5, Samuel Colt's Patent Fire-arms Manufacturing Company signed the very first government contract for producing rifles, issued by Colonel James Ripley of the Ordnance Department for 25,000 stands of arms. On September 2, Hotchkiss & Sons, located in Bridgeport and Sharon, delivered its first order of cannon projectiles. A day later, Hartford's Sharp's Rifle Company delivered its first shipment of 300 shoulder arms, the first installment in the company's eventual sale to the government of approximately 100,000 rifles and carbines during the conflict. On October 28, the Savage Arms Company of Meriden delivered 500 Savage pattern revolvers. By the end of December, the Eagle Manufacturing Company and Mowry, both of Norwich, had received contracts for 25,000 arms and 30,000 rifles, respectively.[77] There were also businesses within the state that, as in modern times, took advantage of war to advertise themselves.

In the immediate aftermath of Bull Run, Lincoln ordered General George McClellan to take command of the new three-year recruits, soon to be called the Army of the Potomac. Both the Union and the Confederacy continued to build their armies, accepting that the war would be longer than either side had originally thought.

Much was expected from the young McClellan. Yet he proved to excel at preparing an army that was never quite ready for action, always believing that Confederate forces outnumbered his own—even when in October 1861, for example, his forces in and around Washington were 120,000 to the enemy's mere 45,000. The historian James McPherson noted that Mc-Clellan was afraid to risk failure and suffered from "Bull Run syndrome," a paralysis that prevented movement.[78] Thus troops like the 5th CVI stayed in the general vicinity of the nation's capital, first in Maryland and then in Virginia, building breastworks in the vicinity of Ball's Bluff, where the Union had lost another battle in poor style. They were joined in their waiting in October by the 8th and 10th CVI.[79]

The Union also considered broader strategies, opting to implement the Anaconda Plan of the aged General Winfield Scott. The plan called for a naval blockade of Southern ports in an attempt to choke the South's trade, including its purchase of weapons. Some 3,500 miles long, the Confederate coastline included ten major ports and an additional 180 inlets, bays, and rivers. By midsummer, the Union was employing three dozen vessels to patrol these waters and cut off Southern supplies. Here, again, Connecticut industry proved instrumental to the Union's ultimate success. Mystic shipbuilding companies, which had thrived on the cotton trade, quickly converted to military production. The Mallory shipyard, George Greenman & Company, and Maxson, Fish & Company all built vessels for the Union. In 1861 alone, Greenman produced three steam transports for the Navy, and in August, Maxson contracted to build an ironclad war ship.[80] One historian noted that Mystic produced fifty-seven steamships, which "represented a full 5 percent of Northern steamships constructed during the war, and they were crucial to the war effort." The local paper, the *Mystic Pioneer*, remarked in August that visitors to the town "could not fail to be struck with the importance of this place as a shipbuilding and ship owning locality." New England vessels also performed odd but useful duties. In November and December, some forty-five old vessels, many of them whaling ships, were loaded with heavy rocks from the region's ubiquitous stone walls. The stones were transported to Charleston and Savannah and sunk in the harbors to snag blockade runners.

The blockade strategy required that the Union seize Southern ports to serve as bases of operation for the North. The first target was Pamlico Sound on the coast of North Carolina, which offered vessels a protected interior waterway. On August 29, the Union Navy bombarded the two forts guarding the Hatteras inlet. The next mission was to capture Port Royal, South Carolina, which was guarded by Fort Walker and Fort Beauregard.

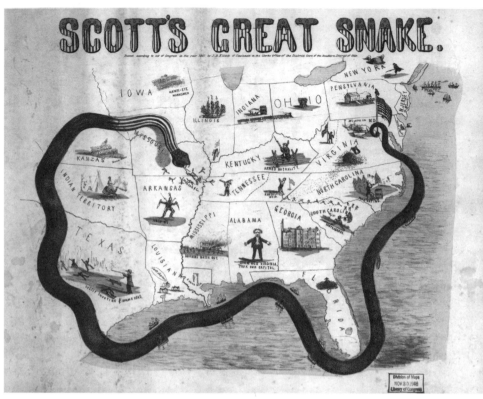

"Scott's Great Snake," by J. B. Elliott, Cincinnati, 1861. Library of Congress Geography and Map Division, LC Civil War Maps (2nd ed.), 11

On November 7, Union naval forces under the command of Flag Officer Samuel du Pont silenced the forts in a mere four hours. General Thomas Sherman then sent troops, including the 6th and 7th Connecticut, to take possession of the forts. Private Stephen Walkley noted in his history of the 7th Regiment that its men were the first to land at Port Royal and enter Fort Walker: "The Seventh regiment had the honor to establish the stars and stripes and the three-vined flag of Connecticut side by side on the sacred soil of South Carolina in place of the stars and bars and the Palmetto flag of that state."[81]

Their entry into Fort Walker was not all about flag waving or, as Walkley put it, like "dress parade." These new soldiers also saw the true face of war for the first time. The naval guns had wreaked havoc on the Confederate defenders, and Private Charles Cadwell of the 6th Regiment wrote that "many of the dead were literally torn to atoms and some were half

Connecticut in the American Civil War

buried where they fell; guns were dismounted, army wagons smashed . . . knapsacks, blankets and rifles lay in confusion all around." Walkley, too, recognized that death could have claimed him and his comrades, remembering that they "had been tossed on a raging sea in danger of foundering until hope almost fled," and "later we saw the strong fort and powerful armament which we believed we must face in deadly assault." Even after the brief battle, while reconnoitering Hilton Head Island (a popular tourist destination today), some men could think of little but home. Walkley wrote of one soldier who was "deathly homesick," and commented to his wife about the monotonous, never-ending sand: "The face of nature presents the utmost possible contrast with breezy, sparkling, ever changing New England." The soldiers were also mobbed by runaway slaves, prompting one soldier to remark: "The negroes glorify us into saints. Let men in high places or low do what they please, this army will not fight for slavery; and the war is a war for liberty."[82] What he meant was white liberty against tyrannical Southerners.

———•———

The beginnings of war in the western theater also captured Connecticut's attention. Although no Connecticut troops were stationed there, a Connecticut native, Nathaniel Lyon of Eastford, became the first Union general to die in battle. Under the command of the intrepid explorer General John C. Frémont, Lyon and his troops had entered St. Louis to quell attempts to take over the arsenal there and disband an encampment of rebel sympathizers. Shortly after, he rode further west, and on August 10, 1861, fought at the Battle of Wilson's Creek, just south of Springfield, Missouri. Lyon's horse was shot out from under him, and he was wounded several times before a bullet finally pierced his heart. News of his death shocked Connecticut. His body was returned home for burial, and some ten thousand mourners paid their respects.[83]

General Frémont's activities in the west also raised questions about the wider aims of the war, questions that some residents of Connecticut wrestled with. On August 30, Frémont declared martial law in Missouri, and as part of his edict announced freedom for the slaves of all Confederates engaged in the war. Lincoln responded immediately and negatively, writing Frémont that the Union was in delicate negotiations with Kentucky, which had not seceded, and that freeing slaves would "alarm our Southern Union friends, and turn them against us — perhaps ruin our rather fair prospect for Kentucky." The president ultimately revoked Frémont's order and, for this and other reasons, removed him from his command.

Yet problems regarding slaves had arisen immediately after the attack on Fort Sumter. In May, three slaves belonging to a Confederate colonel had crossed General Benjamin Butler's lines at Fortress Monroe, Virginia. When the colonel attempted to regain his property under a flag of truce, citing the fugitive slave law, Butler refused, labeling the slaves contraband of war and putting them to work in his camp. Thousands more slaves crossed Union lines in the months that followed. Butler's contraband doctrine might have been what former governor of Kentucky Charles Morehead had in mind when, as noted previously, he wrote that secession would do more damage to slavery than abolitionism would. Butler's decree was part of a new concept regarding the law of war, one that allowed a government to engage in extraordinary acts that would have been illegal in peacetime.[84]

Lincoln ultimately upheld Butler's contraband policy. The *Hartford Times* marveled at such actions and warned Connecticut's citizens that freed slaves would make their way to the North and destroy its society: they will "come in conflict with the free labor of the North—those of them who do not pass into our poor-houses and become burthens upon society. ... Here is an evil at our doors of great magnitude."[85] The policy of labeling slaves contraband of war, however, was as far as Lincoln was willing to go at this stage of the conflict. When General Frémont went a step further, the president balked, even though radical Republicans, the abolitionist wing of the party, were pushing hard to make the war about slavery. Lincoln simply wasn't ready. Of Lincoln's caution, Joseph R. Hawley—who had served as an editor of the *Hartford Evening Press* and marched directly out of his office upon hearing the news of Fort Sumter to help organize and enroll in the 1st CVI—wrote to Gideon Welles: "Permit me to say *damn* the border states. . . . A thousand Lincolns cannot stop the people from fighting slavery."[86]

Other Republicans did not necessarily agree. The *Courant* addressed the issue on October 7, reporting: "The expediency of using the war-power of the National Government, to emancipate the slaves in the rebellious States, is much discussed." The paper continued: "That such a step may become necessary, is possible; lapse of time alone, can settle that point." But, seeming to understand Lincoln's hesitancy, the paper stated: "At *present* it does not appear to become necessary; nay, it would be a suicidal policy—unworthy any statesman." Only a few weeks later, the *Courant* came out with a mixed message of abolitionism and Free Soil doctrine, proclaiming the hope that it was "the Almighty's programme that black slavery shall be utterly *abolished* from the face of the earth," but adding:

Connecticut in the American Civil War

"*We* would rather see this glorious Union, from Maine to Mexico, filled with white men and women, all free and industrious, than to see it as it now is, through a large extent, given over to be inhabited by negroes, with a sparse population of poor whites and idle slaveholders. If that is 'Abolitionism,' then make the most of it!"[87]

The very idea of abolition ignited a fire within the offices of the *Hartford Times*. "The enlistments have not been made with reference to an Abolition war," thundered the paper; "The Administration decides it is not an Abolition contest—the Constitution sanctions nothing of the kind—and such a war could not be successfully waged." In a later article, the *Times* criticized Massachusetts Senator Charles Sumner, who "devoted his speech to a plea for the conversion of the war into a crusade against slavery." In another article, published in mid-December and titled "The Everlasting Negro," the *Times* exploded over the never-ending talk of Republicans in Congress: "They serve up their favorite dish, the African, in every imaginable style—they bring him out fired, roasted, parboiled, scalloped, fricasseed, boiled, baked, steamed, and stewed. . . . All other subjects of legislation are given the go-by."[88]

Such harangues had little effect on those who began to question the North's views on slavery. The *New Haven Palladium* described what might be called the malaise of Northern slavery thought. Referring to the "fossilated compromisers" of the North, the *Palladium* insisted that the North had become complacent and begun to "superstitiously believe" in the propriety of Southern slavery. "Every age has its epidemic delusions," observed the paper, "and the American people have been for thirty years in a sort of a trance, on this subject of slavery. Nothing but the cannon balls that rattled upon Fort Sumpter [sic] could have roused them from their stupor. That thunder did break the spell." In making this assertion, the paper seemed astonished that, at that time, "the Government will not make the freedom of slaves an issue in this contest; for it started in the war for no purpose of *re-moddeling* [sic] *the Government*, but simply to restore it to the precise condition in which it was left by its makers." Then, focusing on the rather odd rationale for carrying out certain aspects of the war but not others, such as emancipation, the *Palladium* pointed out that the Union could shoot Southerners and take their cotton, wheat, and corn, their cattle and their cash, "but to take their slavery property is barbarous, unconstitutional, and in violation of many sacred compromises! We are all *abolitionists* when we come to that! Queer, isn't it?"[89]

In a December sermon delivered in Litchfield, Charles Weatherby raised the same issues. Noting that Northerners had become accustomed to accepting Southern dictation, Weatherby declared: "The North is becoming conscious of its past sinful submission to the slave power. The present war is showing us the extent of the wrong as no other agency could have done." Discussing military necessity, he dismissed the traditional rationale that the Constitution protected slavery and returned to the question of the North's ability to forge its own path: "This subserviency must and will be overcome. It shows a want of moral dignity, and confidence in the right necessary to insure success. Taking our position at different stand points, we find our faith growing stronger that the coming day of freedom is surely drawing near."[90]

That day of freedom was not to occur in 1861. In fact, the war itself had barely begun. By late summer, many residents of Connecticut had reached the conclusion that the conflict would be long and bloody. The *Courant* put it simply: "The rebel understands the meaning of powder and ball; and no shorter argument can be used. . . . That's the duty of the day, with us of Connecticut; there's no use in talking."[91] Gone were the spring days when some had poked fun at the very idea of secession, or mockingly believed Southerners would flee the field of battle and quickly return to the Union. Bull Run had dashed such hopes. It had also sparked a significant peace movement, which revealed that not everyone in the state supported a war to coerce Southern loyalty. Some believed that Connecticut, Hartford especially, was a nest of traitors. If true, it was not enough to stop the much more widespread patriotism that poured forth from around the state. When Lincoln called for additional troops, the three-month veterans fanned out to search for recruits, and war meetings took place in town after town. Connecticut provided some 15,000 men and much-needed war materials. Women formed aid societies and collected every conceivable item for those who served. It was all necessary. For 1862 promised a river of blood.

CHAPTER THREE

A Recognition of Death

1862

If 1861 and the defeat at Bull Run steeled the Union minded citizens of Connecticut to the necessity of a prolonged war, 1862 taught them the bloody realities of such convictions. It also presented the less bloody, but very real, soldiers' deaths caused by any number of diseases. And though many at home may have snapped to attention in supporting the enlistment of troops, procuring supplies, and organizing aid societies, it did not mean that the wheels of government were adequately prepared to usher hundreds of thousands of men and vast quantities of materials into an efficient military organization. Nor had the government fully mapped out its military strategy or found a leader who could achieve victory. Beyond efforts for the Union's survival, few in Connecticut knew what this war of such immense proportions entailed. Winfield Scott's Anaconda Plan was designed to strangle the South, but to work, it required time and Union control of major waterways both on the coast running to Florida and throughout the Gulf of Mexico, as well as the internal route of the Mississippi River. Then there was the defense of Washington. With so many roads into the nation's capital, its protection required a formidable army. The surrounding areas, Virginia and Maryland, would surely be bloody.

While Connecticut troops were baptized by fire, those back in New England were tasked with the continued necessity of maintaining a strong home front. This required a virtual river of supplies, maintained by both soldiers' aid societies and individual families. There was also the importance of holding down the Democrat peace movement and maintaining Republican political control. With the governor's term of office lasting only one year, Governor Buckingham and Republicans had to do battle each spring lest they lose the political war at home. In this sense, the military and political engagements had a symbiotic relationship. The ebb and flow of Union success naturally influenced voters' confidence in the state's administration, and the health of the government at home and its ability to keep "traitors" in check had a resounding effect on the confidence of soldiers in the field. It was a delicate balance that was often made more difficult by the actions of the federal government and the Union military.

When President Lincoln announced his preliminary Emancipation Proclamation in September 1862, Democrats renewed their onslaught against the war. They had charged from the outset that abolition and what they called "negro philanthropy" were the true Republican goals. Lincoln's proclamation opened the door for more such Democratic assaults, even though he and other Republicans argued that emancipation was a means of winning the war, not an end in itself. Nonetheless, the very idea of emancipation created a tempest, and, combined with the shocking bloodletting at battles like Antietam and Fredericksburg, the Union was at a low ebb by the end of the year.

The Anaconda Plan required control of a vast coastline dotted with inlets, bays, creeks, swamps, and bayous, any one of which could allow blockade runners to slip away from Union pursuit or gain access to the South. And, of course, the region was the Confederates' backyard, and they knew, far better than any Yankee, how to navigate the watery morass. Nonetheless, in late 1861, the Union Navy sailed south to shut down rebel trade. The first engagements involved the taking of Pamlico Sound as well as Fort Walker and Fort Beauregard.

Even with these early successes, the arrival of Union troops in the South was plagued by disasters. Brigadier General Ambrose Burnside's North Carolina Expedition force, which included the 8th, 10th, and 11th Connecticut Regiments, was caught in a horrendous storm off the always turbulent Cape Hatteras. From late November into January, Union ships were unable to reach the safety of Pamlico Sound. The men of the 8th were stuffed into the hold of a ship that had no berths and reeked of bilge water. Some of the men slept on deck, wrapped in blankets, as the sea erupted over the gunwales. The 10th was crowded into a filthy schooner that had recently transported coal, and the men did not have nearly enough clean water. Captain Benjamin Pardee of the 10th wrote of the weeks at sea: "How can I describe them? Days of weariness and danger; no news to cheer us; disasters all around us; the skies black and unpromising; the surf beating sullenly the solemn requiem of the lost; sickness on all the vessels; epidemics rapidly extending; deaths frequent; no comfort for the sick; scant food for the well; water, tainted with kerosene, served out in limited quantity; our expedition a seeming failure!" The 11th fared little better. A giant wave beached their vessel on Hatteras, and the men escaped only moments before it was dashed to pieces.[1] It was hardly an auspicious beginning.

The 8th and 10th were part of the roughly 7,500 Union troops that finally landed at Roanoke Island on February 7. They quickly pushed the Confederates back and, with no blankets, spent a cold, rain-drenched night in the woods. The next day, while the 8th was kept in reserve, the 10th moved forward toward the 3,000 enemy troops that had erected a three-gun battery almost in the center of the island, at its crest. Having never experienced combat, the Confederates got their first taste of battle from the 9th New York and 25th Massachusetts, which led the assault. Captain Pardee wrote: "Men came by with stretchers, carrying the brave Massachusetts boys, frightful with bleeding wounds. We see the dead lying beneath trees on either side. Surgeons were busy at their vocation." As the 10th moved into position, continued Pardee, the road "brought us right in front of the rebel guns, and in perfect range. They had three pieces of artillery fronting and commanding this clearing; and large numbers of riflemen perched in trees, behind the turfed walls, and under all possible covers." As Confederate guns opened up, the men were ordered to lie on the ground for cover. Pardee wrote that the "bullets and grape-shot flew thick over the men as they lay. There was a constant 'Hst, hst!' as the musket-bullets whispered past, cutting twigs from the bushes not two feet above their heads, or striking the trees behind which they were sheltered."[2] The regiment's commander, Colonel Charles Russell of Derby, was no sooner finally convinced to seek cover than he was hit with a bullet that entered his shoulder and pierced his heart. He was one of four men killed. More than fifty men of the 10th were wounded. Still, the Union won the battle and with it, control of Albemarle Sound, which served as the watery front door to North Carolina. As the 10th, along with the 8th and 11th, moved on to New Berne, North Carolina, Lieutenant Colonel Albert Drake, the regiment's new commander, wrote: "Good-by, dirty, muddy, swampy, brackish, diseased, and deathful Roanoke!"[3]

It took a month for General Burnside to put his troops in motion again, but on March 13 they arrived at New Berne, located on the Neuse River and providing an entrance into the North Carolina interior. Union forces, numbering 12,000, marched twelve miles through the swamps to arrive just two miles below the Confederate defenses. The rebel lines stretched over two miles, from the Neuse to the Atlantic & North Carolina Railroad, and consisted of some 8,000 men, with forty-one heavy cannons, and nineteen pieces of field artillery. Lieutenant Henry Ward Camp wrote that the next morning, as the 10th Regiment moved forward, "a loud, swift whiz went through the air, sounding as if some one had torn a thousand yards of canvas from one end to the other at a single pull." Suddenly, a huge limb fell from a tree, lopped off by an artillery shell. "The line advanced, under a constant fire, up the slope, in plain sight of the rebel batteries, with their flaunting flags, and approached to within three hundred yards before returning the fire. Then a long line of unwavering musketry, broken here and there by howitzers, flashed and roared in angry response."[4] Lieutenant Joseph Converse noted that after the order to charge was given, "from the curtain of the woods up sprang thousands of blue-coats, — a glittering wave of steel flashing in front, — and rushed forward with loud huzzas, and invincible line." Colonel Drake reported that in less than ten minutes, "we saw the American flag coming along the left into their battery. It went in, and was planted there. Whipped, poor traitors!" Five men from the 10th were killed, and twenty wounded. The 11th suffered six deaths and sixteen wounded, while the 8th captured some 500 prisoners and had two men killed and four wounded.[5]

While the 8th, 10th, and 11th made headway in the middle Atlantic, farther south the 6th and 7th Connecticut Regiments had moved from taking Fort Walker and Fort Beauregard to preparing a siege at Fort Pulaski, on the Savannah River in Georgia. The expedition was almost entirely a Connecticut affair. Designed by the New Haven–born General Joseph Totten, the fort took eighteen years to build, from 1829 to 1847, with granite and sandstone blocks quarried in Connecticut and New York. For fourteen of those years, from 1831 to 1845, the work was overseen by Lieutenant Joseph K. F. Mansfield, also from Connecticut, who was Totten's cousin. When the Civil War began, Confederate Colonel Charles Olmstead, whose family was originally from Connecticut, was in command of the fort.[6] With such a lineage, it was only fitting that Connecticut regiments should force the fort to surrender. Boasting walls seven feet thick and twenty-five feet high, the fort was considered by its designer to be impenetrable. Such a belief, however, was based on traditional notions of military science — notions that the Civil War soon dashed to pieces with the invention of new, devastating weapons. Fort Pulaski was the first victim of the Union's new rifled Parrot guns, whose grooved barrels permitted deadly accuracy and penetration, even of a structure like the fort.

Yet the guns still needed to get as close as possible to the fort, and this is where the 7th Connecticut came in. Ordered to Tybee Island, which was little more than a strip of muddy, insect-infested swamp, the 7th spent the months of December to April moving guns and mortars, some of which weighed eight and a half tons each, two and a half miles so that they could be placed just 1,672 yards from the fort. It was an arduous, dangerous affair. With no roads to the island, the 7th was forced to pull the giant guns by sling cart, with wheels higher than a man, and it took 250 men, trudging through mud that was at times twelve feet deep, to move the guns into position. All of this was done in mere whispers under the cover of night, lest the enemy discover the batteries and fire on the exposed men.

Stephen Walkley, who had written of the regiment's longing for home while at Hilton Head, noted that at Tybee, "more fatal diseases than homesickness awaited the regiment." With swarms of mosquitoes, malaria was rampant, and Walkley devoted two full pages to the itchy, unrelenting fleas that infested this former hog pasture. He concluded: "Though profanity is never excusable, fleas are extenuating circumstances."[7] When the batteries were finally ready, and after Colonel Olmstead had refused to surrender, the first shot was fired on April 10, at 8:15 in the morning by Captain Oliver Sanford of Meriden. He included a special message on the shell, referring to Connecticut's nickname as the Nutmeg State: "A nutmeg from Connecticut; can you furnish a grater?" The next day, the 7th watched as the walls of this state-of-the-art fort, which had taken nearly two decades to complete, crumbled under the precision effects of rifled artillery. The Union captured forty-seven heavy guns, a large store of ammunition, 40,000 pounds of gunpowder, and 360 prisoners. The 6th Regiment served at the same siege, erecting batteries on nearby Jones Island.[8]

Victory at Fort Pulaski did not promise control of the interior of Georgia or South Carolina. Charleston, the seedbed of the war, lay only miles away, but Union forces moved with amazing sloth, something that became an all-too-persistent problem for the North. On June 10, the troops arrived on James Island, where they waited another six days before moving on Secessionville, which lay on the path to Charleston. By this time, the 1st Connecticut Heavy Artillery (formerly the 4th CVI) had joined the 6th and 7th. Confederate defenders had had plenty of time to prepare for battle, and the Union attack was botched from the start. General H. W. Benham ignored the advice of his division commanders and ordered a frontal assault on the strongest part of the enemy's defenses. At the center of the line, the Confederates placed a howitzer stuffed with bottles, old chains, spikes, horseshoes, and any other scrap metal available.

"Fort Pulaski, Ga. Interior view of breach," photograph by Timothy H. Sullivan, April 1862. The ruins of the fort show the effects of rifled artillery fire. Library of Congress, LC-DIG-cwpb-00777

Though the big gun certainly inflicted punishment, the great killer of the day was grape shot. Something of a euphemism, the term describes a mass of lead balls that resembled a cluster of grapes fired from a cannon. Once launched, the balls exploded outward in a lethal hail. Colonel Joseph Hawley of the 7th reported that "grape and rifle shot came in showers," and that Lieutenant Thomas Hooten was hit in the right thigh with grape that traveled up into his body. Sergeant Andrew Upson was also hit: "grape took off three fingers and dashed his right shoulder." Hawley reported that Captain Edwin Hitchcock was "enthusiastically cheering on his men" when he was severely wounded in the thigh. He continued cheering until he was hit by a musket ball, square in his upper lip. Two other men were injured while trying to carry Hitchcock to safety, and he was left to die on the field. The men also witnessed gore from rather bizarre episodes. "I saw a shell explode inside the body of a horse, scattering fragments of flesh and bones in every direction, and covering his rider with gore from head to foot," a member of the 1st Artillery reported.[9]

The 7th was particularly hard hit, with eleven men killed and sixty-two wounded. Three men were captured. For issuing such foolish commands, which in fact were contrary to his own orders, and as a result of the death that ensued, General Benham was arrested, relieved of duty, and transferred. Captain William Lusk of the 79th New York epitomized the anger that the men felt toward the general: "I will not enumerate half the examples of imbecility he has shown, or the wickedness of which he has been guilty."[10] The 6th and 7th were now happy to return to sandy Hilton Head, where they remained encamped until October. Colonel Hawley proceeded home to Connecticut, where he sought enlistments to replenish the 7th's ranks, returning with fifty new recruits in early September. In October, both the 6th and 7th engaged in minor operations in and around St. John's Bluff, Florida, and fought in the battle of Pocotaligo, South Carolina, where they attempted to destroy part of the Charleston & Savannah Railroad. The 6th suffered its first casualties, with five men killed and thirty wounded, among them Colonel John Chatfield.[11] The two regiments remained in the Hilton Head and Beaufort area for the rest of the year.

***

The Union operations along the coast from North Carolina to Florida comprised the first elements of the Anaconda Plan. Farther south, efforts were made to shut down Confederate trade in the Gulf of Mexico, especially in the New Orleans region, and extending all the way up the Mississippi River, above New Orleans itself. Late in 1861, General Benjamin Butler created a New England Brigade that assembled in Massachusetts and made its way to a staging area on Ship Island, Mississippi, about fifty miles east of New Orleans. In late December 1861, the 9th Connecticut arrived on the island. This was a special regiment, made up solely of Irish and Irish Americans. At the outset of the war, the General Assembly rescinded an obnoxious 1855 edict, inspired by the Know Nothings, that had made it illegal for Irish immigrants to serve in the militia. Allowing them to serve, however, was by no means the same as embracing these immigrants. The regiment was treated poorly from the start, receiving limited supplies, and no guns, uniforms, or tents. Half the men arrived at the island with no shoes or shirts. They stood in sharp contrast to other regiments, which, as one historian noted, "would have been amusing if it were not humiliating." While on Ship Island, the men finally received their Enfield rifles, and Colonel Thomas Cahill appropriated a shipment of shoes for the soldiers.[12] The regiment was ultimately joined by the 12th, 13th, and 23rd Connecticut Regiments.

April was a glorious month for the Union. Naval Flag Officer David Farragut steamed up the Mississippi on board the USS *Hartford* together with twenty-four warships carrying 245 guns, heavy mortars, and 15,000 troops. The Union forces took New Orleans with relative ease, and the first troops to enter the city were the men of the 12th. It was a woeful disappointment to the South. The fiery Virginia secessionist Edwin Ruffin wrote: "The recent disaster at New Orleans & probable consequences have operated to depress my spirits more than all the previous losses to our arms & cause."[13] The South feared that the Union's spring victories all along the East Coast, the capture of Fort Donelson and the narrow victory by General Ulysses Grant at Shiloh, both in Tennessee, and the seizure of New Orleans spelled disaster for the rebellion. Over the next several weeks, the Union Navy continued its run up the Mississippi River, capturing Baton Rouge, Natchez, and Memphis. Connecticut regiments — the 9th, 12th, 13th, and 23rd, and later the 24th, 26th, and 28th — moved in and around the New Orleans region for the remainder of the year, safeguarding this gem of Union victory. Many Connecticut troops were stationed at Camp Parapet, about ten miles north of the city. Little real fighting occurred there; the real killer was disease. In the 13th alone, some forty men died of typhoid fever during the hot Louisiana summer. The 12th's Captain John William De Forest wrote about malaria, noting that "the evening resounds with mosquitoes; a tent hums with them like a beehive," and "the night air is as heavy and dank as that of a swamp, and at daybreak the rotten odor of the earth is sickening."[14] In such circumstances, the men actually longed for combat.

De Forest's descriptions of a soldier's life are amazingly detailed. An author from Seymour, Connecticut, he kept a journal throughout his military service that depicted in striking detail the ups and downs of the war, from camp life to marching and battle. He noted early on the vast number of escaped slaves — contraband — who flocked to Union camps when the military arrived. "Five hundred Negroes arrived," he wrote in a letter, "and they drift hither in gangs every day from the plantations. . . . Rations are issued to all, and a roll of names is kept by our provost marshal, who is

*Captain John William De Forest
of the 12th Connecticut Volunteer
Infantry, 1868, photograph by
Cowell's, New Haven, Conn.*

amusingly 'sick of niggers.' What would happen to the creatures if we should leave? I begin to think that the government will be driven to enlist them as soldiers." He added: "Everybody has come over to the notion of enlisting the darkey's." His comments were remarkably prescient, as the enlistment of black troops became a major controversy throughout the nation and in Connecticut. As his service in the South continued, De Forest reported that he had never met a Negro who was hostile to Union soldiers, "but meanwhile they were not vindictive toward their masters, at least not to the extent of insurrection, or massacre, or murder."[15]

While Farragut and Grant effectively wrapped up the war in the west, General McClellan focused on Richmond. The Peninsula Campaign of April and May did not give the Union forces access to the Confederate capital, but it did force the evacuation of Yorktown and Norfolk, forcing the rebels to relinquish the important navy yard and access to the James River. One consequence of this victory was the South's reluctant destruction of the famed CSS *Virginia* (formerly known as the *Merrimac*), which only two months earlier had clashed with the USS *Monitor* in the first battle between two ironclad vessels, and in doing so had changed the course of naval warfare.

All looked gloomy for the Confederacy as spring burst forth in fragrant blooms. Yet that same cyclical renewal also brought rebirth to a beleaguered South, beginning in the Shenandoah Valley. In late May, the famed Stonewall Jackson defeated the Union's General Nathaniel Banks at Winchester, Virginia, driving his troops across the Potomac River into Maryland, and causing panic that Washington was vulnerable to attack. In mid-June, the newly appointed commander of the Army of Northern Virginia, Robert E. Lee, sent Jeb Stuart's cavalry to ascertain McClellan's position. Remarkably, Stuart rode all the way around the Army of the Potomac without the loss of a single man. It was an embarrassment to McClellan and made Stuart famous.

The embarrassments continued for the Union outside of Richmond. During the Seven Days Battles of late June and early July, Lee attacked while McClellan stood still, unwilling to go on the offensive, paralyzed by his persistent belief in Lee's overwhelming numbers. Many in the North had expected a great victory in time to celebrate the nation's birthday, July 4. Instead, the *Hartford Courant* reported: "Richmond became a gaping hell, from which myriads of infuriated devils have been poured forth, breathing slaughter and death." The "reverse, serious but by no means overwhelming," said the paper, "has dashed our cup of exultation to the ground just as it touched our lips and closed the door of victory just as our feet were upon the threshold."[16] The defeat marked the end of the Richmond campaign. It was a shock to the North and a lucky escape for the South. Events did not improve for the Union as the summer wore on.

In the west, Union forces kept a covetous eye on Vicksburg. This "Gibraltar of the West," as Confederates called it, sat at a looping bend in the Mississippi River, atop a 200-foot bluff heavily fortified with artillery. Even with Farragut's fleet, the city could not be taken without a major land assault from the east. Thus the Union adopted a new strategy. In late June, the Irish of the 9th Connecticut Regiment, along with troops from Massachusetts, Vermont, and Wisconsin, began digging a vast canal that cut across the neck of the river's bend, with the intent of diverting the mighty Mississippi, stealing away Vicksburg's waterfront perch, and thereby rendering its artillery fortifications useless. Digging the canal was a nightmare. W. A. Croffut and John M. Morris noted simply: "The Ninth again suffered greatly."[17] Laboring in temperatures as high as 115 degrees, the Irish immigrants hacked away at the muddy, malarial muck, satiating their thirst with nothing but murky water from the river, and surviving on a diet of pork and hard tack — a sort of biscuit baked to be so hard and dry that it could literally last for years.

Of the 350 members of the 9th who helped dig the canal, nearly half of them—153 men—died. Captain Lawrence O'Brien of New Haven reported: "We could not give a funeral escort to the dead; the few who were able to do guard and picket duty could not attend to any extra duty. . . . I saw men drop out of line exhausted, and when we returned many of them would be dead." The regiment's official historian observed that the men "died for their country just as truly as if they had fallen in the forefront of the battle."[18] When the Mississippi's water level dropped in early August, it made the canal plan untenable, and the work was abandoned as quickly as it had begun. The Union's hope of capturing Vicksburg ended too, for a time.

Nor was this the only disappointment in the west. The Union might have slid rather easily into Tennessee and Mississippi in the spring, but summer revealed that Confederate forces were unwilling to simply walk away. Rebels threatened Kentucky, destroyed railroads and bridges in Tennessee, and even endangered Nashville. Union forces were kept busy, and Northerners were continually uneasy about the direction of the war.

Northern fears were further realized when actions in the east went poorly for the Union. On August 5, Stonewall Jackson defeated General Nathaniel Banks at the battle of Cedar Mountain, outside of Culpeper, Virginia. Part of Banks's army was the 5th Connecticut, which endured its most significant combat losses in a single day for its entire service during the war. Out of some 380 men engaged in battle, thirty-five were killed, among them the regiment's major, Edward Blake of New Haven. About seventy-one men were wounded and fifty-nine captured, including Colonel George Chapman of Hartford, and Lieutenant Colonel Henry Stone of Danbury. In all the regiment's eight companies, only three officers avoided death, injury, or capture.

The bloodletting began as the 5th charged across a rough wheat field. "The battery in front belched grape and canister, mowing their ranks," wrote Croffut and Morris; the Union troops suffered a "murderous fire from every quarter." Fifty men were struck within two minutes, as the "narrow field was swept by all the engines of destruction."[19] Wounded men dove behind wheat stacks and rocks. Some were shot again and again. The *Courant* reported that Captain George W. Corliss of New Haven "was struck by ten shots, and fought as long as he could stand." Remarkably, he survived. "The color-bearers of the 5th suffered terribly," the paper wrote in a later article; "every man who raised [the colors] was shot. . . . The State and regimental flags, shattered and torn to shreds, were brought safely off by the brave men who had sworn to defend them."[20]

Cedar Mountain turned out to be only a precursor to a bigger, more demoralizing Union loss, which occurred on the same ground that had inaugurated the war and that had seen the Union's first defeat — Bull Run, or Manassas, as Southerners referred to the battlefield. For three days at the end of August, Union and Confederate armies once again bloodied the Virginia soil, and again rebel forces got the better of the North. Connecticut regiments were not engaged in the battle, though the 5th, still battered from Cedar Mountain, was held in reserve. In the aftermath of the collision, the *Courant* announced: "The second battle of Bull Run has been fought, our army repulsed if not defeated, and the rebel hordes, cooped up in and around Richmond for months, and which we had fondly imagined incapable of holding on even there much longer, have not only advanced so as to threaten Washington in front, but crossing the Potomac, have taken possession, with the airs of conquerors, of the second city of Maryland."[21] The paper could not have better described either the tactical situation or the North's shock at the ability of the South to rise again and again. Much of its success was due to Lee's tenacity and risk taking, as well as the bickering and lack of coordination among Union generals.[22]

The stage was set for a campaign that might very well seal the Union's fate, a fate that had as much to do with foreign views of the war as with the clatter of arms and men on the battlefield. Britain and France took great interest in the American conflict One of the Confederacy's goals had always been to gain foreign recognition, as Southerners ceaselessly believed in the power of "King Cotton" and the demand of British textile mills for the indispensable white staple. The North was equally dedicated to preventing that recognition. Immediately after the second defeat at Bull Run, the *Courant* lamented: "This is sufficiently humiliating, and will doubtless cause John Bull [the British] . . . to put forth with renewed pertinency and vigor their special plea for intervention, on the score of the evident impossibility of our ever conquering the South."[23] Thus the crossroads for the Union war effort converged at the little town of Sharpsburg, Maryland, where the great Potomac River met a little creek named Antietam.

The battle of Antietam was fought on September 17, the single bloodiest day of the entire war. Between 6,300 and 6,500 soldiers, both Union and Confederate, were killed or mortally wounded. Another 17,000 were injured. The historian James McPherson wrote that "the number of casualties at Antietam was four times greater than American casualties at the Normandy beaches on June 6, 1944," and more than twice the combined death

"Antietam, Md. Another view of Antietam Bridge,"
photograph by James F. Gibson, September 1862.
Library of Congress, LC-DIG-cwpb-01133

---

toll from the War of 1812, the Mexican War, and the Spanish-American War.[24] Men from four Connecticut regiments — the 8th, 11th, 14th, and 16th — spilled their blood on the fields surrounding Sharpsburg.

Lieutenant Joseph Converse of Stafford, in the 11th, remembered later that "the day passed like a shrieking shell. The sky was filled with unearthly sounds, — the howl of fiendish missiles, the crash of falling trees, the horrible discharge of hundreds of cannons. Along our entire front, rebel batteries were constantly discovered, till a long line of cannon could be seen though the murky canopy, panting with deadly heat." The regiment's commander, Colonel Thomas H. C. Kingsbury of Franklin, was shot in the foot and then in the leg while attempting to cross the twelve-foot-wide stone bridge (which became known as Burnside's Bridge) that forded Antietam Creek. While being carried off the field, he was hit again, this time receiving a fatal blow to the abdomen. Converse reported that "companies were squads without officers, and officers with broken swords and battered uniforms, but without commands." The 11th had thirty-six men killed and 112 wounded, including every field officer.[25]

The 16th was in the same brigade as the 11th, and also fought at Burnside Bridge. Unlike the 11th, however, the 16th was a brand-new regiment, having been mustered into service on August 24. The men had received little training and were totally unprepared for the slaughter. William Relyea of Suffield remembered: "The way was strewn with the signs of deadly conflict. This altered our view of things mightily. Torn fences, broken tree limbs, wrecked wagons, scattered blankets, abandoned knapsacks, and wounded men, now and then the dead body of a man or horse, ammunition teams, baggage wagons, prisoners and moving troops completely blocked up the roads and made it exceedingly difficult for us to get along." He continued: "Little did any of us think as we trudged along that in a few hours many of us would be stiff and cold in death as the bodies that we saw dressed in blue and gray lying by the roadside."[26]

When the troops arrived on the front line, Corporal Benjamin Blakeslee of Hartford recalled, "we were suddenly ordered to 'Attention!' when a terrible volley was fired into us from behind a stone wall. . . . We were ordered to fix bayonets and advance. In a moment we were riddled with shot." "The most helpless confusion ensued," he continued: "Men were falling on every hand. The survivors at last extricated themselves from the fatal field, and fled, broken and decimated, back to cover near the bridge."[27] Private Relyea remembered the same moment, fixing bayonets and firing a volley: "I had loaded and was going to fire the third time when, happening to look around, I saw only dead men laying where they fell. I very quickly decided it was no place for me." Relyea described the intensity of the enemy's heavy fire as he sprinted back across the field: "The Johnnies [Confederates] kept plowing up dirt around me so thick that it kept me spitting mud and rubbing out of my eyes so much so that I got angry and turning shook my fist in impotent rage."[28] When the men in the 16th were finally able to ascertain the regiment's condition, they counted forty-four dead, one missing, 159 wounded, and nineteen captured. It was an appalling start to their wartime experience.

The 8th Connecticut suffered from the 16th's disorder. After having pushed the Confederates back slightly, the 8th was confronted with a counterattack and no reinforcements to stem the rebel tide. The regiment suffered its single largest loss of the entire war, with thirty-three men killed, 145 wounded, and twenty-three captured. The day after the battle, one of the regiment's members was found on the field, "shot through the body, still laying on his back, just as he had fallen. The fierce sun of the day

Connecticut in the American Civil War

"The Battle of Antietam, Md. Sept. 17th 1862," hand-colored
lithograph, Currier and Ives, New York, 1862 or 1863.
Library of Congress, LC-USZ62-13998

before had blistered and blackened his face. His tongue, swollen to five times its usual size, protruded from his open mouth. He was sightless and speechless, yet breathing."[29]

The Connecticut 14th, also a new regiment with little training, fought on the other side of the battlefield, in the infamous cornfield, facing what became known as Bloody Lane. Samuel Fiske, a minister from Madison, Connecticut, who wrote prolifically and movingly under the pseudonym Dunn Browne, told of the approaching battle and his fellow soldiers as they watched the cannon fire: "A few stand quietly, and watch the field to see where the missile strikes. Some shout, some swear, some, I hope, pray. Some would skedaddle if they dared to, I doubt not." As they were ordered to form battles lines and move into the cornfield, it was, wrote the regiment's official historian, "perhaps the supreme moment of their experience, as there shot through the minds of the men the thought of loved ones at home; the terrible possibilities of the engagement . . . some indeed would be wounded, some slain outright; there must inevitably be suffering and death . . . they wondered who it would be." It didn't take long to find out. As they emerged from the cornfield that partially masked the regiment's movement, "there burst forth a perfect tempest of musketry." Fiske wrote that "the battle itself was a scene of indescribable confusion.

Captain Samuel Fiske of the 14th Connecticut Volunteer Infantry.
Courtesy of the Charlotte L. Evarts Memorial Archive,
Madison, Connecticut

Troops didn't know what they were expected to do, and sometimes, in the excitement, fired at their own men." Captain Jarvis Blinn of Rocky Hill was the first officer to be listed as having died. As his company was ordered to fall back, he was shot in the heart and made a single exclamation: "I am a dead man!" The 14th suffered nineteen killed, 103 wounded, and one man missing.[30]

After hours of battle with no water and nothing to eat but hard tack, the fighting finally ceased and the smoke cleared, revealing a perfect orgy of destruction. Sergeant Benjamin Hirst of the 14th awoke on the battlefield. Writing home, he remarked that he "saw War without romance, there was dead men lying around everywhere some with their head shattered to Pieces, others with their bowels protruding while others had lost their legs and Arms. [W]hat my feelings were, I cannot describe, but I hoped to God never to see such another sight again." The reality of the war was striking. In a subsequent letter, Hirst wrote to his wife what he hoped was a simple truth: "Dear Sarah when we do come Home, we shal [sic] know how to appreciate the Blessings of Home, and I think it will make us Wiser and better men."[31]

Another man from the 14th, Private George Hubbard of Middletown, wrote: "It is enough to make a fellow exclaim horrors of horrors, to go upon a battle field, and see the wounded and killed. Some with their head [sic] blown to atoms by shell while others are killed in different ways. . . . Here we sit around our fire to night 7 of us, but little do we know how soon some one of us may be separated from the rest. We are living at present chiefly upon Hard-Tack, Salt Pork and Faith, the last article being our chief subsistence."[32]

Fiske witnessed the same scenes of death: "I have at last turned over a new and bloody leaf in my experience, and seen a battle, and am now writing you, sitting in a newly plowed field all strewn with the dead of our gallant Union soldiers, still unburied, lying as they fell." He continued: "Think, now, of the horrors of such a scene as lies all round us, hundreds of horses too, all mangled and putrefying, scattered everywhere! Then there are the broken gun carriages, muskets everywhere, clothing all torn and bloody, trees torn with shot and scarred with bullets." He noted that "the air grows terribly offensive from the unburied bodies; and a pestilence will speedily be bred if they are not put under ground."[33] And someone needed to do the burying. That gruesome duty fell to those who survived. "The day is a never to be forgotten one to me," related one member of the 16th; "when the day was over and all that could be found had been covered by mother earth I was glad to rest from the horror of it all. For six months following, everything I ate, drank, or smelled had an odor of dead men in it."[34]

When news of the battle arrived in Connecticut, the *Hartford Evening Press* expressed shock at the death toll and Confederate tenacity, exclaiming: "What strange missiles were those the rebels killed us with at South Mountain and Antietam, horse shoes, twisted telegraph wire, stones, brass

"*Antietam, Maryland. Burying the dead Confederate soldiers*,"
photograph by Alexander Gardner, September 1862.
Library of Congress, LC-B811-561B

buttons, knobs, railroad iron, hammers, and legitimate shell. . . . Is there any glory in beating insanity?"[35]

With such horrific losses to both the Union and Confederate armies, it was difficult to determine which side actually won the battle of Antietam. But because Lee retreated and took his troops back over the Potomac into Virginia, McClellan, who held the battlefield, claimed victory. This was true, even though he failed to pursue Lee's army, as Lincoln had ordered, and thus did not deal it a death blow. McClellan's caution once again got the better of him. He simply couldn't move with any sense of urgency or, more importantly, with the will to smash Lee's army. By October, Lincoln had enough. Aware of McClellan's popularity, however, Lincoln waited until after the congressional elections to remove McClellan and replace him with Burnside. The new commander of the Army of the Potomac planned to renew the assault on Richmond, and he moved quickly until

Connecticut in the American Civil War

he got caught at the Rappahannock River in Virginia, with no pontoons to get across. This gave Lee just enough time to mass his own troops on the heights of Fredericksburg.[36]

Burnside should have withdrawn. Lee's forces were positioned at the rear of the town atop Marye's Heights, a plateau that rose 150 to 200 feet above ground level and wrapped itself around Fredericksburg, so that cannon positioned there could easily fire from several directions at any advancing troops. The Confederate infantry was protected in trenches on the face of the ridge. Yet Lincoln and the North expected action, so Burnside moved forward on December 13. Taking the town was no great difficulty, but advancing on the heights was impossible. Though Connecticut had seven regiments at Fredericksburg, only the 14th and the 27th made the charge. "Who can depict the horrors of that scene?" wrote the 14th's regimental historian; "The belching of two hundred pieces of artillery seemed to lift the earth from its foundation, shells screeched and burst in the air among the men as if possessed by demons and were seeking revenge, the shot from tens of thousands of musketry fell like rain drops in a summer shower."[37] Fiske, who had watched his comrades suffer so greatly only three months earlier, lamented: "Oh! My heart is sick and sad. Blood and wounds and death are before my eyes; of those who are my friends, comrades, brothers. . . . Another tremendous, terrible, murderous butchery of brave men." When the slaughter ended, Fiske wrote: "The city is filled with pieces of brave men who went whole into the conflict. Every basement and floor is covered with pools of blood. Limbs, in many houses, lie in heaps; and surgeons are exhausted with their trying labors."[38] Fredericksburg ended the Union's struggle for 1862.

Yet the battles fought on southern and western fields were not the only conflicts of the war. The home front too had its skirmishes and trials. The face of war, the enlistment of new soldiers, the dizzying preparation and movement of supplies, wagons, muskets, ammunition, and all the other accouterments of death were evident in every community. Newspapers were filled with the news of war—troop movements, battles, casualty lists, and death notices. And then there were the wounded and dead who returned to their homes for healing or burial. It is fair to say that no one in Connecticut, or other parts of the North, escaped the realities of the rebellion. The historian John Niven wrote: "Connecticut had the appearance of an armed camp from Sumter through Appomattox."[39]

The reality is that the federal government was unable to cope with the massive needs of the war. It was only through the work of soldiers' aid societies, of which some seventy existed throughout Connecticut, that soldiers were able to survive. The Hartford Soldiers' Aid Society became a central organizer, working with the other societies in the state to make sure that supplies made their way to Connecticut troops. Virgil Cornish of New Britain agreed to stay in Washington and coordinate the flow of materials to the front. It was a daunting task, dealing with literally thousands of items, boxes upon boxes sent on a weekly basis; the collection and disbursement of funds to destitute soldiers; and the chartering of vessels to deliver supplies. Yet Cornish still found time to visit Washington area hospitals, sit with the sick and wounded, even those from other states, often leaving them with a small token from Connecticut.[40]

As the Union began to run into stiff Confederate resistance in the summer, casualties mounted and the injured made their way home. In June, in an article titled "More Work for Women. — The Wounded Soldiers," the *Courant* explained that though the U.S. Sanitary Commission and other federal agencies would take care of the men, "there is much that private beneficence and attention can do for them. . . . Any woman, any lady, with a little leisure, a needle, and a kind heart can make herself of service." "Let no woman waste any time while this war lasts," announced the paper in a patriotic appeal, "the sex cannot fight, (not in regiments we mean), but they can serve their country equally effectively otherwise."[41]

The summer also brought the need for additional troops. Fearing that yet another call from the federal government might make the Union's situation seem forlorn, Secretary of State William H. Seward met with Northern governors on June 30 and arranged for them to "request" that the president issue a call for another 300,000 three-year recruits. This was done, and new enlistments began in July. "Men of Connecticut! Rally once more at your country's call," urged a letter in the *Courant*.[42] Then, in August, the government called for 300,000 more men — this time, nine-month recruits — adding that if quotas were not met, a draft would be instituted. This threat helped spur enlistments, in part because draftees would not receive the generous bounties offered to recruits. In Connecticut, as elsewhere in the nation, men came forth slowly, and though Governor Buckingham postponed a draft three times, he finally instituted it on September 10. The War Department legitimately exempted some specially skilled workers, such as those at arms manufacturers like Colt, Sharps, and Eli Whitney. Other men found less noble ways of avoiding service. Out of some 1,303 men drafted in Connecticut, 913 were exempted through medical certificates. The most notorious of the exempting doctors

Connecticut in the American Civil War

was a Litchfield surgeon named Josiah G. Beckwith, who excused men for everything from "heart disease," "weak and feeble constitution," "general weakness," and "great nervousness" to "enlarged and diseased scrotum, of *long standing*." Joining Beckwith was Dr. P. W. Ellsworth of Hartford, who exempted some 600 out of 1,600 men.[43]

There were also other ways around military service. In a letter to Governor Buckingham, Timothy Dwight, a professor of divinity at Yale University and the grandson of a former Yale president, cited a 1745 Connecticut charter that excused both faculty and students from military conscription. Theodore D. Woolsey, then president of Yale University, embraced this argument and threatened to sue if the governor failed to abide by the charter.[44] Additionally, if medical exemptions and claiming special status as a student or faculty member failed to work, one could always escape service by paying for a substitute or fleeing into Canada.

As fall came, the need for supplies and donations continued. The *Courant* announced that "public anxiety to learn what is going on has never been surpassed," and at the same time reported the U.S. surgeon general's request for cotton lint used to pack wounds, as well as other hospital stores. The paper noted that such a request "tells its own fearful story," urging: "Let no one slacken exertion, for the position of the armies must necessitate bloodshed, and we may hear at any moment of wide-spread collisions, involving awful suffering to the wounded. The Soldiers' Aid people have the best advisors, and will see that what is sent to them reaches the right spot."[45] The following week was Antietam, the greatest test thus far of the military and home front war machine.

The *Courant* published a pleading article in late September, titled "An Appeal for Help for the Wounded," asking: *"Citizens of Hartford, Will You Respond?"* The article related the trip of Samuel E. Elmer and two other men, who had left Connecticut immediately following Antietam and returned with a number of wounded men from the 16th and 11th Regiments. "Some of them were taken to their homes," reported the paper, "and others were provided with quarters at St. John's Hotel, and will be sent to their friends in the country." The *Courant* lamented that some of the wounded had received little help upon their arrival: "Quite a number of the badly wounded will arrive to-day, and on almost every train for days to come. They should be met at the depot by agents of the Aid Society, or by a committee of citizens, and those who are in transit to their homes should be provided with temporary quarters, and others who have no good homes to go to, should be taken to our hospital. A movement should be made at once in this matter."[46]

The necessity of sending wounded soldiers home revealed the state's and nation's lack of adequate hospitals. On May 24, the General Assembly had passed a resolution appropriating $3,000 to the General Hospital Society for the care of sick and wounded soldiers, but that was hardly enough and additional appropriations followed. After Antietam, the Army made arrangements to rent the hospital in New Haven and appointed Dr. Pliny Jewett as director, renaming the facility Knight U.S. Army General Hospital, after Jonathan Knight, president of the board for the General Hospital Association and a professor at Yale University. Soon after that, the Army announced the pending arrival of some 250 soldiers.[47]

Along with the wounded, Antietam brought a wave of dead to Connecticut. Though the *Courant* had offered a single proclamation that "Connecticut has reason to feel proud of the conduct of her sons in the terrible battle at Antietam Creek," the newspaper was peppered with notices and announcements that better reflected the impact of that battle. Perhaps most telling was the letter from John Burnham, the adjutant officer for the 16th Regiment, who supervised the burial of the regiment's dead and offered very specific directions for their retrieval: "I give you also a minute description of the locality in which we placed the dead, in order that their friends may find their bodies if they wish. . . . The bodies lie near a large tree standing alone, and which I had blazed on all sides so that it can be easily discovered."[48] The letter revealed two stark realities: first, the military had no logistical ability to deal with death on such a massive scale, and second, it was left to those at home to arrange for the return of their loved ones' remains.

Over the next several weeks, bodies poured into the state, and those at home attended funeral after funeral. Some were held in churches, others in private homes. Privates George W. Corbit and Samuel L. Talcott were buried in Coventry. The *Courant* reported: "These two victims of this accursed rebellion were members of Co. D, 14th Reg't, and were wounded in the battle of Antietam, and after lingering for some four weeks amid great pain and suffering have since died." The church was draped in black and filled to overflowing. "Never before have the citizens of Coventry been called upon to perform a more painful duty," the paper commented. The funeral of Gilbert R. Crane of the 11th was held at his mother's home, 526 Main Street in Hartford. On October 11, the *Courant* announced that "W. W. Roberts, undertaker, of this city, had returned, as we stated yesterday, from the battle-field of Antietam." He brought with him the bodies of eight men, one of whom was Captain Jarvis Blinn, who had announced his own death on the battlefield after being shot in the heart. As the dead continued to arrive, the *Courant* lamented: "It is seldom that we are called upon to bury so many braves in so short a space of time. Their friends have the satisfaction of knowing that they have the sympathies of the city with them, and that their loved ones died in a glorious cause."[49]

———•———

What exactly was that glorious cause? For many, the answer was simple: the preservation of the Union. Yet an underlying issue had always been, and continued to be, slavery. Democrats had charged Republicans with abolitionism long before the war began, and Republicans just as quickly repudiated the label, arguing that free labor, the rights of white men, and the aggressive Slave Power were the sources of their animosity toward the South. Some Democrats had steadfastly opposed the war, and peace meetings had been widespread throughout the state. By 1862, these move ments had largely died out, and the Democratic Party had split into two distinct wings: Peace Democrats continued to repudiate any aggression toward the South, insisting that Southerners had a right to secede and that any reconciliation had to be accomplished through peaceful means; War Democrats supported the Union's struggle against secession. Where the wings came together was on the issue of slavery, as neither group supported the freeing of slaves under any circumstances.

Tensions naturally existed between the two factions. When a meeting of War Democrats was announced in Hartford on July 10 and it was erroneously reported that Thomas Seymour was vice president of the gathering, he utterly rejected the idea, declaring that such a meeting "ignores peaceful remedies of any sort, as a means of restoring the Union, and calls loudly for men and means to aid in the subjugation and consequent degradation and overthrow of the South. I follow gentlemen, in no such crusade, neither will I contribute, in any way, to the accomplishment of such bloody purposes."[50]

Still, the Democrats attempted to form a united front for the spring elections, hoping that they might unseat Governor Buckingham. With patriotic sentiment surging in April, they failed rather miserably. The Democratic candidate, James C. Loomis, lost by a margin of 9,148 votes, and Republican newspapers wasted no time in writing epithets for what they considered a dead party: "In no northern state has the spirit of secessionism been so rampant and malignant as in Connecticut. In none has its rebuke, since the war began, been so signal and overwhelming. . . . And if the party is buried, it cannot complain that we have not given it a splendid funeral."[51] Democrats, in turn, insisted that the party "is on a solid foundation. Your principles are just. You sustain the Constitution, which *is the government* of the United States, as you have ever sustained it. You oppose those who make war upon that Constitution, no matter where they belong—whether they are secessionists in arms, or abolitionists with wily talk and insidious ways, ever encroaching upon its principles of compromise and of justice."[52]

Comments about supporting the Constitution were aimed directly at abolitionists. Before the war, Democrats and most Republicans had recognized the Constitution's protection of slavery, but soon after hostilities began, many Republicans questioned the sanctity of that protection when the South had repudiated its allegiance to the Union. Governor Buckingham's May message to the General Assembly following his reelection made this exact point. "Slavery has forced us into a civil war," proclaimed the governor, "but insists that we have no right to use the war power against her interest. Slavery has repudiated her obligations to the Constitution; and yet claims protection by virtue of its provisions. . . . He who refuses to obey its requirements, must not expect its benefits." Buckingham went on to espouse an almost messianic vision of the war, with a providentially inspired destruction of slavery.[53] In August, the governor traveled to Washington with a delegation to deliver an emancipation petition to President Lincoln.

For other Republicans, dismantling slavery was justified by more practical considerations. Slave labor was a distinct wartime asset for the Confederacy. Should not the Union reduce the enemy's ability to fight by every means possible, including the abolition of slavery? It was a politically delicate question. Democrats argued for what they called "the Constitution as it is" and the Union as it was. The *New Haven Register* complained that "the radical anti-slavery presses and orators now openly disavow all respect for the old Union, and their aversion to its reconstruction." Some Democrats charged that the war was actually a revolution to overthrow the Union established by the nation's Founders.[54]

Democrats had plenty of ammunition for such attacks. On March 13, the Republican-controlled Congress enacted a new article of war, forbidding army officers from returning escaped slaves to their masters; this was essentially an official extension of General Butler's earlier contraband policy. In that same month, President Lincoln sent a special message to Congress urging a joint resolution offering "pecuniary aid" to "any state which may adopt gradual abolishment of slavery." Lincoln had also been encouraging the border states to enact gradual emancipation plans. In April, Congress abolished slavery in the District of Columbia. Is it any wonder that Democrats saw an abolitionist onslaught? The *Hartford Times* lamented that such measures would make matters worse, arguing: "It is important, *if our Union is really to be preserved*, to impress upon the minds of the people of the South—those who are not uncompromisingly dissolutionists—the fact, if it is a fact, that this is *not* an abolition war."[55]

When they heard about emancipation in the nation's capital, members of Connecticut's black community gathered at the Temple Street Church, in New Haven, where Amos Beman and others addressed the excited crowd. One reporter called it "probably the largest and most spirited meeting ever held in the State of Connecticut." The state's Republican newspapers greeted the news with equal excitement. The *Hartford Evening Press* announced: "Let all men rejoice and take courage—the policy of the government is on the side of Freedome!" The *Courant* exulted that "the American nation is no longer responsible for what remains of Slavery in the United States," and though regretting that the "war is tremendously expensive, in life, blood, hearts, [and] treasure . . . it is the genius of America to make everything pay; and we see no way in which the South can be made to pay its fair share of the outlay, except by confiscating the property of all rebels in arms, and emancipating every negro in a contumaciously rebellious State."[56]

The *Courant*'s comments were actually more nuanced than they might seem at first. It was not abolition that the paper hailed, but emancipation. The difference lay in the purposes of the measure. Abolition placed the slave before the Union; emancipation, the Union before the slave. Abolition denoted a sense of equality for blacks, something not involved in emancipation. Though the terms were often used interchangeably, the distinction was readily evident to men like Major Henry Ward Camp of the 10th Connecticut regiment. While no supporter of slavery, he insisted that "it is the maintenance of the Government that I consider the object, and the only object of the war; abolition [emancipation], one of the means, but no more. . . . I fight for the preservation of the republic, not for the abolition of slavery, because I consider the former the nobler and more important object." McPherson detected this sentiment among many Northern men, remarking: "Not many Union soldiers were principled abolitionists, but a growing number of them were becoming pragmatic emancipationists."[57]

Lincoln, too, was a pragmatist. In August he sent a now-famous letter to Horace Greeley, the editor of the *New York Tribune*, declaring: "My paramount object in this struggle is to save the Union, and is not either to save or to destroy slavery. If I could save the Union without freeing any slave I would do it, and if I could save it by freeing all the slaves I would do it; and if I could save it by freeing some and leaving others alone I would also do that. What I do about slavery, and the colored race, I do because I believe it helps to save the Union."[58]

The president had been particularly careful at the outset of the war to refuse to endorse the emancipation decrees issued by various generals. There was an important reality at play. Lincoln worried that such a measure might influence the undecided border states. His opposition to such measures at that time did not mean that he failed to consider them. In fact, as Frederick Douglass, the famed black abolitionist, argued, there were tangible reasons for emancipation: "The very stomach of the rebellion is the negro in the condition of the slave. Arrest that hoe in the hands of the negro, and you smite the rebellion in the very seat of life."[59]

There were other reasons for freeing slaves. Worried that England and France might recognize Southern independence, Lincoln insisted in early 1862 that he "can not imagine that any European power would dare to recognize and aid the Southern Confederacy if it became clear that the Confederacy stands for slavery and the Union for freedom."[60] Thus by July, the president had concluded that the Union's survival necessitated the death of slavery. Yet he fully recognized that the Constitution provided him with no such authority, and he therefore acted under his war powers as commander-in-chief. Years later, Gideon Welles, the Connecticut-born Secretary of the Navy, wrote that Lincoln insisted emancipation was "a military necessity, absolutely essential to the preservation of the Union." Yet, ever the pragmatist, the president also realized that the timing had to be perfect, coinciding with a Union victory, lest recent defeats make emancipation look like an act of desperation.[61]

And then came Antietam. Lincoln had hoped for a more decisive victory, but after the tough going of the summer, he took what he could get. McClellan's holding the field of battle made Antietam a Union victory, and Lincoln announced his preliminary Emancipation Proclamation five days after the battle, on September 22: "That on the first day of January in the year of our Lord, one thousand eight hundred and sixty-three, all persons held as slaves within any state, or designated part of a state, the people whereof shall then be in rebellion against the United States shall be then, thenceforward, and forever free."[62]

Within days, a somber but thankful Governor Buckingham wrote to the president: "Not that I think your declaration of freedom will of itself bring liberty to the slave or restore peace to the nation, but I rejoice that your administration will not be prevented by the clamors of men in sympathy with rebels from using such measures as you indicate to overpower the rebellion even if it interferes with and overthrows their much loved system of slavery."[63] Buckingham presented no thunderous, God-inspired disavowals of slavery, as he had in his May message to the General Assembly. He recognized that for Lincoln, emancipation was principally a war measure.

Other Republicans in Connecticut seemed to recognize the same point and exhibited a subdued propriety. No one bellowed for freedom. The proclamation was about emancipation, not abolition. The *Hartford Evening Press* wrote: "We freely confess that whilst we have no scruples about owning slave property, and have no sympathy with the abolitionists in their course in regard to it, still we have ever been prepared to meet that or any other question and decide upon its merits in connection with its bearing on the perpetuity of the Union. *What ever stands in the way of its accomplishment must go by the board.*" The *Courant* remained strangely silent on the merits of the proclamation, making its first real mention to it only in connection with its partisan effects: "The President's proclamation is to be seized by the Democratic party all over the North . . . and the men who love slavery more than they do their country's cause, are about to take open and avowed opposition grounds." It was not until the *Courant* was assailed by an anonymous letter writer, "Honestus," and asked directly, "Do you approve of the President's proclamation? Do you mean to stand by it? And do you believe the Constitution *as it is* can be preserved without it?" that the *Courant* addressed the matter. And even then its response was supportive, but decidedly lukewarm, announcing the hope that the proclamation's "moral effects will penetrate even where our soldiers may not be able to go, and that it will hamstring the South." As for whether the Union could have survived without emancipation, the *Courant* answered minimally—"probably not"—contending that the president would not have issued the proclamation otherwise.[64]

The Democratic press also hesitated in responding to the proclamation, though not nearly so long as Republican papers. On September 27, the *New Haven Register* took a customary Democratic tack and blasted Republicans as the most radical of abolitionists, charging: "The Republicans having now so generally taken the Abolition ground, openly and even boastingly, cannot any longer find fault, as they have in the past, if they are known as, and called, Abolitionists. Our future divisions must therefore be Constitutionalists and Abolitionists."[65] The *Hartford Times* announced: "We do not believe the Government and Union can be sustained by, breaking the Constitution, which is the Government. It is no way to save the Constitution, to break, destroy, or violate any part of it." The paper added that the Emancipation Proclamation "is a REVOLUTION-ARY act! . . . that so far as the *Times* is concerned—and in this we can speak for all Democrats as well—we shall never approve, or attempt to justify such a measure!" The *New Haven Register* thought the proclamation an "inhuman measure," that encouraged slaves to rise up and engage in "indiscriminate butchery." In a later article, the paper blamed "New England fanaticism" and insisted that the freed slaves would have little more than "the cold charity of the Abolitionists to rely on."[66]

In many ways, Lincoln's proclamation was exactly what the Democrats needed to revitalize and unify their beleaguered ranks. Having been beaten down by patriotism in late 1861 and well into the summer of 1862, they now had a rallying cry. The *Courant* had recognized this fact immediately, expressing concern that the proclamation would be "seized" by the party. Democrats, now derisively called Copperheads after the venomous snake of the North, immediately prepared to battle the administration. In Connecticut, as elsewhere in the nation, they focused on two things: winning elections, and fighting Lincoln's curtailment of civil liberties.

The first step to Democratic political control of Connecticut was winning the upcoming November town elections, which would provide a springboard to the April 1863 gubernatorial campaign. Republicans charged that Democrats were attempting to "claim that there had been a change of public sentiment, especially since the publication of the President's proclamation."[67] Whether or not emancipation was the actual cause, Democrats succeeded in capturing several important towns, including Hartford, New Haven, and Bridgeport.[68] Democratic papers crowed with victory. "The ballot box has proven that the North is not *all* abolitionized, and the UNION MAY YET BE RESTORED," trumpeted the *New Haven Register*, adding: "There is great joy throughout THE NORTH! Joy among friends of the Constitution and the Union, for the RIGHT HAS TRIUMPHED, and the evil sectional party of abolition, and so called Republicanism, *has received its death blow*." In a later article, the paper said that "the President's greatest mistake is in supposing that the negro has the remotest connection with the restoration of the Union." The *Hartford Times* declared: "The result is a most gratifying one as it rebukes the Abolition Proclamation."[69]

The Democratic victory allowed the party to renew its earlier failed attempt to protest the war, and one of the first goals was attacking Lincoln's suspension of the writ of habeas corpus. The constitutionally guaranteed writ prevents the unlawful arrest and prolonged detention of any citizen

"Christmas Eve," by Thomas Nast, Harper's Weekly, 1862. The illustration
shows a Northern wife and husband separated on Christmas Eve. While their
children are sleeping, the woman prays for her husband's safety. Away at war,
the husband clutches a letter from home as he tries to stay warm by the fire.

without formal charges and arraignment. Lincoln had suspended the
act in Maryland at the outset of the war, and on September 24, 1862,
he extended the suspension to cover the whole nation. His actions were
unconstitutional. The *Hartford Times* commented on the "incarceration
of American citizens in dungeons for political opinion's sake," and Democrats, after their November victories, proposed a resolution in the General
Assembly "to protest the suspension of the writ of Habeas Corpus . . . as an
unwarrantable imputation upon the loyalty of our Courts and people — an
unjustifiable interference with the liberty of our citizens, and an assump-
tion of power dangerous as a precedent."[70]

With Republicans still firmly in control of the Assembly, there was no
hope of the measure's passing. In fact, Republicans not only killed the
resolution, but they replaced it with another "expressing confidence in
the patriotism and integrity of the President of the United States, and
pledging to him the support of the people of this State, for the suppression
of the Rebellion." Governor Buckingham promptly sent the resolution to

President Lincoln. Nonetheless, the Democrats' attack signaled a rebirth of opposition to the war and opened the door for a more vocal denunciation of military failures as well, such as the Christmastime bloodletting at Fredericksburg. The *New Haven Register* blasted "the stupid management," "the imbecility of the Administration," and the toil "expended on miserable schemes of negro philanthropy, and political engineering, whilst the best blood of the country is being sacrificed to no purpose."[71]

Thus ended 1862. What began as a promising year for the North had by early summer become one of repeated Union losses. The intensity of the fighting shocked both those on the battlefield and those at home. Antietam, while nominally a Union victory, was so horrific that it brought an avalanche of wounded and dead into Connecticut. Life on the home front was full of funerals, treating the injured, and meeting the needs of soldiers in the field, with the rapid accumulation of supplies at home and shipping them off, only to start all over again. Calls for additional troops, more men being sent off to war, draft dodgers, the never-ending political battles and mudslinging—no one could escape the war. The year ended with the Union merely hanging on. The mood may have been best expressed by Private Justus Silliman of the 17th CVI, who wrote home on New Year's Eve: "Well the old year is dying and to night the wind is already moaning its requiem, through the bare branches of the old trees, and the moon shines drearily through the heavy clouds. So passes off the old year, a year of sadness and desolation long to be remembered. I hope and pray that tomorrow's dawn will usher in a bright and happy new year."[72]

CHAPTER FOUR

The Union Crucible

1863

On January 1, 1863, President Abraham Lincoln instituted a revolutionary change in the nation's history by signing the Emancipation Proclamation. He justified his decision "by virtue of the power in me vested as Commander-in-Chief, of the Army and Navy of the United States," and "as a fit and necessary war measure for suppressing said rebellion."[1] The proclamation also opened the door for blacks to serve in the military. Although Lincoln had issued a preliminary proclamation in September 1862, many Americans still wondered if emancipation would become a reality. It created divisions throughout the North, causing many War Democrats who had previously tried to work with the Republican administration to turn their backs on it, outraged over abolition and the clear avowal that the war was no longer just about saving the Union. Emancipation, violations of habeas corpus, suppression of newspapers, the conscription of soldiers — all of these acts, argued Democrats, pointed to Lincoln's despotism as the true source of the nation's destruction. The Emancipation Proclamation, more than any other act, served as the catalyst that reinvigorated the Democratic Party.

With both Northern and Southern armies toughing out the winter season, the next major military campaigns did not begin until late spring. When they did commence, the North finally achieved a string of victories, most notably Vicksburg in the west and Gettysburg in the east, which presaged ultimate disaster for the Confederacy. The successes came as a result of better commanders, better soldiers, and a thinly spread Confederate military. By 1863, both the Northern and Southern soldiers had become battle-hardened veterans who fought valiantly in spite of suffering the sorrow of fallen comrades, the hardship of relentless marching, and hunger, many times appeased by little more than hardtack and coffee. Connecticut soldiers often commented on the beauty of the Virginia countryside, only

"Emancipation," by Thomas Nast, Harper's Weekly, *January 24, 1863.*
In the center, slaves celebrate news of their emancipation. At the left is the past,
with slave auctions and whippings. At the right is the future, with black
children attending school and black men working for themselves.

to mourn its destruction by the unrelenting hand of war. They repeatedly wrote of their desire for the war's end, yet they expressed conviction that duty to the Union bound them to continue fighting until it was secure. They looked to those at home for sustenance in the form of continued provisions sent by the many soldiers' aid societies and the U.S. Sanitary Commission, letters from family and friends, and, most importantly, an unremitting patriotism. But patriotism was something that was not always forthcoming. As Americans have learned in every war, soldiers in the field cannot fight, bleed, and die without the confidence and support of those at home.

Combating the Democratic resurgence in Connecticut, then, proved to be as important as any military battle. The coming spring elections pitted Governor Buckingham against the formidable Thomas H. Seymour. Had Seymour won, all hopes for Connecticut's continued participation in the war effort might have crumbled, and many worried that it would lead to a chain reaction throughout the North. Thus the first campaign of the

Connecticut in the American Civil War

new year was not military, but a political battle upon which everything else depended. Those at home knew it, and the soldiers in the field did, too. Buckingham's narrow victory, followed only a few months later by the amazing Union military successes of the summer, revealed 1863 to be the Union's crucible.

———

Free blacks in Connecticut greeted news of the Emancipation Proclamation with excitement. In New Haven, a huge celebration was held at the Temple Street Church. So many people arrived that the church could not hold the crowd. The *Palladium* announced: "That class of our citizens of whom a certain judge [Chief Justice Roger Taney] once extra-judicially decided that 'they have no rights that white men are bound to respect,' held a jubilee. . . . The platform, desk, and surroundings, were handsomely draped with American flags." The meeting was described as "conducted in a very orderly and credible manner."[2] The celebration had been a long time coming. Previously, black abolitionists such as Amos Beman and James Pennington had advocated that blacks observe what they called the Negro Fourth of July, British West Indian emancipation, on August 1, and boycott July 4th.[3]

Nor were black Connecticut residents alone in celebrating Lincoln's proclamation. In Norwich, Mayor James Lloyd Greene ordered the raising of the town flag, the tolling of church bells, and a hundred-gun salute for January 2. Everything did not go smoothly, however. When the mayor later presented to the city council the $98 bill for the celebration, several town residents filed for and received an injunction from the state's Superior Court in New London, stopping the mayor from collecting the money. The *Norwich Aurora* supported the court's decision and insisted that the mayor had violated the city's charter and "the feelings of three-fourths of our tax-payers." The *Norwich Morning Bulletin* opposed the injunction and concluded that "the whole movement was undoubtedly gotten up for political effect in the coming State and City elections," and that "the movers in this matter have placed themselves in a very foolish and contemptible position."[4]

Such disputes accurately reflected the larger division in Connecticut over the war and the issue of slavery. The Democratic Party used the Emancipation Proclamation as an opening wedge in its political attack on the Republicans. Democrats had always argued that the Constitution guaranteed slavery's protection and that Republicans were rabid, dangerous abolitionists who wanted to upset the proper racial balance of white superiority. In the eyes of Democrats, the Emancipation Proclamation confirmed such arguments. The *New Haven Register* announced that the Republican "programme is now being unmasked, with brazen effrontery." Throughout January, Democratic papers published vitriolic attacks on abolition and fervent defenses of slavery. Charging abolitionists with "sham philanthropy," the *Register* thundered: "Men of America! Behold the picture of Abolition barbarism! THE PROGRAME OF ABOLITIONISM IS, ALL THINGS CONSIDERED, THE MOST MONSTROUS AND BLOODY PROJECT EVER INVENTED BY THE BRAIN OF MAN OR FIEND!" The *Hartford Times* accused Lincoln of violating his oath of office to defend the Constitution and asserted that Republicans had now "openly proclaimed" the war "is a John Brown raid on a gigantic scale." In another article, the *Times* described a "grand Emancipation celebration" at Cooper Institute in New York, and lamented: "The noble old Flag, so dear to the heart of every true American — the starry Banner that was once the symbol of Power, and the enforcer of respect, among all foreign nations — is indeed sadly lowered and foully prostituted when it waves over a broken, weakened and warring country, and is *cheered* by the disciples of [William Lloyd] Garrison!"[5]

In making such arguments, the Democrats appealed to their loyal base, those who had always been opposed to abolition and Republicans. Yet the Democrats also cast a wider net in an attempt to aggravate the underlying racism that was as ubiquitous as the stone walls that dotted Connecticut's landscape, and which Republicans had so markedly revealed when making their earlier arguments for war on the grounds of free soil and white rights. Democrats refocused the race issue by attacking the Emancipation Proclamation's announcement of mustering black troops. Commenting on the fact that blacks would serve under white officers, the *New Haven Register*, announced "what everybody knows to be the case, socially and politically, at home, that the negro race are unfit associates for the officers, who are to be white men; and it also declares the insulting outrage, that these negroes, unfit as they are for the companionship of officers, are just fit for the associates and fellow soldiers of the rank and file of our gallant and patriotic army. The Representatives who thus voted for the equality of the negroes with the rank and file, were sent to represent a people who at home do not admit the negro to either social or political equality."[6]

The *Hartford Times* expressed equal exasperation: "A negro army! To fight the battles of this once mighty Nation! If anything remained that could humiliate us still more before the world, these 'Architects of Ruin,' now in power, have surely found it, in this measure. The project is a very

degrading one. It is a confession of weakness." It is for the purpose of calling "an inferior race to do for us what we are unable or unwilling to do for
ourselves!" The paper continued in a subsequent article: "The measure is
demoralizing to the army, as well as humiliating to the Union" and "this
whole scheme of negro soldiers, will fall, as the emancipation proclamation must inevitably fall, after doing much more harm than good."[7]

The Republican press, of course, responded to Lincoln's proclamation
with a markedly different outlook, one that challenged its own views as
expressed in the 1850s. In a lengthy article on January 2, the day after the
proclamation, the *Hartford Courant* proclaimed: "Now, for the first time
in its history, the Government stands unequivocally committed to the
support of the fundamental principles on which it was originally founded.
Hitherto our national life has been disfigured by a glaring inconsistency.
To justify the revolution which established our independence, we pro
claimed our belief in certain inalienable rights as common to all men;
to subserve the ends of self-interest we have suffered a sixth part of the
population of the land to groan under despotism that repudiates every
liberal maxim, and is still upheld by the gravest sanction of constitution
and law. Nowhere else has such an anomaly in government ever existed.
Here it exists no longer."[8]

Although the *Courant* accurately captured the inherent paradox of accepting slavery at the nation's founding, it failed to adequately explore
that very inconsistency, suggesting instead that Jefferson and the other
Founders of the nation had included blacks in the promises of the Declaration of Independence. Nor did the paper confront the equally challenging problem of slavery's constitutional sanction. Even worse, the
Courant's sudden enthusiasm for emancipation and freedom conflicted
with its previous racism and much-argued indifference to black rights,
views it had espoused, at times viciously, during the Free Soil 1850s. Still,
recognizing that some in Connecticut might cringe at the thought of black
equality, the *Courant* theorized that no immediate, radical changes would
take place, even remarking: "Centuries of degradation debase the qualities of manhood. Races do not spring at a bound from the lowest plane
of humanity to a participation in the pride, and hopes, and thirsts which
grow up with civilization. We incline strongly to the belief that the negro
himself, will remain passive."[9]

Months later, at the end of March, the *Courant* published another article championing freedom. Once again, it paid no heed to its previous
antagonism toward blacks, and it began to depict a mythic moral North
opposing an oppressive South: "We are now passing through a crisis which

is to affect materially the destiny of the race. Two antagonistic systems have joined in mortal combat. On the one side, is liberty supported by the maxims of philosophy and the truths of religion; on the other, an enormous system of oppression that drags the only apologies for its existence from the rubbish of past ages and long exploded theories." The paper continued, however paradoxically: "America is the home of freedom. Our Government is based upon an acknowledgement of the fundamental and absolute equality of man." As the *Courant* continued with its racial amnesia, it at least acknowledged the difficulties of the Constitution's protection of slavery: "Practically we have denied what theoretically we claimed to be a self-evident truth. Had the supporters of human slavery observed the obligations of the Constitution, this strange anomaly might have continued for many years to come." The only way around the Union's foundational document, explained the *Courant*, was for the South to choose war: "They put themselves without the pale and protection of the Constitution," and "that crime sealed the death warrant of bondage in America."[10]

In April, the *Courant* once again addressed the issue of the North's moral opposition to slavery by citing William H. Seward's famous 1858 "irrepressible conflict" speech in Rochester, New York, in which he had argued that the march toward abolition was unstoppable. Connecticut, of course, along with the *Courant*, had never embraced such arguments, but in 1863 the paper announced that "the idea of freedom in the northern mind had become irrepressible," and "the North would have sinned against their deepest convictions in permitting slavery to encroach further upon the domains of freedom." The nurturing of a vast, mythical, Northern moral crusade against slavery was in full march. Yet the *Courant* revealed its earlier racist thinking when it insisted that if slavery had not been stopped, it would have ultimately caused an economic blight in the South that would have forced all whites to move North: "The continuance of slavery would end ultimately in giving up the whole southern country to the dominion of the negro. But crushed out now, the peculiar civilization of Africa will never usurp possession of any portion of the territory of the United States."[11]

In the months and years to come, Democrats and Republicans continued to spar over questions of freedom and racial equality, but by the end of January 1863, the parties had hunkered down and were focused on the immediate prize of the state's governorship. Control of the executive office might mean the future of Connecticut's — and, perhaps, the Union's — war efforts. Therefore, the eyes of the nation, including President Lincoln's, were on the Nutmeg State. It was a contest as important as that in 1860, when Buckingham's victory secured the state's support at the outset of the war. This time, however, not everyone was at home and able to vote. Connecticut's 1818 constitution specifically stated that electors had to meet in their respective towns, and when Governor Buckingham asked the state's Supreme Court justices to consider the constitutionality of a law allowing soldiers to vote in the field, he was told without qualification that it would be unconstitutional. The General Assembly passed an amendment in 1864 that allowed soldiers to vote, but this did nothing for them during the contested and very important 1863 campaign.[12]

The concerns and opinions of the soldiers ultimately became a primary focus of the news coverage. In addition to reporting on the parties' nominating conventions, the two principal state papers, the *Courant* and the *Times*, devoted page after page to letters from soldiers, with each paper claiming that the men were on its party's side. As the date of the election crept closer, the *Courant* in particular devoted itself to the battle by filling lengthy columns with numerous letters. The ensuing struggle was the most concentrated, sustained political effort of the war, both at home and in the field. The many letters and resolutions sent to the papers by various regiments revealed that everyone in and from Connecticut was consumed by the possibility of Republican defeat.

The Republicans held their party convention on January 21 in New Haven, where Governor Buckingham easily received the nomination. Yet only a portion of the delegates who might have attended were present, and this made many believe in the party's further vulnerability. Three weeks later, the state party's Central Committee published a lengthy appeal, declaring: "A State Election is soon to take place more important than any which has occurred since the foundation of our Government. Connecticut is to declare on the first Monday in April, whether she is in favor of a *dishonorable peace — submission to the demands of armed traitors*, and a *dissolution of the Union*, or whether she is determined at every hazard, to defend the honor of our National Flag and the Union of these States."[13]

The state's Democrats gathered at Touro Hall in Hartford on February 17, with the actual convention the next day. Thomas H. Seymour, the party's stalwart, uncompromising opponent of the war, received the nomination. At the convention, speakers like William W. Eaton of Hartford, a representative in the General Assembly, regaled the audience with heartfelt denunciations of the war and President Lincoln: "Is any man so low as to be loyal to any man — to Abraham Lincoln, the accidental

President? The Democrats of Connecticut will not sustain war waged for the destruction of the Union. We will tell Lincoln that he cannot come into Connecticut, and take men from their homes; that he cannot come into Connecticut and compel men to serve in the army."[14] Another speaker, Henry H. Barbour, revealed the very real danger for Republicans should Seymour win election: *"We are against the War.* The elections of other States have not been understood by the President. *There have been too many War Democrats chosen.* When Thomas H. Seymour is elected, *the President will understand what that means."*[15] The threat was no further Connecticut support of Lincoln's war.

These and other arguments caused Republicans to seethe with indignation. The *Courant* proclaimed that prominent men of the Democratic Party spoke for hours and "not one solitary word or sentence was uttered in condemnation of the rebellion, or of the crimes of its leaders. . . . Such is the shameful position of the Democratic party of Connecticut."[16] In a stroke of propaganda genius, Republicans tainted the meeting with the notorious epithet "Hartford Convention."

The *Hartford Evening Press* also entered the fray, charging that the Copperheads of Connecticut—a term that compared Northern Democrats to the venomous copperhead snake—"have put themselves squarely against the war, and picked out as their candidate about the only public man in New England who has been from the first openly and notoriously *with* the South and *against* the North in this struggle. It is not possible to show that he occupies any different ground than Jeff Davis, except in daring." The paper asked, "What Do 'Peace Men' Want?" And it provided the answer: "It would seem that their great desire is to humble the North, to permit its conquest in this war, to strike down democracy and erect on its ruins the aristocratic rule of slaveholders."[17]

The first of the soldiers' letters home appeared on January 20, when the *Times* published an article titled "The Soldiers and Their Feelings," which included an anonymous letter stating: "The feeling here is that the Rebs can never be conquered by fighting—the soldiers are disheartened." The *Courant* responded on February 9, in "What Some of the Soldiers Say," offering two letters. The first came from an officer of the 15th CVI, "formerly an active Democrat from New Haven," who wrote: "The feeling of the North, which we hear is growing more and more strong against the war, is doing an incalculable amount of injury in this army, and I hope it may soon give way to a feeling of sincere patriotism. Remember and do your duty in voting for Buckingham for Governor." Another soldier wrote: "I was once in favor of compromise, conciliation, concession, but

"The Copperhead Party—In Favor of a Vigorous Prosecution of Peace!"
Harper's Weekly, *February 28, 1863. Three Copperheads advance on Columbia,*
who holds a shield labeled "Union." Library of Congress, LC-USZ62-132749

that was before the hellish act of firing on our country's flag had been consummated; but now I stand up unbroken and unbent, and my voice is for War! War!! War!!!" Eleven days later, the *Times* published a letter from a Republican soldier, who insisted: "I think it full time this war was over; there have been money and lives enough lost, and we are no better off than we were a year ago; and all for the cussed nigger. We have lost sight of the real object we all commenced the fight for, the Constitution and the Union."[18]

By March, the competition of soldiers' letters was going strong. Democratic and Republican newspapers together printed more than forty letters that month, with the majority appearing in the *Courant*. Additionally, that paper published eight sets of resolutions sent in by various Connecticut regiments, all of which were in favor of fighting the war and in support of Buckingham. The *Times*, of course, published letters challenging the veracity of the resolutions.[19] The 20th CVI sent in one such set of resolutions, which announced: "We are amazed to find that, in opposition to us, while here before the foe, and in hostility to the measures which have been adopted for the preservation of our liberties, there are at home men who attempt to conceal their sympathies with the rebellion by a cowardly clamor for peace." The soldiers warned: "When we have crushed the foe in front, we will ourselves, if necessity requires, take care of the more cowardly ones in the rear, who are heaping contempt upon our cause and insult our efforts." Another soldier demanded: "How would you and you [sic] loving wife or sister like a bloody war in Connecticut in consequence thereof [of a Seymour victory]?"[20]

An officer from the 15th CVI wrote: "I am astonished beyond measure that the democrats of Connecticut should be so bold in their disloyalty. . . . I cannot believe that you will allow them to do it. It would be a burning disgrace to the State, and a source of sorrow and mortification to the whole loyal country." Another soldier wrote: "You have and can have no idea of the feeling that the bare possibility of the election of such a man [as Seymour] has upon the soldiers. . . . I hope the people of Connecticut have not so far degenerated, as to allow the election of an arch traitor." Other soldiers expressed the same sentiments: "Nothing in all our trials has given us such a *chill*, as the late Copperhead movement in Connecticut. . . . I tell you, the Seymour platform is loudly denounced, by Democrats as well as Republicans." The letter continued: "We say to the Copperheads of Connecticut, if you cannot come down here and shoulder your muskets with us, in defence of your Government, for God's sake and the sake of your country, don't arrange your batteries on the side of Jeff. Davis." Soldiers from the 19th CVI, later the 2nd Heavy Artillery, implored those at home: "We pray you not to crush our resolution, and palsy our arms, by electing for your Governor, *and ours*, a man who hopes for our defeat and humiliation!"[21] One soldier of the 27th sounded the same note: "I hope, in all favor, that our friends will not allow Tom Seymour to be elected Governor of Connecticut. DON'T DO IT! For mercy's sake, don't let him be Governor." A man in the 22nd continued the barrage, expressing amazement at his state's apparent disloyalty: "Do not elect T. H. Seymour, for I do not want to come home to Connecticut and have such a man as that holding the position that those anti-war Democrats—those slimy copperheads—do to a State which ought to be loyal. For Heaven's sake, what is Connecticut coming to?"[22]

One of the most significant resolutions, purely because of what it represented, was a statement from the Ninth Army Corps, comprising the 9th, 12th, 13th, 23rd, 24th, 25th, 26th, and 28th Connecticut Regiments, all then stationed in the Louisiana area: "You sent us here (did you not?) to bear onward the stainless folds of Connecticut's flag, side by side with

Connecticut in the American Civil War

the glorious Stars and Stripes, until perjured Secession shall be ground to powder beneath the iron heel of war. And we will do it; but do not place us between two fires. To-day treason is more dangerous in Connecticut than in Louisiana."[23]

Democrats too sent letters to the press, often charging that the *Courant* fabricated the true sentiments of soldiers and that many were coerced into adopting regimental resolutions. A soldier from the 22nd claimed: "Almost to a man, rank and file, HEARTILY ENDORSE THE NOMINATION OF Gov. Seymour, and daily wish and pray that he may be elected. I never saw in my life a set of men so unanimous for Seymour." He noted that a group of state Republican Party leaders had suddenly appeared in camp to talk about the election and, he wrote, "to unmask this vile Niggerhead plot, with its underground work arrangements . . . to make it appear that the soldiers endorse niggerism." He concluded that the regiment's resolutions are "a willful, DELIBERATE LIE." Another soldier from the same regiment stated that the men had held an informal ballot, with Seymour the victor.[24] In reaction, the *Courant* peppered its columns with soldiers' letters denying such statements about the 22nd, and announcing that a regimental ballot had been conducted, with 607 soldiers participating and the vast majority, 431, voting for Buckingham—while only 176 voted for Seymour.[25] Other soldiers' letters countering Democratic claims followed, with one Democratic soldier insisting: "I have not turned Black Republican or nigger worshiper—nothing of the kind—far from it; but Jeff. Davis and his cursed followers want fight, and they shall have it as long as I can play a 30-pound shell at them."[26]

Although there was clearly a propaganda component of the newspaper coverage—in fact, one so large that it strains the ability of the reader to separate fact from fiction—similar sentiments regarding the 1863 election and concerns over patriotism at home appeared in the writings of several Connecticut soldiers. Samuel Fiske, the minister from Madison who wrote under the pseudonym Dunn Browne, bristled at the conduct of Connecticut Democrats, writing: "Give me a 'Hartford *Times*,' or some other appropriate receptacle, for I am nauseated; I am sick, poisoned; have taken something, that, most emphatically, doesn't agree with me; have swallowed the vile and traitorous resolutions of the recent Democratic Convention at Hartford." He continued: "If the dear old State doesn't spew out of her mouth this ill-savoring Tom Seymour Democracy at the coming April election, we of the army will march North, instead of South, to get at the heart of the Rebellion. Talk about demoralization of the army!"[27]

*Sergeant Fred Lucas of the
19th Connecticut Volunteer
Regiment, which later became the
2nd Connecticut Heavy Artillery.
Courtesy of Ernest Barker*

Fiske's views were meant for publication, in the *Springfield Republican*, but his fellow soldier, Fred Lucas — from the 19th CVI, soon to become the 2nd Heavy Artillery — wrote private letters to his mother. This remarkable set of correspondence, owned by the Goshen Historical Society, includes hundreds of letters in which the usually affable young Lucas tells of his experiences in and around Washington, D.C. The only time the correspondence shows even a hint of animosity or anger has to do with traitors at home. Lucas revealed a grudging respect for Southern rebels, but he had no patience for those in Connecticut: "Would to God, we in the field could return but to deposit our votes at the coming election and if possible prevent the election of the traitor Tom Seymour. His election will inspire the Confederacy with fresh hope and courage. Shame, shame, that Conn. should ever permit such an outrage and insult to her soldiers. But mind you the soldiers, some of them, will return. And they will not forget that while absent from home and unable to protest their rights there, by their own presence and their own votes, there were men so depraved, so vile, so treasonable as to make use of the opportunity thus afforded, to injure, abuse, and insult them, by advocating such measures and endorsed by the Tom Seymour party of Conn." Lucas promised "just retribution," and remarked: "We can have some little respect for an armed traitor in the enemy's ranks but for those who sympathise with treason at home we can have none but for them we have the greatest and deepest disgust. It is owing in great measure to their efforts that the war continues."[28]

Although not as frequently, the Democrats' point of view also appeared in private letters home. Sergeant Benjamin Hirst of the 14th wrote to his wife: "They are having a high old time in Conn about Politics, but I think Tom Seymour will be the next governor if they do call him a Copperhead. They got up some Humbug Resolution in our Regiment the other day in which they try to make it appear that the 14th are to a man in favour of Buckingham but I think if they will Vote the Regiment by Ballot they will find it a little differant [sic] to what they expect."[29]

Soldiers' sentiments were not the only political weapon in the party arsenals. In late March, as the election grew closer, Democrats held another mass gathering at Touro Hall, again denouncing abolitionism and violations of the Constitution. The *Times* followed with more charges that Republicans "prostitute the war into an Abolition raid."[30] Republicans countered with the unorthodox use of a female political speaker, a Quaker from Pennsylvania named Anna Dickinson, who arrived in Connecticut on March 24 and traveled the state for twelve days, appearing every night before audiences that were both supportive and hostile. Dickinson was a mesmerizing orator who, apparently, withstood the attacks of hecklers easily and playfully. The *Times* sneered that Republicans had fallen so low they "actually procure a 'woman' for aid," and the *New Haven Register* scoffed: "Nothing popularizes any cause as a petticoat."[31] There was no denying, however, that Dickinson made an impact. Moreover, her inclusion by Republicans might have indicated a further movement toward abolitionism: Dickinson was devout in the cause and associated with William Lloyd Garrison.[32]

Only days before the April 6 election, Republicans published broadsides to clarify the significance of a Buckingham victory. When the results came in, Buckingham was victorious, but with a narrow margin of just 2,634 votes.[33] It was an outcome that could have been easily reversed had the Republicans slackened their efforts for even a moment. The *Courant* exulted in the result, declaring that "one of the most hotly contested political campaigns ever witnessed in Connecticut has just closed in a magnificent triumph for the Union. . . . Domestic treason has received a withering rebuke," and "the whole nation will exult over the verdict pronounced in this State, yesterday." Under the headline "Victory! Victory!" the *Hartford Evening Press* wrote: "It was a voice for war. Let there be no mistake about it. Connecticut, small but compact and invincible puts her foot indignantly on every proposal of dishonorable peace. The South will well understand it."[34]

Democrats understood it, too, at least insofar as concluding that the election had been rigged. They charged that only Republican soldiers were

"A Vote for Buckingham," the Hartford Courant,
April 4, 1863. This Republican advertisement tells
readers what a vote for Buckingham would mean.

given furloughs to go home and vote, and that vast amounts of money had poured into the state at the direction of the Lincoln administration. The *Times* made such charges clear in several articles: "The Democracy of Connecticut gallantly contended on Monday against all the virulent Abolitionists, the haters of the Union," yet Republicans utilized "the whole power of the federal administration; with MONEY in unlimited quantities . . . with over 2,000 *selected* soldiers from the army sent home to vote. . . . A FREE AND FAIR EXPRESSION OF THE POPULAR WILL WOULD HAVE RESULTED IN A DEMOCRATIC AND CONSTITUTIONAL TRIUMPH. But foul corruption and vile oppression — proved, and not denied — have been sufficient to turn the scale against us. . . . The Administration interfered directly in this election."[35] The *Register* concurred: "It is very evident from the election returns that the Democrats have been cheated out of it. Buckingham's majority of less than 2,500 falls short of the number of furloughed soldiers sent home to vote for him."[36]

There may have been some truth in Democratic accusations. Painfully aware of the nation's misgivings concerning the war, Lincoln looked to

Connecticut with trepidation, as he had in 1860. In February, he summoned Thurlow Weed, a New York political boss, to the White House, writing him: "We are in a tight place. Money for legitimate purposes is needed immediately; but there is no appropriation from which it can be lawfully taken. I didn't know how to raise it, and so I sent for you."[37] Only days later, Connecticut's Gideon Welles, the secretary of the Navy, wrote in his diary that Weed was in town: "He has been sent for, but my informant knows not for what purposes of government. It is, I learn, to consult in regard to a scheme of Seward to influence the New Hampshire and Connecticut elections."[38] Although Weed's role is not proof of corruption in the election, anything was possible in a political contest fraught with such dire consequences had Republicans lost.

Not long after the election, Governor Buckingham delivered his annual May address to the General Assembly. He said little of the political contest, noting only that "this commonwealth has not faltered in devotion to the government, or withheld sympathy and support from her sons now battling for the national life." He then moved onto the business of state: finances, debt, and banking. Yet he came back to the war and its meaning by echoing the arguments that Republicans had made during the election: "The conflict, inaugurated at Sumter, must go on until the government shall conquer or be conquered. Let no one be deceived by the artful device of securing peace by a cessation of hostilities or by yielding to the claims of our enemies." He also stated that the causes of the war did not matter at the present time: "Slavery or Abolitionism, by ambition or interference with states rights. . . . The fact that it [the war] exists as a verity forces upon us the duties of the hour."[39]

As the Connecticut political home front was secured for the Union, the blustery winds of winter gave way to spring, and a renewal of military campaigns in the south and west. Connecticut troops were spread throughout the nation, experiencing all that the Confederacy and the landscape had to offer. Indeed, the men's various locations presented them with markedly different experiences. In Louisiana, the troops faced snake-infested swamps that released swarms of malarial-laden mosquitoes in warm weather. Captain John De Forest, a novelist before and after the war, insisted that these buzzing vermin drew more blood than rebel cannons. He lamented over uniforms so dirty and tattered that they could not be washed lest they disintegrate, and marches that produced horrid blisters. "I do not mean a single blister, as big as a pea," he wrote, "but a series of blisters, each as large as a dollar, or, to judge one's sensations, as large as a cartwheel. . . . Heat, hunger, thirst, and fatigue are nothing compared to this torment." Still, hunger too was an ever-present concern, and at one point De Forest and his comrades dined on "Louisiana *potage*," alligator soup. He concluded that the war was taking a moral toll: "The men are not so good as they were once; they drink harder and swear more and gamble deeper." He concluded that the essayist Thomas de Quincey was correct: in De Forest's paraphrase, "if homicide is habitually indulged in, it leads to immorality."[40]

Along the coast of South Carolina and Florida, the men faced similar difficulties, but they also, at least in South Carolina, had to deal with a more entrenched enemy and constant attempts to run the Union blockade. The 7th Regiment drilled in small-boat landing techniques in the surf, while the 17th performed picket duty on Folly Island, where they ate so many oysters that they were almost sickened.[41] Further north, troops stationed in and around Washington had remarkably varied duty. Samuel Fiske of the 14th marveled at the beauty of Virginia, which "does really seem to be too lovely to be the seat of a horrid war." He also wrote of the men's "wet feet every day of the march, the cold ground to lie upon, and insufficient food for them to eat." He complained that many will go home "poor bloated inebriates," and that it would take more moral courage to issue an "alcoholic *habeas corpus*" than the Emancipation Proclamation. He concluded of his war experience up to the end of 1863 that "it is hard to be a private, hard to be an officer, hard to march, hard to fight, hard to be out on picket in the rain, hard to live on short rations and be exposed to all sorts of weather, hard to be wounded and lose legs and arms and get ugly scars on one's face, hard to think of lying down in death without the gentle hand of love to smooth one's brow."[42]

In marked contrast, Fred Lucas of the 19th did not see battle in 1862 or 1863. Instead, he and his compatriots guarded Washington, visited the nation's unfinished Capitol, and periodically rode out to Mount Vernon, George Washington's estate. He witnessed the beginnings of Arlington Cemetery, and, not yet knowing true battle, measured the martial ardor and readiness of his regiment by writing satisfyingly of the immense work that went into cleaning their arms: "Every minute part of the metal, every screw head is polished so bright we can see our faces in them," and "every part of our dress must be in the neatest order, belts & boots highly polished, and whites gloves perfectly clean."[43] What a contrast to John De Forest, who could not even wash his uniform. Once Lucas had seen battle in 1864, he laughed at his earlier, inexperienced musings.

Connecticut in the American Civil War

Although the men's service differed in some respects, there were common experiences that confronted all soldiers. Foremost was death, which could come from a minor skirmish or a major battle, a sniper's rifle or an artillery shell. Even the naive young Lucas witnessed death, seeing soldiers dying of disease in hospitals, and remarking that his colonel, Elisha Kellogg of Derby, told him: "'It is hard to see the boys die here. It seems like a sacrifice of life without recompense. I can watch men fall on the field of battle without a twinge,' said the Col. 'But it is hard to see them die here.'"[44] For many, the opportunity for an honorable death, and perhaps victory, came with the spring season.

With that military effort, however, came the need for an intense operation on the home front, one that was conducted almost solely by women. As noted earlier, the Hartford Soldiers' Aid Society served as a central organizer for a wide variety of other societies located throughout Connecticut. The columns of the *Courant* were full of mentions of the societies' operations. Sarah S. Cowan of the Hartford society peppered the paper with appeals such as: "It is hoped that the battles which are now being fought, and those constantly impending, may stimulate the humane public to new efforts in behalf of our sick and wounded soldiers." The societies raised money and collected a wide assortment of garments, medical supplies, and books, as well as food. Really, they collected just about everything, and they often received letters from soldiers, regimental chaplains, and surgeons requesting specific items. Nathan Mayer, the assistant surgeon of the 16th, noted: "The papers and old magazines are very useful, and of good influence. Without good reading matter supplied from home, the soldier is too apt to purchase trashy novels, which are the sole stock of the book vendors here."[45]

On occasion, women slipped notes into the boxes or garments they sent to soldiers. For example, Ellen M. Sprague of Andover stuffed the following message into a sock: "My dear Friend and brother in our Country's cause: To your care and keeping I commit these socks, and trust they may never be disgraced by any conduct of their wearer. Loyal fingers fashioned them, and may a patriot's tread, whose very step shall tell against our rebel foes, wear them threadbare (if need be) in crushing the wicked rebellion. In every stitch is knit a prayer for our nation's weal, and the hope that peace may smile upon our land long ere these be unfit for use."[46]

In early September, the Hartford Soldiers' Aid Society announced that in the past sixteen months it had received $15,000 in donations, and "all the moneys intrusted to them are rapidly converted into garments, medicines, and delicacies for the sick and wounded. . . . The ladies of Hartford

"Our Women and the War," by Winslow Homer,
Harper's Weekly, *September 6, 1862. This illustration*
accompanied an article of the same title, which explained:
"The moral of the picture is sufficiently obvious; there is no
woman who can not in some way do something to help the army.
. . . This war of ours has developed scores of Florence Nightingales,
whose names no one knows, but whose reward, in the soldier's
gratitude and Heaven's approval, is the highest guerdon
woman can ever win." The women in the illustration
are sewing, washing, praying, and writing home
on behalf of a wounded soldier.

and vicinity have performed an immense amount of gratuitous labor for the relief of our suffering troops." The society announced in a subsequent article that "the amount of suffering relieved by this and similar associations, is beyond computation. Their agents are on the battlefields before the cannons have ceased to roar. . . . So long as the defenders of the Union are exposed to peril and pain, thousands of noble women of the land are ready to toil without weariness or recompense, to mitigate their hardships."[47]

Yet the home front effort was not solely about the relief of suffering, or providing the material comforts of home. Another part of Connecticut's workforce diligently produced every means of destruction. Already home to a remarkable array of arms and munitions companies before the war, which were joined by a host of newcomers once hostilities broke out, the little Nutmeg State was a virtual arsenal unto itself. Best known are Colt, Eli Whitney, Jr., Sharps, and Savage Fire Arms, yet others dotted the state, such as the Connecticut Arms Company in Norfolk, William Muir in

Connecticut in the American Civil War

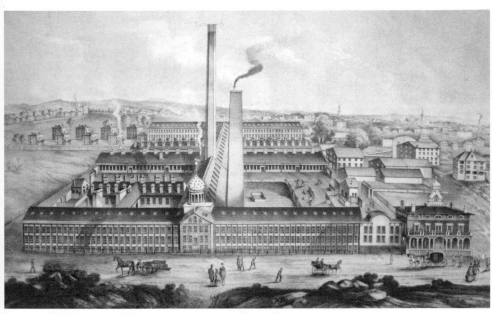

The Colt Factory, Hartford, 1862. Courtesy of the Museum
of Connecticut History, Connecticut State Library

Windsor Locks, and the Norwich Arms Company. There were also a host of smaller subcontractors.[48] Additionally, companies like Collins & Co., in Collinsville, the same company that had made some of John Brown's infamous pikes, produced swords and bayonets, and Hotchkiss & Sons manufactured all sorts of newly designed artillery shells. One arms historian has written: "Connecticut's firearms industry achieved an unrivaled degree of success during the Civil War, manufacturing enough firearms to equip a large portion of the Union armies."[49] Moreover, many of the state's manufacturers developed innovations. Between 1862 and 1863, more than seventy patents were issued to Connecticut inventors, some 75 percent of them for weaponry. Most were related to firearm and cartridge improvements, but there were also items such as Alexander Twining's patent for "armor cladding" for ships to "resist and/or repel Missiles," and James Lyons's new gun carriage that allowed a cannon to swivel 360 degrees.[50]

Yet Connecticut did not produce only the destructive implements of war. The state's manufacturers created a vast array of nonlethal war related items: socks (*lots* of socks) and stockings, cloth, shirts, hats, and uniforms, brass buckles, brass insignia of every variety, rubber ponchos, blankets, and haversacks.[51] Patents were also issued for a soldier's folding

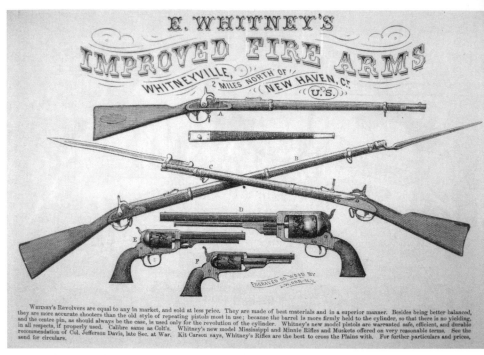

*E. Whitney Improved Firearms, company advertisement. Courtesy
of the Museum of Connecticut History, Connecticut State Library*

cot; a folding chair; a folding knife, fork, and spoon combination; and a "camp bed."[52] Much of Connecticut manufacturing was all about war, all the time. Without this massive production, it is doubtful that the Union could have adequately supplied its armies. Nor were the benefits one-sided: the state's manufacturers made huge profits. Contracts over the course of the war for these sorts of items totaled close to $4 million. In 2008 dollars, that is almost $56 million.[53]

All of this preparation and production was needed as President Lincoln attempted to turn the tide of 1863 with yet another new commander for the Army of the Potomac. Lincoln had removed the troublesome, overly cautious McClellan and replaced him with Burnside, under whom the Union received a drubbing at Fredericksburg. On January 26, Burnside was supplanted by Joseph Hooker, popularly known as "Fighting Joe." He also inspired other epithets. Charles Francis Adams Jr. noted that Hooker's headquarters was "a place which no self-respecting man liked to go, and no decent women could go. It was a combination of barroom

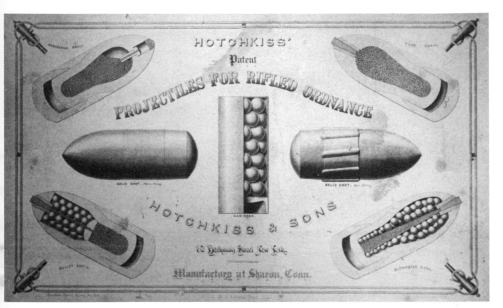

Hotchkiss' Patent Projectiles for Rifled Ordinance, company advertisement.
Courtesy of the Museum of Connecticut History, Connecticut State Library

and brothel," out of which came the term "hooker" for the prostitutes, or Hooker's girls, who frequented the camp. Nonetheless, Hooker addressed many of the problems about which the soldiers had been complaining, such as the lack of supplies and low morale.[54] Unfortunately, he did not live up to the "fighting" in his nickname.

The battle of Chancellorsville occurred in the opening days of May. Hooker had been preparing a major offensive southward, but he wanted to avoid the Confederate trenches that had proved so deadly when Burnside unwisely attempted to storm Marye's Heights at Fredericksburg. Therefore, Hooker split the Army of the Potomac into three parts. The cavalry crossed the Rappahannock well north of Chancellorsville, then rode south to cut Lee's supply lines. The main force of 70,000 infantrymen also crossed upstream and then marched to the Confederate flank, while 40,000 more feinted at Fredericksburg to keep its rebel defenders tied down there. Hooker was certain of forcing Lee to retreat; indeed, he seemed more focused on that than on actually fighting. The difficulty came when Lee stood fast and Fighting Joe, like McClellan, became unnerved.

On May 1, the armies met at Chancellorsville, Virginia, where Hooker stood still, retreated, and stood still again. Lee moved swiftly and effectively, once again gambling that he could split his forces and carry out an end run while the Union Army hesitated. The historian James McPherson wrote: "Hooker seemed in a daze even before a cannonball hit his headquarters and knocked him unconscious in mid-morning."[55] Unfortunately for his troops, the general woke up just in time to do nothing, and Lee knew it. Even after Union officers held a war council on May 5, voting to go on the attack, Hooker demurred and then retreated across the river. On hearing the news, Lincoln exclaimed: "My God! My God! What will the country say! What will the country say!"[56] Chancellorsville was yet another disastrous defeat for the Union.

Five Connecticut regiments fought at Chancellorsville — the 5th, 14th, 17th, 20th, and 27th. The prolific Samuel Fiske conveyed his exasperation at Hooker's inability to act, writing a series of comments in his journal on May 2:

> Eleven, A.M. — Nothing done yet in the way of fighting since seven o'clock.
> Three, P.M. — Still nothing done!
> Six, P.M. — Hard fighting again, terrific musketry and cannonade from the enemy.
> Eight, P.M. — We have met a serious reverse. Our eleventh corps, and the twelfth perhaps, have most shamefully run; and we are in danger of defeat, which the Lord forbid! We shall have a hard time, and nobody knows who will live through it. I don't know as I want to, if we are now shamefully defeated.[57]

In the ensuing days, as the battle continued, Fiske was ultimately captured by, as he put it, "the brownest and most illiterate looking vagabonds that I ever set eyes on, — every one of them with a gun in his hand."[58] As often happened in battle, the tide turned briefly. Union forces overran a Confederate position, and Fiske regained his freedom.

Yet the experience of having been among the rebels and observing their condition gave him a new perspective. "Their supply and ammunition trains look like a congregation of all the crippled California emigrant-trains that ever escaped off the desert," he wrote; "The men are ill dressed, ill equipped, and ill provided, — a set of ragamuffins that a man is ashamed to be seen among, even when he is a prisoner and can't help it. And yet they have beaten us fairly; beaten us all to pieces." After witnessing the condition of the rebel army, Fiske was convinced that "all we have to do is to make up our minds not to run before an equal number of the enemy; to keep cool, and save our ammunition to shoot something besides trees with; and, when the Butternuts [Confederates] find we don't run away, they will."[59]

Of the Connecticut troops, the 17th, 20th, and 27th suffered most at Chancellorsville. The 17th was part of the 11th Corps that had fled, and the regiment suffered 106 casualties during the rout. The 20th lost a full third of its men, with twenty-six killed, forty-nine wounded, twenty-two wounded and captured, and an additional seventy-three taken prisoner. Worst off was the 27th, which was ensnared during the Union retreat; some 272 men out of the regiment's 293 were captured. Many of them were sent to the notorious Libby Prison.[60]

There were inspiring moments even in the midst of the slaughter. A colonel from the Pennsylvania 132nd Regiment remembered what he described as "one of the most heroic deeds I have saw done to help stem the fleeing tide of men and restore courage, was not the work of a battery, nor a charge of cannon, but the charge of a band of music!" The colonel was writing of the Connecticut 14th's regimental band, noting that they "went right out into that open space between our new line and the rebels, with shot and shell crashing all about them, and played the 'Star Spangled Banner,' the 'Red, White, and Blue' and 'Yankee Doodle,' and repeated them for a full twenty minutes." "They never played better," continued the colonel; "Did that require nerve? It was undoubtedly the first and only band concert given under such conditions. Never was American grit more finely illustrated. Its effect upon the men was magical."[61]

Although May started poorly for the Union, the coming weeks promised better outcomes. Most notably, General Ulysses S. Grant proved to be what most other Union commanders were not: determined to crush the enemy. Still intent on capturing Vicksburg, that Gibraltar of the West that had eluded him in 1862, Grant tried every conceivable strategy. He briefly renewed work on a Mississippi canal; attempted to move gunboats through snagged bayous choked with fallen trees and inhabited with every sort of swamp creature; and ultimately, in mid-April, pursued the risky strategy of running Union gunboats down the Mississippi past the gauntlet of Confederate artillery that protected the city. The plan was for the Navy to ferry troops, who had marched down the west side of the river, across the river and thirty miles downstream. Grant then had the troops loop around and launch a land assault from the southeast. Part of the general's success (much like Lee's) was his daring, in this case his decision to break away from a secure line of supply and allow the army to forage. McPherson wrote: "Thus had Grant wrought in a seventeen-day campaign during which his army marched 180 miles, fought and won five engagements against separate enemy forces . . . inflicted 7,200 casualties at the cost of 4,300, and cooped up an apparently demoralized enemy in the Vicksburg defenses."[62]

Now came the siege, a massive bombardment that lasted for more than a month. Though Jefferson Davis implored Lee to send reinforcements, he refused, insisting that they were needed for his own campaign into Pennsylvania. On July 3, Vicksburg's rebel commander, General John Pemberton, asked for surrender terms, and the next day he capitulated. Upon learning of the Union victory, Lincoln reportedly said: "Grant is my man, and I am his the rest of the war."[63]

The Vicksburg victory was tremendously important for a variety of reasons. It helped to further secure the Mississippi River for the Union, it demoralized the South, and it ended the Union siege at Port Hudson, Louisiana, where the Connecticut 12th, 13th, 24th, 26th, and 28th regiments, along with other Union forces under the command of General Nathaniel Banks, were attempting to take the only other city besides Vicksburg that still offered resistance along the great river. As with Grant's assault further north, the initial attack on Port Hudson was repulsed, and the Union Army settled in for a prolonged bombardment. From May 21 to July 9, the army tried repeatedly to capture the city. When news of Vicksburg's surrender arrived, the Confederate commander, General Franklin Gardner, recognized the futility of continuing and surrendered.

Captain De Forest of the Connecticut 12th wrote eloquently of the Port Hudson days, providing a remarkable window into one of the new facets of war. Trench warfare has been widely associated with World War I, but it began at places like Vicksburg and Port Hudson. De Forest wrote of the trenches: "Danger is perpetually present. The spring is always bent; the nerves never have a chance to recuperate; the elasticity of courage is slowly worn out. Every morning I was awakened by the popping of rifles and the whistling of balls; hardly a day passed that I did not hear the loud exclamations of the wounded, or see the corpses borne to the rear; and the gamut of my good-night lullaby varied all the way from Minié rifles to sixty-eight pounders." De Forest also told of the amazing proficiency at arms displayed by soldiers in both armies. Separated by 150 yards, at one point the rebels "held up a hoe handle to test our marksmanship, it was struck by no less than three bullets in as many minutes." A captured officer from the Second Alabama "told me that most of their casualties were cases of shots between the brim of the hat and the top of the forehead." De Forest noted that men killed one another by sending their bullets through tiny portholes cut through trees that fortified the front of the trench. "Several of our men were shot in the face through the portholes as they were taking aim," he wrote, and "it must be remembered that these openings were but just large enough to protrude the barrel of a musket and take sight along it."[64]

July was a glorious month for the Union. Grant and Banks had tightened the noose around the Confederacy in the west, and all that remained was an equally significant victory in the east. Remarkably, it came at exactly the same time that Vicksburg surrendered.

Gettysburg is perhaps the best-known battle of the war. As always, Lee opted for a daring, risky strategy, invading Pennsylvania in the hope that a single campaign would dishearten the North, encourage the Copperhead movement, move foreign nations to recognize the Confederacy, and, just as important, allow his army to resupply itself in the fertile Northern countryside. In one bold move, Lee hoped to sting the Union so severely that it would be forced to make peace.[65]

Thus Lee made his way across the Potomac for the second time and poured his troops into the North, concentrating his army there and striking fear and panic into the hearts of Pennsylvania civilians, who had grown accustomed to letting Virginia soil run red with blood. The *Hartford Courant*'s headline in mid-June said it all: "The Rebel Raid — Call to Arms! Excitement in Philadelphia."[66] The two great armies ultimately met at the little town of Gettysburg. The geography was something of an accident. The Confederate General A. P. Hill had gone there because it was reported that a supply of shoes could be had for his barefooted men. Prior to his arrival, however, a Union cavalry officer, John Buford, had ridden in and immediately recognized Gettysburg's strategic importance, with a dozen roads converging on the town. He wisely posted troops, armed with breech-loading carbines, on the heights to the north and west of town, where they held off the initial Confederate advance.[67]

As news of the armies' movements reached Washington, Lincoln recognized the opportunity to deliver a fatal blow to the South and pushed Hooker to act. Yet the president quickly recognized that Fighting Joe was not the man for the job, and on June 28, Lincoln appointed General George Gordon Meade as commander.[68] Hill's men had gone for the shoes on the morning of July 1, and by midday more and more men from both armies had converged on the area. Once their total forces had arrived,

Meade commanded some 90,000 troops to Lee's 75,000. The Confederate general's failed hope was to rout the Union line quickly, but by the evening of July 1, the Union was well entrenched in a semicircle on Cemetery Ridge, just south of the city. Confederate General James Longstreet surveyed the enemy line and concluded that it was far too formidable to attack. Lee insisted, however, and so the battle began the next day, with Confederate forces attempting a two-pronged assault on the ends of the Union line: on the right, at Cemetery Ridge and Culp's Hill, and on the left, at Little Round Top. Union troops held their positions, with their commanders reinforcing the lines and counterattacking at just the right times. On July 3, Lee opted to gamble everything with a harrowing charge just to the right of the Union center. General George Edward Pickett led some 12,000 men directly into the heart of the Union defenses. A barrage of 150 Confederate cannons preceded the charge in an attempt to soften the enemy; it was with the single largest Southern bombardment of the war.[69]

For Connecticut regiments, Gettysburg was both horrific and heroic. The six units that were involved in the battle — the 2nd Light Artillery, and the 5th, 14th, 17th, 20th, and 27th Infantry — sustained significant losses but fought valiantly.[70] The 14th, in particular, which had suffered so grievously at earlier battles, played an important part in fending off Pickett's charge. Positioned at a stone wall directly to the left of Cemetery Hill, at a spot called the angle, the 14th experienced the massive but ineffectual cannonading that preceded the grand charge. The regiment's historian wrote: "I utterly despair of giving any idea of the various diabolical sounds to which we listened, the howling of the shell [sic] as they sped through the air was like the voice of the tornado upon the ocean, and the sound of their bursting like incessant crashes of the heaviest thunder."[71] The blasts were heard a hundred miles away.

As the smoke cleared, the sun shone on the field, revealing Pickett's columns. In his official report, Major Theodore Ellis of Hartford wrote: "As far as the eye could reach could be seen the advancing troops, their gay war flags fluttering in the gentle summer breeze, while their sabers and bayonets flashed and glistened in the midday sun. Step by step they came, the music and rhythm of their tread resounding upon rock-ribbed earth. Every movement expressed determination and resolute defiance, the line moving forward like a victorious giant, confident of power and victory. . . . The advance seems as resistless as the incoming tide. It was the last throw of the dice in this supreme moment of the great game of war."[72] As the brigades surged forward, the 14th opened a withering fire. Two com-

THE BATTLE OF GETTYSBURG, Pᴬ JULY 3ᵈ 1863.

This terrific and bloody conflict between the gallant 'Army of the Potomac', commanded by their great General George G. Meade, and the hosts of the rebel 'Army of the East' under General Lee, was commenced on Wednesday July 1ˢᵗ and ended on Friday the 3ᵈ at 5 O'Clock P. M. — The decisive Battle was fought on Friday, ending in the complete rout & dispersion of the Rebel Army. A Nations thanks and undying fame ever crown the Army of the heroic soldiers, who fought with such unflinching bravery in this long and desperate fight.

"The Battle of Gettysburg, Pa. July 3d. 1863," hand-colored lithograph, Currier and Ives, New York, 1863. The caption reads: "This terrific and bloody conflict between the gallant 'Army of the Potomac,' commanded by their great General George G. Meade, and the hosts of rebel 'Army of the East' under General Lee, was commenced on Wednesday July 1st and ended on Friday the 3rd at 5 O'Clock P.M. The decisive Battle was fought on Friday, ending in the complete rout & dispersion of the Rebel Army. A Nation thanks and undying fame ever crown the Army of the heroic soldiers, who fought with such unflinching bravery in this long and desperate fight." Library of Congress, LC-USZ62-13961

panies carried new Sharps breech-loading rifles, and the men worked in pairs, one loading and the other firing. One of the soldiers recalled later: "So rapid was the firing that the barrels became so hot that it was almost impossible to use them, some using the precious water in their canteens to pour upon the overworked guns." The rebels continued to drive forward and came within a hundred yards of the 14th's position. The regiment's historian wrote that in an area "no larger than a football field, came some of the most vicious hand-to-hand fighting of the Civil War."[73] The men of the 14th leaped over the stone wall and poured into the enemy's ranks, driven to a frenzy by the effectiveness of the Union fire and intent on stealing rebel battle flags, the prizes of combat. Sergeant Edward Wade of New Britain remembered afterward: "By this time the Fourteenth were all excited: they remembered Antietam, Fredericksburg, and Chancellorsville, and over the wall they went; nothing could stop them, and soon they were fighting hand-to-hand with the rebels. We captured six battle-flags and forty prisoners; and over one hundred prisoners came in afterwards. . . . Oh, it was a glorious day for the old Fourteenth!"[74]

The once disheartened Samuel Fiske felt exactly the same way, writing immediately after the battle: "I have at last had the desired opportunity of seeing a battle in which there was real fighting; hard, persistent, desperate fighting; a fighting worthy of a noble cause and the confidence of a gallant people, and of the glorious anniversary that is upon us. . . . With a tremendous shout, catching from regiment to regiment along our line, our boys sprang up over the fence and down the slope upon the wavering enemy, with a rush that nothing could withstand. The enemy fled, throwing away everything. We captured thousands of prisoners, — among them two generals, scores of colors, and arms of all descriptions without number. . . . Hurrah for the gallant old 14th! She is getting some of the pay for Fredericksburg and Chancellorsville."[75]

The 14th lost ten men killed, fifty-seven wounded, and four captured, but the regiment had restored both its reputation and the men's belief in an ultimate Union victory. Three men from the regiment received the congressional Medal of Honor for their valor in capturing flags, and *Harper's Weekly* wrote of the regiment's service: "So ended the battle of Gettysburg, and the sun sank to rest that night on a battle-field that had proved that the Army of the Potomac could and would save the people of the North from invasion whenever and wherever they may be assailed."[76]

The glory of the Gettysburg battlefield buoyed the North and elated President Lincoln.[77] Yet as the smoke cleared and the cheers subsided, the reality of 23,000 Union and 28,000 Confederate casualties hit the Northern soldiers like a hammer. Private Loren Goodrich of the 14th wrote to his family in New Britain that his elation quickly turned to compassion for the fallen rebels: "It was a horrible sight to see those poor fellows lying there who a few hours before were in the full bloom of manhood. One man who lived two hours after the battle was holding in his hand the picture of his wife and children. There he died with no loving hand or kind friend to soothe or cheer him with kind words, grasping in his death clutch the picture of those innocent ones who will be left fatherless." The regiment's chaplain, Henry Stevens of Cromwell, wrote that the dead were "in some

"Incidents of the War. A Harvest of Death, Gettysburg, July, 1863,"
photograph by Timothy H. Sullivan, July 1863, in Alexander Gardner,
Gardner's Photographic Sketchbook of the War *(Washington: Philip*
& Soloman, 1866). Library of Congress, LC-B8184-7964-A

places so numerous that the ground appeared covered by them, and one could walk for distances stepping only on the bodies of the slain."[78]

A private in the 17th, Justus Silliman of New Canaan, described a field hospital: "Three thousand wounded in our hospitals[,] hundreds have had limbs amputated. The barn more resembled a butcher shop than any other institution. One citizen on going near it fainted away and had to be carried off." Silliman added: "The groans of the wounded are sounding through the camp night and day. I will not shock you with the details of the terrible sufferings of these martyrs for their country. Neither will I write of the scene I witnessed in passing over the battlefields. . . . Since the battle, Gettysburg has been an extensive coffin mart & embalmers harvest the field. [T]he coffins were stacked on the streets blockading the sidewalks. [T]hese coffin speculators made an enormous profit."[79]

Like Antietam, Gettysburg inspired a sense of emergency on the home front. In "An Urgent Appeal," the Hartford Soldiers' Aid Society announced that it would "forward immediately all the hospital stores on hand for the relief of our noble bleeding army; the ghastly wounds of husbands, brothers and sons, dear to thousands of loyal hearts, call upon us for aid. Let a hearty response be made at once from the bloodiest battle-field of the war." Just days later, the society issued "another call upon the women of the North for aid to our wounded. Thousands of our brave soldiers are at this moment suffering from all the agonies that flow from war — loss of limbs and members, and wounds from bullets, bombs and bayonets, in all parts of their bodily frames. These again produce fever, exhaustion, and innumerable complications of disease."[80]

In addition to this horror, there were other aspects of Gettysburg that went poorly. Rather than quickly pursuing the defeated rebels, General Meade opted for caution, moving slowly and thereby allowing Lee to escape across the Potomac. Lincoln was dismayed, and so were men like Samuel Fiske, who wrote of the army's inactivity: "Now I have scarcely a doubt the enemy has taken himself away from us. . . . The men universally were eager, anxious, panting, to be led on to complete triumph, and utterly crush the defeated and despairing enemy." He added that a Confederate was now "sitting on the other side of the river, performing various gyrations with his fingers, — thumb on his nose." Still, July was an incredible month for the Union, with the victories of Vicksburg and Port Hudson in the west and Gettysburg in the east. Fiske concluded: "Let the country have it in remembrance. The empty sham of Rebellion is collapsing fast and finally. Let Northern Copperheads beware!"[81]

Fiske's blend of joy at victory with anger toward Democrats was not uncommon. The young Fred Lucas, of the 19th, made exactly the same connection, writing home: "How does the glorious news which comes pouring into us today from Meade north of the Potomac & Grant at Vicksburg affect them [the Democrats]?" He continued: "Oh, if we could only meet the traitors at home and annihilate the fire in the rear."[82] Nor was this merely a residual fuming about the spring elections. As Union armies bled in the summer fields, new examples of disloyalty at home were revealed. Foremost were the actions of those who rebelled against the March 3 Enrollment Act, which authorized a federal draft. Only a week after Gettysburg, New York City witnessed the infamous draft riots, in which mobs protested the unequal nature of the draft because a $300 commutation fee allowed wealthy men to escape service. Bloodshed and destruction were unleashed in the streets. Federal troops had to be called in and martial law declared to quell the insurrection. Writing of the disturbance, Fiske remarked: "We are coming home soon, and we shall not

Connecticut in the American Civil War

fire *blank cartridges* at riotous 'friends' who resist laws, and fill our streets and houses with blood."[83]

The conscription act was actually far more about inducing men to volunteer and in doing so receive town and state bounties, than actually implementing an efficient draft. It was more a threat than a reality. Of those who were eventually drafted, only a tiny portion — around 7 percent nationwide — ever served. The vast majority of draftees were deemed unacceptable for military duty. This was the case in Connecticut as well as more generally. Governor Buckingham implemented a draft on July 18, shortly after the New York draft riots — and did so only after he had secretly issued guns to loyal citizens in the areas where the draft was to take place. Of the 11,530 Connecticut men drafted in 1863, some 8,000 were exempted, and 2,248 men who were not exempted paid substitutes to take their place. Once mustered in, many of the substitutes deserted as quickly as possible. Some set fire to the conscript camp in New Haven, some jumped from moving trains, and others assaulted guards to make an escape. Ultimately, out of almost 12,000 men drafted, only 248 actually served.[84] This was hardly an efficient way to replenish troops.

Arguments over conscription had actually begun immediately after the Enrollment Act's passage and were made a part of the spring election arguments. The *Hartford Times* had insisted: "The bill gives to Abraham Lincoln the power to draft men when and where he chooses . . . [and this is] a gigantic stride toward a Central, Abolition DESPOTISM." The connection to abolition was now standard Democratic practice and continued to appear in subsequent articles, such as when the *Times* charged that the draft proposed that "Negroes are to be mixed in with white men. A negro party with a negro policy, has come to that."[85] The paper also expressed disgust that rich men could buy their way out of military service, or pay someone else to be a substitute, when poor men had no such opportunity. And once again agitating racial animosity, the *Times* reprinted a salacious story entitled "A Nigger Selling White People," reporting that a black man had "four white men, offering them for sale as substitutes. He put on immense airs . . . and cut a monstrous swell about the streets, with his slaves tagging along behind. He was a genuine specimen of that happy class who derive exquisite enjoyment in this nigger millennium. We have not heard how he made it with his chattels, but [we] suppose they met with a ready sale in the Lincoln market. Isn't this a great country?"[86] Obviously, the intent was to show the reversal of fortunes: whites were now the slaves. Such articles cleverly blended criticism of the draft and the hiring of substitutes with an attempt to fan the underlying racism in Connecticut society. The connection was more than mere propaganda. There existed a genuine link between the president's Emancipation Proclamation authorizing the enlistment of black troops and the subsequent conscription act. In the most overt sense, both were about manpower to crush the rebellion. Yet they were also, as the *Times* duly noted, about race: the connection between the two races, the abilities of blacks to better themselves within white society, and what that actually meant to American society in the long run.

The famed black abolitionist Frederick Douglass had written: "Once let the black man get upon his person the brass letters, U.S.; let him get an eagle on his button, and a musket on his shoulder and bullets in his pocket, and there is no power on earth which can deny that he had earned the right to citizenship."[87] The *Hartford Daily Post* noted of the Emancipation Proclamation: "As a result of this declaration the shackles have fallen from the limbs of four millions of slaves; and this vast multitude, with no recognized political status in the community stands before the nation, seeking from the power which has accorded the boon of emancipation, the bestowal of the right of suffrage." "This," concluded the *Post*, "constitutes the 'negro question.'"[88] Thus black freedom, military service, and citizenship — the overall issue of race — was part of the larger context of the war, whether in the form of arguments over conscription, the willingness of whites to serve with blacks, or the conduct of blacks in the military.

The first service of black troops came in January of 1863, when Massachusetts Colonel Thomas Wentworth Higginson, an avid abolitionist, led a regiment of volunteer black soldiers in a minor skirmish in South Carolina. He reported afterward to the War Department: "Nobody knows anything about these men who has not seen them in battle. . . . No officer in this regiment now doubts that the key to the successful prosecution of the war lies in the unlimited employment of black troops." The *New York Tribune* commented that such reports were sure "to shake our inveterate Saxon prejudice against the capacity and courage of negro troops." In March, Massachusetts Governor John Andrew authorized the enlistment of what became the famous 54th all-black regiment, with white officers. Jefferson Davis's response to the Emancipation Proclamation that authorized such actions was that it represented "the most execrable measure in the history of guilty man," and he promised to turn over captured Union officers to state governments as "criminals engaged in inciting servile insurrection."[89] The punishment was death.

Connecticut soldiers readily recognized that the struggles over the issues of military necessity and race were related to the enlistment of

Connecticut in the American Civil War

blacks and forced conscription of whites. Fred Lucas wrote: "I saw the negro regiment yesterday drilling and a body of fine, smart, intelligent looking darkies they are. They learn rapidly and I think will soon make good soldiers. I infer from what the papers say that the subjects to draft at the north are all willing to have the blacks armed now although many strongly opposed the measure one year since." As much as he looked approvingly at black soldiers, Lucas refused to serve with them, telling his mother: "I could secure a commission in the colored troops if I desired one but I do not by any means. I choose to serve my country where I am to mixing so freely with the negros. I cannot see any temptation to prompt a man to aspire to shoulder straps [an officer's insignia] in such a position and under such circumstances; although I respect the colored troops very much and rely on their bravery." Lucas also connected the wider manpower issue directly with the need for black soldiers. He blasted draft dodgers, asking: "Where is the boasted Loyalty, Patriotism, and Love of Country?" He criticized the "the soldier traffic"—the use of substitutes—and concluded: "Darkey soldiers may possibly shield their [white substitutes'] persons from draft, and their pockets from wounds, but time will one day return the old soldiers home and then, I fear, those who now escape by means of black substitutes bought with little money, will have old sores opened, if not new ones formed."[90]

John De Forest was also offered promotion if he led a black regiment, but he too declined. Moreover, he presented on numerous occasions unflattering views of blacks, referring to "Ball's servant, a fat and dirty nigger" and "Lieutenant Berry's man, a blubber-lipped loafer called John Bull," and remarking: "I then got a little yellow vagrant named Harry."[91] Other Connecticut soldiers had equally sharp words for black troops. William Van Deursen of the 24th wrote: "Yesterday a negro regiment arrived here from down the river, about 1000 strong. Some of the officers are black and some white. They are a dirty looking lot enough. I suppose they are good enough to dig trenches." In other letters he reported that "an orderly Sergt. of the 25 Conn. Vols. has been put in Capt. of one company [of black soldiers]. I would sooner go private in ours. They are a dirty looking set and I don't believe will ever make soldiers," and "how government can expect white men to live in such a spot I cannot tell."[92]

The most heralded test of black troops came during the Union attempt to take Charleston, and especially Fort Wagner, during the summer. It was here that the Massachusetts 54th charged the fort's wall and fell in large numbers, their commander Colonel Robert Gould Shaw also succumbing to the deadly rebel fire. The *Courant* wrote about the regiment's service, noting that the 6th Connecticut had supported the 54th, and in another article included a letter from a soldier in the 10th Connecticut, who wrote: "The 54th Mass. (colored) led the charge, and I tell you they did well; they demonstrated that negroes can fight as well, if not better, than white troops."[93] Interestingly, the Connecticut 7th had, a full week before the 54th, gotten over the wall at Fort Wagner but had been forced to retreat when no reinforcements came to their aid.[94] Although the 54th failed to take the fort, the regiment's heroism was publicized widely. The battle for Charleston ultimately turned into a siege that lasted from mid-August to November, during which Fort Sumter, seen as the epicenter of the rebellion, was pounded into rubble.[95]

The glowing accounts of the 54th's action drew heavy criticism and charges of fabrication from Connecticut Democrats. The *Hartford Times* scoffed: "It must have been evident to all impartial observers that the flaming accounts of 'negro bravery' with which . . . the administration journals were simultaneously filled, were the products of a pre-arranged and systematic plan." After arming the Negroes, "the abolitionists found it necessary to proclaim, as a matter of course, that they were heroes. Hence the flaming lies paraded in the [New York] *Tribune* and papers of that class."[96] Democrats could not deny, however, that the reports of black bravery and assistance to the Union influenced public opinion in the North. Months earlier, it would have been impossible to broach the idea of a black Connecticut regiment, but by late in the year even that extreme measure in the land of steady racism seemed possible. Accordingly, on November 13, at a special session of the General Assembly, Colonel Dexter R. Wright from New Haven, formerly the commander of the 15th regiment, proposed—and Colonel Benjamin S. Pardee, formerly of the 10th, and also from New Haven, seconded the proposal—a bill authorizing Governor Buckingham to organize a regiment of "colored infantry."[97]

Democrats exploded in opposition. Henry Mitchell of Bristol called the bill "the greatest monstrosity ever introduced into Connecticut," and William W. Eaton of Hartford railed against it for an hour, exclaiming: "I am opposed to raising negro soldiers; it is against the spirit of the age. The whole thing is rotten from beginning to end." "It is the most disgraceful bill ever introduced into the Connecticut Legislature," he continued; "If it must pass it should be amended so as to include Camanchee [sic] and Ojibway Indians. . . . [I] would sooner let loose the wild Camanchees than the ferocious negro. He is both ferocious and cowardly, and ferocity and cowardice go hand in hand." Eaton then unleashed a blast that foreshadowed the South's postwar Jim Crow propaganda and that, for many, justified segregation: "You will let loose upon every household south of Mason and Dixon's line a band of ferocious men who will spread lust and rapine all over the land. . . . Lust is to be legalized by this bill. The African cannot be controlled, possessing, as he does, all the elements of a brutal civilization. You offer a bid for the vilest crimes known to man."[98] The *Hartford Times*, once again connecting black troops with the larger issues of substitutes and conscription, added that the bill was little more than a scam by New York brokers to sell "shoddy implements of war" to Connecticut.[99]

To such impassioned declarations as Eaton's, the *Hartford Courant* responded that "the experience of the war had dispelled all such hallucinations. The armed negro is not a brutal and ferocious being, let loose to ravage and plunder. He has shown himself to be docile, humane and generous. He fights bravely, meeting dangers and death with alacrity, not merely for himself, but with the ennobling purpose of striking the manacle from the hands of his race. . . . It is but just that the blacks should be allowed their share in removing a degredation and an iniquity." On the same day it was proposed, the bill passed and paved the way for the creation of the 29th and later the 30th Connecticut Negro Regiments. Beginning on December 11 and for several days thereafter, the *Courant* ran announcements for enlistments.[100] Connecticut had indeed come a long way in 1863.

The sniping between the two parties had little effect on the willingness of the state's black community to come forward and enroll. By January 1864, some 1,249 men had enlisted in the 29th, and another 469 formed the 30th, which later became part of the 31st Regiment United States Colored Infantry. The 29th was mustered into service on March 8, and a week later the soldiers received a flag presented by the colored ladies of New Haven. The regiment then left for Annapolis, Maryland.[101]

The level of black participation in Connecticut regiments was astounding, considering that the 1860 census revealed only 8,726 blacks living in the state, and of them only 2,206 were men between the ages of fifteen and fifty (the most likely ages for service). This meant that some 78 percent of eligible black men enrolled in the 29th and 30th regiments. Just over 15 percent of these men died as a result of the war.[102]

Determining the motivations for black enrollment in the army is difficult. It is tempting to conclude that the opportunity to take part in striking down slavery was the essential factor, but enlistment bounties and steady pay (motivating factors for some white soldiers) may also have played a part. The lack of sources on the 29th and 30th prevents an accurate assessment of the men's motivations, although two brief sketches of soldiers in the 29th do exist. Alexander Newton and Isaac Hill, both ministers, and neither of whom were born in Connecticut, wrote of their time in the 29th. Newton was an abolitionist before the war and active in the underground railroad, writing after the war: "Although free born, I was born under the curse of slavery, surrounded by the thorns and briars of prejudice, hatred, persecution and the suffering incident to this fearful regime." His book's introduction noted that Newton was "doing what he could on the battlefield to liberate his race." Isaac Hill does not comment on his reason for enlisting in the last company of the 29th, though he begins the preface to his work by stating, "The author of this has for a long time been greatly concerned for this land and nation, and for the human family in general, but more particularly for the unfortunate African, both in this and every other part of the world."[103]

As fall arrived, many in the North believed they could detect the faint stench of defeat coming from the Confederacy. This was true even though Union General William Rosecrans, after initially driving rebel forces out of Tennessee and into northern Georgia, was repulsed in late September at the Battle of Chickamauga. He was forced to flee all the way back to Chattanooga, where he was besieged by Confederate General Braxton Bragg. Fortunately for Rosecrans, on October 17, Lincoln appointed Grant commander of the newly created Military Division of Mississippi, and the general quickly ordered Hooker and William Tecumseh Sherman to bring Rosecrans reinforcements, and then joined them to supervise the campaign. By late November, Union forces had once again pushed Bragg's troops out of the area.[104]

On the same day that the president appointed Grant commander in the west, he also called for an additional 300,000 troops. The *Courant* responded quickly: "One more grand rally, and the rebellion will bite the dust." Governor Buckingham called a special session of the General Assembly to coordinate the raising of additional men. "The call of the President for more troops to reinforce our armies," proclaimed the governor, "is one of great encouragement, furnishing as it does new evidence of his determination to use all power which the constitution has placed in his hand to maintain national authority unimpaired."[105]

Some Northerners even began to consider the basis of reconstruction, or how the South might rejoin the Union. William Ellsworth, a longtime state politician and a four-term governor (1838–42), wrote to the *Courant*: "When these States return to the Union, it will be, if at all, under a sense of their mistake and folly; and when they have repealed their secession ordinances and given up their resistance to the lawful government, they shall be received into the government which they endeavored to destroy." These strong words were buoyed by Republican amnesia of the war's causes and the North's alleged commitment to freedom. Failing to acknowledge that the Constitution had in fact protected slavery, Ellsworth insisted: "Let it ever be remembered that it is the opponents of the administration and no others who are dissatisfied with the constitution as it is," following with the recurring idea "that the *North* is compelled now to persevere in the cause of liberty, and that freedom is sure to triumph in the end." He concluded: "And here let me say, I do most sincerely approve and admire the [Emancipation] proclamation of President Lincoln, which has been so curtly and unjustly criticized by gentlemen who are opposed to the war. It is one of the greatest, wisest, and most heoric [sic] acts of all time, and will grow in the favor of wise men, while the world lasts."[106]

Although Ellsworth may ultimately have been correct about the wisdom and heroism of Lincoln's action, such arguments did not go unchallenged in Connecticut. The war was not over, and neither the South nor its Copperhead supporters were ready to throw in the towel. In September, in anticipation of the November town elections, the *Hartford Times* once again proclaimed; "If this Proclamation is sustained, the Union will be broken. The old Union *will no longer exist.*" In November, the *Times* somewhat disingenuously announced: "All Democrats are ready to give the last dollar and the last man to maintain the Constitution and restore the Union; but not a dollar nor a man, unless legally compelled to do so, to aid in a war for the abolition of slavery — a war for the destruction of the Union. If this is treason, make the most of it." The paper continued its onslaught well into December, with an article entitled "The President's 'Greatest Folly,'" in which it again attacked emancipation and asked: "Have the American people a desire for a continuation of this official Punch and Judy show at Washington?"[107]

Yet Lincoln was hardly done. He focused on winning the war and honoring those who served the Union. He called forth additional troops, announced a national day of thanksgiving, and — in the now-famous Gettysburg Address — memorialized the blood-soaked battlefield and the sacrifices of so many.[108] And on December 8, the president announced a plan of pardon and amnesty to those who took an oath to the United States and accepted emancipation. This was a long shot, but he hoped it would convince those in the South who had grown tired of war to capitulate sooner rather than later. In taking such a gamble, however, the president also challenged some of his own supporters — radicals who were determined to punish the South not merely by freeing slaves, but by completely undoing the South's social and economic structure.[109]

———•———

And so ended 1863, a year that proved to be the Union's—and Connecticut's—crucible. Governor Buckingham had narrowly won the April election, and with it had secured the state's continued loyalty to the nation's cause. The summer campaigns, from Vicksburg to Gettysburg, revealed that Northern armies could indeed rout the dreaded rebels. Lincoln had found his man in Grant. Union soldiers found a renewed confidence. Samuel Fiske said it best: "This is the best thing I know about the Army of the Potomac. The spirit of patriotism, and the confidence in our cause and in our final and speedy victory, is a perfect contrast to the feelings of discouragement and impatience and growling that prevailed a year ago, and, later, after Fredericksburg."[110]

This optimism, however, did not foretell immediate Northern victory. The Union still faced a tough and very bloody eighteen months before it finally defeated the Confederacy. Then there was the issue of reconstruction and slavery, the latter of which had dominated the Northern consciousness ever since Lincoln had issued the Emancipation Proclamation. Democrats, in particular, connected the decree—and the rabid abolitionism that allegedly inspired it—to everything negative they could think of in an attempt to tap into the underlying racism of Connecticut society. For their part, many Republicans conveniently forgot their party's previous denunciations of blacks and the Free Soil rhetoric of the 1850s. They were now the stalwart defenders of freedom and liberty.

Ultimately, the *Courant* struck exactly the right chord in looking back over the past months: "The year 1863 has been a year of campaigns and battles. It has brought a series of Union triumphs that have few parallels in the history of wars. Occasionally the tide of success has been momentarily interrupted by bloody defeat. But the victories of the enemy have proved showy, rather than substantial, and according to rebel confessions, have, with hardly an exception, turned to ashes on the lips."[111]

CHAPTER FIVE

Expensive Victory

1864-65

Hope for the Union was mighty in 1864. After the victories of the previous year, many in the North anticipated the Confederacy's quick collapse. This was not to be. Robert E. Lee proved to be what he had been so many times before — a tenacious, resourceful commander who could rally his ragged, battle-worn soldiers, getting them to fight against what seemed impossible odds. The war dragged on for another sixteen bloody months.

The fighting continued to be horrific, the death tolls remarkable. The Union's new commander, Ulysses S. Grant, had come to the head of the conflict with a new strategy. It was simple but powerful: destroy the enemy's ability to fight and kill Confederate troops at all costs. Unlike previous Union generals who refused to engage the enemy, or sought to win strategic victories that controlled territory, Grant went after armies. His conclusion was that if Union soldiers were to die anyway — and they would, through any number of diseases and ailments — then why not trade their lives for military success? This was Grant's simple, effective, and very bloody plan. He would chase Lee down, run his army into the ground, destroy the South's ability to resupply or reinforce its troops, and in doing so put a noose around the Confederacy's neck. Grant also attempted to utilize Union forces strategically, making sure that the various Northern armies positioned around the nation worked in concert, so that Lee could no longer shift his men around to confront military hotspots. All the theaters of war were now engaged.

For the modern reader, it is easy to see Grant's bold initiatives as the beginning of the end. We know the war's outcome. Yet for much of 1864, the North remained worried about the prospect of a Southern victory. Home front morale was at an all-time low as casualty figures battered the war-weary nation. The conflict had already gone on far longer than anyone could have imagined. No one escaped its effects. Even those far from the fields of battle were confronted by death on a daily basis and exhausted by the conflict. The need for supplies from the home front never abated. In the midst of this gloom, politics reared its ugly head, as it had so many times before. Fortunately for Connecticut, the 1863 gubernatorial election was as close as the Copperheads ever came to controlling the state. They never posed another serious threat to Governor Buckingham. Yet 1864 offered a far more dire situation: a presidential election that pitted Abraham Lincoln against General George McClellan. Even Lincoln believed that he could not carry the nation, and if he lost the presidency, the possibility of an undivided future for the Union would be lost, too.

Democrats predicted four more years of unrelenting bloodshed should Lincoln win, and they focused specifically on his abolitionist policies as the source of continued Northern suffering. Seizing rumors of peace talks, Democratic editors in Connecticut and around the nation insisted that the war could be over if Lincoln dropped his insistence that slavery come to an end. The fact that he refused, they argued, revealed that the war was, as they had always insisted, an abolitionist revolution—one that would ultimately, as it had already begun to do, place "niggers" on an equal footing with whites. Such arguments were both sincere denunciations of Lincoln's war policies and calculated political attacks to tap into Northern racism.

For Republicans, the issues of race, slavery, and the meaning of the war continued to shift. The principal goal was still preservation of the Union. Emancipation had been advocated on the basis of achieving that singular mission, and thus many had attempted to make a clear distinction between emancipation and abolition. Yet in the immediate aftermath of the Emancipation Proclamation, some Republicans lauded the edict as the promise of a freedom they had always sought. Such sentiments stood in stark contrast to their prewar views. This trend continued in the last months of the war, and it remains exceedingly difficult to determine the degree to which some in the North had truly come around to an enlightened acceptance of slavery's evil, or if the years of bloodshed and suffering had hardened their attitudes toward the South and made eradicating slavery more a punishment than a moral goal. No doubt both views existed. Republican newspapers did begin in 1864 to admit that their views regarding slavery had changed during the course of the war. Whatever the impetus, many had come to embrace the war as a revolution to blast slavery from the continent.

For some Connecticut troops, the fighting began early in 1864. Ordered to Florida in February with the plan of cutting that state off from the Confederacy, the 7th CVI under the command of Colonel Joseph Hawley engaged the enemy at Olustee. Although initially successful in driving the rebels back, the battle ended as so many others had, in a stalemate that left the two forces in close proximity to one another but with neither desiring a heavy engagement. The initial part of the battle had, however, shown the effectiveness of rapid-fire, breech-loading rifles. Hawley had gone North and purchased on his own credit 400 Spencer seven-shot rifles. He wrote that his men "moved forward rapidly, the discharges of their seven shooters making a continuous roll like the musketry of a whole brigade."[1]

If this one bright spot highlighted the effectiveness of Northern arms innovation, the overall battle revealed that the Confederacy retained enough strength in the deep South to immobilize and endanger Union forces. Even farther north, the Confederacy could on occasion flex its muscle. To some extent, the Union had been complacent since its initial success in capturing strategic areas. Winfield Scott's Anaconda Plan had resulted in some early successes in controlling important ports in North Carolina and interrupting Confederate supply lines, but by 1864 Union forces stationed at New Berne, Washington, and Plymouth in that state had ceased offensive operations and were satisfied to simply occupy territory with units thinly spread out over the area. This made them sitting ducks for a Rebel attack. When Robert E. Lee finally released some of his troops for operations further south, they joined Confederate General Robert Hoke, who also had the advantage of possessing a new ironclad steamer, the *Albemarle*. On April 17, Hoke advanced with 10,000 men on Plymouth, where 1,600 Union defenders were stationed, 400 of them from the 16th Connecticut. It was hardly a contest, though the 16th put up a good fight for the next three days. On April 20, they surrendered, and if it had not been for what occurred next, it is likely that history would not have paid much attention to this rather minor engagement.[2]

There are two stories. First, realizing their impending capture, members of the 16th opted to hide their regimental flag by tearing it into pieces and distributing it among the men rather than have it fall into enemy hands. They carried these pieces throughout the remainder of the war and many years later reassembled what was left of the flag. It continues to stand in the Hall of Flags at the Connecticut State Capitol — a testament to honor and sacrifice.[3] And sacrifice is exactly what the men of the 16th did. The second story is their incarceration at the notorious Andersonville Prison. William Croffut and John M. Morris wrote in 1869 that "of the four hundred enlisted men, less than two hundred ever escaped to tell the story of the starvation and nameless tortures in the loathsome hell of Andersonville." Sergeant Robert H. Kellogg of Wethersfield survived the ordeal and published an account of it after the war. "As we entered the place," he wrote, "a spectacle met our eyes that almost froze our blood with horror, and made our hearts fail within us. Before us were forms that had once been active and erect; — *stalwart men*, now nothing but mere walking skeletons, covered with filth and vermin." Many charged that the poor treatment of Union soldiers was deliberate, and this has remained a point of historical contention.[4]

The early Confederate military successes were not the only difficulties for the Union in 1864. Internal problems posed an even greater danger. Most pressing was the end of three-year enlistments for many of the regiments. The government tried to induce reenlistments through new bounties, a special chevron (insignia) placed on the soldier's sleeve, and the promise of a thirty-day furlough. Yet only a little over half of the Union troops, about 136,000, signed on for another three years of service. Some 3,347 Connecticut veterans reenlisted, and the 8th, 11th, 12th, and 13th CVI regiments enjoyed a brief visit home at the beginning of the year. To make up for the loss of soldiers, the army turned to men raised during the 1863 draft, as well as substitutes who had taken the hefty bounties promised for service. Connecticut provided 3,849 substitutes in 1864.[5]

Like substitutes from elsewhere in the North, these men were a deplorable lot, universally detested by veterans. The *Hartford Courant* reported on January 30 that of 127 "volunteers" sent to the front from a camp in New Haven, 60 had escaped by crawling through railroad car windows. Samuel Fiske referred to such replacements as "deserters or *dead-beats*, hangers-on at hospitals," and complained of "sending out to us as substitutes the lowest and vilest classes of your population." Fred Lucas agreed: "They are ugly desperate fellows, old sailors, state prison birds, and participators in the late New York riots." It was difficult to imagine how the Union was to battle Lee's hardened troops with men who, as Fiske put it, "come out with no idea of fighting."[6] Nor was the South oblivious to these circumstances, realizing that simply maintaining a stalemate with even minor military successes might allow the Confederacy to hang on long enough for those in the North to grow despondent and give up the war through the ballot box.

The first political test came with Governor Buckingham's reelection

Connecticut in the American Civil War

*A report on the 1864 gubernatorial election in Connecticut
in the* Hartford Daily Courant, *April 5, 1864.*

bid in April 1864. The situation wasn't nearly as desperate as had been the case a year earlier, when Thomas Seymour posed a decided threat to the Republicans. The military successes of 1863 had blunted Copperhead strength, and Democrats chose what they hoped would be a more palatable, pro-war candidate, Origen S. Seymour of Litchfield. The strategy had little effect. Not only did O. S. Seymour lose by 5,658 votes,[7] but the Democrats also lost the New Haven city elections for the first time in eight years, and, more significantly, William H. Eaton of Hartford, an outspoken Peace Democrat, lost his House seat in the Assembly. The results represented a solid victory for the Republicans, and they claimed it as such. "Throw high the cap of liberty! Connecticut has spoken in thunder tones to the nation and the world," announced the *Courant;* "Copperheadism in Connecticut has received its death wound." The South will hear us, insisted the paper. "Realizing the hopelessness of wearying the North into desistance, they will see before them the alternative of speedy submission or annihilation." The *Hartford Evening Press* announced that the Democrats were "finally nailed up and sent home in a box. . . . Union triumphant — no compromise with treason."[8]

Republicans lost little time in relaying the results to Washington. Governor Buckingham wrote President Lincoln immediately: "I beg leave to assure you that the election in this state yesterday may be regarded as a new pledge of the people to sustain your Administration in efforts to preserve national integrity. In the opinion of many our election in 1860 was the pivot on which events turned which led to the election of your Excellency to the Presidency and now if it shall lead to like results none will feel worse than the copperhead sympathisers [sic] with traitors in Conn[ecticut] and none rejoice more or give you a more cordial support than our loyal & patriotic citizens who have rolled up such a majority in favor of overwhelming the armies of the rebellion."[9]

Democrats blamed the losses on furloughed Republican soldiers, Republican treachery, and Democrats who stayed home from the polls. It was this last group that appeared most troubling. "It seems there are some voters who did not know the day on which it [the election] was to be held," lamented the *Hartford Times*; "Why should they slumber now, when the death knell of the Republic is uninterruptedly ringing, it is surprising to us. But they have slumbered this spring. Thousands who do not approve of this war, have not voted." The paper accepted that "the Abolitionists have swept the board by a majority," but reasoned "the people looked upon an active canvass this Spring as useless, reserving their strength for the Presidential contest. In that struggle the great question of the preservation of the UNION will be directly presented, and then the people will rouse and act."[10]

Everyone recognized the dire importance of the coming presidential election. The South sought to hold on and wear down the North. "If we can break up the enemy's arrangements early, and throw him back," wrote Confederate General James Longstreet, "he will not be able to recover his position or his morale until the Presidential election is over, and then we will have a new President to treat with."[11] Northern Democrats craved an election victory that would both reveal the "true" sentiment of those at home and allow an immediate cessation of hostilities, so that negotiations for peace could begin. Republicans hoped that Lincoln's reelection might finally snuff out the fires of rebellion. All of these aspirations hinged on one thing: military success.

———•———

In early 1863, after the dismal military performances of the preceding months, Fiske recognized what he believed was the cause of failed Union efforts. Likening the Confederacy to a mule that needed to be moved, he asked: "Isn't the trouble with our Union team something like this, — that one hitches on to this leg, and another to that one, and another to the slippery tail or ear, and thus act ineffectually or against each other, instead of tackling right around the neck of the beast with one long pull, strong pull, and pull all together?" By 1864, with Grant appointed to the position of general in chief, and Lincoln looking to him for a concerted military effort, the president had come to a slightly different analogy than Fiske: "As we say out West, if a man can't skin he must hold a leg while somebody else does."[12]

Connecticut in the American Civil War

The men's points were the same: victory required a combined strategy that placed the weight of Northern armies squarely on the Confederacy. Grant understood this. Pressure was his mission. His objective for the spring of 1864 was a multifront movement. Thus he ordered Benjamin Butler's Army of the James, Franz Sigel's forces in West Virginia, and Nathaniel Banks's Army of the Gulf to launch simultaneous attacks in their regions, while the Army of the Potomac went after Lee. To respond to the Union's coordinated attacks, Confederate forces would be spread thin and unable to gain reinforcements. If everything had gone as planned, the war might have ended quickly. It didn't. The generals moved with typical Union sloth, and Confederate forces managed once again to box them in or stall their efforts.

Most Connecticut troops served in Butler's forces and the Army of the Potomac. The 8th, 11th, and 21st CVI had been stationed with Butler's army, and the 6th, 7th, and 10th joined them in preparation for a spring push toward Richmond. On May 9–10, the 6th and 7th engaged the enemy at Chester Station, Virginia. Days later, all of Butler's Connecticut regiments fought at Drewry's Bluff, where they and other Union troops were pushed back by Confederate forces under the command of General P. T. Beauregard. The historian of the 21st put it simply: "Whatever the intentions of our commander, they were forestalled by his more nimble adversary. Beauregard commenced the battle that both sides were intending to inaugurate."[13] During the engagement, the 21st suffered sixteen men killed, seventy-one wounded, and a number captured. The 7th fared little better, with seventeen killed and thirty wounded. Major Oliver Sanford of Meriden wrote of a "murderous fire" and "the enemy pouring volley after volley into us."[14] The other regiments had similar casualties, though the 11th was particularly hard hit, with 9 killed, 46 wounded, and 135 captured. At home, newspaper articles initially delivered encouraging news, but after official word of defeat, the *Courant* concluded: "The proof of his [Butler's] incompetency has cost the country dearly."[15]

Generals Sigel and Banks suffered similar fates. The major push then had to come from the Army of the Potomac, which had begun to move at the same time as Butler, in early May. Grant never took his eye off the main prize, the Army of Virginia. "Lee's army will be your objective point," Grant told George Meade, the nominal commander of the Army of the Potomac; "wherever Lee goes, there will you go also."[16] Union forces therefore headed south on May 4, crossing the Rapidan River in the hopes of confronting Lee. With the Union having 115,000 men to the Confederacy's 64,000, Lee fully understood what such a battle would mean. He therefore let

Grant cross unopposed into Virginia and planned a counterattack when the Northern army entered the Wilderness, a dense, pine and oak forest where superiority in numbers would mean little and artillery even less.

The only Connecticut regiment to join the Army of the Potomac on its drive south was the famed 14th, which had suffered so grievously at Antietam, witnessed the horrors of Fredericksburg, and gained laurels at Gettysburg. As the men began the trek into Virginia, Samuel Fiske wrote of his belief that these were to be the "great and terrible battles that are to decide this opening campaign, and probably bring the war to an end." He hoped that "every opportunity may be taken to inspire the patriotism and enthusiasm of our troops, and keep before their minds the great principles which first sent them forth from their peaceful homes to fight for endangered liberty and republican government, for God, and freedom throughout the world."[17]

These were some of the last words that Fiske wrote. The intrepid minister from Madison was shot through the collarbone and right lung on May 6 during the opening battles of the Wilderness campaign and died on May 22, in a Fredericksburg hospital. Unlike so many soldiers killed on the field, Fiske was joined by his wife and family before succumbing to his wounds. Delivering a eulogy, W. S. Tyler, a professor at Amherst College, remembered that Fiske had just been home on furlough and that "he returned to the field of conflict with a sadness that was unusual, perhaps with a distinct presentiment of what was before him." "When he fell," insisted Tyler, "the whole country, and especially New England felt the blow."[18]

Fiske was just one of the many who died in the Wilderness campaign. On May 12, the *Hartford Courant* began the war news with the headline, "THE MOST DESPERATE OF ALL THE BATTLES." It overstated the case, but not by much. Virginia was once again a killing ground. Between May 5 and 12, the Union Army lost 30,000 men and Lee 18,000, along with a third of his corps commanders. The *Courant* noted of Grant's army that "roads, fields and woods are literally swarming with these suffering heroes." Eleven men from the 14th were killed and sixty-two wounded.[19]

Grant pushed on. Previous Union commanders would have retreated or dug in, but he called for additional troops and continued to move. He confronted Lee at Spotsylvania, then moved even further south, sparring along the way, always attempting to draw Lee into battle. On June 1, the two forces met at Cold Harbor. With both sides having received reinforcements, their strengths were roughly what they had been at the Wilderness, Grant with 109,000 men and Lee with 59,000.

"Ruins at Hampton, Virginia showing chimneys, and man standing,"
photographer unknown. Union troops saw ruin and destruction as they
marched through Virginia. Library of Congress, LC-USZ62-103066

Additional Connecticut regiments made up part of these numbers.
Along with the 8th, 11th, 14th, and 21st, the Army of the Potomac now included the 2nd Heavy Artillery, which was pulled from its duty of defend-
ing Washington. The men had never seen combat, and young Fred Lucas
wrote home on May 13 that "all the old soldiers of the regiment are eager
to go to the front and this has become a common subject for grumbling
and complaint." They received orders only days later, and Lucas proudly
announced: "Grant needs us doubtless and we are ready & eager to aid
him. Boys are in high spirits and when next you hear from us Glory may
be mixed with the name of the 2nd Conn."[20]

As they marched through Virginia on their way to join the Army of
the Potomac, Lucas finally had the opportunity to witness what so many
who had marched before him had seen: "This is truly a desolate country.
War has stripped every vistage [sic] of civilization from the land, even the
trees and bushes in the vicinity of the route we have travelled." He noted
that "trains of wounded men are continually coming in from the front and
those who die are buried on the way." Nevertheless, his spirits remained
high: "I am in splendid trim and ready for what ever may come. I like this
chance which I think is now given us of taking part in field service."[21]

Then came Cold Harbor. It was an awful affair. Lee's men were protected by a series of zigzag trenches, many fronted by abatis (a defensive barrier of tree trunks with sharpened points), that led to formidable artillery fortifications along a seven-mile front. For twelve days, beginning on June 1, the two armies tried to annihilate one another, often from close range. Members of the 14th remembered that "the firing became intolerable, the men fell behind the dead bodies of Confederate soldiers, using tin plates and pans to throw earth to cover these dead bodies to serve as protection."[22] The 8th was held in reserve, suffering limited casualties, while the 11th and 21st CVI and the 2nd Heavy Artillery engaged in a series of bayonet assaults on enemy lines. Colonel Griffin Stedman of the 11th wrote in his report that as his men moved forward, "I was the first to enter the open field and see the enemy's lines, a curve. I bade farewell to all I loved. It seemed impossible to survive that fire; but I was spared, while the officers of my staff who followed me closely, were struck down." His regiment suffered eighteen killed, two missing, and eighty-six wounded.[23]

It was the eager 2nd that took the worst mauling, leaving some 322 men on the battlefield, 129 of them dead or close to death. Croffut and Morris wrote that as the men charged forward, "the companies in front became disorganized and broken by the horrible fire which they could neither resist not endure; and the shattered fragments crept back to cover. . . . Only half of them returned, however; for they left nearly two hundred bleeding on the ground."[24] Perhaps the greatest blow was the death of their popular colonel, Elisha Kellogg, who was found on the front of one of the rebel breastworks, shot twice through the head.[25]

Lucas wrote home on June 2, in the midst of the Cold Harbor campaign: "We have now tasted of the Bloody battlefield & done our duty nobly." He had quickly learned a common lesson: "The romance of war is never realized: its reality is far a different thing. The description of brave & impetuous charges, valiant deeds of heroism & personal exhibitions of daring & courage look well on paper and please the public taste but the real battlefield with it's [sic] woe & carnage & bloodshed, pain & misery, groans & cries, curses & prayers of the wounded & dying is indeed a scene which my pen cannot describe." He continued: "Today, as we brought in our dead & wounded and found who they were I witnessed many a sad meeting. Brothers have found brothers among the dead, fathers their sons & sons their fathers & old and familiar friends the same trial."[26] War, Lucas now understood, was nothing to be sought after.

Cold Harbor was a disaster for the Union. In just under two weeks of fighting, the Army of the Potomac had suffered 12,000 casualties, while

Connecticut in the American Civil War

"Cold Harbor, Va. African Americans collecting bones of soldiers killed in the battle," photograph by John Reekie, April 1865. The site was in the main eastern theater of the war during Grant's Wilderness Campaign, May–June 1864. Library of Congress, LC-B8171-7926

Lee had lost between 2,500 and 4,500 men. The worst day for the North was June 3, when Grant ordered a series of full charges on Confederate lines. After only a few hours, 7,000 Union soldiers had fallen to the Confederate's 1,500. Grant remarked later in the day: "I regret this assault more than any one I have ever ordered."[27] Further attacks were useless, and Grant redirected his army to Petersburg in the hope of keeping up the pressure on Lee and taking the city, an important source of supply for the Confederate capital, Richmond.

When Union soldiers arrived in Petersburg, however, their commanders were unable to move them against the city's heavily fortified trenches. The men had learned the effects of concentrated fire and were not eager to try it again. As the historian James McPherson explains: "Cold Harbor syndrome inhibited Union soldiers from pressing home their assaults." In the course of the previous seven weeks, the Army of the Potomac had confronted the enemy like never before, engaging in a series of very bloody battles. McPherson notes that "some 65,000 northern boys were killed, wounded, or missing since May 4. This figure amounted to three-fifths of the total number of combat casualties suffered by the Army of the Potomac during the *previous three years*. No army could take such punishment and retain its fighting edge."[28]

Petersburg therefore became a siege. For the next ten months, Union forces launched attack after attack, dug elaborate trench lines that extended for miles, and attempted novel strategies such as at the battle of the crater, in which Union forces dug a 500-foot shaft beneath Confederate lines and detonated 8,000 pounds of gun powder in it. Connecticut regiments at Petersburg included the 6th, 7th, 11th, and the 21st, as well as the 29th and 30th black regiments, the latter of which had been transferred to the 31st Regiment U.S. Colored Infantry. After being mustered in on March 8, the 29th was ultimately transported to Beaufort, South Carolina, where its men performed guard and picket duty for four months. In August, they were brought to the siege lines of Virginia. The 30th did guard duty in Virginia during the first half of June. Its men then entered the Petersburg trenches and were part of the crater attack on July 30, where they suffered eighty-two casualties in a systematic, racial slaughter by rebel forces. These regiments, along with the rest of the Army of the Potomac, maneuvered before the city in a war of attrition, not achieving success until April 1865, when Petersburg finally surrendered.[29]

The long stalemate frustrated Northerners back home, who had hoped for immediate success from Grant. The bloodletting of the Wilderness and Cold Harbor campaigns shocked everyone, leading some to call Grant a butcher. These frustrations were compounded by General William Tecumseh Sherman's inability to capture Atlanta. Leading a force that consisted of some 93,000 men, including the 5th and 20th Connecticut regiments, Sherman began his operations in May, but stiff resistance kept him from sealing the city's fate. He crept steadily forward, but in mid-July, Atlanta seemed forever out of reach. To make matters worse, from July 6 to 11, Confederate General Jubal Early launched a raid across the Potomac River into Maryland and came within five miles of Washington, D.C. The attack had no real strategic importance other than an attempt to redirect Union efforts and take some of the pressure off Lee at Petersburg. Still, Early managed to cut telegraph wires, burn railroads and private property, and cause general alarm. The *Courant* reported that in Baltimore, "the Greatest excitement prevails here, citizens arming and going out to fight rebel cavalry." The raid certainly didn't help Northern views of the war. McPherson wrote: "The months of July and August 1864 brought a greater crisis of northern morale than the same months in 1862."[30]

The heavy battlefield losses were reflected in the newspapers' attitudes as information about the spring campaigns poured in. Soldiers' Aid Societies once again implored those at home for supplies. The *Courant* reported on May 17 that "Old Linen is in the most *pressing* demand," and announced again a week later: "We are requested to state that our wounded soldiers are suffering for the want of old linen and cotton to dress their wounds." These requests were juxtaposed with advertisements for "Fine Mourning Dress Goods" and "Mourning Millinery." Reports of sick and wounded soldiers in the hundreds appeared, many listing specifics regarding Connecticut regiments and who was killed or injured. Some 250 wounded men arrived at New Haven's Knight Army Hospital in mid-May, and more continued to arrive through June.[31]

As much as the Union army had been battered by its sustained efforts in Virginia, so too were those who cared for the fallen men. After three years of fighting, everyone was worn out. The *Courant* announced at the end of June: "Members of different aid societies are fast giving out from sheer exhaustion and fevers. Many have been forced to give up their labors and return home." A letter from the Hartford Sanitary Association reflected the effects of a fatigued public: "We are in trembling fear lest our supplies of all kinds may give out this summer. Our boxes and packages received are so much smaller than heretofore, and this terrible fighting creates such a demand from the hospitals, that we beg the Aid Societies to work with all their might, and to economize with all their strength." The writer continued: "We are beginning to feel the war at the North, and must actually deny ourselves our habitual comforts, to supply the wants of our brave soldiers. Oh! Such suffering as I hear of through my son, who is a surgeon at Fortress Monroe." Another letter from a woman at Hammond Hospital in Maryland lamented: "Men beg me almost with tears in their eyes for clothing which will be free from vermin. . . . Men going to the front or to the North are almost invariably destitute of shirts, drawers, socks and shoes." Sidney Stanley, a Connecticut diarist wrote: "The war drags hard and heavily; nobody seems to have any feeling of interest for the armies and they are seldom spoken of."[32]

So great was the level of Northern apathy that the *Courant* published an editorial titled "The Great Duty of the Hour," in which the author starkly contrasted what those in the field faced with the difficulties of those at home, and therefore the ensuing obligation owed to soldiers: "Do we, who are citizens of this favored town [Hartford], remote from the field of strife — spared the daily spectacle witnessed in other cities of the maimed, mutilated and suffering victims of this war which is being waged for the unity of *our* country, and for the future well-being of *our* Children — do we fully accept, and faithfully discharge the duties which this solemn crisis imposes upon *us*?" He continued: "Do we follow that long train of ambulances, freighted with suffering humanity, shrieking, groaning, often dying on that dreadful journey, or do we go with them to the hospitals, now filled to over-flowing, with those who have survived these tortures to languish on beds of pain? . . . Every man, every woman, every child, must have their portion of these burdens, and yet, so far as this city of ours is concerned, no extraordinary effort has been made to meet this extraordinary demand." The author closed his long, chastising message by questioning whether good Christian men and women could "shut their eyes and turn their backs upon this, the most imperative duty of the hour?"[33]

If such an editorial seemed particularly hard on those at home, it did not compare to a letter sent by Fred Lucas to his mother. After she had apparently complained of the difficulties in Connecticut, the usually affable Lucas lashed out: "Do you wonder the people are almost discouraged & wish the war to end? You at home think you suffer the calamities of war & growl at taxes, drafts, etc but have you lived for three years where the armies have marched & fought, burned your fences & building, killed your stock, & robbed you of all your household supplies & worst of all — conscripted your husband & sons & taken them forcibly from you? Don't complain then, of your losses or the heavy burdens you have to bear in consequence of this rebellion. Connecticut knows nothing compared to the states of Maryland & Virginia, has suffered nothing at all."[34]

Even the state's arms industry was feeling the exhaustion of war, though for Connecticut's manufacturers this was the result of producing too much. By the end of 1863, the war machine was in full operation, with many newcomers and massive production. The established manufacturers had effectively glutted the market, and most of the new companies disappeared quickly. The stalwarts, Colt and Henry, survived by virtue of their innovative designs and excellent marketing, and the need for high-quality weapons on the western frontier. Nor was the gun industry the only one affected by overproduction. Other Connecticut industries — including gunpowder makers in Canton and East Hartford; the Ames iron foundry, which produced cannons in Litchfield; and ship engine builders in Mystic — suffered, as did the communities that they supported.[35]

Northern depression over the continuing war was exacerbated by midsummer rumors of peace and Democratic manipulation of those reports. The story was that Confederate agents were in Niagara Falls, Canada, bringing overtures from Jefferson Davis. Even Horace Greeley, the estimable editor of the *New York Tribune*, believed the news and implored Lincoln to end the war. The president responded to Greeley in writing, telling him to bring to Washington "any person anywhere professing to have any proposition of Jefferson Davis in writing, for peace, embracing the restoration of the Union and abandonment of slavery." Lincoln knew the Confederacy would never propose these terms, but he also understood the Northern desire for peace and felt compelled on July 18 to send his private secretary, John Hay, along with Greeley to meet with Confederate agents. Lincoln offered the same terms, and the meeting came to nothing. The difference between the two positions was intractable: Lincoln wanted the restoration of the Union and the abolishment of slavery; Davis wanted Southern independence. There was nothing to negotiate. The *Courant* tried to limit the effects of the peace rumors by ridiculing the Confederate agents as "mere adventurers, as destitute of credentials and authority as of character," and Greeley himself stated after the meeting that "the telegraphic stories concerning peace conferences at Niagara Falls, have a slender foundation in fact, but most of the details are very wide of the truth."[36]

Democrats made all they could of the news. The *Hartford Times* announced: "For the first time since this reign of horrors began, *there is a gleam of light* through the black storm clouds which have rested like a funeral pall upon our afflicted country. The South proposes to RESTORE THE OLD UNION!" Yet, continued the paper, "it seems that the proposition of the South is not satisfactory to Abraham Lincoln. This man, whom an inscrutable Fate inflicted upon our unhappy land as its chief magistrate ... demands as a *condition* precedent to its [the Union's] restoration, that the South shall abolish negro slavery! This arrogant usurpation of dictatorial power, and most wickedly unpatriotic use of it, will, if persisted in, be duly attended to by the American people. Abraham Lincoln must not be permitted to stand in the way of a restoration of the Union."[37]

Lincoln's insistence on emancipation allowed Democrats to refocus on what they had asserted from the outset: Lincoln was an abolitionist, and the war had been started to free slaves and make them the equals of whites. The issue of race had always bubbled beneath the surface of the war news.

Throughout the spring and summer, the *Times* littered its columns with stories of black inferiority, abolitionist desires for miscegenation, and the protection from battle, or failure in battle, of black troops.

For instance, on June 6, in an article titled the "Negro's Place in Nature," the paper reported on an English naturalist, Dr. Hunt, who "takes the position that the negro race is intended by Nature to a position of subordination," observing that Hunt "overthrows the whole fabric of modern Abolition philanthropy." The *Times* followed with articles such as "The Negro Everything — White Man Nothing," in which it declared in regard to black troops: "It is about time the 'white trash' should leave the army, and let the gallant Africans win the victory, unencumbered."[38] Another story announced that "the miscegenation journals have made fools of themselves the past year, in their extravagantly overwrought puffs of the Negro troops."[39]

Even more harshly, the *Times* ridiculed the General Assembly's creation of a black regiment, disdainfully commenting on the "philanthropic principle laid down a year ago in the Connecticut legislature . . . that a nigger is just as good as anybody to stop a rebel bullet." The *Times* also blasted the *Courant* for racial hypocrisy, charging that "it used to be the opinion of the *Hartford Courant*, not long after the election of Abraham Lincoln, that 'this government is the government of white men.' But that paper has changed its opinion — (an exploit which experience and practice have rendered easy and familiar) — and it no longer believes the government was made for white men."[40]

Democrats had always been overt in their racism, but the news of peace negotiations unleashed a new tide of vulgarity. They also focused even more heavily on the president's devotion to abolition and repeated their well-worn argument that he had no authority to free slaves. The *Times* insisted that Lincoln had "declared in his official papers, since he became President of the United States, that an African slave is as much property as a horse." In a subsequent article, it argued that "[he has] no more business to demand the abolition of slavery than he has to demand the burning of every dwelling house at the North and South. The Constitution of the United States leaves the slavery question in the hands of the States."[41] Some of this was standard states' rights boilerplate language, but the president's power to emancipate, together with his authority to lay waste to homes, was a trickier matter and actually fell right into Republican hands. Lincoln insisted that emancipation was a war measure, and thus not strictly within the bounds of the Constitution. The same was true of destroying private property, something that was quickly to become a

"I'm not to blame for being white, sir!" probably drawn by Dominique C. Frabronius, printed by G. W. Cottrell, Boston, 1862. The drawing attacks Massachusetts Senator Charles Sumner, the prominent opponent of slavery, by showing him giving a few coins to a black child while ignoring a needy white child. Library of Congress, LC-USZ62-12771

Union war aim. The larger question of permanent emancipation after the war required, Lincoln believed, an amendment to the Constitution. Thus the Thirteenth Amendment was proposed early in 1864 and passed the Senate, but it failed to win a majority of votes in the House. Remarkably, neither the Republican nor the Democratic newspapers in Connecticut made a great deal of the proposal in 1864.

The stalled military efforts throughout the nation, combined with rumors of peace and the Democratic attacks on Lincoln's abolitionism, hampered Republicans' chances of success in the November elections. In late August, Henry J. Raymond, chairman of the party's national committee, wrote the president: "I feel compelled to drop you a line concerning the political condition of the Country as it strikes me." Raymond reported that "the tide is strongly against us," explaining that "two special causes are assigned for this great reaction in public sentiment, — the want of military successes, and the impression in some minds, the fear and suspicion in others, that we are not to have peace *in any event* under this Administration until Slavery is abandoned."[42]

Lincoln too believed that he would lose the presidential election. Still, he refused to back down on emancipation, though he denied that his "sole purpose was abolition." Instead, the president reasserted the rationale of military necessity, insisting that "no human power can subdue this rebellion without using the Emancipation lever as I have done."[43] He also believed that it would be immoral to abandon the promise of freedom given to blacks who had joined the war effort. These issues of freedom and race had plagued Republicans since before the war began. There were disagreements about them within the party, and many Republicans had altered their views with consistent inconsistency. They had initially responded to Democratic charges of abolitionism with outrage, yet by 1863, with the Emancipation Proclamation and the significant military victories of that summer, Republicans more openly embraced the end of slavery as a goal beyond its sheer militarily necessity.

The continuing shift in Republican thought reflected both the historical amnesia inaugurated by the Emancipation Proclamation and a seemingly more reflective acknowledgement that the party's outlook had changed. The *Courant* continued to reflect these shifts, declaring in January 1864: "A few arrogant Southerners provoked the present war for the purpose of perpetuating the enslavement of the African race. Disregarding the moral sentiments of all civilized communities, they avowed the determination to build up an empire founded on slavery as its corner-stone."[44] The paper did not bother to mention that its own "moral sentiments" had been particularly antiblack in the years before the war and even at the beginning of the conflict.

Yet only a month later, in February, the *Courant* seemed more thoughtful, admitting that "at first the North generally desired to restore federal supremacy over the seceded states, without destroying the tenure which bound four millions of blacks to perpetual servitude." As the rebellion continued, however, "it was not long before the Northern mind became convinced of the absolute necessity of uprooting slavery. Inexorable events were the arguments that revolutionized their opinions. It was impossible for honest and thoughtful men to resist the truth, however reluctant to acknowledge past errors by the adoption of new sentiments." The article did not elaborate on the "inexorable events," but in another piece, the paper declared: "It is interesting to watch the steady growth of the anti-slavery sentiment at the North." At the start of the conflict, continued the *Courant*, "the conservative element predominated in numbers, and contended that the war should be so conducted as to destroy the rebellion without damaging slavery. The obstinacy of the enemy, however, gradually dislodged patriotic men from the position. All have come to see that slavery was the cause of the rebellion, and the only way to prevent a repetition of similar conflicts hereafter, is to crush out the system now that the heel of justice is upon it. The institution will not be permitted to survive the war."[45]

These sentiments were further supported at the Connecticut Republican Convention that renominated Governor Buckingham on February 17, 1864. John Rice of Farmington spoke at length about the "issues" connected to the war. Foremost was that "men with wicked hearts have raised their paricidal [sic] hands to overthrow the best government ever vouchsafed to man," yet "another of the issues which is presented, is the question whether the infamous system which led its advocates to rebel, shall not be destroyed. We can never be at peace so long as slavery is allowed to have a controlling power in the affairs of the nation. Shall it not be torn up, root and branch?" In advocating such a measure, Rice specifically addressed the growth of antislavery sentiment, insisting, "We have advanced rapidly upon this question. First, as a military necessity, it has become the subject of deep thought, until we have emancipation inscribed upon our banner." In another version of the speech, he was reported to have said: "We have made a rapid advance. — This position a short time since would have been deemed *radical*. Now it is the most truly *conservative*."[46]

Once victorious in the gubernatorial election, Buckingham, who had always been in favor of abolition, stated firmly: "The disaffection which has led to this terrible civil war, has, in the opinion of many, been caused directly by slavery, and of others, by an unjustifiable agitation of questions relating thereunto, still, nearly all agree that it has been either the direct or proximate cause of the rebellion." He insisted that "the events of the past urge us to adopt some measure which shall terminate in favor of freedom, that controversy which must ever exist so long as a part of the nation remains free and a part enslaved." That measure, declared the governor, was a constitutional amendment. A deeply religious man, Buckingham ended his address in the certainty that "under the guidance of the King of

Kings, this revolution will carry the Nation onward in the path of prosperity, intelligence, and influence, and upward, to a higher level of freedom, civilization, and Christianity, where every citizen, whether high or low, rich or poor, learned or ignorant, of whatever tribe, or race, or nation, shall be protected in all the inalienable rights which God has given him, under our National emblem of Liberty, Union, and Power."[47]

The governor's insistence that the war was now a "revolution" was exactly what Democrats had charged from the outset, arguing long and loud for the protection of slavery under the guise of "the Constitution as it is." Still, as forthright as some Republicans were in their condemnation of slavery and embrace of abolition, it is impossible to paint the entire party with such a broad stroke. As always, much depended on politics. Consider Raymond's August letter to Lincoln discussing the dire situation of the Republican Party and asking if it would be wise to appoint a commission to offer peace to the Confederacy *"on the sole condition of acknowledging the supremacy of the Constitution,* — all other questions to be settled in convention of the people of all the States?"[48] Lincoln briefly considered creating such a commission, but ultimately declined. Union and emancipation had indeed become intertwined; at least if Lincoln won reelection.

Only a week after Raymond sent his earnest letter, news arrived of Sherman's victory at Atlanta, and the North's depression seemed to lift. The *Hartford Evening Press* announced jubilantly: "Gen. Sherman has closed one of the most remarkable and triumphant campaigns in the history of the world by a glorious, crowning success. Atlanta is ours! The prize is grasped[,] the object of the arduous fighting of the whole spring and summer is attained." The *Courant* concurred: "This is the heaviest blow that could befall the rebels. The district of which Atlanta is the center, may be called the very heart of the confederacy." The 5th Connecticut was given the honor of being the first regiment to march through the city, having been heavily engaged in the fighting that led to victory.[49] The announcement of Sherman's success resulted in spontaneous celebrations throughout Connecticut and the rest of the North. In Waterbury, a hundred-gun salute was fired, bands played, and people rallied around bonfires. Similar scenes occurred in Hartford and New Haven.[50]

Equally heartening was General Philip Sheridan's actions in the Shenandoah Valley. Tired of the Confederates' ability to use the area as a conduit to Washington, D.C., and embarrassed by Jubal Early's midsummer jaunt into Maryland, Grant ordered Sheridan to take his cavalry, along with ad-

Connecticut in the American Civil War

ditional troops transferred for the campaign, and "put himself south of the enemy, and follow him to the death."[51] Sheridan did just that. From August to October, he hunted Early, throwing him south in a series of successive campaigns. Joining Sheridan in this chase was the Connecticut 2nd Heavy Artillery, the 9th Irish regiment, and the 12th and 13th CVI. They engaged Early at such places as Opequon (also known as the third battle of Winchester), Fisher's Hill, and Cedar Creek. The first two battles, on September 19 and 21–22, resulted in decided Confederate losses that hurled Early further down the valley. Sheridan followed these victories with a scorched-earth policy so that nothing would be left for the rebels if they should return. Captain John De Forest, who had reenlisted and enjoyed a brief furlough home in February, rejoined the 12th and marched through the valley, bearing witness to the destruction wrought by Union troops. After the infantry had rushed through, wrote De Forest, "behind came the cavalry, in a broad line from mountain to mountain, burning the mills and barns and driving the cattle and sheep." He reported that "over seventy mills and two thousand barns, crammed with flour, wheat, corn and hay, were destroyed. The inhabitants were left so stripped of food that I cannot imagine how they escaped starvation. The valley was thus desolated, partly as a punishment for the frequent bushwhacking of our trains and stragglers, but mainly to prevent Early from subsisting his army in it and marching once more to the Potomac. It was a woful [sic] sight for civilized eyes; but as a warlike measure it was very effective."[52]

The battle of Cedar Creek on October 19 was the final major Union assault in the Shenandoah, and it was initiated by an early morning surprise attack by the Confederates. Jubal Early had taken a page from Robert E. Lee's book and, rather than act on the defensive, turned his troops loose for a harrowing run directly at the Union encampment. It nearly worked. De Forest remarked that the Confederacy "was in such a desperate case that its commanders were driven to risk venturesome campaigns and deliver battles which might fairly be called forlorn hopes. . . . Their only chance of success, or escape, lay in audacity."[53] At the outset of the battle, Union troops took a beating. The 9th suffered its worst losses in any engagement of the war, with two killed, thirteen wounded, and nine captured. The 12th had 168 casualties (23 killed, 55 wounded, and 90 captured), which effectively put an end to the regiment because of its previous losses. De Forest wrote: "I never on any battlefield saw so much blood as on this of Cedar Creek. The firm limestone soil would not receive it, and there was no pitying summer grass to hide it." He also remarked that the Confederate assault had been so sudden and the ensuing Union retreat so quick that "an army of thirty thousand men had disappeared as if an earthquake had swallowed it."[54] De Forest sensed fear from the entire Union command. The 13th regiment did a bit better, losing only two killed, twenty wounded, and nine captured, though the previous battle at Opequan had given the regiment its biggest losses for a single day, with six killed, forty-one wounded, and thirty captured.[55]

Nor was the 2nd Heavy Artillery spared serious loss of life before the rebels were routed. The regiment lost 22 killed, 112 wounded, and 52 captured.[56] By now, only four months into actual combat duty, the Heavies were no longer a green, untried unit, and Lucas no longer judged his comrades' military ardor by the polish of their arms or the perfection of their dress. He wrote home in late August: "The contrast between the general appearance of our regiment today & what it was five months since cannot be described. From 1700 men it has dwindled down to about 700 present for duty & the bright, blue, clean & new clothing highly polished boots, cartridge boxes & belts & the burnished, shining muskets with glittering bayonets & bright brasses & better than all the noble, healthy, stalwart, soldierly look & bearing of all the men is materially changed. Clothing is far from clean, boots & blackening have give way to course [sic], rough army shoes, bright muskets are well covered with the marks of the field & of their exposure."[57]

Only a month later, young Lucas had other news to report. After the battle of Cedar Creek, he wrote once again to his mother. With his usual nonchalance, he noted: "I received your kind letter this afternoon. It found me in rather a hard fix for one who never knew by experience the suffering of wounded men. But you must not worry concerning me, Dear Mother. Thus far I am doing quite well, I think. I have a serious wound but my surgeon tells me it is not fatal nor will I lose my leg if it does well. It is a hole about the size of a man's finger through my thigh about 3 inches below the groin. The missile went clean through coming out behind. It struck the bone but just far enough one side of center to cause it to glance around and not shatter my leg. It is terrible sore & lame and I am tired of lying here with it but I am determined to keep up good spirits and make the best of everything." He concluded: "My turn came and I must bear the torture. Tis only the rough side of soldiering & to be expected. God grant that this bloody war may cease soon & the rebels be whipped effectually & peace restored."[58] Lucas was laid up until February, when he rejoined his regiment.

Sherman's victory at Atlanta and Sheridan's success in the Shenandoah Valley could not have been timed more perfectly. With only weeks to the November presidential election, the North was in a bad way until these victories changed public sentiment. The *Courant* effectively captured the mood: "The political horizon has changed remarkably. During the month of August despondency hung like a pall over the country." "To-day all is changed," continued the paper; "the current of dissatisfaction, and clamor, and gloom, whose treacherous waters were hurrying the nation toward the vortex of destruction, is arrested."[59] Moreover, Sherman capitalized on his success by adopting a daring strategy: cut loose from his base of supply and, with a reduced force of 62,000 men, blaze a trail to the sea. Not only would his march embolden those on the home front even further, but it would allow his army to come up behind Lee and trap him against Grant's Army of the Potomac.

Adding to all of this good news was George McClellan's letter of acceptance for the Democratic presidential nomination. On August 29, the party had met in Chicago and hammered out what became known as the Chicago Platform, an undeniable concession to the South that promised an immediate cessation of hostilities, followed by negotiations. Slavery would surely be secure. Yet in light of the fall of Atlanta, turmoil within his own party, and a belief that accepting such terms would dishonor the many fellow soldiers who had lost their lives, McClellan rejected the platform. In a September 8 letter, he accepted the nomination but agreed to end hostilities only if the South first returned to the Union.[60] It was a great blow to the Peace Democrats and further divided the party.

The Republicans did not miss the meaning of the general's momentous letter. The *Courant* declared that McClellan "has spoken fearlessly for the Union, making its full and complete restoration a condition precedent of peace. . . . He cut loose from the Chicago platform." Two days later, the paper commented: "McClellan's letter of acceptance falls like a wet blanket upon the extreme peace men." Even soldiers at the front gloried in McClellan's letter. Lucas wrote home: "How do the MacClellanites like his letter of acceptance of the nomination at Chicago & his repudiation of the platform built for him to run upon?"[61] In only a matter of weeks, the tide of the election seemed to have turned. The war momentum was re-established, the Democrats were divided, and the *Courant* observed that Democrats had little to focus on besides their continuing and monotonous denunciations of blacks and abolition. Reporting on a Middletown "Copperhead Clam-bake" and the speech of Democratic representative Chauncey Fowler of Durham, the paper announced: "The burden of his

"To Whom It May Concern," Hartford Times,
September 24, 1864. The newspaper printed side by side
two contrasting statements on slavery by Abraham Lincoln.
Courtesy of the Connecticut State Library

song was the nigger — the everlasting uncompromising subject of Democratic oratory."[62]

Although in fact the Democrats had more to lash out against than blacks and abolitionists, the *Courant's* charge was not far off the mark. Democrats had made a mission of warring against both groups, harping on the inferiority of blacks and their pending equality with whites, and the unconstitutional, hypocritical acts of the abolitionists. In an attempt to make the hypocrisy painfully apparent, the *Times* ran simple editorials that placed Lincoln's views before and during the war in stark contrast.[63]

Published only weeks before the presidential election, these broadsides were a last-ditch effort to stem the Republican wave. The core of the Democratic message was racially motivated, in the hope that the continued ridicule of blacks and abolitionists would successfully sway white voters. The *New Haven Register* insisted that Republicans "are inflexibly opposed to a restoration of the Union that does not include 'the abandonment of

Connecticut in the American Civil War

*An editorial urging voters to support the Democratic Party,
the* Hartford Times, *August 19, 1864. Courtesy of
the Connecticut State Library*

slavery,' while Democrats are for the Union just as our fathers made it, with States rights and United States rights unimpaired. *That's* the difference."[64] The paper followed a few days later with typical racist trash: "Old Abe say, he ought to be re-elected, because he has two hundred thousand of nigger troops, now in hand, and they might not be so much in favor, if he and his cabinet were turned adrift in the November election." Other incendiary articles followed, such as "Negro Catchers of White Men," in which the *Register* revealed the reversal of racial fortunes by reporting that "at Elmira, New York, a squad of President Lincoln's *negro soldiers* are engaged hunting up white men who have been drafted. The darkies carry a high head, as, with gun in hand, they drag the white men from their families and march them off to camp, to fight for the freedom of Southern negroes who don't want to be free. All who like this picture, can vote the Republican ticket."[65]

Democrats also focused on the war's duration, promising that reelecting Lincoln would guarantee many more years of bloodshed and that the South could never be subjugated. The *Times* asked readers: "How many more years of war are we to have? How many more drafts? How many more thousands of millions spent? How long are our institutions to be crushed by military rule? How long is labor to be drained by the exhaustion of men and means?" The *Register* complained of taxation on everything: "And all this must be kept up, and be continued, and no one knows how long, to gratify the whim of a smutty joker [Lincoln]."[66]

As the final day of the campaign arrived, after the Democratic Party had organized some three hundred meetings throughout the state in the preceding weeks,[67] the two leading Democratic papers put the issue plainly. The *Times* ran the headline "A Republic or a Monarchy."[68] The *Register* announced: "The argument is closed—the case is made up, and tomorrow the jury will render its verdict,—a verdict upon which rests the fate of the country. Should it pronounce in favor of the election of General McClellan, we shall speedily have restored the Union, with peace reigning throughout our now distracted land; and we can then apply our energies to the work of restoring the happiness and prosperity which prevailed before the fell spirit of sectional fanaticism became a power in the land. Should it pronounce for Lincoln,—it will be an endorsement of the usurpations, corruption and outrages of which the Administration has been guilty—a declaration in favor of uncompromising war for Abolition—for unrelenting conscription and ruinous debt and taxation to carry out the policy of Garrison, Greeley, and Co. Was there ever a more momentous issue committed to the judgment of any people?"[69]

———◦———

Republicans seemed assured of victory almost as soon as Sherman captured Atlanta. It was just the medication needed for an ailing home front, and Connecticut Republicans helped to further reinvigorate the public by holding a series of huge rallies in Hartford. On October 7, thousands marched along the city's streets, raising a succession of flags along the way. The *Courant* reported: "Never before have we witnessed in this city so much enthusiasm, so much manifested devotion to the Union, or a more earnest, popular expression of love for the OLD FLAG."[70] The keynote speaker was General Joseph Hawley, of the 7th CVI, who had been one of the very first men to enroll in the 1st Connecticut Regiment. He had fought at Bull Run and in dozens of other battles, reenlisted in the 7th after his first tour of duty ended, and been unceasingly devoted to his men and the Union. He was also a staunch, radical Republican, and his support of Lincoln quelled rumblings against the president within his own party. While giving a stirring, patriotic speech—imploring: "I appeal to you as men upon whom the world is looking, to do your duty!"—Hawley was jeered by a group of Copperheads. He responded: "I've heard a worse noise than that, and the men who made it fired on me, and I didn't run." The crowd went wild, and the *Courant* noted of the Republican rally, and another held by Democrats: "The contrast between the two meetings was as between Light and Darkness; Loyalty and Treason; Heaven and Hell!"[71] Only a week later, another rally for a "Grand Torchlight Procession" met at the State House, and thousands of people once again marched through the city.[72]

The enthusiasm for the Republican ticket in the election could not be dampened. Yet Republicans nonetheless worried that traitors planned attacks should Lincoln win, with one newspaper reporting that "unless careful precautions are taken, a Northern insurrection will be the certain result of Mr. Lincoln's re-election." Remembering the New York City draft riots, the president heeded such warnings and sent several regiments to the city. On board vessels in the city's harbor were 3,500 Union troops, among whom were the 6th, 7th, and 10th Connecticut regiments. This was as close as they got to home. No trouble ensued, and the men returned to the Virginia front.[73]

Abraham Lincoln won a resounding victory in the election of 1864. His popular vote exceeded McClellan's by almost half a million, and the electoral vote, at 212 to 21, was devastating. The *Hartford Evening Press* derisively commented: "What was that man's name? McClellum, McPendlum, Micklelan, McClinelton—seems as if there was some such man, doing something or other the other day."[74] The barb was not warranted by Connecticut's election returns. Almost 90,000 votes were cast, and Lincoln won by a mere 2,405 votes—a victory almost certainly secured by the fact that the General Assembly had passed an amendment to the state constitution authorizing soldiers to vote in the field.[75] What had been true at the war's outset and throughout the conflict remained true at the end of 1864: Connecticut was divided.

The margin, however, did not ultimately matter. Victory was victory. The *Courant* announced: "The presidential campaign of 1864 has closed in a signal and overwhelming Union victory. . . . The country is saved. In the glorious record of yesterday, traitors will read the doom of the rebellion, and turn in despair from the wicked schemes that have brought them to the gates of death."[76] Governor Buckingham wrote to Lincoln, congratulating "the Nation & the friends of human liberty everywhere that our true able & ever faithful President has been reelected to the highest civil position on earth," and issued a proclamation to the citizens of Connecticut recommending a day of public thanksgiving.[77] The election caused many to believe, as the *Courant* put it, "that the rebellion is on the point of collapse."

Democrats, of course, charged fraud at the polls and continued to predict the nation's downfall. "As we said a week before the election," announced the *Times*, "we say now since that the balloting is finished, there are hundreds of thousands who voted the Lincoln ticket on Tuesday who will sorely regret it before the end of 1865." The *Register* concurred: "Connecticut has voted in favor of a continuance of unrelenting war, conscription, crushing taxation and irresponsible despotism."[78]

Such Democratic views were, to some extent, bolstered by President Lincoln's annual message to Congress, delivered on December 6. He restated his commitment to the war, insisted that the nation possessed abundant resources, and said "we are *gaining* strength, and may, if need be, maintain the contest indefinitely." He also urged Congress to reconsider passing the Thirteenth Amendment abolishing slavery, insisting that in the election "the voice of the people now, for the first time, [was] heard upon the question." The president noted that with the Republican victories, a new Congress would be seated in the next session and it was therefore "only a matter of *time*." He implored those in the opposition to "consider the will of the majority" and again placed the matter in terms of national necessity, insisting that "the common end is the maintenance of the Union; and, among the means to secure that end, such will, through the election, is most clearly declared in favor of such a constitutional amendment."[79] Later in December, the president once more showed his resolve by issuing a proclamation recruiting another 300,000 men. Clearly, Lincoln meant to finish the war. And the military cooperated. On December 22, Sherman reached the sea, sending the president a simple telegram: "I beg to present you as a Christmas-gift the city of Savannah."[80]

Thus closed 1864. Not an easy year for the North, it nonetheless concluded with a sense that the end of the war was near. As the new year arrived, there was no waiting for spring campaigns. The Union acted quickly, on January 15 taking Fort Fisher, North Carolina, which guarded the entrance to Wilmington. After a massive naval bombardment, troops under the command of Connecticut's General Alfred Terry, including the 6th and 7th CVI, stormed the fort. It protected one of the few remaining avenues of supply for Lee's beleaguered troops, the last army standing between the Confederacy and defeat. And Sherman was on his way, blazing a trail through the Carolinas and punishing the seedbed of Southern extremism. Croffut and Morris wrote: "In South Carolina, [the Union troops] reveled, indulging a terrible joy at the thought that the Rebellion was in its last gasp, and resolved to collect principal and interest of the debt long due to justice. The pestilent State was swept with a besom of flame."[81]

The end for the Confederacy was not solely on the military front. On January 31, 1865, sixteen Democrats in the House of Representatives

Connecticut in the American Civil War

voted in favor of the Thirteenth Amendment, providing the necessary two-thirds vote to approve the abolition of slavery. "Slavery is dead," declared the *Hartford Evening Press*; "We can hardly realize the magnitude of the statement." The paper also recognized that a mere four years earlier, many in the North had been willing "to put a clause in the constitution by which slavery never could be touched." The *Courant* declared the amendment "one of the most memorable events of the century." It, too, however, commented on the North's early views of slavery, stating that the institution never would have died had it not been "killed through the folly of its friends. Had the south remained peaceful, the north would never have interfered with their domestic concerns." The paper insisted that slavery would have grown until it "induced a war of races, which would have continued till one of the other was exterminated."[82]

What does such a statement say about the moral imperatives of emancipation? For many Americans, such a question cuts to the core of the Civil War's larger meaning. Certainly, there existed diehard abolitionists devoted to the eradication of slavery. Yet they made up only a small portion of the Northern population and did not control the Republican Party. For other Northerners, the end of slavery was unquestionably tied to the Slave Power — destroying the institution would also destroy the existing political power in the South. Moreover, at the most basic level, ridding the nation of slavery also relieved the political system of its central point of contention, a problem that existed well beyond the Constitution. There is also the distinct reality that many in the North simply wanted to punish the South for the war. Since slavery seemed to be the primary rationale for the Confederate cause, emancipation was a just reward to Northerners who were outraged by the legions of men slain and wounded. Yet it is also a reality that many in the North had come to recognize the evils of slavery. Measuring the extent of these varying motives is difficult, if not impossible. What is certain, however, is that ending slavery did not put to rest the formidable issues attached to race, issues that reverberate to this day.

For Democrats, the question of slavery did not end with the renewed push for the Thirteenth Amendment. They emphatically disputed the legality and efficacy of emancipation. Many argued that it would prolong the war, that it left no room for negotiation with the South, and that it was "merely a vent for the passions of the radical faction." Others insisted that the amendment had been passed by Congress only as a result of corrupt political bargains, and that it would never be ratified by the states. Democrats also continued to sound the mantra of states' rights, insisting that "Congress is given no power, under the organic law of the Union, to meddle with the domestic affairs of any State." Ultimately, some concluded that "the abstract question of slavery is of no consequence; but violation of *the bond* under which our union was formed cannot be too strongly reprobated."[83]

In terms of the larger issue of race, the amendment did nothing to stop — indeed, it exacerbated — Democratic attacks on blacks. In an article entitled "Inferiority of the Negro Race," published in early March, the *Times* blasted the idea that blacks were even marginally equal to whites: "If the negro is 'superior' to the white race, we would ask for the evidence of the superiority." The paper concluded: "The negro, like the native American Indian, points to no such evidences of the superiority of his people, through all the long line of his ancestry extending back to the remotest of days." Where, asked the *Times*, is the evidence of any real civilization? "All is blank — a blankness that is more eloquent than words, for it tells of one unbroken state of savagery and barbarism; of a stationary race, who are to-day just where they were three thousand years ago."[84]

Even Republicans such as Fred Lucas mixed the meaning of black freedom with their own feelings about race. Lucas wrote home: "Congress is doing good work of late. The new amendment to the Constitution regarding the total abolition of slavery, except as a punishment for crime has now become a law subject as yet to the ratification of the several states. This war is gradually effecting mighty results of wiping away forever the causes which promoted it and the evils which originated it. What a glorious peace it will be when it finally dawns, costing so much blood, treasure, and human life, and bring about such permanent radical changes in the minds and sentiments of our people." Yet only two months later, he commented: "Negroes are roaming around all over this region — free and too ignorant to make proper use of freedom, they are become a pest & nuisance to the army and their former masters. The soldiers are impressing them and compelling them to do their work. We have scores about our camp & keep them at labor for us. We have endless sport with these negroes . . . every nigger is dancing & the soldiers laughing at their antics."[85]

———————

As Republicans and Democrats disputed the meaning of the Thirteenth Amendment, the Union troops continued their path toward Richmond. Everyone sensed that the end was near. Lucas, back at the front by early February, wrote letter after letter reporting the desertion of Confederate soldiers, explaining that "the absconding 'Johnnies' usually have to run the gauntlet of fire from their own men & often get hit before they reach our lines. Our boys cheer them on & encourage them, while the bullets whistle musically about them." Once behind Union lines, "they shook our hands and embraced us and all but kissed us so great was their joy to get away." He concluded: "If these runaways could be believed the confederacy is well nigh exploded and peace not far off." McPherson noted that in February the Confederate Army lost a full 8 percent of its men due to desertion.[86]

Grant continued to push his men forward, doing his best to encircle Petersburg and cut it off from all lines of supply. By March, Lee recognized that his army was through if he didn't move, but that meant sacrificing Petersburg, and with it Richmond. On April 3, Union troops entered the Confederate capital and, perhaps as a true sign of the times, black soldiers were among the first in the city. Connecticut was well represented, as soldiers from Companies C and G of the 29th black regiment marched into the heart of the Confederacy.[87] President Lincoln arrived shortly thereafter and sat in the study of Jefferson Davis, only forty hours after he had fled. Lincoln reportedly said to Admiral David Porter: "Thank God I have lived to see this. It seems to me that I have been dreaming a horrid dream for four years, and now the nightmare is gone."[88] Only six days later, on April 9, Grant and Lee met at Appomattox Courthouse and agreed on surrender terms. The war was over, and the *Hartford Courant* announced "glorious news! of peace! Union! Happiness!"[89]

———— • ————

The happiness was short-lived. On April 14, while attending the theater, Abraham Lincoln was shot in the back of the head by John Wilkes Booth. The *Courant* reported the "awful calamity" and announced: "We are called on to write the most heart rending news that has been written since the nation was born, news that will carry sadness and gloom all over the land; that our beloved President Lincoln, who has thus far been so providentially spared, has been assassinated in cold blood by a murderer—a rebel—who, not satisfied with attempts to destroy the life-blood of the nation, has stricken down, with a cowardly hand, the very head of the nation." The paper stated bluntly two days later: "Slavery had murdered Abraham Lincoln."[90]

The news traveled like a shock wave through the Union, both on the home front and among the troops. Lucas wrote that when told of "the murder of our beloved President scarcely an eye in that large audience of rough & sunburnt men but was wet with grief and I might say also that not one among them but felt more than ever before his duty to his

"The Assassination of President Lincoln, At Ford's Theatre,
Washington, D.C., April 14th, 1865," Currier and Ives,
New York, 1865. Library of Congress, LC-USZ62-2073

nation & cause, and a stronger determination than ever to be faithful in
the countries [sic] service." He also recognized that the president's death
had changed everything: "But if terrible to us it is very terrible to the rebel
cause. We can never give our enemies the leniency they might have rec'd.
before. . . . Two weeks ago I could have pardoned even old Jeff Davis himself
I believe; so flushed & pleased were we with the victory & success that all
feeling of animosity was gone almost, but when the saddening news came
to us of the vile murder of our Chief we could not help but give way to the
prompting of human nature and encourage the thoughts of vengeance on
the perpetrators, aiders & abettors of the foul crime. Yesterday at noon the
batteries of our Corps. tolled a requisition for the dead by firing our guns
for half an hour. We are acting History now!"[91]

Justus Silliman of the 17th CVI, stationed in Florida, responded similarly
to Lincoln's death: "We received the sad news and startling intelligence of
the assassination of President Lincoln. . . . So great was our surprise and
grief on hearing it that we could not utter a word. It seemed as though from
the sunshine of our joy we had become suddenly enveloped in a dark and
gloomy cloud that was horrible to contemplate." Silliman's shock quickly
turned to anger, and he reported that "deep threats are heard on every side

Connecticut in the American Civil War

AWFUL CALAMITY!

TERRIBLE LOSS TO THE NATION!

PRESIDENT LINCOLN ASSASSINATED!

ATTEMPT TO ASSASSINATE SECRETARY SEWARD!

He Still Lives.

Headlines in the Hartford Courant,
April 15, 1865.

---

from our soldiers, many of whom have expressed a desire to be led against the enemy under the black flag and carry out a war of extermination but I trust that, as heretofore, we may not influenced by such motives, but that we may be incited by our desire to perpetuate our institutions of justice & liberty & to put down wrong & oppression." He concluded: "In killing Lincoln they have destroyed the mildest of their foes."[92]

Those at home in Connecticut reacted to the news of Lincoln's assassination with equal shock, sadness, and anger. The city of Hartford and other towns throughout the state immediately went into mourning. Homes and businesses were draped in black, flags hung at half mast, and images of Lincoln filled windows. Some state residents suggested that funds be collected for a permanent memorial in Hartford. Charles J. Hoadly, the state librarian, wrote to Governor Buckingham immediately after Lincoln's death that "I have no heart to comment on the sad news this morning." He reported that "the city bells are tolling[,] the flags are all at half mast and the front of the state house on the Main St. side is being hung with black." The *Courant* reported: "The sorrow which has found utterance in hurried exclamations, among neighbors and acquaintances, in homes and on our public streets for four days past, was brought to its height in the solemn observances which took place in the houses of God."[93]

The anger over the assassination was palpable, especially when some dared to rejoice at the president's death. One George Brown allegedly announced: "I don't care G—d—; I should like to dance on his grave." He and others who uttered such sentiments were summarily assaulted. The mourning and anger blended together into toxic mix of emotion. On April 20, a large gathering assembled at Allyn Hall in Hartford, and James G. Batterson, elected president of the group that organized the affair, announced: "We have assembled here today under circumstances of the most painful and heart-sickening character; circumstances which have no parallel in the history of our country." Batterson's opening remarks revealed both the sadness and frustration felt within the wider community, and he used his speech as an opportunity to lash out against the defeated rebels: "What spectacle is this? Why all these weeds of mourning? Why all these tearful eyes and saddened hearts? *Our dearly beloved President is dead!!* Dead—and to-day all that was mortal of him in whom the nation hoped and trusted, has been removed forever from our sight. Dead—and that great warm heart, which never beat in malice, to-day, is cold and still. Dead—and a great nation has become a mourning widow, who like Rachel weeping for her children, refuses to be comforted, for He is not. Dead—and by the hands of that vile power, that most iniquitous sum of all human and infernal villainies, that most stupendous wickedness which has ever entered the hearts of men or devils since 'the morning stars sang together'—*human slavery!*"[94]

Undoubtedly conscious of the razor-thin line separating sorrow from anger, the Democratic newspapers in Connecticut were temperate, if not sympathetic to the nation's loss. The *Times* wrote: "At any time, under any circumstances, the assassination of the Chief Magistrate of the Republic would be considered a great calamity. But at this time, in the present exigency of the Union, with all the surrounding circumstances, that act is of graver significance, and of more appalling interest."[95]

Ironically, before he died from wounds in the Wilderness campaign, Samuel Fiske had contemplated the coming presidential election and, thinking that McClellan might win, had determined that "the least desirable thing in the whole world, it seems to me, is to be an Ex-President." Fiske was disgusted by the scheming, intrigue, and ambition of politicians and concluded that "the man who shall devote himself most earnestly and successfully to the ending of this Rebellion; who shall work with an eye and a heart to that great end, forgetting self in country,—he is the one whose name shall be in the hearts of our children, and his praises on their lips. He shall be greater and better than a President: he could even afford to be an Ex-President."[96] Fiske did not write that he was referring to Lincoln, but his words, nonetheless, have a remarkable prescience.

On May 23, various regiments of the Union Army, including the Connecticut 5th, 12th, 14th, and 20th, marched through the streets of Washington, D.C., in a grand review.[97] By midsummer, most of the men were on their way home. The fighting of the previous eighteen months had proven to be some of the bloodiest of the war. It was an expensive victory. Grant had taken command with a single goal: destroy Lee's army, and with it the Confederacy. Accomplishing this had secured the Union and put an end to the disastrous theory of secession. Slavery was also finished, whether or not that had originally been a Union war aim, and regardless of what the future actually held for blacks. All of this had required a startling sacrifice. Some 360,000 Northern soldiers died, and 5,354 of these were from Connecticut. The little Nutmeg State had sent 55,864 soldiers to war — nearly half of her male population between the ages of fifteen and fifty.[98]

Those at home had borne the burden of every soldier, every battle, and every wound and death. Without the constant stream of supplies from Connecticut, combined with the state's significant war industry, there would have been little chance of Union success. In this sense, the conflict was truly a total war. The same was true of the political scene at home. While soldiers battled in the field, Republicans and Democrats waged a virtually constant fight for political control of the state. The painfully even division from the 1860 election return well through the 1864 presidential contest revealed that Connecticut remained a hotly contested battleground. The continual conflict, both military and political, took its toll on everyone. And although April 1865 brought an end to the war, its memory was just beginning. Surviving the war included surviving the peace.

CHAPTER SIX

Survival's Memory

1865-1965

The memory of war is a tricky thing. It inevitably changes as time marches on and those who actually participated in a conflict pass on. A new generation can never fully experience the fear, despondence, and loss, or the joy, victory, and nationalism of those who came before. Every nation desires to remember and promote the justice of its cause and the sacrifice of those who fought. Even defeat can morph into a living force, a consciousness that honors soldiers and commitment, and that expands on positive rationales for fighting. Such was certainly the case in the South. Belief in the so-called Lost Cause helped spawn an intense Southern nationalism following the Civil War. After a shattering defeat, with their lands devastated, a significant portion of their male population dead or maimed, and the system of slave labor eradicated, Southerners comforted themselves with the belief that their cause had been noble and heroic. They had fought to defend their land from tyrannous Northern invaders. They had fought to defend the true Constitution, untrammeled by Northern manipulation and federal power. The Southern mantra was, once again, states' rights. When the Confederate President Jefferson Davis and Vice President Alexander Stevens wrote books after the rebellion, their focus was on the sanctity of state sovereignty, not on a defense of slavery. The peculiar institution fell into the background of the conflict. Even today, arguments continue over the meaning of the rebel flag—whether it represents states' rights or unadulterated racism.[1]

For the North, the meaning of the war had always, to some extent, been convoluted. At its core was the preservation of the Union. Republicans rallied behind this cause, but the Democratic Party split into war and peace wings—those for saving the Union, and those who believed secession was legal and that the South should not be coerced to stay in the United States. At the outset of the war, even Republicans insisted that it was not about abolition. Their thinking changed as the conflict continued. First they accepted emancipation as a military necessity, and then, by the midpoint of the war, they claimed that they had always been in favor of liberty for blacks. Thus, by the rebellion's end, many in the North, and certainly in Connecticut, saw themselves as liberators of downtrodden slaves, and saw the war as a rebirth, a second revolution that finally realized Jefferson's idealistic declaration that "all men are created equal." To a large extent, modern Americans have internalized this history of the war, going a step further by supposing that it began to free the slaves. Except for a small minority of abolitionists, this simply was not the case.

<hr />

Historians have delved deeply into the memory of the Civil War, some insisting that the South was not alone in perpetuating the myth of the Lost Cause.[2] Some Northerners readily embraced the idea, partly because they desired reconciliation and partly because they were economically motivated to get the Southern agricultural system running again, and reconciliation aided that goal. After four years of conflict, of battles that astounded the entire nation by the extent of bloodshed and death, Northerners simply wanted peace, healing, and movement forward. It was the nobility of sacrifice and the devotion to the nation that captivated soldiers and citizens alike. As time moved on, there was no desire to wrestle with or agonize over the abolitionist sentiment that had developed as the war progressed. There was no clarion call to nurture the former slaves, the freedmen. As the historian David Blight succinctly put it: "Americans faced an overwhelming task after the Civil War and emancipation: how to understand the tangled relationship between two profound ideas — *healing* and *justice*."[3] They chose healing.

The racism of nineteenth-century America precluded the idea of justice. Or, perhaps more correctly, many in the North viewed emancipation as enough justice. Going any further could be equated with promoting black social and political equality, something that few white Northerners condoned. In this sense, there existed a distinct difference between emancipation and abolition similar to what had been articulated at the time of Lincoln's Emancipation Proclamation. And though during the war, some Northerners may have developed a sort of amnesia regarding their prewar views of blacks, or even admitted the errors of those views, in the war's long aftermath, there existed no widespread desire to wrestle with such issues. The reality is that most white Northerners, including many residents of Connecticut, wanted to establish a firm separation between the races.

We think of segregation as primarily a Southern phenomenon, one that developed in the latter half of the nineteenth century and was endorsed by the infamous 1896 Supreme Court decision in *Plessy v. Ferguson*, which legally sanctioned the idea of "separate but equal." Yet devotion to racial separation was also characteristic of Northerners and had developed much earlier.

The disintegration of abolitionist sentiment, the feeling that blacks had already received justice, the distaste for black political and social equality, and the desire for separation between the races — all culminated in one momentous event that steered Connecticut's course into the postwar years. In the spring of 1865, the General Assembly passed an amendment to the state constitution removing the word "white" in determining who could vote, and scheduled an October referendum on the subject. The change was overwhelmingly rejected by Connecticut voters. And it was Republican votes that secured the amendment's defeat. The state's residents may have ultimately supported emancipation, but they were not advocates of black civic equality — they were not abolitionists. The vote was a resolute shift from thoughts of justice and equality to those of healing and reconciliation.

The focus of the postwar years, then, was not racial harmony or the plight of the newly freed slaves, though some speakers periodically highlighted the end of slavery. It was commemoration, a remembrance of all that was noble in the great struggle. The North had guaranteed the Union's survival by crushing the theory of secession along with the Southern armies that carried its message. It was a success of constitutional democracy. Citizen soldiers had risen in a time of dire emergency. Their sacrifices and devotion had become the bond that created a nation, as opposed to merely a Union or league of states. As much as Southern nationalism was born of a failed war, Northern nationalism was born of victory. These are stories that carried through the war's centennial commemoration.

In Connecticut, as well as elsewhere in the North, the people — especially the soldiers — came together to remember and memorialize their sacrifices. This activity did not wait for appropriate anniversaries. It was immediate, overwhelming. As the historian Drew Gilpin Faust has recognized, the degree of death was so immense, so singular in the nation's history, that memorializing the dead through public ceremonies and monuments was unrivaled in the nation's history.[4]

Connecticut stood at the forefront of this movement, in part because James G. Batterson, the founder of the Traveler's Insurance Company, in Hartford, was also one of the country's principal stone and quarry industrialists and a leading supplier of stone for Civil War monuments in both the state and the nation. His best-known Connecticut monument is the Sailor's and Soldier's Memorial Arch in Hartford's Bushnell Park, and he aided in the erection of dozens of statues and obelisks that dot town greens around the state.[5] He also built monuments at the Antietam and Gettysburg battlefields, among others. At the dedication of each of these monuments, people gathered and were regaled with speeches about the meaning of war and sacrifice. The nation also inaugurated Decoration Day, which later became Memorial Day, a time to remember and place flowers or wreaths on the tombs of those who sacrificed themselves that the nation might live. Connecticut also held a grand Battle Flag Day in 1879, during which many of the regimental flags carried into battle by the state's soldiers were returned in a formal parade to the state armory, and later displayed permanently in the state capitol's Hall of Flags. They remain there to this day, though their preservation is an ongoing struggle.[6]

The state also focused on the momentous anniversaries of the war, most notably the fiftieth and hundredth anniversaries. These were times of reconciliation and memorialization of the nobility of the great struggle that had threatened the nation's very survival. At the fiftieth anniversary, beginning in 1911, aging Union soldiers traveled with their families to distant Southern battlefields and met their Confederate counterparts. They remembered the great battles, setting aside — as perhaps they had already done long before — any animosity, and embraced one another as comrades in arms. In many respects, the centennial commemoration, beginning in 1961, was even more important. A full century had passed, and the nation had once again weathered a mighty storm of war, World War II. The anniversary also fell during the momentous and challenging civil rights era, when black Americans battled for the justice that had been so summarily denied them in the years following the war, with the era's failed promises of reconstruction. Yet once again, the nation refused to recognize the complex issues of slavery and race that had led to the war and rippled through the decades that followed it.

We now stand on the threshold of the sesquicentennial, the 150th anniversary of the Civil War. In the long march of time, fifty years may not seem like much, but America has demonstrably moved forward on matters of race. Perhaps the most overt example is the election of a black president, Barack Obama. Historians therefore look to this commemoration differently, hoping that the nation can undertake honest and open conversations about the meaning of slavery, past and present racism in America, the complicity of the North in the existence of slavery, and the fact that the Civil War was not originally fought to secure abolition or civic equality for black Americans.

<hr/>

The issue of black voting rights actually exploded onto the scene before the war ended. Since its 1818 constitution, Connecticut was the only state in New England to bar all blacks from voting. Though several attempts had been made to amend the law in the 1840s and 1850s, all had failed miserably. In the waning months of 1864, another amendment was proposed, simply removing the word "white" from the language describing electors.[7] A vote on it was postponed until the following session of the General Assembly, in May 1865. At the opening of that term, the amendment was announced, and Governor Buckingham—who had been reelected the previous month, once again resoundingly defeating Origen S. Seymour—delivered his final address to the Assembly. He focused on the amendment, declaring: "We are now battling for the inalienable rights of man, without regard to race or color. In this struggle the colored man, hitherto degraded and oppressed, have, in every section of the country, been on the side of the government, and are now in our armies by thousands fighting for freedom under the protection of law. Let us inspire the colored man with self-respect, and encourage him to struggle and hope for a more elevated destiny, by granting him the boon so long withheld."[8]

The rationale used by the governor for giving blacks the right to vote presaged many of the arguments that his fellow Republicans raised in the ensuing weeks and months as the measure was debated. Buckingham believed that the war had provided lessons that cut to the very core of the nation's freedom, and support for the amendment was an important demonstration that those lessons had been learned: "The terrible sufferings caused by the sword have given freemen a more clear understanding of the foundations upon which republican liberty must rest, and have prepared the public to submit to a verdict rendered at the ballot box. If the decision shall be made with reference to the claims of right and universal justice, we may hope for enduring peace."[9] The governor would be sorely disappointed.

If Republicans were forced to wait until May to put the amendment to a vote, Democrats felt no compunction about denouncing it early. In a February 1865 article, the *Hartford Times* put the matter bluntly: "To us it appears that this question of negro suffrage is involved in that of the races. We cannot commingle the African race with the white race without injurious results. If we cannot do this, we cannot admit them to the right

Connecticut in the American Civil War

of suffrage." The paper concluded: "Inferior — made so by the hand of the Creator — the negro cannot be forced to an equality with the whites till the unchangeable laws of God are destroyed."[10] Such arguments were one of the mainstays of the Democratic Party throughout the war, as Democrats continually worked to exploit the underlying racism in Connecticut and prevent the rise of abolitionism.

The *Courant* responded to the Democratic blast in rather lackluster fashion, denying the "inferiority" of blacks, and several days later, the paper charged that the *Times* had "Nigger on the Brain," asking, "Who has heaped degradation and insult on negroes to the extent the democratic party has?" The *Courant* insisted that the primary reason for Democratic opposition to the amendment was that the party would not benefit from black suffrage.[11] Democrats, of course, charged that a principal reason why the Republicans were pushing the amendment was the potential benefit at the polls, with increased Republican voters.

This sparring was merely a precursor to a much larger legislative and newspaper battle that began once the amendment was formally approved in May. Republicans appeared confident of the amendment's success before the vote, with the *Courant* announcing that "the plan of extending the elective franchise to black and white on the same conditions [is] rapidly gaining favor among all classes."[12] The paper and several Republican legislators made a variety of intersecting arguments in favor of the amendment: the essential equality of the races, and the fact that justice demanded such a measure, both because of blacks' service in the military and because of the essential nature of human rights and liberty woven within the fabric of America. In making the latter argument, some speakers cited the Declaration of Independence and insisted that the nation's Founders had actually been in favor of total equality. Republicans also stressed that the vote would have a great impact on the rest of the nation and the future of Reconstruction.

The debates in the state's House of Representatives began on May 19 with the reading of committee reports. A minority report (from a committee of two Democrats) argued against the amendment on the grounds that Negroes possessed "no inventive faculties, no genius for the arts, or for any of those occupations requiring intellect and wisdom," and that the "Supreme Court of the United States has decided the negro to be not a citizen of the United States, and therefore it is unconstitutional to extend the elective franchise to him." This reference was to the 1857 *Dred Scott* decision in which the Court, led by Chief Justice Roger Taney, had determined that no black, whether slave or free, was a citizen. In response, George

Pratt of Norwich, a Republican representative, insisted "that [Supreme Court] decision was notoriously a mere *obiter dictum* [a determination on an issue that was not actually being considered by the Court], and it should not be allowed to influence our action, or to effect [sic] our judgments." Representative Henry Harrison of New Haven concurred, stating that the Supreme Court's decision could "hardly be recognized as having the weight of authority."[13]

Dismiss the issue as they might, Republicans nonetheless desired a formal answer on the point, and on June 15 and 16, they passed legislation requiring the Connecticut Supreme Court to "give an opinion on the subject of negro citizenship."[14] The court obliged with remarkable swiftness, determining a mere twelve days later that "in their opinion a free colored person born in this State is a 'citizen' of this State, and of the United States, within the meaning of the amendment of the constitution referred to." The judges provided no elaboration of "within the meaning of the amendment."[15] The very fact that they provided an advisory opinion was unusual.

While such matters were under consideration, the debates within the Assembly continued. Pratt argued that "the question of the rights of the colored race has greatly changed in the popular mind within the last three or four years. The nation has been saved, and its salvation comes not alone from the endurance and valor of its white population; the black man has been called on, and thousands of his race have rushed to the rescue and to them are we greatly indebted for the victories which have been given to our arms."[16] The *Courant* agreed and went further, insisting: "There is no reason why mere color should disqualify a person to vote. If the negro on the average rises to an equality of intelligence and virtue with the white, let him enjoy equal privileges." The paper also reminded readers of the impending issues of Reconstruction in the aftermath of the war, concluding: "We cannot reasonably appeal to the South to perform duties which we neglect ourselves."[17] This was an important point that would be further highlighted in the aftermath of the vote.

On May 24, the House engaged in its longest day of debate regarding the amendment. Most flamboyant was the ever ready showman, P. T. Barnum, who had only recently been elected to the legislature — solely, as he said, "because I wished to have the honor of voting for the two constitutional amendments — one for driving slavery entirely out of our country [the Thirteenth Amendment] — the other to allow men of education and good moral character, to vote regardless of the color of their skins." Barnum delivered a long, engaging speech with quick-witted jibes aimed at his Democratic opponents, addressing concerns over interracial marriage, the barbarity of blacks, and their potential for the future. He also revealed, even in supporting the amendment, the deep-seated racism that existed in nineteenth-century Connecticut. Responding to a Democrat who had expressed concerns about intermarriage, the showman said: "The gentleman expresses apprehension that more and more will continue to be asked by the negro until by and by his sons will be trying to marry negro girls, and that would not suit him. I perfectly agree with the gentleman in his tastes. I should not like to associate with or have my children marry with negroes, but, the gentleman may remember that when his sons propose to marry with negroes the black girls may have a word to say in objection to such a proposition."[18]

Barnum's clever ripostes filled the legislative hall with laughter, but he was not merely joking. His speech expressed a sincere conviction that blacks, no matter what their previous circumstances, could be raised up. He insisted that "if the colored man is indeed a *man*, then his manhood, with proper training, can be developed. His soul may appear dormant, his brain inactive, but there is a *vitality* there, and if you will give her the opportunity *nature will assert herself.*" Barnum's dismissal of black intellect was actually a minor slight considering what followed. And whether his remarks were merely an attempt to connect with the decidedly racist element of the state, or sincere beliefs on his own part, they nonetheless reflected an essential bigotry that permeated American society. "Their race has been buried for ages in ignorance and barbarism," announced Barnum, "and you can scarcely perceive that they have any more manhood or womanhood than many orang-outangs or gorillas. You look at their low foreheads, their thick skulls, their woolly heads, their thick lips, their broad noses, their dull lazy eyes, and you may be tempted to adopt language of this minority committee and exclaim, surely these people have 'no *inventive* faculties, no genius for the arts, or for any of those occupations requiring *intellect* and *wisdom*.' But bring them into the light of civilization, let them and their children come into the genial sunshine of Christianity, teach them industry, self-reliance and self-respect, and the human soul will begin to develop itself."[19] Although layered with racist rhetoric that is shocking to modern sensibilities, Barnum's overall message was one of hope, of a better future for both races — one that required some level of magnanimity on the part of whites.

One of the other powerful speeches in the House was from John Douglas of Middletown, a Republican, who strenuously denied charges of black inferiority and asserted that military service had revealed the capabilities of blacks and justified their rights. These were hardly new arguments, and thus it was Douglas's insistence on the complete equality of the races and his rather strained views concerning the beliefs of the nation's Founders that gave his speech an explosive quality. He insisted that when the nation was created, the Founders "expressly declared that all men were created equal, and we accept that proposition to-day and give it our most hearty endorsement." Though the Founders could not fully strike down slavery at the time, they nonetheless looked to its future demise, insisted Douglas. He cited the abolishment of the African slave trade as evidence, "so that it [slavery] might die out and in a few years and become extinct." He continued: "So when we look at the opinions of the founders of the government, we find them in favor of the equality of man. . . . The ultimate equality of all men was the inspiration that moved them."[20]

Douglas's assertions were debatable. Although there is little question that some of the nation's Founders had hoped for slavery's death over time, to argue that they believed in total, or even partial, equality among the races is outlandish. The Democrats did not fail to respond. Announcing that "fanatics are constantly harping on this sentence in the Declaration of Independence—all men are created equal," the *Hartford Times* reminded its readers: "Let us notice that the signers held slaves. . . . One of two conclusions we must come to: either that they did not consider negroes the equals of white men in the sentence quoted, or that they were hypocrites, and did not believe what they had subscribed to—otherwise they would have immediately liberated their slaves and entitled them to those rights referred to."[21] Surely, the *Times* evaluation of the Founders' intent was as unsubstantiated as Douglas's, yet the paper's message was one that Democrats had highlighted for years, and it helped to place in stark contrast the steady insistence of Republicans that the Declaration of Independence had really been meant to include blacks.

Douglas's arguments about equality did not stop with his shoddy historical analysis. He also attempted to carry the issue by storm, thundering that "equality, equality, is the word which sounds out from every humble lip," and warning the state's residents: "If Connecticut fails to strike this blow for equality—if she fails to do justice to the men she called upon to fight her battles, it will be a more decisive blow in favor of despotism, ingratitude and aristocracy than her whole history shows her to have given in favor of partial freedom." He ended his speech by recognizing the immense magnitude of little Connecticut's vote on the remainder of the nation: "The decision we make may have material weight in settling this question in our sister states, and from this house may go out that which

Connecticut in the American Civil War

shall induce, at an early day, a radical change in the constitutions of the states of this Republic, so that all men, black and white, shall stand equal in making laws under which they live."[22]

If Douglas could argue for his understanding of the Founders' views, so too could Connecticut Democrats. Most notably, Judge Harris Munson, a representative from Seymour, took great issue with the convoluted musings of his opponents and announced firmly: "The Constitution ought to stand without mutilation." Focusing specifically on the intent of Connecticut's founders, Munson insisted that their inclusion of the word "white" left no question as to where they stood on matters of race: "The language of the Constitution clearly precludes any intention on the part of its framers of admitting the black man to the right of citizenship or political equality." Munson did not bother to deal with the fact that the insertion of "white" occurred in 1818, an act that actually took the vote away from some blacks. Rather, he remained certain that "our fathers regarded the mingling of the black man with the white race with abhorrence. And when the great social compact was made, it was made by and between white men. Negroes were not parties to that contract; but they were positively and intentionally excluded from becoming parties to it."[23]

Munson also denied that whites had "downtrodden" the Negro, insisting that, "so far from treading down the negro race, we have been constantly raising and lifting them up. If the race is still low down in the valley, it is not our fault; it is because nature's God has placed them there." This continual Democratic focus on inferiority belied the essential Republican argument that blacks were equal, and that it was merely environment and opportunity that had left them intellectually behind. Munson countered this idea, insisting: "The negro of this State owes all the civilization and culture and education which he now has, to white men," and adding the truly offensive remark that "in this State we have made him a favored pet." He concluded by heralding the grandeur of American citizenship and warning that it would mean little if fanatical men forced a change in the state's constitution: "Pass this amendment, and this proud distinction looses [sic] all of its attractions. We curb the noble ambition of our youth, and point them down to the negro's level." The *Hartford Times* noted of Munson's speech that it was an "able exposition" and that he displayed "firmness in opposing a measure for mongrelizing the best race on earth."[24]

Resolutely racist as these comments seem, they pale in comparison to a series of longer articles that placed the amendment firmly on the line of racial separation. In a remarkable commentary that presaged by thirty years the Supreme Court's 1896 *Plessy v. Ferguson* decision, the *Times* insisted that "neither the white nor the colored can be benefitted by legislative enactments to force equality that nature itself had forbidden." The *Times* also foreshadowed another of the Jim Crow era preoccupations—interracial sex: "White supremacy is not adhered to in any spirit of intolerance towards the inferior race, but only as a means to preserving our own race from the deplorable consequences of *hybridism*, and of saving our country from that *mongrelism*." The *Times* argued that the amendment would place blacks on an equal footing with whites in every regard, not merely in terms of voting, maintaining the black man's "right to mingle freely in general society and form family ties without distinction to color or race." The paper insisted on the amendment's larger meaning to the nation, arguing: "The action of Connecticut will become significant. . . . Negro suffrage once conceded can never be recalled."[25]

Although impassioned, resolute, and decidedly racist, the arguments of Democratic opponents to the amendment had little bearing on the outcome of the General Assembly vote. On May 25, the House approved the amendment by a vote of 157 to 77. In response, the *Courant* announced: "Freedom marches on from victory to victory. . . . But the voters of the State must remember that the work is not yet fully accomplished."[26] The next hurdle was the Senate, where days later Republicans once again claimed that justice was due to the black man because of his mistreatment at the hands of whites, his admirable service in the nation's defense, and the fact that "our fathers did not mean to make 'color' an article of disqualification." With a fully Republican Senate, the vote on May 31 was unanimous: twenty-one in favor of the amendment.[27] The date for the public referendum, which was required to enact a constitutional change, was scheduled for the first Monday in October, at the same time as town elections.

Over the next four months, Republican and Democratic newspapers attempted to influence the decisions of the state's voters. The core of the matter was how Connecticut residents viewed racial equality. The arguments put forth followed those made during the debates in the General Assembly and, in reality, those paraded ad nauseam by both parties during the latter part of the war.[28]

Had abolitionist thought truly changed the underlying racism in Connecticut? Or had those living in the "land of steady habits" accepted emancipation but reached a line they refused to cross regarding race? The issue, as one historian put it, was a "crucial test" of Republican policy, for "Connecticut was one of the few states where the issue squarely faced

An article attempting to sway voters
before the referendum on the amendment
to the state constitution that would allow blacks
to vote, Hartford Times, *September 26, 1865.*
Courtesy of the Connecticut State Library

voters" and "by September, Republicans realized the necessity of carrying the state."[29]

Little Connecticut once again played a mighty role. The *New York Times* noted that "the result of this vote will be awaited with considerable interest. Now that slavery has been abolished, it is certainly just and right that all the prejudices and hostilities of race which it engendered should give place to sentiments of justice and equal rights. Whether they have done so, or not, to any considerable extent in Connecticut, will be determined by this vote."[30] As the time of the election grew closer, Republicans within the state were worried. William Grosner of New Haven wrote to Massachusetts Senator Charles Sumner on September 5, remarking that many "feel that the influence of a defeat here in retarding the course elsewhere would be disastrous," yet "a great many Republicans flinch, especially in the country towns, and curiously enough in abolition districts. Some of our oldest radicals are more weak on this issue than the late converts from Democracy." Grosner also reported that in some towns, the Republican committees were hostile, and that "all this is unpleasant."[31]

The *Times* seemed to sense a chink in the Republican armor. In an article titled "Prejudice," the paper blasted the *Courant*, charging: "It is prejudice that does not permit the editor of the *Courant* to invite negroes to dine with him, commingle in the parties given by the family, and to associate intimately with his children." "He wars upon the prejudice against blacks," continued the *Times*, "and nurses a prejudice in his own heart." The newspaper repeated the argument that the white race would be degraded if it were mixed with the black race and blasted one of the key Republican arguments about black military service having saved the nation: "It is a humbug of proportions too monstrous." It was whites who "fought terrible battles and sacrificed thousands of lives," continued the *Times*, and "the white race owes the black nothing on account of the war. If the negro is not satisfied with the sacrifices that the whites have made for him, and the result of those sacrifices, he will be satisfied with nothing short of the abandonment of this government by the whites and the inauguration of his race into the sole control of it."[32]

The *Times* published a flurry of articles in the latter half of September that went utterly unmatched by the *Courant*. The Democratic press continued its arguments about white degradation, mongrelization, the lies of black military service, and blacks not being a party to the white social compact.[33] Only days before the vote, the *Times* peppered readers with a series of short pieces on the issue, each one promising that Republicans would never be satisfied with the suffrage victory: rather, "they will keep up the irrepressible negro conflict." The paper's editor cut to the core of what many voters themselves ultimately determined: "Slavery is abolished, and negro agitation ought to cease. But the fanatics are determined that it shall not. They mean to keep it alive and if they can carry the amendment on Monday, they will then bring the negro into political agitation in all our elections. To end this agitation, let the amendment be defeated."[34]

On October 3, the day after the election, the *Hartford Courant* did not give the outcome but listed only the results of towns that had announced their returns. The *Hartford Post* did not wait. "Connecticut has decided by a majority sufficient to be emphatic," announced that paper, "that the negro is not a man, that he has no political rights which white men are bound to respect." The next day the *Courant* admitted the amendment's defeat, by more than 6,000 votes, but—in a kind of damage control—insisted: "This is not considered by either side as a test of party strength, but merely as showing the firm hold which the old-time prejudice against the negro has upon the voters of our State."[35]

The *Times* did not delay in heralding what it viewed as a great victory. In an article titled "A White Man's State in New England," the paper announced that "Negro suffrage is defeated," continuing: "It is scarcely possible to overestimate the importance of this result, in its influence on the destiny of the nation. The ultras see it, and howl. . . . It is a triumph of

Connecticut in the American Civil War

CONNECTICUT.----THE RESULT.

A White Man's State in New England.

Negro suffrage is defeated. Whether the
majority against it proves to be Two or Five
Thousand is a matter of secondary importance.
The great fact stands out, that Connecticut, a
New England State, puts her seal of condemnation upon this mischievous scheme; and this
has been done essentially, by the conservative
Republicans, in spite of unusually severe
efforts of the Republican party managers to
whip them into a strict partizan vote.

The beginning of an article announcing the results
of the referendum, Hartford Times, *October 4, 1865.*
Courtesy of the Connecticut State Library

principle. It is more than the mere election of men to office."[36] The next
day, the *Courant* responded to Democratic crowing by, rather remarkably,
declaring: "What is the use of ascribing high and lofty motives to those
who voted either for or against the measure, when the greater number on
each side were without doubt actuated by no more sublime considerations
than at any other election."[37] Although the paper's earlier argument about
party strength was accurate — Republicans had largely swept the state in
town elections — it was Republican districts that had defeated the amendment. Apparently, some Republicans had voted against the measure and
others had refused to vote for or against it.[38] The assertion that the outcome reflected no "high and lofty motives" was an absurdity. Republicans
had held up the amendment as an essential testament of justice, equality,
and, very importantly, one of the key meanings of the war itself. That the
amendment lost so decisively left no doubts about where Connecticut
residents stood on matters of racial equality.

Nor was this fact missed by those outside the state. The *New York Times*
presented a lengthy analysis of the amendment's failure, announcing:
"The people of Connecticut have decided by about 5,000 majority, that
they will not permit negroes to vote. They are to be excluded from suffrage, not because they lack intelligence or capacity, but solely and simply
because they are black. That there is any reason for so broad and hostile
discrimination, scarcely anyone pretends. . . . The decision is purely due to
prejudice — to an unreasonable, unjust and cruel prejudice — against the

negro."[39] In addition to racism, the paper listed two additional reasons for the vote.

The first was that people had grown tired of the frenzied push for black rights and concluded that emancipation was reward enough. "It is the natural reaction of the anti-slavery excitement which has culminated in the war and in the abolition of slavery," explained the *New York Times*, and now that freedom has been realized, "appeals on his [the black man's] behalf have thus lost half of the force which slavery gave them. The nation has done so much for the negro and at such a cost, that it does not feel called upon just now to do much more."[40]

The second reason was the way Republicans went about pushing or, rather, forcing their message on the voters. "There can be no doubt that the country is tired and disgusted with the extreme and extravagant style in which the claims of the negro have been pressed," asserted the paper. "The claims, interests, courage and character of the whites have been made wholly subordinate to those of the blacks. There must in the nature of things be a reaction to all this — and the Connecticut election indicates that it has begun."[41]

William Lloyd Garrison's Boston-based *Liberator* was far less philosophical about the outcome. In the 1850s, Garrison had referred to Connecticut as the "Georgia of New England." Now, in an article titled "An Evil Decision," he wrote: "This exhibition of meanness on the part of a New England State will be of priceless value, it is so quotable in support of slavery, prejudice, and injustice, which form the sum of their political creed, and in their combination are known as Democracy." Garrison's insinuation regarding "Democracy" was that the Democratic Party had successfully defeated the amendment. He was wrong: Republicans were largely responsible. Regardless, Garrison recognized the imposing potential ramifications of the vote, stating: "If we should apply the Connecticut policy to the South, we must expect to lose most of the benefits we have derived from the war, and the conflict we had thought decided will have to be fought all over again."[42]

For the time being, the issue was finished in Connecticut. The 1870 passage of the Fifteenth Amendment to the federal Constitution, which said that a citizen could not be denied the right to vote based on "race, color, or previous condition of servitude," ultimately negated Connecticut's "whites only" clause. Nonetheless, it took the state until 1876—another six years — to actually adopt an amendment removing the word "white" from its own constitution.[43]

With the abandonment of black suffrage, Connecticut voters had turned their backs on justice and instead focused on healing, to use the words of David Blight cited previously. Remembrance and commemoration were the intimate companions of the war. Emancipation was not forgotten — the gaining of black freedom had been achieved through the sacrifices of Northern soldiers. Yet the echoes that resonated through time were more about the noble actions and sacrifices of those men than the strained, and untrue, abolitionist notion that they had fought primarily for liberation and equality.

The realities of the war, with all its bloodshed and death, instilled in the nation a ready understanding that much of the ground on which the fighting had occurred was hallowed. President Lincoln visited Gettysburg immediately after the great battle there and announced solemnly: "We have come to dedicate a portion of that field, as a final resting place for those who here gave their lives that the nation might live. It is altogether fitting and proper that we should do this." Fred Lucas, who witnessed the birth of Arlington Cemetery while helping defend Washington from the Confederates, had written home in December 1863: "This is a beautiful ground and is kept up in elegant style by the government. It already contains thousands of graves. It will doubtless be one of the memorable places connected with this rebellion, noted as is Gettysburg; and a place to be visited by travelers as well as relatives of the brave men who sleep there."[44] Thus, even before the war was close to an end and while its outcome was still unknown, people understood the great sacrifices it involved and realized that the men who fought deserved to be honored and remembered.

This understanding was no stranger to Connecticut. On July 28, 1863, the town of Kensington dedicated the state's, and certainly the North's, first Civil War monument. The town had lost six men in the previous two years of the war, and Reverend Charles B. Hilliard of the Congregational Church, an ardent supporter of the war, initiated a movement to create the memorial. The congregation raised $350, though many who were asked to contribute refused on the grounds that the South's cause was just and that secession was legal. Nelson Augustus Moore designed the twenty-foot-high stone obelisk, a fitting funerary design to memorialize death, carved from Portland, Connecticut, brownstone. The finished monument included Connecticut's seal and motto — *qui transtulit sustinet* (he who transplants still sustains) — the names of the deceased soldiers, and a simple message to remember those who had fallen:

Kensington Civil War Monument.

Soldiers

Erected to commemorate the death
of those who perished in suppressing
the Southern Rebellion.
"How sleep the brave who sinke to rest
By all their country's wishes blest."
1863.[45]

Kensington Civil War Monument showing
detail of the Connecticut State Seal.

On the dedication day, U.S. Senator Lafayette S. Foster spoke of the dead, declaring that "the wicked ambition of Southern leaders had brought upon [our] fair land all the horror and suffering we have been called upon to pass through during the last two years." The *Hartford Courant* reported that "the monument had been erected by the people of Kensington to the memory of those who have sacrificed their lives upon the altar of their country," and "its purpose is a noble one, to carry down to posterity, in an endurable form, the names of the brave heroes who fought and died in defence of their country, when a wicked and causeless rebellion armed itself to destroy the liberties of a free people. No better fame could award the true and brave."[46]

The next monuments erected in Connecticut came in the war's immediate aftermath. In 1866, four towns — Bristol, North Branford, Cheshire, and Northfield, whose monument is commonly referred to as being in Litchfield — dedicated obelisks to the memory of those who had died. The Bristol monument, in keeping with the theme of honoring the dead,

Bristol Civil War Monument.

was placed on the highest hill in the town's West Cemetery, and was also made of Portland brownstone, this time supplied by James Batterson. The obelisk was crowned with a large carved eagle, the traditional symbol of American nationalism. The names of the deceased solders were inscribed on the shaft, along with the names of the battles in which they died, and there were inscriptions that the monument was erected in "grateful re-

Connecticut in the American Civil War

Cheshire Civil War Monument.

membrance," and that "the sacrifice was not in vain." The North Branford monument, located on the town green adjacent to the Congregational church, was simpler in design, with no crowning features, though it offered greater detail on the memorialized soldiers, giving their names, units, places of death, and ages at death. The Cheshire obelisk, similarly simple in design and again located on the town green adjacent to the local

Northfield Civil War Monument.

Congregational church, was unique among the early monuments because it included the names Lincoln and Foote (referring to the president and to Admiral Andrew Foote, born in New Haven) on the pedestal. Originally, it included just fourteen names; on it was inscribed "erected to the memory of those who enlisted." The Northfield monument, located in Litchfield County, was slightly different, with a finial at the top, out of which pro-

North Branford Civil War Monument.

truded a flame. It too included Lincoln's name, as well those of the soldiers who had perished, and bore an inscription: "that the generations to come/ might know them."[47]

These early monuments show the overarching themes of the many memorials created in the coming decades. In his admirable 1993 study for the Connecticut Historical Society, David Ransom investigated 136 monuments spread throughout the state, virtually all of which were built between the end of the Civil War and the 1920s.[48] There appears to be no unifying building period or specific design elements. As early as 1867, designers had already developed memorials that moved away from the traditional funeral obelisk and were located away from cemeteries or churches. Still, the vast majority continued to use words such as "memory," "tribute," "honor," and "gratitude" or "grateful recognition." Very few of the structures, even those built in the twentieth century, referred to the war as the "Civil War." Rather, they referred to "the War of Rebellion" or "the War for the Union," or noted that the men had fought in "Defense of the Union" or to "Preserve the Nation," or—echoing Lincoln's words in the Gettysburg Address—that the "brave men . . . gave up their lives that the republic might live."[49] Two monuments, in East Hartford (1868) and Stratford (1889), quoted Andrew Jackson's famous statement, "the union must and shall be preserved," made in response to South Carolina's infamous 1831 attempt to defy the federal government.

Many of Connecticut's monuments focused on the idea of sacrifice, patriotism, and loyalty to the Union or the flag. Branford's 1885 tribute featured a standardbearer—a soldier holding a flag—atop a tall granite pedestal with the words "one country—one flag." Plainville erected a similar structure in 1913, inscribed "defenders of the flag," and Winsted's 1905 monument, technically in Winchester, was inscribed "loyalty to the flag of their country." The Winsted monument also focused on another important theme, the soldiers' patriotic service and the message to posterity that young men should follow their example if the nation was once again imperiled:

> This monument has been
> erected that all who come
> after them may be mindful of
> their deeds and fail not in the
> day of trial to emulate
> their example

Guilford's 1877 memorial highlighted the same point with its inscription: "that their example may spread to coming generations." And Watertown's 1908 granite column capped with a bronze eagle announced that the soldiers had earned "the admiration of succeeding generations and a place among the nation's heroes."

Some of the monuments also used the words "liberty" or "freedom," though not in reference to slavery or blacks. Farmington's 1872 obelisk

Thomaston Civil War Monument.

in Riverside Cemetery stated that "they gave their lives for our country and freedom," and Derby's 1877 bronze soldier on a granite pedestal commemorated the "defenders of liberty and nationality." Bridgeport's 1876 Seaside Park memorial proclaimed a "new birth of freedom," but connected it to the idea of maintaining a democratic government, and New Haven's 1905 Civil War Monument on Broadway referred to those who "offered their lives on the altar of constitutional government and human liberty." This is as close as any of the tributes got to anything more than a generalized democratic liberty, and even here liberty was connected to the idea of government.

This does not mean that there were no monuments related to colored soldiers or race, but they were few in number. The Hartford monument dedicated to Charles Weld and erected in the late 1860s is really a tombstone; located in the Old North Cemetery, it notes Weld's service as a lieutenant colonel in the 41st U.S. Colored Troops. The John Benson Marker in Stratford, erected around 1884, is also a tombstone and located in a cemetery; it observes that Benson was a member of the Connecticut 29th Colored Regiment.[50]

Certainly one of the two most significant commentaries on slavery and the more imposing issues of race connected to the Civil War is the Sailors and Soldiers Memorial Arch, created by Batterson and located in Hartford's Bushnell Park. Designed by George Keller and completed in 1886, it was the first triumphal arch in the United States. It is Connecticut's largest Civil War memorial, standing 160 feet tall, with each of its two towers 67 feet in circumference. Keller attempted to tell the story of the war and its commemoration in terra cotta friezes that included almost a hundred life-size figures, representing the many citizens of Hartford who had gone off to war. There are also six statues on the exterior of the towers, five of which depict a farmer, blacksmith, student, carpenter, and mason—the common men who dropped the tools of their trade and picked up rifles instead. The sixth statue, originally slated to be a merchant, was changed at the last minute to a slave, his shackles broken, holding a slate with the letters A, B, C on it—representing the educational uplifting of his race.[51]

The other significant reference to slavery on a Connecticut monument is Waterbury's Soldiers' Monument, under construction at the same time as the Hartford arch and completed in 1884. It is difficult to determine which structure first engaged the issue of slavery. The forty-eight-foot-high Waterbury pedestal with Lady Liberty at the top also includes four bronze figures, one of which is a woman seated with a book in her lap, in front of an eagle with the word "Emancipation" in its beak. The figure's foot is placed on a cannon, next to which is a broken shackle, and to the left of the woman's knee is a schoolboy, who is directly adjacent to a black child seated on a cotton bale and reaching for the book. The symbolism of the chains, cotton, and education is powerful, and uncommon for a Connecticut monument.[52] Indeed, it took more than a hundred years, in 2008, for the creation of a monument paying tribute to the state's black residents who fought in the war. In that year New Haven unveiled a memorial honoring the 29th regiment.[53]

The designs of Connecticut's Civil War monuments vary as greatly as the dates when they were completed and the organizations (private citizens' groups, community organizations, the state, the Grand Army of the Republic, and others) that supported their construction. Three towns — Madison (1897), Windsor Locks (1891), and Old Lyme (1921) — built memorial halls. In 1871, Wesleyan University created its Memorial Chapel. Other tributes focused on specific groups or offered particularly unique designs. New Haven's 1870 Knight Hospital monument focused on the work of that important institution and the men who died there. Danbury created an 1894 monument to "soldiers and sailors in unknown graves," and Winsted (1900), Canton (1903), and West Hartford (1904) all paid tribute to those "whose bodies were never brought home."

There were special tributes, too. Litchfield's 1894 monument called Mustered Out had a unique design, with a large granite drum signifying the drummer's tribute to those who left the service through death. Lebanon's 1922 memorial to five wars lionized Governor William Buckingham. The 1902 Mothers' Soldiers' Monument in Union was dedicated "to the mothers who gave their sons." Two memorials were specifically designated for those who died as a result of being interned in the Andersonville Prison Camp. The Banning and Rowe Monument in East Hartland (1870) commemorated John Banning and Rodolphous Rowe, both of the 16th CVI and both captured at Plymouth, North Carolina. Banning's inscription noted that he was "a martyr to this unholy rebellion." The other prison memorial, the 1907 Andersonville Boy statue, is located on the grounds of the state capitol and is a replica of the original placed at Andersonville, in Georgia, the same year. Both are dedicated to the "Connecticut men who suffered in Southern military prisons."[54]

Griffin A. Stedman is the only Connecticut soldier to whom two monuments are dedicated; the one at Barry Square in Hartford (1900) also marks the spot on which many regiments encamped before going to the South. Also particularly interesting is the Petersburg Express monument (1902), located at the entrance to the grounds of the state capitol — a

Sailor's and Soldier's Memorial Arch, Hartford.

Sailor's and Soldier's Memorial Arch showing detail of a slave.

thirteen-inch Sea Coast mortar used by the 1st Heavy Artillery during the siege of Petersburg, Virginia.

Some of the Connecticut monuments to Civil War soldiers were erected for specific occasions. Six monuments were built during the fiftieth anniversary of the war (1911–15). The most significant was Yale's 1915 marble hallway, inscribed with the names of the men who had attended the university and fought in the war. The inscription reads: "that their high devotion may live in all her sons and that the bonds which now unite the land

Waterbury's Soldiers' Monument.

*Waterbury's Soldiers' Monument showing detail of children
with a seated figure representing emancipation.*

may endure." The message was clearly about reconciliation, and the names inscribed on the walls included those Yale men who had fought for the Confederacy.[55] Another Confederate monument — really a tombstone — was erected in New London in 1977 to Major General G. W. Smith Stone, a Southerner who had married a woman from the town.

This brief discussion of the state's Civil War monuments would not be complete without a mention of my favorite monument, erected in New Britain in 1900. Located in the city's center, it is a particularly beautiful, fifty-one-foot-high limestone tomb crowned with a bronze winged Victory and featuring elegant architectural details. A remarkably comprehensive inscription conveys virtually all of the many themes seen in other monuments, along with noteworthy quotes from important historical figures:

New Britain Civil War Monument.

Oh rare and royal
was the sacrifice

With malice toward none
with charity for all
with firmness in the right
                    —Lincoln

This monument is built in
grateful remembrance of
the soldiers and sailors
who in the war to maintain
the union offered their
lives in the cause of mankind
that coming generations
taught by their example may
cherish the fruits of their
valor and devotion and make
their memory immortal

For you and me they
put their armor on

Let us have peace
            —Grant

For you and me they
stood in grim array
liberty and union
now and forever
one inseparable
            —Webster

They joined the mortal
struggle and went down

To heroes living
and dear martyrs dead
            —Lowell[56]

The New Britain monument represents something strikingly important about the many memorials' contemporary relevance. Do they continue to succeed in passing on the lessons of sacrifice and patriotism, as their creators hoped they would? How many people drive past this imposing structure in downtown New Britain each day, giving it little more than a glance?

When the various monuments throughout the state were erected, their dedications were imposing ceremonies at which thousands — sometimes tens of thousands — gathered to remember as a community the sacrifices of previous generations. Indeed, that was the point. With so much death, the people of Connecticut needed to know that the sacrifices, the sufferings, and the seemingly endless bloodletting had not been in vain. This is what they were told over and over again, as they attended dedication ceremonies and placed flowers each year on Decoration (or Memorial) Day on the graves of the Civil War dead.

———·———

The nation and Connecticut adopted the first formal, annual ritual of recognition and remembrance in 1868. Variously known as Memorial Day (the name we now use) or Decoration Day, it was observed on May 30, when towns and cities across the Union honored the dead by decorating their graves with flowers. The Grand Army of the Republic, a rapidly growing veterans' organization, was determined to make sure that "the loyal people . . . thronged to the heroes' graves and . . . vied with the surviving veterans in rendering homage to the beloved dead."[57] The *Hartford Courant* heartily endorsed the observance, noting that "we hope to see general observance on the part of our citizens of 'decoration day,'" and announcing that "all returned soldiers and sailors, the ladies, and citizens generally, are invited to join." The *Hartford Times* offered a rather curmudgeonly view of the day's purpose, decrying the "bands of music, military escorts, speeches, poems, &c." Instead, the *Times* wrote, "we cannot but think that the ceremony would be much more impressive, if the comrades of the deceased would go quietly and alone, in the early morning, and lay their offerings on the graves."[58]

These ceremonies, along with the continual stream of monument dedications, offered the residents of Connecticut a way of understanding the war. Certainly the most sought-after speaker at such events was General Joseph R. Hawley, a man who, as noted in chapter 5, epitomized devotion to the Union. He had marched out of the *Hartford Evening Press* office the moment that news had arrived of the firing on Fort Sumter, helped organize the 1st Connecticut Regiment, and then reenlisted in the 7th once his initial term of duty ended. He served throughout the war, sometimes coming home to recruit more troops, acquire supplies for his men, or help to rally an often dissent-ridden Republican Party. In 1866, he ran for governor and, despite his tremendous popularity, beat his Democratic opponent, James English, by a mere 455 votes. Hawley also chaired the 1868 Republican national convention in Chicago, served as president of the U.S. Centennial Commission in Philadelphia, and headed the national exhibition there in 1876. He served three terms in the U.S. House of Representatives (1872–73, 1874–75, and 1879–81), and he spent the last twenty-four years of his life in the U.S. Senate (1881–1905).[59]

The historian Ellsworth S. Grant noted that "almost a Hawley cult existed," and his speaking at commemorative events was essential. In 1886, a newspaper claimed that "no civic rite since the war has been thought complete unless the people were addressed by Senator Hawley."[60] His was a patriotism that knew no limits. He once announced: "I believe in the Fourth of July all over, from the crown of my head to the sole of my feet . . . I believe in the flag." His devotion also included the state: "I have no sovereign but Connecticut and Uncle Sam," and "Connecticut had the proudest history in the world." In dedication speeches, such as the one at Manchester in 1872, Hawley told crowds that Europeans claimed the United States "had no history," but that the Civil War had provided an even "nobler history" than the Old World's. The nostalgic storyteller loved to talk about the state's patriotic past. At the dedication of Hartford's Memorial Arch, Hawley went all the way back to Thomas Hooker and the Fundamental Orders, which he saw as Connecticut's great contribution to free government.[61]

Hawley's speeches invariably focused on American democracy — which he called "the grand experiment of government by the people" — and insisted that the war's meaning extended far beyond the borders of the United States. In Greenwich in 1890, he proclaimed: "We were fighting the battle of the centuries and the world . . . it was *for* the North, *for* the South, *for* the slave, *for* the master, for the whole people and *all* people. It was the battle of the World and of Humanity." At Mystic's Dedication Day in 1883, Hawley insisted that "failure of the republic would have put the world back a century," and that "some day this is to be the form of government for the world."[62]

Hawley's sweeping tributes to freedom and republican government rarely mentioned slavery, though he was a committed abolitionist even before the war. In a particularly long address at Springfield in 1886, he said that slavery was "the underlying cause" of the nation's "calamities" and that "universal liberty was established" with emancipation.[63] Yet these were only passing references. No one wanted to hear about the contentious racial issues connected to the war. Instead, people wanted to hear about national unity, the great sacrifice and devotion of the many who had lost their lives, and the labors of those on the home front. The many ceremonies held throughout Connecticut and the nation were about the nation's success, due to those who had come to her need in a time of great peril.

These ideas were never more apparent than at the momentous Battle Flag Day Parade on September 17, 1879. Hawley, of course, served as the grand marshal for the event, during which Connecticut's eighty war banners, the flags that had waved in victory and defeat over dozens of Southern battlefields, were carried from the State Arsenal to the newly completed State Capitol in Hartford. The General Assembly had passed a resolution in March 1879 directing that various regimental and battle flags should be prominently displayed in the capitol, and in September, tens of thousands of citizens packed Hartford streets as some ten thousand veterans marched.[64]

<hr />

These scenes of triumph and tribute were in obvious contrast to scenes of loss. But the ceremonies were meant to convey that loss, too. The war, so traumatic, was still a daily memory. Four years of such tremendous magnitude could not be easily forgotten. The reminders walked the streets of virtually every city and town. Though medical records from the war are dreadfully incomplete, Northern surgeons reported that some 21,753 men survived amputations; Congress promised them prosthetic limbs free of charge.[65] The *Courant* periodically ran articles on how to purchase or replace these devices.[66] Men bearing the scars of the conflict were constant reminders of war and sacrifice.

There were also those who bore no outward marks but who still suffered, some perhaps even more than those who had been physically wounded. We have only recently come to understand the concept of post-traumatic stress disorder. Before the Vietnam War, combat stress had been referred to as "shell shock" or "battle fatigue." During the Civil War, it was known as "soldier's heart." It is hardly surprising that men who watched their friends and relatives literally explode in front of them, men who saw the dead piled upon the fields of carnage, men who marched back over those fields months later and saw the remains of the fallen protruding from their shallow graves — that these men would be victims of a lasting and

Connecticut in the American Civil War

dreadful trauma. The outward manifestation of this suffering was seen in suicide, alcoholism, excessive opium use, public outbursts, and violent behavior. The great difficulty was that in this age of premodern medicine, few understood the sources of such behavior and little attention was paid to treating what today is understood as a psychological ailment.

There are very few histories of Civil War veterans and their mental illnesses, and none involving Connecticut soldiers.[67] As part of the ongoing study of Connecticut's Civil War experience, researchers have attempted to investigate the fates of more than a hundred soldiers who were treated at the Connecticut Hospital for the Insane, founded in Middletown in 1868 and today known as Connecticut Valley Hospital (CVH). Many of these veterans suffered from what was described as "alcoholism," "inebriety," "mental paralysis," "imbecility," "dementia," and "mania," all common terms of the time for what today would be recognized as potential symptoms of post-traumatic stress disorder. In an attempt to gain more information about these men, in 2009 scholars requested access to CVH patient records. These requests were denied based on the claim of physician/patient privilege. The scholars then filed a Freedom of Information Act request with the Connecticut Freedom of Information Commission, arguing that the hospital had been created and the men in question treated at a time when no physicians were licensed in Connecticut, and no recognized field of psychiatry existed. Because neither licensure nor confidentiality in this context existed in the late nineteenth and early twentieth centuries, the physician-patient privilege could not exist for records created at that time. Nonetheless, the researchers assured both the hospital and the commission that all soldiers' files would be treated with the utmost respect and that an effort would be made to track down the men's living descendants and gain their permission to publish information about their Civil War ancestors. The commission released its decision in April 2010, determining that the files cannot be withheld from researchers. This work is currently underway, but it could not be incorporated into the current study.[68]

That a great deal more needs to be learned about post-traumatic stress disorder among Connecticut Civil War veterans does not mean that no information currently exists. For example, Daniel Copperhilt was an English immigrant who joined the 15th CVI and was discharged in 1864 due to insanity. He lived for a time at Fitch's Home, the state and nation's first soldiers' home, located in Darien. Copperhilt ultimately escaped the facility in 1884 and, six years later, was found wandering aimlessly near his former home. Diagnosed with imbecility, he was transferred to the Hospital for the Insane. He had been a carpenter before the war. James Herrick, a teacher, was discharged in January 1863 from the 5th CVI on the ground of insanity. He was treated at Fitch's Home for mania and was transferred in 1891 to the Hospital for the Insane. He died soon after. Caleb Trowbridge was listed as an inebriate and was expelled from Fitch's Home nine times for alcohol possession, opium possession, and behaving violently toward the staff. During the periods when he was banned from Fitch's, Trowbridge was arrested four times. These stories are hardly unique, and are striking examples of the toll that war can take on the minds of men.[69]

It is obviously impossible to address in a single chapter the huge range of issues that faced veterans as they returned from war. It is, however, no exaggeration to argue that after the Civil War, Americans confronted the largest postwar adjustment in history, even to this day. Nothing can compare, on the front or at home, with the sheer scope of this conflict. That is why Decoration and Memorial Days, monuments, and the many speeches at their dedications, mattered so much. All were instrumental to the healing process. All Americans needed to know that their sacrifices had not been in vain. The monuments repeatedly told them so. And those monuments continued to be erected through the fiftieth anniversary of the conflict.

That semicentennial was the last great remembrance of the Civil War generation. Even a cursory examination of newspapers from the period reveals that veterans were dying at a steady rate in the early part of the twentieth century. The nation had changed a great deal in the intervening years. The war itself had resulted in a true explosion of industrialization, and the years that followed witnessed an increased shift from agricultural life to urban life, with a large influx of immigrants arriving on the nation's shores.

These changes did not dampen the ardor of Civil War memory. As the days grew closer to mid-April 1911, the *Courant* announced: "FIFTY YEARS SINCE THE FIRING ON SUMTER" and reported on a Grand Army of the Republic campfire to commemorate the event, at which Governor Raymond Baldwin and other dignitaries would speak. The paper noted that the anniversary fell on the coming Friday, and observed: "There was a lively Friday fifty years ago, when Fort Sumter was fired upon. If you doubt it, ask some one who remembers the excitement at that time. . . . Hartford, like the rest of the country, was stirred with indignation . . . the first shot carried the people into a frenzy."[70]

On April 12, the day of the firing on Fort Sumter, the *Courant* announced

Connecticut in the American Civil War

that "it would be appropriate if Hartford's welcome to the veterans of the Civil War today included the lifting of the hat [when passing] one of the country's defenders of a half-century ago." Over the ensuing months and years, many articles appeared, announcing veterans' gatherings, reminiscences, and the deaths of those who had served. Not everything that accompanied the commemoration, however, was flag waving and nostalgia. The paper also reported on April 21, 1911, that a veteran had committed suicide by hanging himself. Perhaps the stirring up of so many memories was too much.[71]

Other veterans reveled in the fanfare. Many of them had met on an annual basis since the war ceased, but they nevertheless understood that fifty years was a significant anniversary and that many of their comrades might not survive beyond the commemoration period. Age was now their most merciless foe. Still, they flocked to the streets and to the famous battlefields, such as Antietam and Gettysburg. They met with their Northern and Southern comrades. They remembered together. The Connecticut General Assembly even appropriated $10,000 to pay for the state's veterans to attend the Gettysburg anniversary. The *Courant* announced: "Blue and Gray Camp as Friends at Gettysburg."[72] President Woodrow Wilson spoke to the men, emphasizing the reconciliation that had occurred and the greatness of America. He insisted that the intervening years "have meant peace and union and vigor, and the maturity and might of a great nation. How wholesome and healing the peace has been! We have found one another again as brothers and comrades in arms, enemies no longer."[73]

There were also special events in Connecticut, events that remembered remembering. The state's first Civil War monument, in Kensington, was celebrated as a milestone of dedication and memory. As early as February 1913, plans were underway for a ceremony on July 29.[74] Governor Baldwin was present, along with U.S. Senator George P. McLean and a number of state politicians. Some 1,500 people gathered on the town green to, as the *Courant* described it, "honor a shaft of stone and the ideal that the shaft had represented for fifty years."[75] The many speeches echoed the themes of reconciliation, national unity, and the sacrifices of those who fell. McLean, the state's governor from 1901 to 1903, remarked that the Kensington monument, as a "little dull red shaft of Connecticut valley sandstone which we have met to talk about today may be a very indifferent object in itself but, when we read its message, and listen to its story, where will we find a grander and more beautiful memorial? This little block of stone has been preaching the sermon of ages."[76]

"The Blue and the Gray at Gettysburg, Assembly Tent, Gettysburg Celebration, Pennsylvania," 1913. Library of Congress, LC-USZ62-88416

But the senator did more than pontificate about nationalism and service. He also discussed the causes of the war, briefly, but with certainty. In what was almost a drum roll of questions, McLean pushed his audience, asking: "Have we forgotten the covenant which ran with the soil which this army redeemed with its life blood?" He answered his own question: "This little shaft of sandstone tells us today, as with tongue of flame, that the boys in blue died by the thousands for a stranger. . . . They died to square the account we had with the black man. It was a fearful price to pay but justice cares nothing for cost." So convinced of that was the senator that he repeated: "The boys in blue died to give the black man liberty and a chance in the world."[77]

It is ironic to read the senator's assurance that abolition was the war's purpose. Yet that irony extends far beyond the causes of the Civil War. By 1913, the Constitution included the Fourteenth Amendment, which defined citizenship and included black Americans in it, and the Fifteenth Amend-

Connecticut in the American Civil War

ment, which gave black men the right to vote. Yet in 1877, the North and South had agreed to a deal ending Southern reconstruction and pulling Northern troops out of the South. This was the product of the infamous presidential stalemate of 1876, when neither Rutherford B. Hayes nor Samuel Tilden garnered enough electoral votes to become president. The great compromise of the day netted Hayes the presidency in exchange for the end of military occupation and essentially the government's abandonment of the freemen. In 1896, the Supreme Court sanctioned segregation as constitutional, as long as it was "equal." But it wasn't, and the physical separation was merely an overt example of the unequal opportunities open to blacks since the end of the war. Add to all this the explosion of racial violence perpetrated by groups like the Ku Klux Klan and the very real terror of daily lynchings throughout the South, and Senator McLean's musings about giving the black man "liberty and a chance in the world" dry up and blow away far more easily than the sand that made up the stone of the Kensington monument.

The senator had insisted that "justice" had been the cause of the war. There is some element of truth in this, at least insofar as emancipation freed the slaves. Yet this was not the original rationale for the war, and many slaves took justice into their own hands by freeing themselves. Lincoln ultimately stepped up to the plate by issuing the Emancipation Proclamation, but that was initially a war measure, not an act of abolition. When the war ended, most white Americans concluded that emancipation was justice enough. The desire for the end of the fighting, for a physical and psychological peace, trumped any efforts to extend the war's justice to black Americans. Healing and reconciliation became the nation's focus. Emancipation was not wholly forgotten. It was the war's gift, and eventually many came to believe, as did Senator McLean, that the gift meant more than it really did. As David Blight noted so poignantly in discussing these issues, especially in the time between the war's end and its fiftieth anniversary, "romance triumphed over reality, sentimental remembrance won over ideological memory."[78]

Nor did things change with another fifty years of distance from the Great Rebellion. When the centennial arrived, the nation was in the midst of the largest racial turmoil since the Civil War period. The civil rights movement had begun to percolate during the 1950s, and by the start of the centennial commemoration in 1961, it had exploded onto the national scene. Black Americans were finally insisting on the completion of Civil War abolition, at least as far as basic rights of equality before the law. In 1954, the Supreme Court had agreed with them, in *Brown v. the Board of*

Education striking down *Plessy v. Ferguson* and declaring that separate was not equal.

Those commemorating the centennial of the Civil War did not take much notice. Their avoidance of slavery and race was conspicuous. Robert Cook's *Troubled Commemoration: The American Civil War Centennial, 1961–1965* admirably dissects the many difficulties connected with the anniversary.[79] Two of the larger issues were dodging the continuing sectional tensions and a rather rabid, crass commercialism. Moreover, the commemoration did not seem to resonate with the public. One critic noted that "the Civil War centennials are proving to be rather sedate affairs," adding in relation to the tensions within the national Civil War Centennial Commission that "there probably have been louder rebel yells in committee rooms than on the fields of glory."[80] Perhaps part of the reason why most Americans did not connect with the centennial was that they had just lived through World War II and the Korean War, and the conflict in Vietnam was rapidly heating up. Commemorating a war, even one that defined the nation, may have simply been too close to the recent conflicts.[81]

Connecticut was one of the many states that formed an official centennial commission. On August 27, 1959, Governor Abraham Ribicoff announced the appointment of fifteen men to the Connecticut Civil War Centennial Commission. Six came from the Hartford Civil War Roundtable, including the commission's chairperson, Albert Putnam, and such Hartford notables as J. Doyle Dewitt, president of Travelers Insurance, and John R. Reitemeyer, publisher and president of the *Hartford Courant*. Also among the group was the Pulitzer Prize–winning author Robert Penn Warren.[82] The commission focused on both public commemorations and academic productions. It published "The Connecticut Civil War Centennial: A Manual for Its Observance in the Towns and Cities of the State of Connecticut" and inspired the creation of some thirty-five committees in towns around the state.

The pamphlet was as much a marketing guide as a consideration of the war, though it clearly stated that all events should be tasteful, avoid commercialization, and highlight the war's meaning. It asked pointedly: "Why Commemorate the Civil War?" Part of the answer was that "the Civil War, like any other war, was a tragedy. Therefore its 100th anniversary, the Civil War Centennial, is not a celebration. It is a commemoration." Yet, continued the pamphlet, "the chief purpose of the Centennial is to strengthen the unity of the country through mutual understanding — an understanding derived from the realization that there was dedication and devotion on both sides. North and South, there were those who gave all they had in support of what they sincerely believed."[83] The commission also focused on the character of those who fought, the ideals of democracy and service to the nation, and the lessons of the war for modern Americans.

The reconciliation tradition continued. There was no mention of the war's causes; no mention of slavery; no mention of emancipation or race. A hundred years after the war, such topics remained taboo. A draft of the pamphlet was explicit: "The Centennial is no time for finding fault or placing blame or fighting issues all over again. . . . This is the time to recognize these divisive forces; but this is also the time to honor dedication and devotion, courage and honor, integrity and faith — qualities plentifully demonstrated in the War of 1861–1865 — and so needed for our survival in the years to come."[84]

The point was made even more clearly in a 1962 letter from James I. Robertson Jr., the executive director of the National Civil War Centennial Commission, to Albert Putnam, the chair of Connecticut's commission: "Only those of us actively engaged in commemorating impartially a war that drove wedges of dissension and defiance among our grandfathers can understand the ominous, awesome task we have. Clearly, the only way in which such an extended observance can be carried out with proper dignity and due reverence is to emphasize the accord that superceded animosity, and to treat with equal homage the sacrifices of blue and gray — both American as much then as now."[85]

Therefore, the Connecticut commission helped plan commemorative activities, created an extensive speakers' bureau, encouraged the *Hartford Courant* to run a yearlong series of articles in 1961, and produced a number of informative pamphlets on Civil War leaders like Joseph Hawley, John Sedgewick, and Andrew Foote, along with works on Lincoln's visit to Hartford and Connecticut doctors who served during the war. It also commissioned the writing of John Niven's *Connecticut for the Union.*[86]

Yet the commission could not always avoid racial issues. When planning for the hundredth anniversary of the Emancipation Proclamation and a ceremony to be held at the State Library, Colonel Egbert White, a member of the commission, wrote: "Would it not be fitting to have a negro read the Proclamation? The names that come to mind are Martin Luther King and Thurwood Marshall who is a Federal Judge. I am told Marshall is a talented speaker and of course King is also."[87] The fact that White got Marshall's name wrong (it was Thurgood) may have been a simple oversight, but it was one that spoke to the larger omissions of the centennial. Secretary of State Ella Grasso, later Connecticut's first female governor, read the Emancipation Proclamation.

Race continued to stalk the commission. When in 1963 the new governor, John Dempsey, was presented with an opportunity to appoint five new members, he received a letter from Republican State Chairman A. Searle Pinney, who noted that "no Negro is represented among the prominent writers, historians and Civil War authorities who make up the commission." Given the fact that "the Negro soldier, you will recall, played an important role in the war between the states," and that "deserved attention is being given to Negroes who have made notable contributions to society, the appointment of Connecticut Negro representatives to the commission would be particularly appropriate." Pinney even recommended some "splendid citizens."[88]

The letter inspired one Robert Maule to write the *Courant*, agreeing with Pinney but insisting that "a Negro civic organization submit names." Venting some of his disgust at the Democratic Party and the failure of blacks to stand up for themselves, Maule wrote: "As a Negro, I am quite concerned to think that in this century and year of 1963, here in Connecticut, we still find such bigoted conditions accorded people of color, and yet, not one Negro leader has come forth to ask why. It is inexcusable that such men as these who set themselves up to be leaders and represent the people, make such a mockery of themselves."[89] Governor Dempsey ultimately named eight new members to the commission, though only one of them, John E. Rogers, was among the "Negroes" suggested by Pinney. One other black resident of the state, Daniel I. Fletcher, was also appointed.[90]

Although the commission as an official body avoided addressing the war's causes and the racial issues that grew out of them, not all its individual members did so. At the opening of the commemoration in 1961, one commission member, Robert Penn Warren, published *The Legacy of the Civil War: Meditations on the Centennial*, in which he addressed the continued fascination with and importance of the war. He began simply: "The Civil War is, for the American imagination, the great single event of our history. Without too much wrenching, it may, in fact be said to *be* American history." Warren believed that there existed certain objective facts about the war, one of which was that "we became a nation, only with the Civil War." America's perpetuity, at least from within, would never again be challenged. Secession was dead. Another truth, he insisted, was that "the Civil War abolished slavery, even if it did little or nothing to abolish racism."[91]

It was here that Warren accurately stripped the vagueness from the nation's memory by dissecting what he called the South's "Great Alibi" and the North's "Treasure of Virtue." The "Great Alibi" was a potent aspect of the Lost Cause tradition, which excused Southern prejudice as noble. The "Treasure of Virtue" was the Northern myth that abolition had always been a goal of the war, that "slavery was the *sine qua non* of the War." Warren noted that "when one is happy in forgetfulness, facts get forgotten." He stated plainly that at the start of the war, Lincoln and the Republican Party had pledged to protect slavery where it existed, that Congress had stated that the war had not been started to interfere with the institutions of any states, and that the Emancipation Proclamation promised slavery's protection before it promised a slave's freedom, if only the rebelling states would return to the Union. Warren reminded readers who had forgotten that "racism was all too common in the liberating army. It is forgotten that only the failure of Northern volunteering overcame the powerful prejudice against accepting Negro troops, and allowed 'Sambo's Right to be Kilt'—as the title of a contemporary song had it." He also reminded Americans that they had "forgotten that racism and Abolitionism might, and often did, go hand in hand." "The Great Alibi and Treasury of Virtue," concluded Warren, "are maiming liabilities we inherit from the Civil War." Although the book was favorably reviewed for its "skillful and subtle analysis," it was a meditation that few wanted to ponder. Thus the centennial came and went, providing little more than the continued memory of reconciliation and healing. Justice was still elusive.[92]

When the Civil War ended, most Connecticut residents wanted relief from four years of shock and trauma. The aftermath of the war focused on precisely that reconciliation and healing. One symbolic example of reconciliation was the return of the portraits of former Democratic governors Thomas H. Seymour and Isaac Toucey to the walls of the state Senate chamber. They had been cut from their frames in the heated early months of the war, when both men had been outspoken in their opposition to fighting the South. The resolution removing them had allowed their return when the Senate was satisfied of the men's loyalty to the Union.[93] In the war's aftermath, it is uncertain what loyalty actually meant. For the South, it had been coerced at the point of a bayonet and the roar of the cannon. For the North, including Connecticut, it might have meant the acceptance of emancipation. It certainly didn't mean the acceptance of abolition, with its deeper pronouncements of racial equality and black rights. The state's residents gave remarkable testament to this fact when they defeated a referendum to remove the word "white" from the state's constitution. Black liberation had been enough of a reward for the heavy cost in blood.

The memory of the war, then, turned toward tribute to those who had served the nation. The monuments, Decoration Days, and the many dedications and speeches trumpeted a resounding message of service in time of peril. This was a noble and meaningful message. It was how the nation survived the awful, haunting realities of so much death. The many Connecticut monuments continue to stand. They continue to be refurbished, and in some places, new monuments are being erected. All provide ample evidence that the Civil War continues to resonate in the American mind. We continue to wrestle with its meaning and legacy.

Nothing reveals this more than attempts to commemorate its anniversary. The semicentennial and the centennial commemorations bore witness to these struggles. The centennial was by far the more controversial of the two, coinciding as it did with the 1960s civil rights movement. The commemoration sat like a lid on a boiling pot, which caused Warren to ask simply, but poignantly, if in 1961 Americans had yet learned the racial lessons of the war. "Sadly, we must answer no," he concluded; "We have not yet achieved justice. We have not yet created a union which is, in the deepest sense, a community. We have not yet resolved our deep dubieties or self-deceptions. In other words, we are sadly human, and in our contemplation of the Civil War we see a dramatization of our humanity; one appeal of the War is that it holds in suspension, beyond all schematic readings and claims to total interpretation, so many of the issues and tragic ironies — somehow essential yet immeasurable — which we yet live."[94] It remains to be seen if the commemoration of the 150th anniversary will reveal greater understanding and progress.

Epilogue

Connecticut's experience during the Civil War offers a window into a remarkable period in the state's history. Perhaps never in Connecticut's long past was there a time that revealed more division and more commitment. The war represented a national rift, which also played itself out within the state and its towns and cities. Connecticut's citizens both reviled the war to preserve the Union and reveled in it. Their disagreements were often violent. In the end, the state's support for the Lincoln administration depended upon the often narrow success of the Republicans and their critical attention to party politics. The most serious events were the elections of 1860 and 1863, in which a loss by Governor Buckingham could have spelled disaster for Connecticut's involvement in the war. The voting revealed the harrowing, razor-thin margin of support for the war.

For those who did come to the Union standard, the war demanded a striking degree of commitment and sacrifice. On both the military and home fronts, the people sacrificed for the nation. When President Lincoln called men to arms, Connecticut quickly organized three full regiments, not just the one he had requested. In all, the state provided thirty regiments, along with cavalry and artillery units. Almost half—47 percent—of men between the ages of fifteen and fifty served in the military. They fought, bled, and died in every major battle of the war. They served valiantly at Bull Run and covered the Union retreat there, battered down the seemingly impenetrable walls of Fort Pulaski, suffered horribly at Antietam and Fredericksburg, gained victory and redemption at Gettysburg, and drove the Confederacy to a slow, merciless death at Cold Harbor and Petersburg.

The men who fought the war—men like Samuel Fiske, Fred Lucas, and John De Forest—left us an important legacy: they wrote a constant stream of letters home, telling of the shock of battle, the misery of war, the importance of duty, the frustration with those at home, and the hope for peace. Not all survived or returned home uninjured. Fiske died—surrounded by his wife and family—at Cold Harbor. Lucas received a bullet through his leg that glanced off the bone and left him hobbling for months. He survived the war, returned home, and married Jennie Wadhams. They had corresponded for more than two years, since Jennie handed Fred a "testament" when he enlisted in 1862 and marched from Litchfield to the regimental encampment on the edge of town. De Forest survived the war uninjured and presented his experiences in a novel, *Miss Ravenel's Conversion from Secession to Loyalty*, which described warfare in all its horrible reality. His book, no doubt, was as cathartic as it was literary.

Nor was it merely men who fought the war. Women coordinated a massive home front operation. They created the nation's first soldiers' aid society in Bridgeport and formed others throughout the state. They provided a steady stream of every conceivable item, from linens, blankets, and shirts to food, books, and writing paper. It is no exaggeration to say that the war could not have been waged without their extraordinary efforts. They also received and cared for the flood of wounded and dead.

Connecticut's industry also poured forth a steady stream of support, from the deadly war materiel produced by Colt, Sharps, and the Eli Whitney Company to the patented artillery projectiles of Hotchkiss and Company, gunpowder from Hazardville, and ships from Mystic and New London. There was also less lethal production from the brass and rubber industries, as well as plenty of textiles for uniforms. All of this revealed an impressive industrial capacity that continued well after the war.

Those who sacrificed themselves "that the nation might live" — as Lincoln first said in the Gettysburg Address — represented a potent symbol of American nationalism. Their commitment to the Union's survival did more than anything else to carry the war forward. And the Civil War they fought defined our nation. It sealed the Union's permanence. It also sealed the fate of slavery, ending the peculiar institution forever.

Yet we should not take the confluence of the nation's survival and slavery's death to mean that the nation somehow aligned those two objectives during the war. As I have tried to make clear throughout this book, slavery was amazingly controversial in Connecticut. Milo Holcomb's letter in 1860 advocating slavery throughout the North; the Free Soil, Free Labor arguments of the 1850s; and the sometimes rabid disputes over race and slavery that occurred throughout the war years all reveal that fighting on behalf of black freedom and civil rights was not the primary motivator for most Connecticut residents. Even as emancipation came to be recognized as a military necessity, the idea of abolition, with its support of equal rights for blacks, was largely shunned. That was clear in the constitutional referendum of 1865, when the state's voters defeated the attempt to remove the word "white" from the definition of who could vote. In the years that

Connecticut in the American Civil War

followed, most people sought to forget the war's troubling legacy of race, and focus instead on remembrance and sacrifice.

Nonetheless, the controversy over slavery and race that preceded the war, accompanied the war, and followed the war (try as Americans did to deny it) continues to roil beneath the surface as one of the war's legacies and continues to be a monumental issue for the nation. That harsh truth challenges what many in the North today would like to believe: that the war was inaugurated on behalf of black freedom, and that Connecticut was a leader in that movement.

As the 150th anniversary of the Civil War begins, the significance of slavery as a factor in the war and the nation's present attitude toward racial inequality will continue to generate discussion. Indeed, they appeared the moment America elected its first African American president, in 2008. The *New York Times* columnist Thomas Friedman wrote in an article titled "Finishing Our Work": "And so it came to pass that on Nov. 4, 2008, shortly after 11 p.m. Eastern time, the American Civil War ended, as a black man — Barack Hussein Obama — won enough electoral votes to become president of the United States."[1] This simple statement reveals with poignancy the degree to which the American story continues to be defined by the racial impact of the Civil War.

Whether or not Friedman is correct in his conclusion is a matter of debate. One event — even the election of a black president — cannot erase the indelible impact of race-related events that have poured over this nation like a succession of monstrous waves.[2] The legacy of race, both nationally and in Connecticut, was and continues to be shaped by the institution of slavery and the catastrophic war that was connected to it. As one historian put it: "Too often, in too many ways, the enduring legacy of slavery, the Civil War, Reconstruction, Jim Crow, and even the modern civil rights era stick like a fishbone in the nation's throat."[3]

To some extent, America has been trying to dislodge that fishbone ever since the civil rights era. That watershed period changed the views of many. Still, it took another forty years for our nation to officially address the continuing tensions over its slave past. In July 2008, the U.S. House of Representatives approved a resolution apologizing for slavery and racial segregation, announcing that a "genuine apology is an important and necessary first step in the process of racial reconciliation."[4] A year later, in June 2009, the U.S. Senate followed suit. "It's long past due. A national apology by the representative body of the people is a necessary collective response to a past collective injustice," Iowa's Senator Tom Harkin insisted, arguing that "it is both appropriate and imperative that Congress fulfill its

moral obligation and officially apologize for slavery and Jim Crow laws."
Both resolutions included statements prohibiting slave reparations, the
payment to African Americans for the enslavement of their ancestors, a
topic that has been hotly debated.[5]

The apologies generated mixed reactions among both white and
black Americans. Many whites questioned the wisdom and meaning of
apologizing for something that happened long before they were alive;
indeed, even before their grandparents were alive. Slavery was something
to which they had no direct ties and for which, logically, they could not
be held accountable. Many black Americans considered the resolutions
"feel good" statements that were without real meaning if they were devoid
of reparations.[6] Perhaps the comments that garnered the most attention
were those of Chris Matthews, an MSNBC talk show host, who blasted
Tennessee Congressman Steven Cohen. "You're from what state?" asked
Matthews. "Tennessee. You're from a Southern state that was part of fighting the Civil War from the other side. What about people from Pennsylvania whose ancestors went down and fought, and fought the Civil War and
got killed? We lost 600,000 men in that fight in the Civil War who died
at point blank range. These guys were killed fighting the evils of slavery,
and now you want them to apologize. It makes no sense to me." "Why,"
demanded Matthews, "should the whole country apologize for what a
good half or more of the country got killed opposing, sir? I mean you're
from Tennessee. Maybe you should apologize first before you ask the rest
of the country to. Why should Pennsylvania apologize for something it
fought and died . . . you're laughing! It's not funny! Why should anybody
apologize for your sins?"[7]

From my perspective, Representative Cohen at that moment appears
to understand the history of slavery and race in America better than Chris
Matthews does, and Cohen tried to explain that past, to little effect. And
therein lies the problem. Matthews represents what many contemporary
Americans today believe about the North's involvement in the Civil War —
the Northerners were the good guys, motivated by morality to fight the
evils of slavery. If only it were that simple.

Connecticut too is confronted with these issues. On June 19, 2009,
the General Assembly passed a joint resolution "Expressing the Profound
Regret of the Connecticut General Assembly for the History of Wrongs
Inflicted upon Black Citizens by Means of Slavery, Exploitation and Legalized Racial Segregation, and Calling on All Citizens to Take Part in Acts of
Racial Reconciliation." Connecticut was the seventh state to pass such an
act, and the first in New England.[8] The apology, which generated the same

type of reaction that the national resolutions did, is yet another indicator of the degree to which the Civil War and the legacy of slavery continue to affect our nation today.

Thus there should be no question why historians see the sesquicentennial as perhaps the most important commemoration of the great war that has yet occurred. As the scholar David Blight has written: "This time, we must commemorate our Civil War in all its meanings, but above all we must commemorate and understand emancipation as its most enduring challenge. This time, the fighting of the Civil War itself should not unite us in pathos and nostalgia alone; but maybe, just maybe, we will give ourselves the chance to find unity in a shared history of conflict, in a genuine sense of tragedy, and in a conflicted memory stared squarely in the face."[9]

It will not be an easy task. On one level, the legacy of slavery affects even the planning of commemoration events, revealing clear and immediate divisions concerning how history should be told and who should tell it. Look at what happened nationally when the Republican governor of Virginia, Bob McDonnell, proclaimed April 2010 as Confederate History Month and made no mention of slavery. Instead, he announced the need to "understand the sacrifices of the Confederate leaders, soldiers and citizens during the period of the Civil War." Only later, after an uproar in the media, did he say that "there were any number of aspects to that conflict between the states. Obviously, it involved slavery. It involved other issues. But I focused on the ones I thought were most significant for Virginia." McDonnell later apologized, saying that the proclamation had "contained a major omission" and adding to it the statement: "It is important for all Virginians to understand that the institution of slavery led to this war and was an evil and inhumane practice that deprived people of their God-given inalienable rights . . . all Virginians are thankful for its permanent eradication from our borders, and the study of this time period should reflect upon and learn from this painful part of our history."[10]

Nor are such difficulties solely a Southern concern. When I met with the Connecticut Freedom Trail Commission in the summer of 2009 to discuss the commemoration and elicit both support for and participation in the statewide Connecticut Civil War Commemoration Committee, I was asked bluntly how many people on the committee are black. The answer at that time was zero, and I tried to explain that the committee was in the initial stages of organizing and that my visit to the Freedom Trail Commission that day was to expressly address the issue of African American participation. I also noted that the committee had been trying for some time, without success, to engage the Connecticut chapter of the

National Association for the Advancement of Colored People. Still, the commission's reaction was that the failure to contact it earlier was merely another example of black exclusion and meant that "others are attempting to tell our history." Shortly after the meeting, I received a concerned e-mail message from a colleague at Central Connecticut State University: "Active and prominent members of the Greater Hartford Community questioned me about the History dept's role in the Freedom Trail and the absence of a member(s) of the committee who 'looked like them' or a person of color pertinent to this history on your(?) committee. Needless to say, I was taken aback since I had no knowledge of the project and there was upset, consternation and unhappiness on the part of those who confronted."[11]

There is no question that the history of the Civil War as it relates to slavery and race is deeply personal and not always seen clearly by any one group. Mistakes can be made — and, given good intentions, rectified. Perspectives on history can vary, and if people are genuinely interested in engaging the past, they can learn much. One of the major challenges in understanding the Civil War is that it was not solely about slavery. As much as the topic interests me as a scholar, it is not the primary area of focus for many Civil War historians and buffs. Not all studies of the conflict address it. And though slavery and its importance to the conflict is certainly woven throughout the pages of this book, I have also attempted to tell the story of the amazing sacrifices by the men and women of Connecticut who rallied to the nation's defense, as well as the story of those who voiced their dissent.

I have tried to accurately tell Connecticut's story in this great and troubling history, and in the process bring to the fore the importance of slavery and race, showing how people in Connecticut saw those issues then and see them today as part of the larger meaning of the struggle. No matter what its causes or consequences, the Civil War was a shared struggle that has shaped our nation in ways both good and bad. Unless we recognize that our history is a shared history and the war was a shared struggle, I fear the war's more negative legacies will continue.

NOTES

Introduction

1 Milo A. Holcomb to Abraham Lincoln, July 29, 1860, Abraham Lincoln Papers, American Memory, Library of Congress, http://memory.loc.gov/ammem/alhtml/malhome.html.

2 William Lloyd Garrison to Amos A. Phelps, December 16, 1835, in *The Letters of William Lloyd Garrison, 1822-1835*, ed. Walter M. Merrill (Cambridge, Mass.: Belknap Press of Harvard University Press, 1971), 1:578.

3 Russell B. Nye, *Fettered Freedom: Civil Liberties and the Slavery Controversy, 1830-1860* (East Lansing: Michigan State College Press, 1949), 162. Leonard L. Richards (*Gentlemen of Property and Standing: Anti-Abolition Mobs in Jacksonian America* (New York: Oxford University Press, 1970], 40) concurred that "Connecticut remained the most inhospitable of the New England states."

4 *Norwich Courier*, July 31, 1833.

5 Quoted in *A Statement of Facts, Respecting the School for Colored Females, in Canterbury, Ct.* (Brooklyn, Conn.: Advertiser Press, 1833), 8–10. See also Jarvis M. Morse, *A Neglected Period of Connecticut's History, 1818-1850* (New Haven, Conn: Yale University Press, 1933), 195.

6 Quoted in Samuel J. May, *Some Recollections of Our Antislavery Conflict* (1869; repr., New York: Arno, 1968), 47. At a second meeting, the town selectmen declared that Crandall's school was designed "to promulgate their disgusting doctrines of amalgamation and their pernicious sentiments of subverting the Union" (quoted in Lawrence Bruser, "Political Antislavery in Connecticut, 1844–1858" [Ph.D. diss., Columbia University, 1974], 56).

7 *Journal & Inquirer*, May 2, 1857; quoted in Bruser, "Political Antislavery in Connecticut, 1844–1858," 365; [Thomas Day], "Sam and Sambo," *Hartford Daily Courant*, March 6, 1856.

8 "Connecticut Legislature — Special Session," *Hartford Daily Courant*, November 14, 1863.

9 "CONNECTICUT — THE RESULT. A White Man's State in New England," *Hartford Times*, October 3, 1865; "The Question of Negro Suffrage," *New York Times*, September 12, 1865; "The Connecticut Election," *New York Times*, October 4, 1865.

10 Niven, John, *Connecticut for the Union: The Role of the State in the Civil War* (New Haven, Conn.: Yale University Press, 1965).

11 According to 2000 U.S. Census figures, the population of Bridgeport is 139,529; New Haven, 123,626; Hartford, 121,578; Stamford, 117,083; Norwalk, 82,951; and Danbury, 74, 848.

12 The earliest source for figures on Connecticut soldiers is William A. Croffut and John M. Morris, *The Military and Civil History of Connecticut during the War of 1861–1864* (New York: Ledyard Bill, 1869), 800, which states that 54,882 soldiers served. Another work, Frederick H. Dyer, *A Compendium of the War of Rebellion* (Cedar Rapids, Iowa: Torch Books, 1908) has become an indispensable source on the history of regiments throughout the nation; Dyer gives 55,864 as the number of Connecticut soldiers. (Dyer's statistics are available on two websites: "The Civil War Archive," http://www.civilwararchive .com/unionct.htm, and "The Civil War Homepage," http://www.civil-war .net/searchstates.asp?searchstates=Connecticut.) Population figures and calculations are based on the 1860 U.S. Census for Connecticut, 36–41 (http://www2.census.gov/prod2/decennial/documents/1860a-04.pdf). Most recently, Blaikie Hines, *Civil War: Volunteer Sons of Connecticut* (Thomaston, Conn.: American Patriot, 2002), xii–xiii, states that 43,837 men from Connecticut enlisted, with 39,395 of them serving in Connecticut regiments.

13 Population figures and calculations are based on the 1860 U.S. Census for Connecticut. The census lists 6,726 persons as black, and 1,901 as mulatto, for a total of 8,627. Men accounted for 4,136, and of these, 2,206 were between the ages of fifteen and fifty. Just as with white troops, it is impossible to be certain how many of these men were actually from Connecticut. A look at the regimental muster roles does list the vast majority of men as from Connecticut towns. Still, this is not definitive. See *Record of Connecticut Men in the War of Rebellion, 1861–1865* (Hartford, Conn.: Case, Lockwood and Brainard, 1889).

Chapter 1. Connecticut within the Nation, 1776-1860

1 The archaeologist Warren Perry and colleagues noted: "The discovery of New Salem Plantation in southeastern Connecticut belies the myth of small-scale and benevolent African enslavement in New England" (Janet Woodruff, Gerald F. Sawyer, and Warren R. Perry, "How Archaeology Exposes the Nature of African Captivity and Freedom in Eighteenth Century Connecticut," *Connecticut History* 46, no. 2 [Fall 2007]: 155–83).

2 Jackson Turner Main, *Society and Economy in Colonial Connecticut* (Princeton, N.J.: Princeton University Press, 1983), 176–81, table 5.1, indicated that there were more than 6,000 slaves in Connecticut at the time of the American Revolution. Lorenzo Greene, *The Negro in Colonial New England, 1620–1776* (New York: Columbia University Press, 1942), 74–75, stated that the highest number of slaves within the state was 6,273, in 1782. See also

Joanne Pope Melish, *Disowning Slavery: Gradual Emancipation and "Race" in New England, 1780–1860* (Ithaca, N.Y.: Cornell University Press, 1998); Guocun Yang, "From Slavery to Emancipation: The African Americans of Connecticut, 1650s–1820s" (Ph.D. diss., University of Connecticut, 1999). Bruce Stark disputes the figure of over 6,000, noting that the actual figure for 1774 is 5,083 because Native Americans had been incorrectly counted as slaves ("Slavery in Connecticut: A Re-Examination," *The Connecticut Review* 9 [November 1975]: 75–81).

3   Winthrop Jordan, "The Influence of the West Indies on the Origins of New England," *The William and Mary Quarterly*, 3rd ser., 18, no. 2 (April 1961): 243–50; Main, *Society and Economy in Colonial Connecticut*; Myron O. Stachiw, "For the Sake of Commerce: Slavery, Antislavery, and Northern Industry," in *The Meaning of Slavery in the North*, ed. David Roediger and Martin H. Blatt (New York: Garland, 1998); Jay Coughtry, *The Notorious Triangle: Rhode Island and the African Slave Trade, 1700–1807* (Philadelphia: Temple University Press, 1981); *Traces of the Trade*, directed by Katrina Browne (Boston: Ebb Pod Productions, 2008); Anne Farrow, Joel Lang, and Jenifer Frank, *How the North Promoted, Prolonged, and Profited from Slavery* (New York: Ballantine, 2005); Paul E. Rivard, *A New Order of Things: How the Textile Industry Transformed New England* (Hanover, N.H.: University Press of New England, 2002).

4   The paragraph reads: "He has waged cruel war against human nature itself, violating its most sacred rights of life & liberty in the persons of a distant people who never offended him, captivating & carrying them into slavery in another hemisphere, or to incur miserable death in their transportation thither. This piratical warfare, the opprobrium of infidel powers, is the warfare of the CHRISTIAN king of Great Britain. Determined to keep open a market where MEN should be bought & sold, he has prostituted his negative for suppressing every legislative attempt to prohibit or to restrain this execrable commerce: and that this assemblage of horrors might want no fact of distinguished die, he is now exciting those very people to rise in arms among us, and to purchase that liberty of which he has deprived them, & murdering the people upon whom he also obtruded them; thus paying off former crimes committed against the liberties of one people, with crimes which he urges them to commit against the lives of another" (Thomas Jefferson, rough draft of the Declaration of Independence, Papers of Thomas Jefferson, http://www.princeton.edu/~tjpapers/declaration/declaration.html).

5   Melish, *Disowning Slavery*; Greene, *The Negro in Colonial New England*; Leon Litwack, *North of Slavery: The Negro in the Free States, 1790–1860* (Chicago: University of Chicago Press, 1961); Edgar J. McManus, *Black Bondage in the North* (Syracuse, N.Y.: Syracuse University Press, 1973).

6 Yang, "From Slavery to Emancipation, 38–39; Charles J. Hoadly, ed., *Public Records of the Colony of Connecticut* (Hartford, Conn.: Brown and Parsons, 1850–90), 4:40. The records are also available online (http://www.colonialct .uconn.edu).

7 "Act for the Punishment of Those that Receive Money from Negros, etc.," in Hoadly, ed., *Public Records of the Colony of Connecticut*, 5:52–53. Other slave regulations appear in 6:390–91 and 7:290.

8 Greene, *The Negro in Colonial New England*, 312–13. Some scholars have questioned whether this law was ever effectively enforced. See Barbara W. Brown and James M. Rose, *Black Roots in Southeastern Connecticut* (New London, Conn.: New London County Historical Society, 2001).

9 "An Act for the Punishment of Negros, Indian and Molatto [sic] Slaves, for Speaking Defamatory Words," in Hoadly, ed., *Public Records of the Colony of Connecticut*, 7:290.

10 "An Act for Prohibiting the Importation of Indian, Negro or Molatto Slaves," in Hoadly, ed., *Public Records of the Colony of Connecticut*, 14:329. See also David Menschel, "Abolition without Deliverance: The Law of Connecticut Slavery 1784–1848," *Yale Law Journal* 111, no. 1 (October 2001): 191–94. Menschel notes: "The 1774 law was not motivated by humanitarian impulses — at least not humanitarian toward slaves. The preamble to the Act states that 'the increase of slaves in this Colony is injurious to the poor and inconvenient.'" For additional commentary on restrictions imposed on slaves, see Greene, *The Negro in Colonial New England*, 138; McManus, *Black Bondage in the North*, 73, 75.

11 Melish, *Disowning Slavery*, 69–70. The law stipulated: "No Negro or Molatto [sic] Child, that shall, after the first Day of March, One Thousand seven hundred and eight-four, be born within this State, shall be held in Servitude, longer than until they arrive to the Age of twenty-five Years, notwithstanding the Mother or Parent of such Child was held in Servitude at the Time of its Birth; but such Child, at the Age aforesaid, shall be free; any Law, Usage or Custom to the contrary notwithstanding" ("An Act Concerning Indian, Molatto, and Negro Servants and Slaves," in *Acts and Laws of the State of Connecticut in America* [Hartford, Conn.: Elisha Babcock, 1786], 233–35).

12 Menschel, "Abolition without Deliverance," 186–87. Menschel also noted: "In some senses, the 1784 law made slave life more uncertain because the law created incentives for slaveholders to export their bondspeople from Connecticut."

13 The historian James Essig questioned both the commitment and the effectiveness of this first abolition society, arguing that it was founded as much in response to a growing crisis over the churches' social relevance as because of as any great desire to fight on behalf of slaves. Meeting minutes show that

members denounced slavery in the South but insisted that slavery in Connecticut "was always distinguished by that mildness and clemency which accorded the characters of their masters." Essig concluded that to the men in the society, "the existence of slavery was distasteful, even embarrassing, but not really alarming; slaves were sad to be in bondage, but happy to be in Connecticut" (James D. Essig, "Connecticut Ministers and Slavery, 1790–1795," *Journal of American Studies* 15 [April 1981]: 7–44). Another author noted that the early abolition sentiment in the state may have died off as the free black population grew. See John J. O'Connell, "The Abolitionist Movement in Connecticut, 1830–1850" (master's thesis, Trinity College, 1971), 19.

14   "An Act for the Abolition of Slavery in this State, and To Provide for the Education and Maintenance of Such as Shall be Emancipated Thereby," 1794, Misc. Papers, Ser. 2, Vol. 1, Doc No. 56, Connecticut State Library, Hartford; "An Act in Addition to An Act Entitled 'An Act Concerning Indian, Mulatto and Negro Servants and Slaves,'" in Charles J. Hoadly, ed., *Public Records of the State of Connecticut* (Hartford, Conn.: Brown and Parsons, 1850), 9:38–39. For instance, the following acts became law: "An Act to Repeal Part of An Act Entitled 'An Act for the Punishment of Defamation,'" in Hoadly, ed., *Public Records of the State of Connecticut*, 9:91; and "An Act to Repeal Certain Paragraphs of An Act Entitled 'An Act Concerning Indian Mulatto and Negro Servants and Slaves,'" 9:92.

15   Menschel, "Abolition without Deliverance," 208–13; Melish, *Disowning Slavery*, 90, 101, 102, 104; Litwack, *North of Slavery*, 15.

16   Melish, *Disowning Slavery*, chapter 2, has an extended discussion of gradual emancipation and, in particular, Levi Hart's 1775 gradual emancipation plan, called "Some Thoughts on the Subject of Freeing the Negro Slaves in the Colony of Connecticut, humbly offered to the Consideration of all friends of liberty & Justice." See also Arthur Zilversmit, *First Emancipation: The Abolition of Slavery in the North* (Chicago: University of Chicago Press, 1967); Menschel, "Abolition without Deliverance," 190–91, 198.

17   1818 Constitution of the State of Connecticut, art. 6, sect. 2, http://www.sots .ct.gov/sots/cwp/view.asp?a=3188&q=392280. Connecticut was the exception in New England, where other states enfranchised free blacks. The exclusion of black voting rights actually began in 1814, when the General Assembly enacted a law that defined a "freeman" as a free white man. See "An Act in Further Addition to An Act Entitled An Act for Regulating the Election of the Governor, Lieutenant Governor, Assistants, Etc.," in Hoadly, ed., *Public Records of the State of Connecticut*, 17:49. See also David W. Wills, "Beyond Commonality and Plurality: Persistent Racial Polarity in American Religion and Politics," in *Religion and American Politics: From the Colonial Period to the 1980s*, ed. Mark A. Noll (New York: Oxford University Press, 1990), 205.

18 David Waldsteicher, *Slavery's Constitution: From Revolution to Ratification* (New York: Hill and Wang, 2009); John P. Kaminski, ed., *A Necessary Evil? Slavery and the Debate over the Constitution* (Madison, Wisc.: Madison House, 1995).

19 *Selections from the Letters and Speeches of the Hon. James H. Hammond, of South Carolina* (New York: John F. Trow, 1866), 317. See also C. Wayne Smith and J. Tom Cothren, eds., *Cotton: Origin, History, Technology, and Production* (New York: Wiley, 1999); South Carolina Cotton Museum, *The History of Cotton* (Virginia Beach, Va.: Donning, 2005), distributed by the University of South Carolina Press; Thomas R. Beardsley, *Willimantic Industry and Community: The Rise and Decline of a Connecticut Textile City* (Willimantic, Conn.: Windham Textile and History Museum, 1993).

20 Donald R. Hickey, *The War of 1812: A Forgotten Conflict* (Urbana: University of Illinois Press, 1989).

21 Matthew Mason, *Slavery and Politics in the Early American Republic* (Chapel Hill: University of North Carolina Press, 2006), 61, introduction.

22 Mason, *Slavery and Politics in the Early American Republic*; Robert Pierce Forbes, *The Missouri Compromise and Its Aftermath: Slavery & the Meaning of America* (Chapel Hill: University of North Carolina Press, 2007).

23 There was a second Missouri Compromise in 1821, which was essentially an agreement that Missouri would not pass a constitutional amendment barring free blacks from entering the state. Many Northerners viewed this as a fundamental denial of the rights in the federal Constitution: "The citizens of each state shall be entitled to all privileges and immunities of citizens in the several states" (art. 4, sect. 2). This, of course, begged the question of whether or not blacks, even free blacks, were citizens, something that would be decided some twenty-five years later in the infamous 1857 *Dred Scott* decision.

24 Historians have remarked that much of the nation was focused more on the effects of a major recession, the Panic of 1819, than it was on the sectional battle in Congress. This may have been true of Connecticut. Some Northerners viewed the Missouri crisis as an opportunity for a Federalist resurgence, a comeback to permit revenge on the Republicans for earlier losses. This idea played a role for some Northern legislators, causing them to vote for compromise measures in the belief that a speedy resolution was needed to stop any Federalist plot. Newspapers from Pennsylvania to Maine addressed this issue, some insisting that another Hartford Convention had come to pass. See Glover Moore, *The Missouri Controversy, 1819–1821* (Lexington: University of Kentucky Press, 1953), 160, 188–89.

25 "Slavery," *Connecticut Courant*, March 14, 1820; "The Slave Question," *Hartford Daily Times*, March 21, 1820; Forbes, *The Missouri Compromise and*

Its Aftermath, 99–100. Mason (*Slavery and Politics in the Early American Republic*, 210, 217) questioned the degree to which voting for or against the compromise affected a politician's political future.

26   Quoted in *Connecticut Courant*, May 9, 1820. The *Courant* responded to Governor Wolcott's speech, stating: "When the vote of the House of Representatives, which yielded an extension of slavery to Missouri, was first communicated to the inhabitants of this state, a universal burst of indignation flowed from all, without distinction of party. It was a spontaneous effusion of feeling, which resulted from the native abhorrence to slavery" ("Governor's Speech," *Connecticut Courant*, May 16, 1820).

27   "Prohibition of Slavery in Missouri," *Congressional Globe*, No. 481, Senate, 16th Cong., 1st Sess., January 18, 1820.

28   Thomas Jefferson to John Holmes, April 22, 1820, Library of Congress, http://www.loc.gov/exhibits/jefferson/159.html.

29   Richard P. McCormick, *The Second American Party System: Party Formation in the Jacksonian Era* (New York: Norton, 1973); Michael F. Holt, *The Political Crisis of the 1850s* (New York: Norton, 1978); Donald B. Cole, *Martin Van Buren and the American Political System* (Princeton, N.J.: Princeton University Press, 1984).

30   Mathew Carey, *Letters on the colonization society; with a view of its probable results, under the following heads: the origin of the society; increase of the coloured population; manumission of slaves in this country; declarations of legislatures, and other assembled bodies, in favour of the society; situation of the colonists at Monrovia and other towns . . . Addressed to the Hon. C.F. Mercer . . .* (Hartford, Conn.: P. B. Gleason, 1832); O'Connell, "The Abolitionist Movement in Connecticut"; Donald M. Bishop, "The African Colonization Movement in Connecticut, 1816–1840" (master's thesis, Trinity College, 1967). The historian George F. Frederickson noted that moderate antislavery proponents were attracted to colonization (*Black Image in the White Mind: The Debate on Afro-American Character and Destiny, 1817–1914* [Middletown, Conn.: Wesleyan University Press, 1987]).

31   Jonathon Mayhew Wainwright, *A Discourse, on the Occasion of Forming the African Mission School Society, Delivered in Christ Church, in Hartford, Connecticut on . . . August 10, 1828 . . .* (Hartford, Conn.: H. and F. J. Huntington, 1828), 18. See also Melish, *Disowning Slavery*, 216.

32   "American Colonization Society," *Norwich Courier*, October, 28, 1829. The author also quoted a speech made by Reverend Thomas Hopkins Gaulladet, principal of the Deaf and Dumb Asylum at Hartford, who insisted: "The southern gentlemen ought not to have all the blame attached to them for the sin of slavery; even at this moment . . . in my own native state of *Connecticut*, we have about 30 slaves!" Regarding emancipation, he remarked: "We did

not do it until it was found quite convenient; and then what provision was made for the poor black? Let our State Prison records answer the question."

33 "An Act Concerning Crimes and Punishments," *The Public Statute Laws of the State of Connecticut* (Hartford, Conn.: John L. Boswell, 1839), May session, 1830, chap. 1, sect. 19; Jarvis M. Morse, *A Neglected Period of Connecticut's History, 1818-1850* (New Haven, Conn.: Yale University Press, 1933), 192.

34 O'Connell, "The Abolitionist Movement in Connecticut," 20–27, provides a good breakdown of societies by town. See also Lawrence Bruser, "Political Antislavery in Connecticut, 1844–1858" (Ph.D. diss., Columbia University, 1974), 49, 50, 59.

35 Hugh Davis, *Leonard Bacon: New England Reformer and Antislavery Moderate* (Baton Rouge: Louisiana State University Press, 1998); James Brewer Stewart, *Abolitionist Politics and the Coming of the Civil War* (Amherst: University of Massachusetts Press, 2008); David E. Swift, *Black Prophets of Justice: Activist Clergy before the Civil War* (Baton Rouge: Louisiana State University Press, 1989).

36 Simeon Jocelyn, *Constitution of the American Society of Free Persons of Color for Improving their Condition* (1831, n.p.), Yale Slavery Pamphlets #86, Beinecke Rare Book and Manuscript Library, Yale University, New Haven, Connecticut.

37 "Negro College," reprinted in *Connecticut Courant*, September 20, 1831. See also Hilary J. Moss, "Education's Inequity: Opposition to Black Higher Education in Antebellum Connecticut," *History of Education Quarterly* 46, no. 1 (Spring 2006): 16–35.

38 Quoted in "For the Norwich Courier to the American Colonization Society," *Norwich Courier*, March 27, 1833.

39 Quoted in Samuel J. May, *Some Recollections of Our Antislavery Conflict* (1869; repr., New York: Arno, 1968), 47. A second meeting of the town selectmen declared that Crandall's school was designed "to promulgate [abolitionists'] disgusting doctrines of amalgamation and their pernicious sentiments of subverting the Union" (quoted in Bruser, "Political Antislavery in Connecticut," 56.).

40 *A Statement of Facts, Respecting the School for Colored Females, in Canterbury, Ct.* (Brooklyn, Conn.: Advertiser Press, 1833), 8–10.

41 "An act in addition to an Act entitled 'An Act for the admission and settlement of Inhabitants of Towns," Connecticut General Assembly (http://www.yale.edu/glc/crandall/02.htm); Morse, *A Neglected Period of Connecticut's History*, 195.

42 "An act in addition to an Act entitled 'An Act for the admission and settlement of Inhabitants of Towns,'" Connecticut General Assembly (http://www.yale.edu/glc/crandall/02.htm); Leonard L. Richards, *Gentlemen of Property and*

Standing: Anti-Abolition Mobs in Jacksonian America (New York: Oxford University Press, 1970), 39–40; Morse, *A Neglected Period of Connecticut's History*, 195. At least one historian has noted that the Crandall affair caused some Northerners to question slavery and join the opposition to it. See Bernard Steiner, *History of Slavery in Connecticut* (Baltimore: Johns Hopkins University Press, 1893), 67. See also O'Connell, "The Abolitionist Movement in Connecticut," 13–14.

43 Melish, *Disowning Slavery*, 137. Morse wrote: "The [Crandall] affair demonstrated very forcibly that most Connecticut people were not at all kindly disposed to the negroes within their doors" (*A Neglected Period of Connecticut's History*, 196). And Mason wrote: "What held white Northerners and Southerners together on the American Colonization Society was a conviction that free African Americans posed an unacceptable risk to the American social order. In most public and moderate documents, its leaders depicted free blacks as degraded, discontented, and thus dangerous 'banditti,' arguing that colonization was as much an act of self-interested patriotism as humanity" (*Slavery and Politics in the Early American Republic*, 113). Litwack also noted that "emancipation could not erase the idea that blacks were inferior" (*North of Slavery*, 15).

44 William Lloyd Garrison to Amos A. Phelps, December 16, 1835, in *The Letters of William Lloyd Garrison, 1822–1835*, ed. Walter M. Merrill (Cambridge, Mass.: Belknap Press of Harvard University Press, 1971), 1:578.

45 Richards, *Gentlemen of Property and Standing*, 40. See also David Grimsted, *American Mobbing, 1828–1861: Toward Civil War* (New York: Oxford University Press, 1998). Though these numbers are certainly significant, it is unclear how many people overall belonged to the anti-abolition movement, or the extent to which it represented general opinion in Connecticut. See Morse, *A Neglected Period of Connecticut's History*, 196–97, for examples of anti-black mobs. The historian David Swift noted that "when black efforts to 'elevate the race' took hold in Connecticut, assisted by white abolitionists, white opposition was occasionally vehement and violent" (*Black Prophets of Justice*, 181).

46 *Norwich Courier*, July 31, 1833.

47 "Negro College." Others engaged in a similar amnesia regarding slavery in Connecticut. Leonard Bacon of New Haven announced: "Slavery never existed here to any considerable extent, and for years it has been a thing unknown" (*A Plea for Africa, Delivered in New-Haven, July 4, 1825* [New Haven, Conn.: T. G. Woodward, 1825], 12). See also Melish, *Disowning Slavery*, 214–15.

48 *Connecticut Courant*, August 31, 1835. See also *Connecticut Courant*, August 12, 1833: "There are few, we believe, who will seriously contend that Congress

can adopt measures for the abolition of slavery, or that this result can be brought about in any other way than the voluntary action of the masters themselves. It would seem, therefore, that the inexpediency of any course which only tends to irritate and inflame those who alone have the power to emancipate the salver, must be sufficiently obvious. The effect cannot fall to aggravate the condition of the slave, and render his prospect of freedom darker than ever." It should be noted that the newspapers quoted represent both Democratic and Whig viewpoints, indicating that both parties attacked antislavery agitation.

49 "Public Disturbance," reprinted in *Connecticut Courant*, December 10, 1836.

50 Morse, *A Neglected Period of Connecticut's History*, 193. For antislavery sentiment in Middletown, see Thomas E. La Lancette, *A Noble and Glorious Cause: The Life, Times and Civil War Service of Captain Elijah W. Gibbons* (Middletown, Conn.: Godfrey Memorial Library, 2005), 5.

51 Quoted in *Connecticut Courant*, January 18, 1836.

52 On the refusal of the use of Hartford's City Hall, O'Connell concluded: "This violent opposition to one of the most important antislavery meetings in the State's history was symptomatic of the pervasive hostility of the majority of Connecticut citizens which had been present since the first abolition stirrings in the State" ("The Abolitionist Movement in Connecticut," 29). This opposition and violence was also seen in a number of places: in 1839 the Wolcott Congregational Church was burned the day before an antislavery meeting was scheduled; in the same year, Gerrit Smith, speaking in New Haven, was accosted by a crowd and pelted with rotten eggs; in 1842 in Madison, a committee was formed to discourage abolitionist lectures; in 1848, a mob of three hundred people attacked the office of the antislavery newspaper, the *Charter Oak* (34–35).

53 Quoted in "Meeting at New Haven," *Connecticut Courant*, September 21, 1835.

54 "Governor's Message," *Connecticut Courant*, May 9, 1836.

55 Swift, *Black Prophets of Justice*, 196.

56 "An Act for the fulfillment of the Obligations of this State, Imposed by the Constitution of the United States, in Regard to Persons Held to Service or Labor in One State Escaping into Another, and to Secure the Right of Trial by Jury, the Cases Herein Mentioned," *The Public Statute Laws of the State of Connecticut*, May session, 1838, chap. 37.

57 "An Act to Repeal an Act Therein Mentioned and for Other Purposes," *Public Acts Passed By the General Assembly of the State of Connecticut*, (Hartford, Conn.: Office of the Secretary of State, 1844), May session, 1844, chap. 27. Pennsylvania had enacted an 1826 law similar to Connecticut's 1838 statute.

The Supreme Court's ruling was somewhat ambiguous. The Court said that the fugitive slave recovery process was controlled by the Constitution and that, therefore, Pennsylvania's process was unenforceable. On the other hand, the Court said that the Constitution does not require state officials to take any action to assist in enforcement of the federal process. The decision effectively left it up to the states to decide whether to require state officials to be involved (*Prigg v. Pennsylvania*, 41 U.S. 539 [1842]). Whether intentionally or not, this created a loophole for the antislavery states.

58 *Report of the Joint Select Committee to Whom Was Referred Sundry Petitions Relative To the Subject of Slavery* (Hartford, Conn.: Patriot Office, 1839), 6, 5. This report is particularly remarkable because it came from a Whig-dominated General Assembly. The report also sounded like a precursor to the Supreme Court's 1896 *Plessy v. Ferguson* decision in its insistence that giving blacks rights was an innovation in the social system. The Court stated: "If no such equality exists — if in social concerns and relations of society, the colored population is regarded as a distinct and inferior race, the proposition to admit them to a full participation of political power, can be regarded in no other light, than a proposition to promote by legislation, an equality in social condition, between the two races." And the report argued that most residents of Connecticut were opposed to interfering with the domestic concerns of other states and that it was fanatic abolitionists who were agitating about the issue. See also Bruser, "Political Antislavery in Connecticut," 60–61; Morse, *A Neglected Period of Connecticut's History*, 331.

59 Howard Jones, *Mutiny on the Amistad: The Saga of a Slave Revolt and Its Impact on American Abolition, Law, and Diplomacy* (New York: Oxford University Press, 1988). See also Morse, *A Neglected Period of Connecticut's History*, 197–203; O'Connell, "The Abolitionist Movement in Connecticut," 36.

60 *Hartford Daily Courant*, January 18, 1840.

61 Quoted in Ralph Foster Weld, *Slavery in Connecticut* (New Haven, Conn.: Yale University Press, 1935), 28; "An Act to Prevent Slavery," in *The Revised Statutes of the State of Connecticut* (Hartford, Conn.: Case, Tiffany, 1849), 584.

62 Quoted in "Mass Meeting," *Colored American* (New York), November 20, 1841, Item #17430, Amos Beman Scrapbooks, Beinecke Rare Book and Manuscript Library. The scrapbooks are available online, via http://www.library.yale.edu/beinecke/.

63 Swift, *Black Prophets of Justice*, 197.

64 Amos Beman, James Pennington, and Joseph Brown, "To the Good People of the State of Connecticut," *Hartford Daily Courant*, September 29, 1847. See also Swift, *Black Prophets of Justice*, 198.

65 William C. Fowler, *Local Law in Massachusetts and Connecticut: Historically Considered; and The Historical Status of the Negro in Connecticut* (Albany, N.Y.: Joel Munsell, 1872), 145.

66 "An Act for the Assessment and Collection of Taxation," *Public Acts Passed by the General Assembly of the State of Connecticut* (Hartford, Conn.: Office of the Secretary of State, 1872), May session, 1851, chap. 47, sect. 6.

67 Quoted in Swift, *Black Prophets of Justice*, 272–73.

68 "Colored Men's Convention," Frederick Douglass' Paper, May 4, 1855, Item #64672, Amos Beman Scrapbooks. See also in Amos Beman Scrapbooks: "Rev. A. G. Beman, and the Connecticut Legislature," Frederick Douglass' Paper, June 22, 1855, Item #65084; and "Equal Suffrage in Connecticut," Frederick Douglass' Paper, June 29, 1855, Item #65122.

69 Swift, *Black Prophets of Justice*, 274.

70 The historian Eric Foner stated: "If any event in American history can be signaled out as the beginning of a path which led almost inevitably to sectional controversy and civil war, it was the introduction of the Wilmot Proviso" ("The Wilmot Proviso Revisited," *Journal of American History* 56, no. 2 [September 1969]: 262). See also Joel H. Silbey, *Storm over Texas: The Annexation Controversy and the Road to the Civil War* (New York: Oxford University Press, 2007); Frederick Merk, *Slavery and the Annexation of Texas* (New York: Knopf, 1972); Michael A. Morrison, *Slavery in the American West: The Eclipse of Manifest Destiny and the Coming of the Civil War* (Chapel Hill: University of North Carolina Press, 1997). Even with this growing anti-Southern sentiment, opposition to abolition remained strong. In Waterbury, Reverend David Root of the First Church was voted out of the congregation for speaking out against slavery. See Joseph Anderson, "The First Church from 1826 to 1864," in *The Town and City of Waterbury, Connecticut, From the Aboriginal Period to the Year Eighteen Hundred and Ninety-Five*, ed. Joseph Anderson (New Haven, Conn: Price and Lee, 1896), 590–92.

71 Morrison, *Slavery in the American West*; Jean H. Baker, *Affairs of Party: The Political Culture of Northern Democrats in the Mid-Nineteenth Century* (Ithaca, N.Y.: Cornell University Press, 1983); David M. Pletcher, *The Diplomacy of Annexation: Texas, Oregon, and the Mexican War* (Columbia: University of Missouri Press, 1973).

72 Morrison, *Slavery in the American West*, 42–44, 59–64.

73 Eric Foner, *Free Soil, Free Labor, Free Men: The Ideology of the Republican Party before the Civil War* (New York: Oxford University Press, 1970), 124–25.

74 Bruser, "Political Antislavery in Connecticut," 64.

75 Augustus Washington to the editors of the *Tribune*, July 3, 1851, in Carter

G. Woodson, ed., *The Mind of the Negro as Reflected in Letters Written During the Crisis, 1800-1860* (Lancaster, Penn.: Lancaster Press, 1926), 133. The Washington letter is also available online as "African Colonization By a Man of Color," http://teachingamericanhistory.org/library/index.asp ?document=621. See also O'Connell, "The Abolitionist Movement in Connecticut," 46–67.

76 "Texas," *Hartford Daily Courant*, February 21, 1845; "State of the Texas Question," *Hartford Daily Courant*, March 8, 1845.

77 *Hartford Daily Courant*, November 2, 1847; "Explanations," *Hartford Daily Courant*, November 18, 1847. See also "The Test of Public Policy," *Hartford Daily Courant*, January 27, 1847.

78 *Hartford Times*, September 25, 1844.

79 Holt, *The Political Crisis of the 1850s*, 106–10.

80 Holt, *The Political Crisis of the 1850s*; Tyler G. Anbinder, *Nativism and Slavery: The Northern Know Nothings and the Politics of the 1850s* (New York: Oxford University Press, 1992); Robert D. Parmet, "The Know-Nothings in Connecticut" (Ph.D. diss., Columbia University, 1966); Carroll John Noonan, *Nativism in Connecticut, 1829-1860* (Washington: Catholic University of America, 1938).

81 Holt, *The Political Crisis of the 1850s*, 102–5.

82 Morrison, *Slavery in the American West*, 124–25; James M. McPherson, *Battle Cry of Freedom: The Civil War Era* (New York: Oxford University Press, 1988), 70–71.

83 "An Act to Amend, and Supplementary to, an Act Entitled 'An Act Respecting Fugitives From Justice and Persons Escaping From The Service of Their Masters,' Approved February Twelfth, One Thousand Seven Hundred and Ninety-three," *Congressional Globe*, Thirty-First Cong., 1st Sess., September 18, 1850, 462–63.

84 Quoted in Bruser, "Political Antislavery in Connecticut," 174. See also, William B. Allen, *Rethinking Uncle Tom: The Political Philosophy of Harriet Beecher Stowe* (New York: Lexington, 2009).

85 Bruser, "Political Antislavery in Connecticut," 124, 139. A meeting of colored citizens in Hartford held at the Talcott Street Church quoted the Declaration of Independence and promised: "We will resist the enforcement of the Fugitive Slave law . . . believing that it violates a man's natural rights, the instincts of our nature, the spirit and letter of the Constitution, and the express injunctions of the Holy Writ, and is entirely subversive of the ends of government" (quoted in "For the Courant," *Hartford Daily Courant*, October 24, 1850).

86 Quoted in Strother, *The Underground Railroad in Connecticut*, 102. Strother noted that Connecticut and the North witnessed a large exodus of free blacks to Canada (103–5).

87 Bruser, "Political Antislavery in Connecticut," 116, 140; "Fugitive Slave Law," *Hartford Daily Courant*, October 4, 1850. In another article, the paper stated: "All laws passed in constitutional form must be obeyed until they are repealed. Any other course is criminal, and other doctrine leads to direct anarchy" (October 19, 1850).

88 T. E. Graves, letter to the editor, *Hartford Daily Courant*, November 20, 1850; quoted in Strother, *The Underground Railroad in Connecticut*, 98. See also "Fugitive Slave Bill," *Hartford Daily Courant*, August 30, 1850. Alfred Burr, editor of the *Hartford Times*, wrote that slaveholders "assume that a slave is legal property, and among the most valuable they have . . . they are as quickly and sensitively roused when a negro is stolen from them, as we at the North are when cattle and horses are stolen from us. Thus they have a right under the Constitution to hold these slaves. . . . We, at the North, must look at these things as they are" (quoted in Bruser, "Political Antislavery in Connecticut," 162).

89 Quoted in Bruser, "Political Antislavery in Connecticut," 165.

90 Morrison, *Slavery in the American West*, chapter 5; John R. Wunder and Joann M. Ross, eds., *The Kansas-Nebraska Act of 1854* (Lincoln: University of Nebraska Press, 2008).

91 "Speech of Mr. Truman Smith," *Congressional Globe*, 33rd Cong., 1st sess., Senate, February 10 and 11, 1854, appendix, 175–78.

92 "Hurl Back the Invaders!" *Hartford Daily Courant*, March 18, 1854; "Stephen A. Douglas," *Hartford Daily Courant*, September 7, 1854; "The Aggressions of a Slave Power," *Hartford Daily Courant*, September 15, 1854. Even the Democratic *Hartford Times* opposed the Kansas-Nebraska Act, insisting: "We cannot advocate for a repeal of the Missouri Compromise for the sole reason that the present administration advocates it. . . . It may be well for us to scrutinize with care the movements of those who are our uniform opponents, THAT ABOLITIONISTS would rejoice to see the fires of discord rekindled by a revival of the slavery agitation, no one can doubt" (June 5, 1854).

93 New Haven *Palladium*, February 20, 1854; Middletown *Constitution*, May 31, 1854; *Norwich Examiner*, June 1, 1855.

94 Michael F. Holt, *The Rise and Fall of the American Whig Party* (New York: Oxford University Press, 1999), 832; "Whig State Convention!" *Hartford Daily Courant*, February 17, 1854; "Connecticut Legislature," *Hartford Daily Courant*, May 17, 1854; "Speeches of Mr. Toucey and Mr. Gillette," *Hartford Daily Courant*, July 14, 1854. See also "Governor's Message," *Hartford Daily Courant*, May 5, 1854.

95 "Speeches of Mr. Toucey and Mr. Gillette," *Hartford Daily Courant*, July 14, 1854.

96 "Speeches of Mr. Toucey and Mr. Gillette," *Hartford Daily Courant*, July 14, 1854.

97 "An Act for the Defense of Liberty in this State," *Public Acts Passed by the General Assembly of the State of Connecticut* (Hartford, Conn.: Office of the Secretary of State, 1872), May session, 1854, chap. 65. For commentary from those who helped pass the act, see Fowler, *Local Law in Massachusetts and Connecticut*, 97.

98 "The Fugitive Slave Case," *Hartford Daily Courant*, May 30, 1854. See also "Connecticut on the Fugitive Slave Law," *Hartford Daily Courant*, June 26, 1854.

99 Bruser, "Political Antislavery in Connecticut," 249. Bruser (333) gives the votes for president in Connecticut in 1856 were: Democrats, 32,704 (49 percent); Know Nothings, 26,008 (39 percent); Republicans, 6,740 (10 percent); and Whigs, 1,251 (1.9 percent).

100 The 1858 election was the first in which the opposition forces coalesced under the Republican banner. Bruser ("Political Antislavery in Connecticut," 456) gives the votes for governor: Republicans, 36,298 (52 percent); and Democrats, 33,544 (48 percent).

101 William E. Gienapp, *The Origins of the Republican Party, 1852–1856* (New York: Oxford University Press, 1987), 299–300, and "The Crime against Sumner: The Caning of Charles Sumner and the Rise of the Republican Party," *Civil War History* 25 (September, 1979): 218–45; *Hartford Daily Courant*, June 3, 1856; "Indignation Meeting at Meriden," *Hartford Daily Courant*, June 4, 1856; "Tribute to the Memory of Charles Sumner," *Hartford Daily Courant*, June 25, 1856.

102 Don E. Fehrenbacher, *The Dred Scott Case: Its Significance in American Law and Politics* (New York: Oxford University Press, 1978); Mark A. Graber, *Dred Scott and the Problem of Constitutional Evil* (New York: Cambridge University Press, 2008).

103 Quoted in Bruser, "Political Antislavery in Connecticut," 356. Alfred Burr, editor of the *Hartford Times*, insisted that the Republican Party "means open warfare on the part of one half of the union against the institutions and rights of the other" (quoted in Bruser, "Political Antislavery in Connecticut," 282). Bruser notes that the Democrats did not attempt to defend slavery or fight against the idea of Free Soil. Rather, they stuck to the traditional argument of the Union's sanctity, the importance of the Constitution and compromise, the wrongness of sectional agitation, and the dangerous nature of the Republicans as a sectional party.

104 "MEETING AT THE CITY HALL LAST NIGHT, TO SAVE THE UNION," *Hartford Daily Courant*, December 15, 1859; "The Manufacturers' Convention at Meriden," *Hartford Daily Courant*, January 19, 1860. Even the abolitionist

Leonard Bacon denounced Brown ("The Moral of Harpers Ferry," *New Eng-lander* 17, no. 4 [November 1859]: 1078). See also John Niven, *Connecticut for the Union: The Role of the State in the Civil War* (New Haven, Conn.: Yale University Press, 1965), 15–17.

105 New Haven *Journal & Inquirer*, May 2, 1857; quoted in New Haven *Palladium*, April 13 and May 27, 1857; "Working Men!" *Hartford Daily Courant*, April 7,1856; "Free Labor," *Hartford Daily Courant*, April 5, 1856.

106 Quoted in "Senator Foster," New Haven *Palladium*, May 23, 1856.

107 Quoted in Bruser, "Political Antislavery in Connecticut," 365. See also "The Day Approaches" and "Working Men, Attention!" *Hartford Daily Courant*, April 4, 1856; "A Question," *Hartford Daily Courant*, April 5, 1856.

108 "Buchanan in Favor of Slavery Extension," *Hartford Daily Courant*, June 24, 1856; *Hartford Daily Courant*, August 23, 1856.

109 "An Address to the People of Connecticut," *Hartford Daily Courant*, March 14, 1857. The paper also expressed the opinion that "the decision is the heaviest blow ever aimed at Free Laborers; being calculated to degrade such men, to the level of Slaves" (*Hartford Daily Courant*, March 17, 1857).

110 [Thomas Day], "Sam and Sambo," *Hartford Daily Courant*, March 6, 1856.

111 Far more research needs to be done on the abolitionist movement within Connecticut so that historians can gain a deeper understanding of its size and impact. The purpose of this chapter has not been to dismiss or diminish the work of abolitionism but, rather, to point out the degree to which anti-abolitionism and racism existed in the state. Even within the abolitionist movement there was so much racist sentiment that one abolitionist wrote: "I have been brought to conclude, and must say: (to the shame of my brethren be it said) that the greatest of all hindrances is the remaining deep-seated and cruel prejudices of the abolitionists themselves" (quoted in O'Connell, "The Abolitionist Movement in Connecticut," 87). O'Connell concluded: "Many Connecticut abolitionists were really not committed to the twin goal of their [antislavery] society—the elevation of the free Negro" (87). See O'Connell, "The Abolitionist Movement in Connecticut," chapter 4, for a broader discussion of abolitionists' racism.

112 "Proceedings of Union Convention," *Hartford Press*, January 15, 1858.

Chapter 2. And the War Came, 1860-61

1 J. Robert Lane discusses the extent to which other states and commercial interests in New York watched and, to some extent, interfered with Connecticut's election (*A Political History of Connecticut during the Civil War* [Washington: Catholic University of America Press, 1941], 109–10). The historian Albert E. Van Dusen concurred: "The spring election campaign attracted national attention since it was considered by seasoned political

observers as a weather vane for the presidential race in the fall" (*Connecticut* [New York: Random House, 1964], 222).

2 "Obituary: Ex-Gov. Thomas H. Seymour, of Connecticut," *New York Times*, September 4, 1868; Thomas H. Seymour, biographical information available on the Web site of the National Governor's Association, http://www .nga.org.

3 "To Young Laboring Men," *Hartford Daily Courant*, March 10, 1860. See also Lane, *A Political History of Connecticut during the Civil War*, 109–10.

4 James A. Briggs to Abraham Lincoln, February 29, 1860, Abraham Lincoln Papers, American Memory, Library of Congress, http://memory.loc.gov/ ammem/alhtml/malhome.html. Lincoln had initially traveled East to visit his son Robert, who was attending Phillips Academy in New Hampshire, and he decided to use the trip to introduce himself to voters in New York voters, the home of his chief rival for the Republican nomination, William H. Seward. Lincoln delivered his famous Cooper Union address and several speeches in New Hampshire before arriving in Hartford. See Gene Leach, "Glimpses of Lincoln's Brilliance," *Hog River Journal* 3, no. 4 (Fall 2005): 26–31; Lewis K. Parker, "Abraham Lincoln in Connecticut," *Connecticut Lawyer* 19, no. 6 (February 2009): 16–21; J. Doyle Dewitt, *Lincoln in Hartford* (Hartford, Conn.: Civil War Centennial Commission, 1961).

5 Quotations are from Lincoln's Hartford and New Haven speeches, March 5 and 6, 1860, in Abraham Lincoln, *Collected Works*, ed. Roy P. Basler et al. (New Brunswick, N.J.: Rutgers University Press, 1953–55). Lincoln's *Collected Works* are available at http://quod.lib.umich.edu/l/lincoln/.

6 "Abe Lincoln at the City Hall!; Another Republican Rally! THE HALL CROWDED TO EXCESS! The Question of Slavery Philosophically Considered! THE DANGER OF INDIFFERENCE," *Hartford Daily Courant*, March 6, 1860; "Lincoln at Meriden; TREMENDOUS ENTHUSIASM! 3000 IN THE TOWN HALL! Torchlight Procession! Extra Train from New Haven!" *Hartford Daily Courant*, March 9, 1860; "The Wide Awakes," *Hartford Daily Courant*, March 3, 1860; "The Wide Awakes," *Hartford Daily Courant*, March 20, 1860.

7 Abraham Lincoln to Lyman Trumbull, March 26, 1860, in Lincoln, *Collected Works*.

8 James F. Babcock to Abraham Lincoln, April 8, 1860, in Lincoln *Collected Works*. See also The Connecticut Register: Being an Official State Calendar of Public Officers and Institution (Hartford, Conn.: Brown and Parsons, 1859–66), 18. On charges of voter fraud, see Lane, *A Political History of Connecticut during the Civil War*, 120–21.

9 William A. Buckingham, *Message of his Excellency William A. Buckingham, Governor of Connecticut, to the Legislature of the State, May Session, 1860* (New Haven, Conn.: Carrington and Hotchkiss, 1860), 17–20.

10   *Hartford Times*, November 7, 1860.

11   Milo A. Holcomb to Abraham Lincoln, July 29, 1860, Abraham Lincoln Papers.

12   James M. McPherson, *Battle Cry of Freedom: The Civil War Era* (New York: Oxford University Press, 1988), 213–16; John T. Hubbell, "The Douglas Democrats and the Election of 1860," *Mid America* 55, no. 2 (1973): 108–33; Robert W. Johannsen, "Stephen A. Douglas and the South," *Journal of Southern History* 3, no. 1 (1967): 26–50.

13   Douglas Harper first compared the collective votes for Lincoln's opponents to the votes for him. See "1860 Election," http://www.etymonline.com/cw/1860.htm. See also John Woolley and Gerhard Peters, "Voter Turnout in Presidential Elections," http://www.presidency.ucsb.edu/data/turnout.php.

14   Quoted in McPherson, *Battle Cry of Freedom*, 235.

15   "Washington Dispatches," *Hartford Daily Courant*, December 22, 1860; "New Items," *Hartford Daily Courant*, December 25, 1860; *Hartford Daily Courant*, December 27, 1860; "Secession and Postage," *Hartford Daily Courant*, January 21, 1861; "Secession Theory of Debt," *Hartford Daily Courant*, January 21, 1861.

16   "A PROCLAMATION," *Hartford Daily Courant*, December 21, 1860.

17   William A. Croffut and John M. Morris, *The Military and Civil History of Connecticut during the War of 1861–1865* (New York: Ledyard Bill, 1869), 56. The state purchased 1,442 rifles from the Sharp's Rifle company, then contracted with Eli Whitney's company. See David J. Naumec, "The Connecticut Contracted '61 Springfield: The Special Model to the 'Good and Serviceable' Arm," *The Bulletin of the American Society of Arms Collectors* 90 (2005): 9–10.

18   "A War Proclamation," *New Haven Register*, January 22, 1861.

19   Horace Staples to William A. Buckingham, April 23, 1861, RG 005, Governor William A. Buckingham, Connecticut State Library, Hartford, Connecticut. All of this is well documented in John Niven, *Connecticut for the Union: The Role of the State in the Civil War* (New Haven, Conn.: Yale University Press, 1965), 41–42. Naumec, "The Connecticut Contracted '61 Springfield," 3, offers very specific information regarding Colt's desire to set up such an armory, noting that Colt even sent one of his agents to Richmond to speak with Henry A. Wise, then governor of Virginia. Colt vociferously denied selling arms to the South, and after a *New York Tribune* article charged the company with such activities, he sent the newspaper a heated letter in which he insisted: "If any persons have assumed to act as my agents, in giving aid to the rebels of the Southern States, they are acting under false pretenses." Quoted in "Col. Colt's Defense," *Hartford Daily Courant*, December 21, 1861. For additional information on Augustus Hazard, see Mark R. Wilson,

"Gentlemanly Price-Fixing and Its Limits: Collusion and Competition in the U.S. Explosives Industry during the Civil War Era," *Business History Review* 77 no. 2 (Summer 2003): 207–34.

20 Charles Henry Mallory to Stephen Mallory, March 1861, Mallory Family Papers, G. W. Blunt Library, Mystic Seaport, Mystic, Connecticut. Also quoted in James Baughman, *The Mallorys of Mystic* (Middletown, Conn.: Wesleyan University Press, 1972), 105.

21 "News Item," *Hartford Daily Courant*, January 22, 1861.

22 "State Items," *Hartford Daily Courant*, January 22, 1861.

23 *New Haven Journal and Courier*, January 7, 1861.

24 *Hartford Daily Courant*, January 26, 1861; "Affairs at Charleston," *Hartford Daily Courant*, January 30, 1861; "The Union Not Disolved [sic]," *Hartford Daily Courant*, January 31, 1861; "Secession Seceding — South Carolina Nullifying the New Nation," *Hartford Daily Courant*, Feb. 19, 1861; *Hartford Daily Courant*, March 4, 1861; *Hartford Daily Courant*, March 20, 1861.

25 Petitions were sent to Congress by the following towns in Connecticut: Bridgeport, Derby, Fairfield, Milford, Mystic, New Haven, New London, North Haven, Putnam, Seymour, Stratford, Wallingford, and Westport. There were probably many more from other towns. All can be found by searching the Senate and House Journals of the *Congressional Globe*, Library of Congress, American Memory collection, http://memory.loc.gov/ammem/amlaw/lwcg.html. The specific petitions referred to are: Senator James Dixon, *Congressional Globe*, February 5, 1861, Senate Journal, 36th Cong., 2d Sess., 185; Senator Stephen Foster, *Congressional Globe*, February 4, 1861, Senate Journal, 36th Cong., 2d Sess., 183; Congressman Burnham, *Congressional Globe*, February 6, 1861, House Journal, 36th Cong., 2d Sess., 275.

26 Quoted in Lane, *A Political History of Connecticut during the Civil War*, 151. Buckingham decided on a delegation of six: ex-governors Roger Baldwin and Chauncey Cleveland, Judge Charles K. McCurdy, General James T. Pratt, Robins Battell, and Amos Treat. See Croffut and Morris, *The Military and Civil History of Connecticut during the War of 1861–1865*, 34–35. The *New Haven Register* was particularly upset that compromise measures were not given a real chance: "We have yet to see the man who will deny that if People were allowed an opportunity to vote on some fair and definitive proposition, like that of Mr. Crittenden, they would decide by a majority overwhelmingly beyond precedent that this sectional controversy should be settled peacefully!" ("Let the People Speak," January 22, 1861).

27 *Hartford Daily Courant*, February 21, 1861.

28 "An Unmanly Front," *Hartford Times*, March 7, 1861.

29 "Navy Movements: The 'Coercion' policy of the Administration To Be Carried

Out," *Hartford Times*, April 5, 1861; "Premature," *Hartford Times*, April 9, 1861.

30 "THE LATEST NEWS. BY TELEGRAPH. A Demand for Fort Sumter and a Refusal! An Attack Expected in the Morning! 7000 TROOPS AT CHARLESTON. War Movements in the South," *Hartford Daily Courant*, April 12, 1861.

31 "The Fight," *Hartford Daily Courant*, April 13, 1861 (see also "The Charleston Rebels," *Hartford Daily Courant*, April 16, 1861); "The News," *Hartford Times*, April 13, 1861; "The Black Day," *Hartford Times*, April 13, 1861 (The *New Haven Register* insisted: "We have not heart for the sickening spectacle that presents itself to the mind, brought upon the country by Northern injustices and Southern resistance — higher law heresies, contempt for the national obligations, and the indulgence of partisan prejudices" ["The Culmination!" April 13, 1861]); Croffut and Morris, *The Military and Civil History of Connecticut during the War of 1861–1865*, 39–41; William A. Buckingham to Abraham Lincoln, April 15, 1861, Abraham Lincoln Papers.

32 Croffut and Morris, *The Military and Civil History of Connecticut during the War of 1861–1865*, 43, 67, 68, 69; Niven, *Connecticut for the Union*, 48; Blaikie Hines, *Civil War Volunteer Sons of Connecticut* (Thomaston, Conn.: American Patriot, 2002), 19–20, 60–61, 78. Hines's work is a tremendous resource for anyone interested in the background of regiments that served in the war.

33 Croffut and Morris, *The Military and Civil History of Connecticut during the War of 1861–1865*, 56–57; "The War Feeling in Hartford!; A Half Million Loan from Hartford Banks to the Governor MOVEMENTS AT THE ADJU-TANT-GENERAL'S OFFICE Response of the Volunteers! — Rifle Companies Forming! The Union Meeting Last Night The Meeting Last Night PRAYER," *Hartford Daily Courant*, April 18, 1861.

34 William A. Buckingham, *Message of his Excellency William A. Buckingham, Governor of Connecticut, to the Legislature of the State, May Session, 1861* (Hartford, Conn.: J. R. Hawley, 1861): 3–17.

35 "An Act to Provide for the Organization and Equipment of a Volunteer Militia, and to Provide for the Public Defense," approved May 8, 1861, *Annual Report of the Adjutant-General of the State of Connecticut* (New Haven, Conn.: Babcock and Sizer, 1863), 325.

36 Virginia seceded on April 17, Arkansas on May 6, North Carolina on May 20, and Tennessee on June 8.

37 Niven, *Connecticut for the Union*, 56–57.

38 "Editorial," *New Haven Register*, May 6, 1861; "New Item," *New Haven Register*, May 21, 1861.

39 "Negroes Contraband of War," *New Haven Register*, June 3, 1861; *New Haven*

Register, June 7, 1861. See also "Editorial," *New Haven Register*, July 5, 1861, in which the *Register* charges that those pushing the war are: "The most detestable traitors are those who hate the Union and have been working for its overthrow for the quarter of a century. . . . We have such traitors now in Connecticut, and throughout the Northern States. They have been long in league with the rabid Abolitionists Garrison and Wendell Phillips."

40 "News Items," *New Haven Register*, May 7, 1861; *Hartford Times*, June 3 and 6, 1861. See also Croffut and Morris, *The Military and Civil History of Connecticut during the War of 1861-1865*, 103; John E. Tallmadge, "A Peace Movement in Civil War Connecticut," *New England Quarterly* 37, no. 3 (September 1964): 306–21.

41 Quoted in "Gov. Seymour's Peace Offering," *Hartford Weekly Times*, July 22, 1861.

42 "A Marked Warning," *Litchfield Enquirer*, June 27, 1861. I have been unable to determine the difference between a white "peace flag" and a secession flag. The Confederate "bars and stars" was not yet in use. A secession flag may have simply been a white flag or a South Carolina palmetto flag.

43 "A Marked Warning," *Litchfield Enquirer*, June 27, 1861. See also Joanna D. Cowden, "The Politics of Dissent: Civil War Democrats in Connecticut, *New England Quarterly* 56, no. 4 (December 1983): 538–54.

44 Niven, *Connecticut for the Union*, 49–57, provides a good discussion of the problems involved in preparing for war. See also Croffut and Morris, *The Military and Civil History of Connecticut during the War of 1861-1865*, 45–54, 58–59, 63, 73; "War Matters in the State," *Hartford Daily Courant*, May 1, 1861.

45 "Advice to South Carolina," *Litchfield Enquirer*, April 16, 1861.

46 *Litchfield Enquirer*, May 5, 1861.

47 Quoted in Croffut and Morris, *The Military and Civil History of Connecticut during the War of 1861-1865*, 96.

48 For a good general description of the battle and casualty figures, see McPherson, *Battle Cry of Freedom*, 339–46. See also William C. Davis, *Battle at Bull Run: A History of the First Major Campaign of the Civil War* (Baton Rouge: Louisiana State University Press, 1981). For specifics of Connecticut troop movements and an evaluation of Tyler, see Niven, *Connecticut for the Union*, 130–43. The specific Connecticut casualty figures are: 1st CVI, five wounded, six captured; 2nd CVI, one killed, two wounded, fourteen captured; 3rd CVI, three killed, one missing, fifteen wounded, seventeen captured (Hines, *Civil War Volunteer Sons of Connecticut*, 21, 61, 80).

49 "Peace Movement in Bloomfield," *Hartford Weekly Times*, August 10, 1861.

50 Quoted in Croffut and Morris, *The Military and Civil History of Connecticut during the War of 1861-1865*, 106.

51 A. A. Pettingill to William A. Buckingham, August 24, 1861, RG 005, Governor William A. Buckingham, Connecticut State Library.

52 A. A. Pettingill to William A. Buckingham, August 24, 1861, RG 005, Governor William A. Buckingham, Connecticut State Library.

53 Croffut and Morris, *The Military and Civil History of Connecticut during the War of 1861–1865*, 100–110, provides an excellent account of the peace movement and the reactions to it. See also Tallmadge, "A Peace Movement in Civil War Connecticut"; Cowden, "The Politics of Dissent."

54 Quoted in Lane, *A Political History of Connecticut during the Civil War*, 180.

55 George A. Oviate to William A. Buckingham, August 27, 1861, RG 005, Governor William A. Buckingham, Connecticut State Library.

56 "A PROCLAMATION: BY HIS EXCELLENCY THE GOVERNOR," *Hartford Daily Courant*, September 2, 1861.

57 On September 3, Carr wrote to Secretary of War Simon Cameron that he had stopped circulation of the *New York Daily News* in New Haven. On the 11th, he reported that the order was being defied by "a noisy secessionist" named George A. Hubbard, who continued to sell the newspaper on trains of the Naugatuck Railroad. Carr requested approval to arrest Hubbard and did so on the 20th. Hubbard's brother, however, had connections in the Republican Party, and Secretary of State Seward ordered his release. See Barruss M. Carnahan, *Act of Justice: Lincoln's Emancipation Proclamation and the Law of War* (Lexington: University of Kentucky Press, 2007), 57.

58 On August 29, Ellis B. Schnabel was arrested and charged with "making treasonable harangues at peace meetings . . . and with publicly denouncing the government" (*War of Rebellion: Official Records of the Union and Confederate Armies*, 2nd ser., 2:620).

59 Phineas T. Barnum to Abraham Lincoln, August 30, 1861, Abraham Lincoln Papers. Barnum also noted: "Those who one week ago were blatant secessionists are to day publicly announcing themselves as 'in for the country to the end of the war.' The 'strong arm' has a mighty influence here."

60 Croffut and Morris, *The Military and Civil History of Connecticut during the War of 1861–1865*, 110, notes that the peace movement was broken.

61 "Forward! Once More," *Hartford Evening Press*, July 23, 1861.

62 Horace Bushnell, *Reverses Needed: A Discourse Delivered on the Sunday after the Disaster at Bull Run, in the North Church, Hartford* (Hartford, Conn.: L. E. Hunt, 1861).

63 "Editorial," *Hartford Daily Courant*, July 29, 1861.

64 "The War is Necessary," *Hartford Daily Courant*, October 5, 1861. See also "Push on the Column!" *Hartford Daily Courant*, August 10, 1861.

65 "Return Home of the First Regiment," *Hartford Daily Courant*, July 29, 1861.

66 Croffut and Morris, *The Military and Civil History of Connecticut during the War of 1861–1865*, 102; Niven, *Connecticut for the Union*, 64; Hines, *Civil War Volunteer Sons of Connecticut*. Enlistment figures are based on Hines.

67 Charles J. Stille, *History of the United States Sanitary Commission: Being the General Report of Its Work during the War of the Rebellion* (Philadelphia: Lippincott, 1866), 39; Jeanie Attie, *Patriotic Toil: Northern Women and the American Civil War* (Ithaca, N.Y.: Cornell University Press, 1998), 34; Nina Silber, *Daughters of the Union: Northern Women Fight the Civil War* (Cambridge, Mass.: Harvard University Press, 2005), 164.

68 Harriet Terry to General Alfred Terry, May 13, 1861, quoted in Lane, *A Political History of Connecticut during the Civil War*, 172.

69 "Local News," *Litchfield Enquirer*, November 6, 1861. See also "Hartford Soldier's Aid Association," *Hartford Daily Courant*, June 21, 1861; "Aid to Volunteers," *Hartford Daily Courant*, July 19, 1861; "Report of the Managers of the Hartford Soldiers' Aid Association," *Hartford Daily Courant*, August 10, 1861; "Local News," *Litchfield Enquirer*, October 17 and 31, and November 14, 1861; "An Appeal For Blankets," *Hartford Daily Courant*, October 4, 1861; "The Sanitary Commission," *Hartford Daily Courant*, October 9, 1861; "The Sanitary Commission," New Haven *Palladium*, November 27, 1861. "Within two months from the commencement of hostilities the patriotic ladies of Middletown organized an aid society, and began their benevolent work of supplying the soldiers in the field with such articles of comfort and such luxuries as the government was not able to furnish" (*History of Middlesex County, Connecticut, with Biographical Sketches of Its Prominent Men* [New York: J. B. Beers, 1884], 83).

70 "The Women and the Soldiers," *Hartford Daily Courant*, November 13, 1861.

71 Benjamin Douglass, "History of Middletown, Conn., in the War of the Rebellion, 1861–65," Manuscript Collection, Connecticut State Library, Hartford, Connecticut.

72 Sidney Stanley quoted in Lane, *A Political History of Connecticut during the Civil War*, 172, note 15.

73 K. Nolin, Civil War Manuscripts Project, MS Civil War Box II, Folder 2, Connecticut Historical Society, Hartford, Connecticut. See also Croffut and Morris, *The Military and Civil History of Connecticut during the War of 1861–1865*, 148–54.

74 "An Act Authorizing the Treasurer to Borrow Money for the Equipment and Payment of the Volunteer Militia, and to Issue State Bonds," approved June 18, 1861, *Public Acts, Passed by the General Assembly of the State of Connecticut* (Hartford, Conn.: J. M. Scofield, 1863), 50. This act authorized

the state's treasurer to issue bonds in connection with authorized borrowing of up to $2,000,000, with interest at 6 percent to be paid in January and June, and the principal to be paid in twenty years (or in ten years, at the discretion of the General Assembly). It also authorized the state treasurer to advertise and sell such a portion of the bonds as the Assembly decided was necessary, and to accept the most favorable proposals offered by bidders, as long as no bids were accepted at less than par. "An Act in Addition to 'An Act to provide for the Organization and Equipment of a Volunteer Militia, and to provide for the Public Defense,'" approved June 27, 1861, *Annual Report of the Adjutant-General of the State of Connecticut* (New Haven, Conn.: Carrington, Hotchkiss, 1865), 17. This act changed the bounty payments and required towns to report to the comptroller the names of all soldiers resident in the town accepted into U.S. service, including the names of each man's wife and children, and the date and term of enlistment. It required the comptroller to pay towns on a quarterly basis the amounts due from the state to families (if town had already paid, it was to be reimbursed by state), and it authorized reimbursement to individuals and committees that have provided uniforms.

75 "An Act Relating to the Direct Tax imposed by the Congress of the United States," approved October 15, 1861, special October session, *Public Act, Passed by the General Assembly of the State of Connecticut* (New Haven, Conn.: Babcock and Sizer, 1862), 4; "An Act in Addition to 'An Act to provide for the Organization and Equipment of a Volunteer Militia, and to provide for the Public Defense,'" approved October 16, 1861, special October session, *Annual Report of the Adjutant-General of the State of Connecticut* (New Haven, Conn.: Carrington, Hotchkiss, 1865), 2.

76 "It Will Stand," *Hartford Daily Courant*, October 19, 1861, "Toucey and Seymour," *Hartford Daily Courant*, October 29, 1861; "CONNECTICUT DISGRACED," *Hartford Times*, October 16, 1861. The resolution allowed the portraits to be restored when the legislators were satisfied of Toucey and Seymour's loyalty to the Union. See Croffut and Morris, *The Military and Civil History of Connecticut during the War of 1861–1865*, 136.

77 Stuart C. Mowbray, *Civil War Arms Purchases and Deliveries: A Facsimile Reprint of the Master List of Civil War Weapons Purchases and Deliveries including Small Arms, Cannon, Ordnance and Projectiles* (Lincoln, R.I.: Andrew Mowbray, 2000), 732, 767, 945, 950; Naumec, "The Connecticut Contracted '61 Springfield," 2, 6.

78 McPherson, *Battle Cry of Freedom*, 365.

79 For the 5th CVI movements, see Hines, *Civil War Volunteer Sons of Connecticut*, 88, 119, 138.

80 McPherson, *Battle Cry of Freedom*, 369; William N. Peterson, *Mystic Built:*

Ships and Shipyards of the Mystic River, Connecticut, 1784–1919 (Mystic, Conn.: Mystic Seaport Museum, 1989), 8.

81 Thomas A. and Charles K. Stillman, *George Greenman & Co.: Shipbuilders of Mystic, Connecticut* (Mystic, Conn.: Marine Historical Association, 1938), 19. *Mystic Pioneer*, September 7, 1861. See also *Mystic Pioneer*, August 24 and September 21, 1861. Part of the stone fleet, some thirteen vessels, was concentrated at New London for repairs. See Croffut and Morris, *The Military and Civil History of Connecticut during the War of 1861–1865*, 146–47. Stephen Walkley, comp., *History of the Seventh Connecticut Volunteer Infantry, Hawley's Brigade, Terry's Division, Tenth Army Corps, 1861–1865* (1905; repr., Salem, Mass: Higginson Book, 1998), 28. See also McPherson, *Battle Cry of Freedom*, 370–71; Niven, *Connecticut for the Union*, 141. Governor Buckingham issued a proclamation upon hearing the news: "The two regiments from Connecticut were the first to land on the hostile shore; and, after the stars and stripes, the flag of Connecticut was the first to wave above the traitorous soil of South Carolina" (quoted in Croffut and Morris, *The Military and Civil History of Connecticut during the War of 1861–1865*, 132).

82 Charles K. Cadwell, *The Old Sixth Regiment, Its War Record, 1861–5* (1875; repr., Charleston, S.C.: BiblioLife, 2009, 27–28); Walkley, *History of the Seventh Connecticut Volunteer Infantry*, 28, 34; quoted in Croffut and Morris, *The Military and Civil History of Connecticut during the War of 1861–1865*, 132.

83 McPherson, *Battle Cry of Freedom*, 350–52. Croffut and Morris, *The Military and Civil History of Connecticut during the War of 1861–1865*, 112–16; "The Death of Gen. Lyon," *Hartford Daily Courant*, August 15, 1861.

84 McPherson, *Battle Cry of Freedom*, 352–58. John Quincy Adams had first broached the idea of the law of war, arguing that one such outcome was the government's ability to emancipate all slaves (Matthew Warshauer, *Andrew Jackson and the Politics of Martial Law: Nationalism, Civil Liberties, and Partisanship* [Knoxville: University of Tennessee Press, 2006], 191). See also Carnahan, *Act of Justice*.

85 "The Slavery Question and the Government," *Hartford Weekly Times*, August 17, 1861.

86 Quoted in McPherson, *Battle Cry of Freedom*, 356.

87 *Hartford Daily Courant*, October 7, 1861; *Hartford Daily Courant*, October 22, 1861.

88 "ABOLITION FANATICISM," *Hartford Times*, September 24, 1861; "ANTI-SLAVERYISM," *Hartford Times*, October 5, 1861; "The Everlasting Negro," *Hartford Times*, December 12, 1861. See also "The Irrepressible Negro — He Troubles His Riders," *Hartford Times*, December 7, 1861. The *New Haven Register* joined the *Times*, arguing that making war for the abolition of

slavery was "to desire a revolution which shall found a new government on the ruins of the old" and that "the idea of immediate abolition based on the doctrine that slave-holding is a sin *per se*, was not accepted and is not now accepted by one in a hundred citizens of the country" (October 25, 1861). See also *New Haven Register*, November 8, 1861.

89 "The Slavery Element of the War," *New Haven Palladium*, November 25, 1861.

90 Quoted in "Local News," *Litchfield Enquirer*, December 5, 1861.

91 "The Duty of the Day," *Hartford Daily Courant*, September 10, 1861. See also, "What Are We Fighting For?" *Hartford Daily Courant*, September 17, 1861.

Chapter 3. A Recognition of Death, 1862

1 Quoted in William A. Croffut and John M. Morris, *The Military and Civil History of Connecticut during the War of 1861–1865* (New York: Ledyard Bill, 1869), 163; see also 164.

2 Quoted in Croffut and Morris, *The Military and Civil History of Connecticut during the War of 1861–1865*, 165–66.

3 Quoted in Croffut and Morris, *The Military and Civil History of Connecticut during the War of 1861–1865*, 170. See also John Niven, *Connecticut for the Union: The Role of the State in the Civil War* (New Haven, Conn.: Yale University Press, 1965), 153.

4 Henry C. Trumbull, *The Knightly Soldier: A Biography of Major Henry War Camp, Tenth Connecticut Volunteers* (Boston: Nichols and Noyes, 1865), 70.

5 Quoted in Croffut and Morris, *The Military and Civil History of Connecticut during the War of 1861–1865*, 163, 170–74; Niven, *Connecticut for the Union*, 155–57. Blaikie Hines, *Civil War Volunteer Sons of Connecticut* (Thomaston, Conn.: American Patriot, 2002) provides an indispensable, brief account of each regiment's movements and the numbers of killed and wounded. Utilized alongside regimental and other histories, it is an important catalog of Connecticut's service in the Civil War. It has been used for the remainder of this chapter to cross-reference other sources.

6 Seth Johnstone, "A General History of Fort Pulaski," National Park Service, http://www.nps.gov/seac/pulaski/0-introduction/index.htm.

7 Stephen Walkley, comp., *History of the Seventh Connecticut Volunteer Infantry, Hawley's Brigade, Terry's Division, Tenth Army Corps, 1861–1865* (1905; repr., Salem, Mass.: Higginson Book, 1998), 38, 43.

8 Niven, *Connecticut for the Union*, 143–44; Walkley, *History of the Seventh Connecticut Volunteer Infantry*, 38–44.

9 Quoted in Croffut and Morris, *The Military and Civil History of Con-*

necticut during the War of 1861–1865, 200, 201. For more on this battle, see Walkley, *History of the Seventh Connecticut Volunteer Infantry*, 51; Niven, *Connecticut for the Union*, 146–47.

10 Quoted in Niven, *Connecticut for the Union*, 149. See also, "General Benham Dismissed," *Hartford Daily Courant*, August 16, 1862; "General H. W. Benham," *New York Times*, August 16, 1862.

11 "Fill up the Old Regiments. Recruits Wanted for the Seventh," *Hartford Daily Courant*, August 9, 1862; Hines, *Civil War Volunteer Sons of Connecticut*), 99; "The Attack upon the Charleston and Savannah Railroad," *Hartford Daily Courant*, October 30, 1862.

12 Hines, *Civil War Volunteer Sons of Connecticut*, 122–23; Thomas Hamilton Murray, *History of the Ninth Regiment, Connecticut Voluntary Infantry, "The Irish Regiment," in the War of the Rebellion, 1861–1865, The Record of a Gallant Command on the March, in Battle and in Bivouac* (New Haven, Conn.: Price, Lee, and Adkins, 1903); quoted in Croffut and Morris, *The Military and Civil History of Connecticut during the War of 1861–1865*, 140–41.

13 Quoted in James M. McPherson, *Crossroads of Freedom: Antietam* (New York: Oxford University Press, 2002), 26. See also McPherson, *Battle Cry of Freedom: The Civil War Era* (New York: Oxford University Press, 1988), 419–20.

14 John William De Forest, *A Volunteer's Adventures: A Union Captain's Record of the Civil War*, ed., with notes, by James H. Croushore (New Haven, Conn.: Yale University Press, 1946), 38. See also Croffut and Morris, *The Military and Civil History of Connecticut during the War of 1861–1865*, 306.

15 De Forest, *A Volunteer's Adventures*, 39–40, 56–57.

16 "The Prospects and the Duty of the Day," *Hartford Daily Courant*, July 4, 1862. For a discussion of these campaigns, see McPherson, *Battle Cry of Freedom*, 454–76; Clifford Dowdey, *The Seven Days: The Emergence of Lee* (Fairfax, Va.: Fairfax Press, 1964).

17 Croffut and Morris, *The Military and Civil History of Connecticut During the War of 1861–1865*, 310.

18 Quoted in Murray, *History of the Ninth Regiment*, 111, 146. Murray, *History of the Ninth Regiment*, 156.

19 Croffut and Morris, *The Military and Civil History of Connecticut during the War of 1861–1865*, 218.

20 "Bravery of the Fifth Connecticut, *Hartford Daily Courant*, August 14, 1862; *Hartford Daily Courant*, August 13, 1862; See also "Official Report of the Culpepper Fight," *Hartford Daily Courant*, August 15, 1862; Hines, *Civil War Volunteer Sons of Connecticut*, 90. For evidence that Corliss survived, see the *Catalogue of Connecticut Volunteer Organizations, with Additional*

Enlistments and Casualties to July 1, 1864. Compiled From the Records in the Adjutant-General's Office (Hartford, Conn.: Case, Lockwood, 1864), 226, which lists him as having resigned on January 21, 1863.

21 "Letter from Washington," *Hartford Daily Courant*, September 15, 1862.

22 McPherson, *Battle Cry of Freedom*, 528–34; McPherson, *Crossroads of Freedom*, 80–84; John J. Hennessy, *Return to Bull Run: The Campaign and Battle of Second Manassas* (Norman: University of Oklahoma Press, 1999).

23 "Letter from Washington," *Hartford Daily Courant*, September 15, 1862.

24 McPherson, *Crossroads of Freedom*, 3. See also McPherson, *Battle Cry of Freedom*, 544; John Michael Priest, *Antietam: A Soldier's Battle* (New York: Oxford University Press, 1989).

25 Converse quoted in Croffut and Morris, *The Military and Civil History of Connecticut during the War of 1861–1865*, 265, 267; see also 273. Killed and wounded numbers based on Hines, *Civil War Volunteer Sons of Connecticut*, 142.

26 William H. Relyea, *16th Connecticut Volunteer Infantry: Sergeant William H. Relyea*, ed. John Michael Priest (Shippensburg, Pa.: Burd Street, 2002), 18–19.

27 Quoted in Croffut and Morris, *The Military and Civil History of Connecticut during the War of 1861–1865*, 270–71.

28 Relyea, *16th Connecticut Volunteer Infantry*, 37–38.

29 Killed and wounded numbers based on Hines, *Civil War Volunteer Sons of Connecticut*, 183. Croffut and Morris, *The Military and Civil History of Connecticut during the War of 1861–1865*, 274–75.

30 [Samuel Fiske], *Mr. Dunn Browne's Experiences in the Army* (Boston: Nichols and Noyes, 1866), 45; Charles D. Page, *History of the Fourteenth Regiment, Connecticut Vol. Infantry* (1906; repr., Whitefish, Mont.: Kessinger Publishing, n.d.), 36, 40–41; [Fiske], *Mr. Dunn Browne's Experiences in the Army*, 47; Blinn quoted in Page, *History of the Fourteenth Regiment*, 51; killed and wounded numbers based on Hines, *Civil War Volunteer Sons of Connecticut*, 166.

31 Benjamin Hirst, *The Boys From Rockville: Civil War Narratives of Sergeant Benjamin Hirst, Company D, 14th Connecticut Volunteers*, ed. Robert L. Bee (Knoxville: University of Tennessee Press, 1998), 18, 30.

32 George A. Hubbard to Jasper A. Roberts, folder 2, Middlesex County Historical Society, Middletown, Connecticut.

33 [Fiske], *Mr. Dunn Browne's Experiences in the Army*, 49.

34 Relyea, *16th Connecticut Volunteer Infantry*, 31.

35 *Hartford Evening Press*, October 2, 1862.

36 McPherson, *Battle Cry of Freedom*, 570. There was a great deal in the Connecticut press regarding McClellan's removal as commander. Democrats

blamed it on the "rabid abolition part of the Republican party" (see *Hartford Times*, March 13, 14, and 20, 1862).

37 Page, *History of the Fourteenth Regiment*, 85.

38 [Fiske], *Mr. Dunn Browne's Experiences in the Army*, 106–7. The Connecticut regiments presents at Fredericksburg were the 8th, 11th, 14th, 15th, 16th, 17th, and 27th.

39 Niven, *Connecticut for the Union*, 325.

40 "Aid for the Sick and Wounded," *Hartford Daily Courant*, September 9, 1862; "Hartford Soldiers' Aid Society," *Hartford Daily Courant*, November 1, 1862; "What the Sick Soldiers Say about Mr. Cornish and the Hartford Soldiers' Aid Association," *Hartford Daily Courant*, November 4, 1862. See also "Circular," Soldiers Aid, folder 5, Ladies Volunteer Aid Society, Middlesex County Historical Society, Middletown, Connecticut.

41 "More Work for Women. — The Wounded Soldiers," *Hartford Daily Courant*, June 10, 1862. There were many such articles related to soldiers' aid societies and the care of the wounded published during the second half of 1862. See the following from the *Hartford Daily Courant*: "State Items," June 25; "Sick and Wounded Soldiers," July 15; September 2; "Aid for the Sick and Wounded," September 9.

42 "Letter to the Editor," *Hartford Daily Courant*, July 12, 1862.

43 "List of Certified Cowards in Woodbury! As Per Surgeon's Certificates," Museum of Connecticut History, Hartford, Connecticut. This list gives medical exemptions by name and malady. See also McPherson, *Battle Cry of Freedom*, 491–94; Croffut and Morris, *The Military and Civil History of Connecticut during the War of 1861–1865*, 241–45; J. Robert Lane, *A Political History of Connecticut during the Civil War* (Washington: Catholic University of America Press, 1941), 206–8; Jack Franklin Leach, *Conscription in the United States: A Historical Background* (Rutland, Vt.: Tuttle, 1952), 142–43; Niven, *Connecticut for the Union*, 82–86. At the height of the exemption controversy over the notorious Josiah Beckwith, the doctor sent a justification of his actions to the *Litchfield Enquirer*, arguing that "many absurd as well as unjust reports are in circulation in relation to the manner in which certificates of exemption were obtained in the Litchfield office" ("A Card from Dr. Beckwith," *Litchfield Enquirer*, n.d.). The Litchfield Historical Society also owns all of Dr. Beckwith's medical journals, which list the men he exempted and the reasons he gave for doing so (Josiah Gale Beckwith, Journals, Beckwith Family Papers [unprocessed collection], Helga J. Ingraham Memorial Library, Litchfield Historical Society, Litchfield, Connecticut).

44 Timothy Dwight to William A. Buckingham, August 5, 1862, in James W. Geary, *We Need Men: The Union Draft in the Civil War* (Dekalb: Northern Illinois University Press, 1991), 37.

45 "The Situation," *Hartford Daily Courant*, September 1, 1862. Within two weeks so much lint had been gathered that the Hartford Soldiers' Aid Society announced: "The supply of lint and bandages has now become ample for any emergency" ("The Lint Question," *Hartford Daily Courant*, September 9, 1862.) See also "Notice to the Ladies," *Hartford Daily Courant*, September 13, 1862).

46 *Hartford Daily Courant*, September 29, 1862. Some members of the state's soldiers' aid societies immediately left for Virginia and reported: "The Connecticut wounded are so scattered over the country from Antietam to Washington that it is very difficult to find many of them." Nonetheless, the Society insisted that it "will furnish everything necessary to supply the wants of all the sick and wounded Connecticut men" ("The Soldiers' Aid Society," *Hartford Daily Courant*, September 30, 1862.

47 "Connecticut Legislature," *Hartford Daily Courant*, May 24, 1862; *Hartford Daily Courant*, October 7, 1862; "The Knight Hospital," New Haven's Hospitals, http://info.med.yale.edu/library/news/exhibits/hospitals/knighthosp.html.

48 "Our Connecticut Soldiers," *Hartford Daily Courant*, September 23, 1862; "Letter from Adj't Burnham of the 16th C.V.," *Hartford Daily Courant*, September 30, 1862.

49 "Soldiers' Funerals," *Hartford Daily Courant*, October 27, 1862; "Military Items," *Hartford Daily Courant*, October 11, 1862; "Soldier's Funerals," *Hartford Daily Courant*, October 13, 1862.

50 Quoted in Lane, *A Political History of Connecticut during the Civil War*, 205.

51 Buckingham received 39,782 votes, to Loomis's 30,634. The total votes cast were 70,416. This was a distinct drop in votes for Democrats and in overall voter turnout from previous elections. In 1860, Thomas Seymour had received 43,917 (with 88,375 votes cast), and in 1861, Loomis had received 40,986 (with 83,998 votes cast). See *The Connecticut Register: Being an Official State Calendar of Public Officers and Institution* (Hartford, Conn.: Brown and Parsons, 1859–66). Part of this reduction was undoubtedly because some 15,000 soldiers were at the front and thus unable to vote. Democrats claimed that three-quarters of these soldiers were from their party. For this claim and the health of the party, see "The State Election," *Hartford Daily Times*, April 8, 1862. Quoted in *Hartford Evening Press*, April 8, 1862.

52 "The State Election," *Hartford Daily Times*, April 8, 1862. For additional Republicans reactions, see "HARTFORD REDEEMED! Sham Democracy Rebuked. A Gain of 500 Votes!" *Hartford Daily Courant*, April 8, 1862; "Another Victory for the Union! UTTER DEFEAT OF THE REBELS! Wm.

A. Buckingham Re-Elected by from 7,000 to 10,000 Majority!! A UNION SENATOR FROM EVERY DISTRICT! Great Gains in the Legislature!" *Hartford Daily Courant*, April 8, 1862.

53 Buckingham proclaimed: "The decision will not be one of blind chance, but will be directed by God to accomplish His purposes, which, we trust, will be the advancement and more perfect development of such principles of government as are essential to the well-being of our race." See *Message of His Excellency William A. Buckingham, Governor of Connecticut, to the Legislature of the State, May Session, 1862* (New Haven, Conn.: Babcock and Sizler, 1862), 20–23. See also Niven, *Connecticut for the Union*, 281–82.

54 *New Haven Register*, February 10, 1862. For specific charges of revolution, see the *Hartford Times*, October 4, 1862.

55 Quoted in McPherson, *Crossroads of Freedom*, 65; "Abolition of Slavery in Washington," *Hartford Times*, April 19, 1862. See also "Abolition in the District," *Hartford Times*, April 4, 1862; "Abolition Begun," *Hartford Times*, April 11, 1862.

56 Quoted in David E. Swift, *Black Prophets of Justice: Activist Clergy before the Civil War* (Baton Rouge: Louisiana State University Press, 1989), 323; New Haven *Palladium*, April 22, 1862; *Hartford Evening* Press, April 4, 1862; "The District of Columbia Free!" *Hartford Daily Courant*, April 17, 1862.

57 Quoted in Trumbull, *The Knightly Soldier*, 86. McPherson, *Crossroads of Freedom*, 64. In *The Battle Cry of Freedom*, 497 McPherson noted: "While northern soldiers had no love for slavery, most of them had no love for slaves either. They fought for Union and against treason; only a minority in 1862 felt any interest in fighting for black freedom."

58 Abraham Lincoln to Horace Greeley, August 22, 1862, in *The Collected Works of Abraham Lincoln*, ed. Roy P. Basler (New Brunswick, N.J.: Rutgers University Press, 1953), 5:388–89.

59 Quoted in McPherson, *Crossroads of Freedom*, 62.

60 Quoted in McPherson, *Crossroads of Freedom*, 61–62.

61 Gideon Welles, "The History of Emancipation," *Galaxy* 14 (1872): 842–43.

62 "Preliminary Emancipation Proclamation," September 22, 1862, in Lincoln, *The Collected Works*, 5:433–34.

63 William Buckingham to Abraham Lincoln, September 26, 1862, Abraham Lincoln Papers, American Memory, Library of Congress, http://memory.loc .gov/ammem/alhtml/malhome.html.

64 *Hartford Evening Press*, October 1, 1862; "The Lines Are to be Defined," *Hartford Daily Courant*, September 25, 1862; "Questions for the Courant," *Hartford Daily Courant*, November 7, 1862.

65 Quoted in Lane, *A Political History of Connecticut during the Civil War*, 213.

66   *Hartford Times*, October 4,1862; "Retaliation," *New Haven Register*, October 4, 1862; *New Haven Register*, October 8, 1862.

67   Quoted in Lane, *A Political History of Connecticut during the Civil War*, 214.

68   See Lane, *A Political History of Connecticut during the Civil War*, for additional information on Democratic victories. See also "New Haven Election," *Hartford Daily Courant*, November 29, 1862; *Hartford Daily Courant*, November 26, 1862; *Hartford Daily Courant*, December 25, 1862.

69   *New Haven Register*, November 7, 1862; *New Haven Register*, December 22, 1862; *Hartford Times*, November 27, 1862.

70   "A Political Jail Delivery," *Hartford Times*, December 1, 1862; Connecticut Legislature, "Resolution supporting the president; certified December 31, 1862," Abraham Lincoln Papers.

71   Connecticut Legislature, "Resolution supporting the president; certified December 31, 1862," Abraham Lincoln Papers; "The Repulse at Fredericksburg," *New Haven Register*, December 17, 1862. See also Mark E. Neely, Jr., *The Fate of Liberty: Abraham Lincoln and Civil Liberties* (New York: Oxford University Press, 1992); Matthew Warshauer, *Andrew Jackson and the Politics of Martial Law: Nationalism, Civil Liberties, and Partisanship* (Knoxville: University of Tennessee Press, 2006).

72   Justus M. Silliman, *A New Canaan Private in the Civil War: Letters of Justus M. Silliman, 17th Connecticut Volunteers*, ed. Edward Marcus (New Canaan, Conn.: New Canaan Historical Society, 1984), 18. Fiske sounded a similarly woeful note: "This is a time that is trying the spirit of the nation; a time of disappointment, discouragement, and reverses on all hands. . . . The country is indignant, grieved, disappointed, at the waste of its resources, and the general mismanagement of the contest; and is almost desperate as to the prospect of ever getting its armies properly cared for in the camp, or used in the field" (*Mr. Dunn Browne's Experiences in the Army*, 111).

Chapter 4. The Union Crucible, 1863

1   Abraham Lincoln, "Emancipation Proclamation," in *The Collected Works of Abraham Lincoln*, ed. Roy P. Basler (New Brunswick, N.J.: Rutgers University Press, 1953), 6:28–30.

2   "Jubilee of the Colored People of New Haven," New Haven *Palladium*, January 8, 1863.

3   David E. Swift, *Black Prophets of Justice: Activist Clergy before the Civil War* (Baton Rouge: Louisiana State University Press, 1989), 323–25.

4   "Rejoicings," *Norwich Morning Bulletin*, January 3, 1863. See also "The Salute in Honor of the Proclamation—The Aurora and the Injunction," *Norwich Morning Bulletin*, February 9, 1863. Special thanks to Dale Plum-

mer, the municipal historian for Norwich, for providing me with this information.

5 "Abolition or Separation," *New Haven Register*, February 2, 1863; "The Cruelty of Abolitionism," *New Haven Register*, January 14, 1863; "Taxing the People to Pay for Negroes!" *Hartford Times*, January 12, 1863; "Abolitionism," *Hartford Times*, January 8, 1863. See also "Three Grand Mistakes," *Hartford Times*, January 2, 1863; "Abolition Proclamation," *New Haven Register*, January 2, 1863.

6 "Negro Soldiers," *New Haven Register*, February 5, 1863.

7 "The Negro Soldier Bill," *Hartford Times*, February 6, 1863. "NEGRO REGIMENTS," *Hartford Times*, February 16, 1863.

8 "Mr. Lincoln's Proclamation," *Hartford Daily Courant*, January 2, 1863.

9 "Mr. Lincoln's Proclamation," *Hartford Daily Courant*, January 2, 1863.

10 "Slavery and the Constitution," *Hartford Daily Courant*, March 31, 1863. For more on Northern amnesia concerning race and slavery, see Joanne Pope Melish, *Disowning Slavery: Gradual Emancipation and "Race" in New England, 1780–1860* (Ithaca, N.Y.: Cornell University Press, 1998).

11 "The Irrepressible Conflict," *Hartford Daily Courant*, April 22, 1863.

12 1818 Constitution of the State of Connecticut, art. 3, sect. 5, http://www.sots.ct.gov/sots/cwp/view.asp?a=3188&q=392280. The 1864 amendment was passed in August, as Article 13 of the constitution; it applied solely to soldiers during the "present war." See also Josiah Henry Benton, *Voting in the Field: A Forgotten Chapter of the Civil War* (Boston: privately printed, 1915), 175. The *Hartford Times* made a brief mention of the judges' decision in its January 1, 1863, edition.

13 "An Appeal from the Republican State Central Committee," *Hartford Daily Courant*, February 12, 1863. See also J. Robert Lane, *A Political History of Connecticut during the Civil War* (Washington: Catholic University of America Press, 1941), 221–24.

14 "The Convention," *Hartford Times*, February 17, 1863. Eaton referred to Lincoln as an accidental president because he had been elected due to the Democratic Party split; he had not won the majority of the popular vote.

15 "Democratic Caucus. The Administration Denounced. The Rebels not Denounced," *Hartford Daily Courant*, February 18, 1863.

16 "COPPERHEAD SENTIMENTS," *Hartford Daily Courant*, March 12, 1863. See also Lane, *A Political History of Connecticut during the Civil War*, 221–24; Joanna D. Cowden, "The Politics of Dissent: Civil War Democrats in Connecticut," *New England Quarterly* 56, no. 4 (December 1983): 538–54.

17 "The Reaction," *Hartford Evening Press*, February 20, 1863; "What Do 'Peace Men' Want?" *Hartford Evening Press*, February 3, 1863. The *Courant* wrote: "We would like to inquire what plan of settlement the Peace party propose.

Is the Confederate *usurpation* to be indulged in all its demands?" (January 23, 1863). In another article, the *Courant* insisted: "Peace propositions and compromises are a cheat and a snare, cunningly devised by men who have always opposed the Administration and given aid and comfort to the rebels" ("An Appeal from the Republican State Central Committee," February 12, 1863).

18 "The Soldiers and Their Feelings," *Hartford Times*, January 20, 1863; "What Some of the Soldiers Say," *Hartford Daily Courant*, February 9, 1863; "Letter from a Republican Soldier," *Hartford Times*, February 20, 1863.

19 There are too many articles to cite in a single note, though many are cited throughout this chapter, and a thorough search of the *Times* and *Courant* for the month of March will show the letters and resolutions. See also Laura Lawfer, "'Do Not Place Us between Two Fires': Connecticut Soldiers, Connecticut Newspapers, and the Gubernatorial Election of 1863," paper presented at the Symposium on 19th Century Press, the Civil War, and Free Expression, at the University of Tennessee, Chattanooga, November 8–10, 2007. Ms. Lawfer was kind enough to share a copy of her paper.

20 "Echoes from the Army. Address of the 20th Connecticut, Army of the Potomac," *Hartford Daily Courant*, March 2, 1863. "Soldier's Letters," *Hartford Daily Courant*, March 26, 1863.

21 "From the Soldiers," *Hartford Daily Courant*, March 4, 1863; "What the Soldiers Think of the Copperheads," *Hartford Daily Courant*, March 10, 1863; "AN APPEAL TO THE MEN OF CONNECTICUT!" *Hartford Daily Courant*, March 14, 1863; "Soldier's Letters," *Hartford Daily Courant*, March 17, 1863.

22 "How Soldiers Feel," *Hartford Daily Courant*, March 18, 1863.

23 "A VOICE FROM THE NINTH ARMY CORPS. Patriotic Appeal from Five Connecticut Regiments," *Hartford Daily Courant*, March 21, 1863. See also "The 19th Army Corps—A Patriotic Appeal," *Hartford Daily Courant*, March 25, 1863.

24 "The Latest Dodge. REPUBLICAN MISREPRESENTATION OF THE SOLDIERS!" *Hartford Times*, March 12, 1863. "Hear the Soldiers. THE TRUTH AGAINST ABOLITION LIES," *Hartford Times*, March 20, 1863. In response to the letter concerning the 22nd, Private William Pearson wrote: "The writer is very ignorant—not much acquainted with the minds of his fellow soldiers (in Co. B, especially,) or he is awfully addicted to saying and writing that which is not true" ("STILL ANOTHER VOICE," *Hartford Daily Courant*, March 19, 1863). Another soldier insisted: "I wish to say that that article is an unmitigated falsehood, and that the writer has not the courage to make his name known. . . . If a vote was taken nearly every man would vote for Buck" ("Another Voice from the 22d—The Outrageous Course of the *Hartford Times*," *Hartford Daily Courant*, March 19, 1863).

25 "A Statement from Major Glafke," *Hartford Daily Courant*, March 25, 1863; "The Times Rebuked," *Hartford Daily Courant*, March 23, 1863.

26 "What a Soldier Thinks of Seymour's Nomination," *Hartford Daily Courant*, February 27, 1863.

27 [Samuel Fiske], *Mr. Dunn Browne's Experiences in the Army* (Boston: Nichols and Noyes, 1866), 118–19.

28 Frederick A. Lucas, *Dear Mother from Your Dutiful Son: Civil War Letters, September 22, 1862 to August 18, 1865, Written by Frederick A. Lucas to His Mother*, ed. Ernest Barker (Goshen, Conn.: Purple Door Gallery, 2003), 70.

29 Benjamin Hirst, *The Boys from Rockville: Civil War Narratives of Sgt. Benjamin Hirst, Company D, 14th Connecticut Volunteers*, ed. Robert L. Bee (Knoxville: University of Tennessee Press, 1998), 94.

30 "The National Platform! PURPOSES OF THE WAR!" *Hartford Times*, April 4, 1863; See also "A GREAT MEETING. *Outpouring of the Democracy!* IMMENSE ENTHUSIASM. 'Seymour and the Constitution,'" *Hartford Times*, March 20, 1863; *Hartford Times*, March 26, 1863.

31 *New Haven Register*, March 26, 1863.

32 J. Matthew Gallman, "An Inspiration to Work: Anna Elizabeth Dickinson, Public Orator," in *The War Was You and Me*, ed. Joan E. Cashin (Princeton, N.J.: Princeton University Press, 2002), 159–82; J. Matthew Gallman, *America's Joan of Arc: The Life of Anna Elizabeth Dickinson* (New York: Oxford University Press, 2006); Lane, *A Political History of Connecticut during the Civil War*, 232–33; Joseph Duffy, "Anna Elizabeth Dickinson and the Election of 1863," *Connecticut History* 25 (1984): 22–38; Joseph Duffy, "A Quaker Firebrand Swings An Election," *Hog River Journal* 2, no. 4 (August–October 2004), 18–23.

33 There is some minor discrepancy regarding the actual number of votes. I follow *The Connecticut Register: Being an Official State Calendar of Public Officers and Institution* (Hartford, Conn.: Brown and Parsons, 1859-66), which provides the following numbers: Buckingham: 41,031 votes; Seymour: 38,397 votes; total votes: 79,428; margin: 2,634.

34 "THE ELECTION," *Hartford Daily Courant*, April 7, 1863; "WELL DONE, HARTFORD!" *Hartford Daily Courant*, April 7, 1863; "Victory! Victory!" *Hartford Evening Press*, April 7, 1863.

35 "UNWELCOME TRUTHS," *Hartford Times*, April 8, 1863; "The 'Government' Outrage On the People of Connecticut," *Hartford Times*, April 10, 1863. See also "CONNECTICUT ELECTION. THE RESULT," *Hartford Times*, April 7, 1863.

36 "Cheated Out of It," *New Haven Register*, April 8, 1863. The *Register* had written earlier: "The Republicans, knowing well that the popular tide is against them, now depend upon MONEY and a large influx of furloughed

Republican soldiers to carry them through. The Democratic soldiers are to be kept on duty, and the Republicans, to a large extent, sent home to vote. All this won't save them. The PEOPLE are moving" ("Take Notice, Democrats," March 24, 1863).

37 Abraham Lincoln to Thurlow Weed, February 19, 1863, in *The Collected Works of Abraham Lincoln*, 6:112–13.

38 Quoted in *The Collected Works of Abraham Lincoln*, 6:112–13, note 1. See also Stephen F. Knott, *Secret and Sanctioned: Covert Operations and the American Presidency* (New York: Oxford University Press, 1996), 147–48, 222. Lane, *A Political History of Connecticut during the Civil War*, 237, discusses accusations that Mark Howard, a Republican Party insider, raised money for bribery. See also Joanna Dunlap Cowden, *"Heaven Will Frown on Such a Cause as This": Six Democrats Who Opposed Lincoln's War* (Lanham, Md.: University Press of America, 2001), 48–49.

39 *Message of His Excellency William A. Buckingham, Governor of Connecticut, to the Legislature of the State, May Session, 1863* (Hartford, Conn.: J. M. Scofield, 1863), 3, 18.

40 John William De Forest, *A Volunteer's Adventures: A Union Captain's Record of the Civil War*, ed., with notes, by James H. Croushore (New Haven, Conn.: Yale University Press, 1946), 80, 88, 95, 149. De Forest also wrote: "On all sides I can see great patches of bare skin showing through tattered shirts and trousers. I have but one suit, and so cannot wash it. My pantaloons will almost stand alone, so stiff are they with a dried mixture of dust, mud, showers and perspiration" (149).

41 Stephen Walkley, comp., *History of the Seventh Connecticut Volunteer Infantry, Hawley's Brigade, Terry's Division, Tenth Army Corps, 1861–1865* (1905; repr., Salem, Mass: Higginson Book, 1998), 112–15; Justus M. Silliman, *A New Canaan Private in the Civil War: Letters of Justus M. Silliman, 17th Connecticut Volunteers*, ed. Edward Marcus (New Canaan, Conn.: New Canaan Historical Society, 1984), 55.

42 [Fiske], *Mr. Dunn Browne's Experiences in the Army*, 55, 117–18, 290–91, 309–10.

43 Lucas, *Dear Mother from Your Dutiful Son*, 64. For mention of Arlington Cemetery, see 202.

44 Lucas, *Dear Mother from Your Dutiful Son*, 32. Lucas agreed with his colonel: "As for myself rather would I fall by the enemy's hand in mortal combat, than waste away in hospital, the victim of disease. I wish to fall while manfully contending for the cause I have espoused, in the face of the foe, if die I must in course of this war. But let us hope to survive the perils of camp and field, live to return home again to friends we love so well, and to enjoy the hard earned blessings of peace and prosperity again restored: the Rebellion crushed, Right

maintained, and the principles of true republican liberty firmly established, as the governing and controlling powers of the Union" (162).

45 S. S. Cowan, "The Hartford Soldiers' Aid Society," *Hartford Daily Courant*, May 2, 1863; Nathan Myer [sic], "Letter of Acknowledgment from the Assistant Surgeon of the 16th C.V.," *Hartford Daily Courant*, June 9, 1863. See also the following articles from the *Hartford Daily Courant*: "New Haven Hospital," May 2, 1863; "Middletown," May 20, 1863; "The Hartford Soldiers' Aid Association," June 1, 1863.

46 Ellen M. Sprague, "Patriotic Leteter [sic]," *Hartford Daily Courant*, March 14, 1863.

47 *Hartford Daily Courant*, June 9, 1863; *Hartford Daily Courant*, June 13, 1863. See also the following articles from the *Hartford Daily Courant*: "The Hartford Soldiers' Aid Association," August 1, 1863, which lists and thanks the many donors and towns who contributed; August 26, 1863 ("We desire to call the attention of all who wish to contribute to the health, comfort and efficiency of our troops, to the fact that pickles, dried fruit, and krout are at all times among the most useful articles which can be sent to the army. . . . Let everyone, then, who has a garden, put up pickles and sour krout; and every one who has an orchard dry his surplus fruit for our brave defenders. To a soldier threatened with scurvy, or whose digestion has been weakened by camp diet, a few pickles or a tin cup full of dried apples possess a value scarcely calculable in money"); September 7, 1863; "Acknowledgement," September 8, 1863; September 9, 1863; "An Appeal for Our Soldiers," September 30, 1863; "What the Soldiers' Aid Has Done," October 3, 1863, which includes lists of materials sent to the front and the towns that contributed; November 14, 1863.

48 The U.S. Congressional Serial Set provides a detailed index of manufacturing companies throughout the nation. In addition to the Connecticut companies mentioned in the text, the state was home to Horatio Ames; Eagle Manufacturing Co.; Joslyn Fire-arms Co; John P. Lindsay; James D. Mowry; New Haven Arms Co; Parker, Snow & Co; W. W. Welch; Welch, Brown & Co; and A. A. Chapin ("Ordnance Department; Message from the President of the United States in Answer to a Resolution of the house of 15th March Last, Asking for Information Concerning the Ordnance Department and its Transactions, Jan. 14, 1868," U.S. Congressional Serial Set, 40th Cong., 2nd Sess., H. Exec. Doc. 99, 1868).

49 David J. Naumec, "The Connecticut Contracted '61 Springfield: The Special Model to the 'Good and Serviceable' Arm," *The Bulletin of the American Society of Arms Collectors* 90 (2006):16.

50 Dean Nelson, Museum Administrator, Museum of Connecticut History in Hartford, has compiled chronological binders of all patents awarded to Con-

necticut inventors, before, during, and after the war. Patents can be searched by number on google.com/patents. Some of the patents received by Connecticut citizens are: Alexander Twining (New Haven), Patent #39,363, armor cladding; James Lyons (Litchfield), Patent #38,831, gun carriage; C. R. Alsop (director of Savage Arms & C.R. Alsop Arms, Middletown), Patent #37,481, cartridge; B. F. Joslyn (Stonington), Patent #39,405, improvement to a revolving fire-arm, Patent #39,406, a revolver, and Patent #39,407, improvement to breech-loading firearms; B. B. Hotchkiss (Sharon), Patent #37,481, shell fuse, and Patent #38,359, improvement in explosive projectiles.

51 E. J. Coates and F. C. Gaede, *U.S. Army Quartermaster Contracts, 1861–1865,* National Archives, RG 217, Entry 236, includes the following information, which I have grouped into categories (the dates appear to be the contract issue dates):

Socks, bootees, and stockings: A. H. & C. B. Alling (Birmingham), March 11, 1863, 120,000 socks at $.3625 a pair; H. L. Ayres (New Canaan), September 5, 1863, 800 bootees at $2.03 a pair; Lewis Beers (Stratford), August 29, 1862 through January 9, 1863, 13,000 bootees at an average of $2.05 a pair; George Coffing (Salisbury), January 30, 1863, 180,000 wool socks at $.345 a pair, and February 25, 1864, 150,000 stockings at $.3333 a pair, to be delivered at 10,000 pairs per week; M. L. Graham (Salisbury), December 29, 1862, 2,250 socks at $4.00 a dozen, to weigh three pounds per dozen; Hunt, Holbrook and Barber (Hartford), August 17, 1861, 6,000 bootees at $1.87 a pair; William H. Jones (North Manchester), December 27, 1862, 10,000 stockings at $4.00 a dozen; F. M. Marble (New Haven), August 16, 1861, 20,000 bootees at $1.95 a pair; Joseph B. Merrow (Merrow Station), August 26, 1862, 40,000 wool socks at $.30 a pair; Milo Millard (Merrow Station), February 8, 1864, 120,000 stockings at $.32 a pair; John Turkington (Stanford), August 9, 1862, 10,000 bootees at $1.90 a pair, May 4, 1863, 2,000 bootees at $2.11 a pair, and June 14, 1864, 1,000 bootees at $2.19 a pair; Benedict Webb and Co. (New Canaan), August 25, 1864, 5,000 bootees at $2.70 a pair; Charles B. Wheeler (Stepney Depot), eleven contracts from May 13, 1863 to August 13, 1864, totaling 40,000 bootees at $2.06 to $4.47 a pair.

Cloth, thread, and uniforms: Broadbrook Cloth (Broadbrook), August 16, 1861, dark blue, twilled cloth, twenty-seven inches wide, 50,000 yards at $1.18 a yard; Charles G. Day and Co. (Hartford), August 29, 1862, uniform coats for infantry, 14,000 at $7.15 each; Merrick Bro. and Co. (Mansfield), August 16, 1861, 54,000 spools of thread at $.25 each; New Britain Knitting Co. (New Britain), August 26, 1862, 12,000 knit drawers [undershorts] at $.99 a pair, 13,000 knit shirts at $.99 each, and 25,000 knit shirts at $1 each; Reck Manufacturing (Rockville), August 16, 1861, dark blue twilled cloth, 26,000 yards at $1.15 a yard, dark blue kersey, 12,000 yards at $.99 a yard; Nathan Seeley (Bethel), September 18, 1861, 50,000 uniform infantry hats at $1,62 each, and August 28, 1863, 20,000 hats at $1.99 each; H. Stevens and Co. (Naugatuck), August 24, 1861, 25,000 haversacks at $.39 each; Willimantic Linen Co. (Hartford), April 23, 1862, 5,000 200-yard spools of black cotton thread at $.40 a dozen spools.

Brass items: S. M. Buckingham (Waterbury), February 23, 1864, uniform insignia: brass scales, 24,000 at $0, 20,000 for privates at $.50 each, 4,000 for sergeants at $.75 each, company letters, 500,000 at $5.80 a thousand, and numbers one inch long, 50,000 at $5.50 a thousand; George L. Carrington (Waterbury), December 17, 1864, company letters, 300,000 at $7.50 a thousand, trimmings, 300,000 at $7.50 a thousand; Scovill Manufacturing Co. (Waterbury), July 5, 1861, 6,000 coat buttons at $.54 a gross, 2,500 vest buttons at $.34 a gross, trimmings: 30,000 hat bugles at $.14 each, 2,500 crossed sabers at $.02 each, 5,000 crossed cannons at $.15 each, and August 19, 1861, 100,000 A-I, K insignia at $.35 a hundred; Waterbury Brass Co. (Waterbury), August 16, 1861, trimmings: 2,000 gross bugles at $.69 each, 1,400 gross slides for caps at $.32 a gross; Waterbury Hook and Eye Co. (Waterbury), July 6, 1861, 25,000 buttons at $.34 a gross, trimmings: 200 castles at $.06 each, 1,000 trumpets at $.03 each; West Haven Buckle Co. (West Haven), August 16, 1861, 1,400 buckles at $.26 a gross.

Rubber products: Phoenix Rubber Co. (New York, New York, and Naugatuck), eight contracts from May 2, 1863 to February 12, 1865 for ponchos, totaling 174,000 at $2.65 to $4.94 each, fifteen contracts from November 3, 1862 to February 4, 1865 for vulcanized india rubber blankets, totaling 572,000 at $2.75 to $5.25 each.

52 E. W. Pierce and W. J. Clark (W. J. Clark Co., Southington), Patent #34, 089, soldier's folding cot; H. S. Golightly and C. S. Twitchell (New Haven), Patent #37,864, folding chair; James H. Cables (American Knife Co., Plymouth), Patent # 34,712, folding knife, fork, and spoon combination; Lyman Hutchins (Norwich), Patent #36,783, camp bed.

53 These amounts were tabulated by calculating the contracts listed in note 51 and averaging the price of certain goods that had ranges in price. The results are: socks, bootees, and stockings, $467,481; cloth, thread, and uniforms, $394,846; brass items, $28,435; rubber products, $2,947,460; total, $3,838,222. In 2009 dollars, based on the Gross Domestic Product Deflator (GDP), that is $55,900,000. See Samuel H. Williamson, "Seven Ways to Compute the Relative Value of a U.S. Dollar Amount, 1790 to Present," http://www.measuringworth.com/uscompare.

54 Quoted in James M. McPherson, *Battle Cry of Freedom: The Civil War Era* (New York: Oxford University Press, 1988), 585.

55 McPherson, *Battle Cry of Freedom*, 644. McPherson provides an excellent, clear discussion of Union and Confederate strategy at Chancellorsville.

56 Quoted in David Herbert Donald, *Lincoln* (New York: Simon and Schuster, 1995), 436.

57 [Fiske], *Mr. Dunn Browne's Experiences in the Army*, 143–44.

58 [Fiske], *Mr. Dunn Browne's Experiences in the Army*, 147.

59 [Fiske], *Mr. Dunn Browne's Experiences in the Army*, 151, 156.

60 Blaikie Hines, *Civil War Volunteer Sons of Connecticut* (Thomaston, Conn.: American Patriot, 2002), 190, 204, 250–52; John Niven, *Connecticut for the Union: The Role of the State in the Civil War* (New Haven, Conn: Yale University Press, 1965), 227–33. Ironically, the *Courant* wrongly announced a Confederate defeat ("GREAT UNION VICTORY," May 6, 1863). Two days later, the paper reported the Union loss: "Gen. Hooker's Loss Estimated at 10,000 in Killed, Wounded and Missing!" (*Hartford Daily Courant*, May 8, 1863). The paper also wrote of the 27th Regiment: "Much anxiety is felt for the safety of this regiment. The most extravagant rumors have prevailed in reference to it. . . . The regiment took about three hundred men into the Chancellorville [sic] fight, and but one hundred answered their names after the battle was over" ("The Twenty-Seventh Regiment," *Hartford Daily Courant*, May 12, 1863). Nearly all the men in companies D and F were either killed, wounded, or captured. For more on Libby Prison, see James Gindlesperger, *Escape from Libby Prison* (Shippensburg, Pa.: Burd Street, 1996).

61 Quoted in diary of Nelson L. Stowe, 14th Connecticut Infantry, Company B, CHS MS 78010, Connecticut Historical Society, Hartford, Connecticut.

62 McPherson, *Battle Cry of Freedom*, 627.

63 Quoted in McPherson, *Battle Cry of Freedom*, 631. See also 638.

64 De Forest, *A Volunteer's Adventures*, 117, 118–19.

65 McPherson, *Battle Cry of Freedom*, 646–47.

66 "The Rebel Raid — Call to Arms! Excitement in Philadelphia. Movements of Hooker's Army," *Hartford Daily Courant*, June 17, 1863.

67 McPherson, *Battle Cry of Freedom*, 653.

68 "The Change of Command," *Hartford Daily Courant*, June 30, 1863.

69 McPherson, *Battle Cry of Freedom*, 653–63, provides a very clear account of the Confederate and Union strategies. So does Stephen W. Sears, *Gettysburg* (New York: Mariner, 2004).

70 The 2nd Light Artillery arrived at Gettysburg on July 2. It suffered no casualties. See Hines, *Civil War Volunteer Sons of Connecticut*, 73. The 5th was positioned on Culp's Hill, where the men were ordered out of their entrenchments; upon returning, they found their dugouts occupied by Confederates, and in the struggle, they suffered three wounded and seven captured (91). The 17th was attacked at Barlow's Knoll and pushed back to Cemetery Hill,

where it repulsed attack after attack and suffered 206 casualties. After the battle, the regiment helped to pursue Lee (191). The historian Charles P. Hamblen wrote: "The 17th Connecticut had entered Gettysburg on 1 July with 17 officers and 369 men; by the morning of 3 July, it had lost its commander, seven other officers, and 190 men. Only 179 men from Connecticut left Gettysburg on 4 July 1863 with Meade's victorious army" (*Connecticut Yankees at Gettysburg*, ed. Walter L. Powell [Kent, Ohio: Kent State University Press, 1993], 64). The 20th was among the first regiments to arrive and placed on the extreme right, first at Rock Creek and then Cemetery Hill. It suffered five killed and thirty-one wounded (Hines, *Civil War Volunteer Sons of Connecticut*, 205). The 27th was particularly hard hit. Of the seventy-five men who went into battle, twenty-seven were killed, including the regiment's lieutenant colonel and a captain. On July 3, what remained of it was on the main line at Cemetery Ridge, to the left of where Pickett's men charged. The regiment followed Lee and captured 1,000 of his rear guard (250–51).

71 Charles D. Page, *History of the Fourteenth Regiment, Connecticut Vol. Infantry* (1906; repr., Whitefish, Mont.: Kessinger Publishing, n.d.), 150.

72 Quoted in Page, *History of the Fourteenth Regiment*, 151. See also Hamblen, *Connecticut Yankees at Gettysburg*, 102.

73 Quoted in Page, *History of the Fourteenth Regiment*, 152, 154.

74 Quoted in Hamblen, *Connecticut Yankees at Gettysburg*, 107.

75 [Fiske], *Mr. Dunn Browne's Experiences in the Army*, 187–88, 190. Fiske added: "Oh for a glorious Fourth-of-July celebration! not in speeches, firecrackers, and the noise of unshotted cannon, but in earnest, energetic action in pursuing these defeated enemies; in the stern speech of shotted cannon and musketry, thinning the ranks of our haughty invaders, and pushing their columns, torn and bleeding, back to utter rout and destruction" (190).

76 "The Fourteenth at Gettysburg," *Harper's Weekly*, November 21, 1863. The recipients of the Medal of Honor are listed at "The Civil War Soldier: Gettysburg's Medal of Honor Recipients" (Gettysburg National Military Park, United States Department of the Interior, National Park Service, http://www .nps.gov/archive/gett/soldierlife/honor.htm): "Bacon, Elijah W. . . . Private, Company F, 14th Connecticut Infantry. . . . Citation: Capture of flag of 16th North Carolina regiment (C.S.A.); . . . Flynn, Christopher. . . . Corporal, Company K, 14th Connecticut Infantry. . . . Citation: Capture of flag of 52d North Carolina Infantry (C.S.A.); . . . Hincks, William B. . . . Sergeant Major, 14th Connecticut Infantry. . . . Citation: During the high water mark of Pickett's Charge on 3 July 1863 the colors of the 14th Tennessee Infantry C.S.A. were planted 50 yards in front of the center of Sgt. Maj. Hincks' regiment. There were no Confederates standing near it but several were lying down around it. Upon a call for volunteers by Major Ellis to capture this flag, this soldier

and two others leaped the wall. One companion was instantly shot. Sgt. Maj. Hincks outran his remaining companion running straight and swift for the colors amid a storm of shot. Swinging his saber over the prostrate Confederates and uttering a terrific yell, he seized the flag and hastily returned to his lines. The 14th Tennessee carried twelve battle honors on its flag. The devotion to duty shown by Sgt. Maj. Hincks gave encouragement to many of his comrades at a crucial moment of the battle."

77 "FROM GETTYSBURG," *Hartford Daily Courant*, July 3, 1863; "The Invasion," *Hartford Daily Courant*, July 3, 1863; "THE REBEL INVASION. Great and Glorious Victory!" *Hartford Daily Courant*, July 6, 1863.

78 Quoted in Hamblen, *Connecticut Yankees at Gettysburg*, 113, 117.

79 Silliman, *A New Canaan Private in the Civil War*, 45, 46. Sergeant Russell Glenn of the 14th remembered that after the battle he found a dead Confederate soldier, and "in his hand was a daguerreotype. . . . It is certain that the poor fellow lived but an instant after being hit, but in that short space of time his thought was of the picture — probably the face of his sweetheart — and, taking it from his breastpocket, he saw the shattered case, but was permitted to gaze on the features of a loved one as his soul took its immortal flight" (quoted in Page, *History of the Fourteenth Regiment*, 160–61). For more on how the deaths affected the nation, see Drew Gilpin Faust, *This Republic of Suffering: Death and the American Civil War* (New York: Knopf, 2009).

80 "An Urgent Appeal," *Hartford Daily Courant*, July 8, 1863; "Work for Women," *Hartford Daily Courant*, July 13, 1863. See also *Hartford Daily Courant*, July 8, 1863 ("We hope our people will not, in their rejoicing, forget that twenty thousand of our brave heroes are lying bleeding and suffering in Pennsylvania"); "Our Sick and Wounded at Gettysburg," *Hartford Daily Courant*, July 30, 1863.

81 [Fiske], *Mr. Dunn Browne's Experiences in the Army*, 198, 212, 213.

82 Lucas, *Dear Mother from Your Dutiful Son*, 109.

83 [Fiske], *Mr. Dunn Browne's Experiences in the Army*, 213. The draft riots also revealed more deep seated social, economic, and political struggles within society. See Iver Bernstein, *The New York City Draft Riots: Their Significance for American Society and Politics in the Age of the Civil War* (New York: Oxford University Press, 1991); "The New York Riots — Various Incidents," *Hartford Daily Courant*, July 15, 1863; "The Riot in New York. Its Continuance on Tuesday. It Will be Suppressed," *Hartford Daily Courant*, July 15, 1863.

84 Niven, *Connecticut for the Union*, 88–90; William A. Croffut and John M. Morris, *The Military and Civil History of Connecticut during the War of 1861–1865* (New York: Ledyard Bill, 1869), 459; McPherson, *Battle Cry of Freedom*, 605. The *Courant* reflected the idea that volunteering and receiv-

ing bounties was the best way forward ("The Advantages of Volunteering," October 24, 1863).

85 "Something to Think of," *Hartford Times*, February 27, 1863; "'Republican' Law," *Hartford Times*, March 10, 1863. See also, "The Conscription Law. A CONFLICT OF OPINION," *Hartford Times*, March 16, 1863; "THE CONSCRIPTION ACT," *Hartford Times*, March 18, 1863 ("It *classes us with* NEGROES, and I find that my brother laboring men do not like the degradation. I don't certainly.")

86 "A Nigger Selling White People," *Hartford Times*, October 2, 1863. The story came from Dover, New Hampshire.

87 *Douglass Monthly*, August, 1863 quoted in McPherson, *Battle Cry of Freedom*, 564.

88 "National Convalescence," *Hartford Daily Post*, July 19, 1863.

89 Quoted in McPherson, *Battle Cry of Freedom*, 565–66.

90 Lucas, *Dear Mother from Your Dutiful Son*, 113, 117–18, 210–11. Fiske did not make much, if any, mention of black troops, though he did have harsh words for draftees and substitutes: "Yes, come on, even Copperheads; and, if there is the least spark of patriotic life left in your wretched breasts, we'll kindle it with the snap of percussion-caps into a healthy flame, and brace up your system with the wholesome tonic of whistling bullets and bursting shells, till we can send you home recovered and in your right minds, with a leg of an arm less than now, perhaps, but what there is left at least loyal, and not a nuisance and disgrace to the community. . . . Shall our battle-flags, bearing which our best and bravest have gone down on fields of glory, and whose staffs are yet stained with the blood of their dying grasp, be left to the protection of mercenary wretches, who care neither for country nor reputation, who have sold themselves to you only in the hope of deserting to sell over again in endless succession, and who reach the field only because pistols and bayonets have stood between them and flight? . . . Don't heap praises on the courage and devotion of your armies. Don't speak of the glory of the old flag, the sacredness of our cause, or the value of our institutions. It appears that they are altogether worth—a begrudged and reluctant three hundred dollars. Here's to the flag of the Union!—long may it wave!" (*Mr. Dunn Browne's Experiences in the Army*, 227, 239–40, 242).

91 The full quote is: "Ball's servant, a fat and dirty nigger named George Morris, does the cooking passably well, and robs us to feed his friends and wives. Lieutenant Berry's man, a blubber-lipped loafer called John Bull, ran away several days ago for reasons unknown to me and probably not worth mentioning. My mulatto, Charley Weeks, had deserted some time before. I then got a little yellow vagrant named Harry, and promptly dismissed him for never being on hand when wanted. My present waiter is a good-looking and

dccently behaved full-blood who answers to the yell of George! These fellows work well and are fairly faithful till they are paid, when they seem to be taken with an irresistible desire to see the world. I suppose that I should have the same nomadic longing if I had always been shut up on one plantation" (De Forest, *A Volunteer's Adventures*, 77).

92 William Van Deursen, January 25, February 21, and August 14, 1863, Archival Box, Civil War 4, Folder 16, Middlesex County Historical Society, Middletown, Connecticut.

93 "The Colored Troops in Charleston Harbor," *Hartford Daily Courant*, July 31, 1863; "From the Tenth Regiment," *Hartford Daily Courant*, August 17, 1863.

94 McPherson noted that the 54th's charge at Fort Wagner caused many in the North to have a new respect for blacks, and that Lincoln argued that the regiment's action justified his emancipation policy (*Battle Cry of Freedom*, 686). See also Walkley, *History of the Seventh Connecticut Volunteer Infantry*, 75–78.

95 The 7th Connecticut played a major part in the Sumter siege, manning the "Swamp Angel Battery," the largest gun in the bombardment — a 300-pound rifled Parrott. Walkley noted: "No one could witness its performance during the bombardment of Sumter and notice the terrible crushing effect of its huge projectiles upon the masonry of that place, the ease with which it was worked, and its remarkable accuracy at a distance of two and a half miles without being filled with admiration and wonder" (*History of the Seventh Connecticut Volunteer Infantry*, 99). The gun weighed 26,000 pounds. A typical shell weighed 250 pounds, required 25 pounds of powder, and reached the fort in eighteen seconds. In one day, the gun fired fifteen thousand pounds of metal at Sumter (100). Silliman also noted the bombardment's effects: "Our guns are continually thundering on Sumpter [sic] to prevent the rebels from rebuilding. I think when we get through with that fort there will be left scarcely one stone upon another." He continued: "I had a good field glass, could see the fort quite distinctly and our shells bursting around it. It was a mass of ruins. . . . the fort looks more like a huge pile of bricks thrown together, than anything else of which I could think" (Silliman, *A New Canaan Private in the Civil War*, 51, 55). See also "LATEST FROM CHARLESTON. Guns Opened on Sumter," *Hartford Daily Courant*, August 18, 1863. Lucas rejoiced in the news of Sumter's defeat: "They have lost Sumter. Yes Ft. Sumter is ours. Here was the first blow was struck which touched the nation. How quickly was the nations [sic] hand clenched to return the blow. How glorious the result when once more we hold that post in our possession, although a mass of broken, blackened ruins: ruins which are but typical of the future downfall of the Rebellion" (*Dear Mother from Your Dutiful Son*, 153).

96 "Negro Valor," *Hartford Times*, September 19, 1863. See also *Hartford Times*, September 8, 1863: "The bubble of negro bravery seems in a fair way to collapse before it is inflated. Even the *New York Times* confesses that 'the negro like the mule lacks the highest military qualities.'"

97 Croffut and Morris, *The Military and Civil History of Connecticut during the War of 1861–1865*, 460–61.

98 Quoted in "Connecticut Legislature—Special Session," *Hartford Daily Courant*, November 14, 1863.

99 "The Negro Bill," *Hartford Times*, November 18, 1863.

100 "Negrophobia," *Hartford Daily Courant*, November 14, 1863; "GENERAL HEAD-QUARTERS, STATE OF CONNECTICUT—Adjutant General's Office, Hartford, Nov. 23, 1863—*General Orders No 17*—FOR RECRUITING COLORED VOLUNTEERS," *Hartford Daily Courant*, December 11, 12, 16, and 23 1863.

101 Croffut and Morris, *The Military and Civil History of Connecticut during the War of 1861–1865*, 460–61; Hines, *Civil War Volunteer Sons of Connecticut*, 260, 266.

102 Population figures and calculations are based on the Eighth Census, 1860, Population of the United States, State of Connecticut, 36–41, http://www2.census.gov/prod2/decennial/documents/1860a-04.pdf. The census lists 6,726 persons as black, and 1,901 as Mulatto—equaling 8,627. Men accounted for 4,136, and of these, 2,206 were between the ages of fifteen and fifty. Just as with white troops, it is impossible to accurately determine how many of these men were actually from Connecticut. A look at the regimental muster roles, however, does list the vast majority of men as from Connecticut towns. Still, this is not an exact indicator. See *Record of Connecticut Men in the War of Rebellion, 1861–1865* (Hartford: Case, Lockwood & Brainard Company, 1889).

103 Alexander H. Newton, *Out of the Briars: An Autobiography and Sketch of the Twenty-Ninth Regiment—Connecticut Volunteers* (Philadelphia: A. M. E. Book Concern, 1910), xvi; Isaac J. Hill, *A sketch of the 29th regiment of Connecticut colored troops giving a full account of its formation; of all the battles through which it passed, and its final disbandment* (Baltimore: Daugherty, Maguire, 1867), preface. Hill also discusses the idea of manhood in black men who faced whites soldiers on the field of battle.

104 John H. Eicher and David J. Eicher, *Civil War High Commands* (Stanford, Calif.: Stanford University Press, 2001); John Bowers, *Chickamauga and Chattanooga: The Battles That Doomed the Confederacy* (New York: Harper Perennial, 2001); "Great Victory at Chattanooga," *Hartford Daily Courant*, November 26, 1863 ("Gen. Grant has acted with great energy, and has succeeded in infusing a spirit of fiery determination into his entire army").

105 *Hartford Daily Courant*, October 19, 1863; *Message of His Excellency William A. Buckingham, Governor of Connecticut, to the Legislature of the State, Special Session, November, 1863* (Hartford, Conn.: J. M. Scofield, 1863), 6–7.

106 William W. Ellsworth, "The Basis of Reconstruction," *Hartford Daily Courant*, August 25, 1863. A response to those who want a plan for reconstruction refers to them as "croakers," and states: "The course pursued by the loyal States is definite, straightforward, and has for its objects the accomplishment of a certain end. Starting from the fundamental maxim that the Union is indivisible, they meet by force the forcible attempts to subvert it" ("The Road to Peace," *Hartford Daily Courant*, August 17, 1863).

107 *Hartford Times*, September 11, 1863; *Hartford Times*, November 11, 1863; "The President's 'Greatest Folly,'" *Hartford Times*, December 12, 1863. See also "The Union," *Hartford Times*, October 20, 1863. In December, in response to Lincoln's State of the Union address, the *Times* argued: "There can be no Union, under our present form of government, unless the same right is extended to every State. It is certain that the President is vested with no authority, either as a civil or military officer, to define the powers of States, or to abolish any State institution or State law" ("The President's Message," December 10, 1863). See also *Hartford Times*, December 12, 1863. For similar sentiments, see "Abolition Good Times," *New Haven Evening Register*, October 12, 1863; "Mr. Lincoln's Promise," *New Haven Evening Register*, September 8, 1863; *New Haven Evening Register*, December 2, 1863.

108 "The Thanksgiving," *Hartford Daily Courant*, August 6, 1863. Buckingham had advocated a day of thanksgiving in April, following the gubernatorial election ("BY HIS EXCELLENCY, WILLIAM BUCKINGHAM, GOVERNOR OF THE STATE OF CONNECTICUT: A Proclamation," *Hartford Daily Courant*, April 15, 1863). See also "Gettysburg," *Hartford Daily Courant*, November 19, 1863; "The Gettysburg Celebration," *Hartford Daily Courant*, November 20, 1863.

109 Lincoln's plan excluded high-ranking military officers and Confederate governmental officials. Once 10 percent of the population of a given state, based on votes in the 1860 presidential election, took the oath, that state would be allowed to return to the Union. See McPherson, *Battle Cry of Freedom*, 699–700. Even the *Hartford Daily Courant* reacted harshly to Lincoln's amnesty proclamation: "The simple fact that President Lincoln proposes a certain line of policy, does not necessarily impose upon patriotic citizens the duty of favoring it. . . . Shall Jeff. Davis step down from his blood-stained throne, to exercise the highest act of sovereignty under that Constitution for the destruction of which he has brought untold calamities upon the land? . . . To the loyal men of each one of the United States, be they few or many,

belongs the government of such State. Traitors are civilly dead. They are no more to be taken into account than convicts in the penitentiary" ("Mr. Lincoln's Plans," December 18, 1863).

110 [Fiske], *Mr. Dunn Browne's Experiences in the Army*, 310.

111 "The Work Done and to be Done," *Hartford Daily Courant*, November 25, 1863.

Chapter 5. Expensive Victory, 1864-65

1 Quoted in William A. Croffut and John M. Morris, *The Military and Civil History of Connecticut during the War of 1861-1865* (New York: Ledyard Bill, 1869), 508.

2 John Niven, *Connecticut for the Union: The Role of the State in the Civil War* (New Haven, Conn.: Yale University Press, 1965), 184–86.

3 Sergeant William H. Relyea wrote: "Seeing no hope of escape and believing that the next charge would be the last, the sergeant major directed that in order to save our colors from capture they should be stripped from the staffs, which was immediately done" (*16th Connecticut Volunteer Infantry: Sergeant William H. Relyea*, ed. John Michael Priest [Shippensburg, Pa.: Burd Street, 2002], 138). The staffs were rammed down a hole in the breastwork. Color Sergeant Francis Latimer removed the silver plate and sewed it into his shirt, where it stayed during his entire imprisonment at Andersonville: "When finally exchanged about a year later, in the joy of getting clean clothes at Annapolis, he threw away his lousy old shirt coat with the silver plate sewed up in it, and never saw it again, to his undying regret" (139). The flag was torn into pieces and distributed to members of the regiment, who hid it while in prison. It was reassembled years later and was loudly applauded on Flag Day in 1879. The effort to preserve Connecticut regimental Civil War flags is ongoing at the Connecticut State Capitol.

4 Croffut and Morris, *The Military and Civil History of Connecticut during the War of 1861-1865*, 526; quoted in Robert H. Kellogg, *Life and Death in Rebel Prisons: Giving a Complete History of the Inhuman and Barbarous Treatment of our Brave Soldiers by Rebel Authorities, Inflicting Terrible Suffering and Frightful Mortality, Principally at Andersonville, GA., and Florence, S.C.* (Hartford, Conn.: L. Stebbins, 1867), 56. For a good account of the historical controversy over Southern treatment of Union prisoners, see James M. McPherson, *Battle Cry of Freedom: The Civil War Era* (New York: Oxford University Press, 1988), 795–98. See also Lesley J. Gordon, "'Surely They Remember Me': The 16th Connecticut in War, Captivity, and Public Memory," in *Union Soldiers and the Northern Home Front: Wartime Experiences and Postwar Adjustments*, ed. Paul A. Cimbala and Randall M. Miller (New York: Fordham University Press, 2002).

5   McPherson, *Battle Cry of Freedom*, 719–21; Croffut and Morris, *The Military and Civil History of Connecticut during the War of 1861–1865*, 634–636; Niven, *Connecticut for the Union*, 96.

6   "Military Items," *Hartford Daily Courant*, January 30, 1864; [Samuel Fiske], *Mr. Dunn Browne's Experiences in the Army* (Boston: Nichols and Noyes, 1866), 314; Frederick A. Lucas, *Dear Mother from Your Dutiful Son: Civil War Letters, September 22, 1862 to August 18, 1865, Written by Frederick A. Lucas to His Mother*, ed. Ernest Barker (Goshen, Conn.: Purple Door Gallery, 2003), 245; [Fiske], *Mr. Dunn Browne's Experiences in the Army*, 315.

7   Thomas and Origen Seymour may have been cousins. Buckingham received 39,820 votes to Seymour's 34,162 (*The Connecticut Register: Being an Official State Calendar of Public Officers and Institution* [Hartford, Conn.: Brown and Parsons, 1859–66]).

8   "The Result in Hartford!; COPPERHEADISM ON ITS LAST LEGS! Wm. W. Eaton Defeated! A GLORIOUS DAY'S WORK!" *Hartford Daily Courant*, April 5, 1864; "BUCKINGHAM AND UNION," *Hartford Daily Courant*, April 5, 1864; "Victory Again," *Hartford Evening Press*, April 5 1864. See also "The Great Victory," *Hartford Evening Press*, April 5 1864.

9   William A. Buckingham to Abraham Lincoln, April 5, 1864, Abraham Lincoln Papers, American Memory, Library of Congress http://memory.loc.gov/ammem/alhtml/malhome.html.

10 "The State Election," *Hartford Times*, April 5, 1864. See also J. Robert Lane, *A Political History of Connecticut during the Civil War* (Washington: Catholic University of America Press, 1941), 270–72.

11 Quoted in McPherson, *Battle Cry of Freedom*, 721.

12 [Fiske], *Mr. Dunn Browne's Experiences in the Army*, 122–23; quoted in Charles R. Bowery, Jr., *Lee & Grant: Profiles in Leadership from the Battlefields of Virginia* (New York: American Management Association, 2005), 71.

13 *The Story of the Twenty-First Regiment, Connecticut Volunteer Infantry, During the Civil War, 1861–1865* (1900; repr., Whitefish, Mont.: Kessinger Publishing, n.d.), 187.

14 Quoted in Stephen Walkley, comp., *History of the Seventh Connecticut Volunteer Infantry, Hawley's Brigade, Terry's Division, Tenth Army Corps, 1861–1865* (1905; repr., Salem, Mass: Higginson Book, 1998), 138.

15 "General Butler," *Hartford Daily Courant*, May 27, 1864. See also "Gen. Butler's Plans; His Success; complete Surprise of the Rebels," *Hartford Daily Courant*, May 9, 1864; "Butler; Drury's [sic] Bluff Outer Works Captured; RE-enforcements Cut off; The Work Goes Bravely On!," *Hartford Daily Courant*, May 16, 1864. For Connecticut regiments involved in the battle, see Niven, *Connecticut for the Union*, 244–45; and Blaikie Hines, *Civil War*

Volunteer Sons of Connecticut (Thomaston, Conn.: American Patriot, 2002). Hines also provides casualty figures. See also "Military Items; SIXTH REGIMENT SEVENTH REGIMENT EIGHTH REGIMENT TENTH REGIMENT EIGHTEENTH REGIMENT WOUNDED AND MISSING," *Hartford Daily Courant*, May 24, 1864.

16 Quoted in McPherson, *Battle Cry of Freedom*, 722.

17 [Fiske], *Mr. Dunn Browne's Experiences in the Army*, 390.

18 W. S. Tyler, "Captain Samuel Fiske," New Haven *Daily Palladium*, July 2, 1864. See also Croffut and Morris, *The Military and Civil History of Connecticut during the War of 1861–1865*, 598–91; "Obituary," *Frank Leslie's Illustrated Newspaper*, June 11, 1864; Charles D. Page, *History of the Fourteenth Regiment, Connecticut Vol. Infantry* (1906; repr., Whitefish, Mont.: Kessinger Publishing, n.d.), 275–76.

19 "Postscript.—5 A. M.; The Battle Continued Tuesday and Wednesday; THE MOST DESPERATE OF ALL THE BATTLES; GEN. WARREN REPORTED KILLED; OFFICIAL DISPATCH FROM SEC'Y STANTON," *Hartford Daily Courant*, May 12, 1864. See Hines, *Civil War Volunteer Sons of Connecticut*, 170, for the 14th's casualty figures.

20 Lucas, *Dear Mother from Your Dutiful Son*, 263.

21 Lucas, *Dear Mother from Your Dutiful Son*, 265, 266.

22 Page, *History of the Fourteenth Regiment*, 264.

23 Quoted in Croffut and Morris, *The Military and Civil History of Connecticut during the War of 1861–1865*, 597. See also Hines, *Civil War Volunteer Sons of Connecticut*, 144.

24 Croffut and Morris, *The Military and Civil History of Connecticut during the War of 1861–1865*, 588; see also 593.

25 Hines, *Civil War Volunteer Sons of Connecticut*, 65.

26 Lucas, *Dear Mother from Your Dutiful Son*, 269.

27 Quoted in McPherson, *Battle Cry of Freedom*, 735. Historians differ on Southern casualty figures. For more on the battle of Cold Harbor, see Gordon C. Rhea, *Cold Harbor: Grant and Lee, May 26–June 3, 1864* (Baton Rouge: Louisiana State University Press, 2007); Ernest B. Furgurson, *Not War But Murder: Cold Harbor, 1864* (New York: Vintage, 2001).

28 McPherson, *Battle Cry of Freedom*, 741.

29 A. Wilson Greene, *Civil War Petersburg: Confederate City in the Crucible of War* (Charlottesville: University of Virginia Press, 2006); Alan Axelrod, *The Horrid Pit: The Battle of the Crater, the Civil War's Cruelest Mission* (New York: Carroll and Graf, 2007); Richard Slotkin, *No Quarter: The Battle of the Crater, 1864* (New York: Random House, 2009). For Connecticut regiments at Petersburg, see Hines, *Civil War Volunteer Sons of Connecticut*.

30 THE LATEST NEWS; The Raid into Maryland; Injuries to the Baltimore and

Philadelphia Railroad; Gunpowder Bridge Partially Destroyed; Skirmishing near Washington; ESTIMATES OF REBEL STRENGTH; 45,000 Moving Northward," *Hartford Daily Courant*, July 12, 1864; McPherson, *Battle Cry of Freedom*, 760.

31 "Supplies for the Soldiers," *Hartford Daily Courant*, May 17, 1864; "The Ladies of Hartford," *Hartford Daily Courant*, May 26, 1864. For mourning advertisements, see *Hartford Daily Courant*, May 2 and May 11, 1864. For lists of wounded, many by regiment and giving specific names, see "Military Items," *Hartford Daily Courant*, May 12, June 8, June 15, and June 21, 1864.

32 "Army of the Potomac—Occupation of the Weldon Road," *Hartford Daily Courant*, June 30, 1864; "U.S. Sanitary Commission," *Hartford Daily Courant*, July 4, 1864; "Old Soldiers at Hammond Hospital," *Hartford Daily Courant*, August 29, 1864; quoted in Lane, *A Political History of Connecticut during the Civil War*, 275.

33 "The Great Duty of the Hour," *Hartford Daily Courant*, June 27, 1864.

34 Lucas, *Dear Mother from Your Dutiful Son*, 306–7.

35 Niven, *Connecticut for the Union*, chapter 17, provides an excellent discussion of over production and postwar adjustment.

36 Abraham Lincoln to Horace Greeley, July 9, 1864, Abraham Lincoln Papers; "Alleged Peace Negotiations," *Hartford Daily Courant*, July 22, 1864; quoted in *Hartford Daily Courant*, July 23, 1864.

37 "Peace," *Hartford Times*, July 22, 1864. See also, "Peace Negotiation," *Hartford Times*, July 21, 1864; "Propositions for Peace," *Hartford Times*, July 22, 1864.

38 "Negro's Place in Nature," *Hartford Times*, June 6, 1864. "The Negro Everything—White Man Nothing," *Hartford Times*, June 18, 1864.

39 "Negro Troops," *Hartford Times*, July 2, 1864.

40 "Negro Troops," *Hartford Times*, July 2, 1864. See also these other articles from the *Hartford Times*; "How Much Massachusetts Pays for a Negro," August 2, 1864; "Keep Stepping," May 13, 1864; "Amalgamation, North and South," May 6, 1864; "Negro Troops Not Used," May 30, 1864; "Reason from the other side," August 1, 1864; "President Lincoln," August 18, 1864; "The Conscription of Negroes," August 19, 1864.

41 "The Issue," *Hartford Times*, July 28, 1864; "Principles," *Hartford Times*, July 30, 1864. See also "President Lincoln," *Hartford Times*, July 25, 1864.

42 Henry J. Raymond to Abraham Lincoln, August 22, 1864, Abraham Lincoln Papers.

43 Quoted in McPherson, *Battle Cry of Freedom*, 769.

44 "Prospects of the Negro," *Hartford Daily Courant*, January 1, 1864.

45 "Old Fogyism," *Hartford Daily Courant*, January 30, 1864; "Slavery and the Rebellion," *Hartford Daily Courant*, February 17, 1864.

46 "UNION STATE CONVENTION," *Hartford Daily Courant*, February 18, 1864; "Speech of the Hon. John S. Rice, of Farmington," *Hartford Daily Courant*, February 19, 1864.

47 *Message of His Excellency William A. Buckingham, Governor of Connecticut, to the Legislature of the State, May Session, 1864* (New Haven, Conn.: Carrington and Hotchkiss, 1864), 17–19.

48 Henry J. Raymond to Abraham Lincoln, August 22, 1864, Abraham Lincoln Papers. For more on the proposed commission, see McPherson, *Battle Cry of Freedom*, 769.

49 "Atlanta Ours, How to End the War," *Hartford Evening Press*, September 3, 1864; "Atlanta Ours," *Hartford Daily Courant*, September 3, 1864. See also "ATLANTA OURS! Great Battle and Great Victory, Our Advance Enters the City at Noon Friday," *Hartford Daily Courant*, September 3, 1864; Hines, *Civil War Volunteer Sons of Connecticut*, 92.

50 "A Cyclone in the South," *Hartford Evening Press*; November 19, 1864. The *Hartford Daily Courant* was filled for several weeks with articles and notices regarding the celebrations and importance of the Atlanta victory. See, for example, "Rejoicings at Waterbury," September 5, 1864; "Rejoicings over Sherman's Great Union Victory," September 5, 1864; "State Items," September 5, 1864; untitled item, September 6, 1864; "Rejoicings in New Jersey," September 6, 1864; and "Celebration at Boston," September 7, 1864.

51 Quoted in McPherson, *Battle Cry of Freedom*, 758.

52 John William De Forest, *A Volunteer's Adventures: A Union Captain's Record of the Civil War*, ed., with notes, by James H. Croushore (New Haven, Conn.: Yale University Press, 1946), 197.

53 De Forest, *A Volunteer's Adventures*, 215.

54 De Forest, *A Volunteer's Adventures*, 221.

55 Hines, *Civil War Volunteer Sons of Connecticut*, 125, 152–53, 159–61. For news of the Shenandoah campaign, see *Hartford Daily Courant*, October 21, 1864; "Sheridan's Victory," *Hartford Daily Courant*, October 22, 1864; "From Sheridan's Army—The Twelfth Connecticut," *Hartford Daily Courant*, October 29, 1864.

56 Hines, *Civil War Volunteer Sons of Connecticut*, 66.

57 Lucas, *Dear Mother from Your Dutiful Son*, 314.

58 Lucas, *Dear Mother from Your Dutiful Son*, 333–34.

59 "Brightening Prospects," *Hartford Daily Courant*, September 8, 1864.

60 For the Chicago Platform, see McPherson, *Battle Cry of Freedom*, 775–75. See also Charles R. Wilson, "McClellan's Changing Views on the Peace Plank of 1864," *American Historical Review* 38, no. 3 (April 1933): 498–505.

61 "General McClellan's Acceptance," *Hartford Daily Courant*, September 10, 1864; "More Trouble in the Wigwam," *Hartford Daily Courant*, September

12, 1864; Lucas, *Dear Mother from Your Dutiful Son*, 323. See also "The Peace Men Abandoning McClellan," *Hartford Daily Courant*, September 12, 1864.

62 "The Copperhead Clam-Bake," *Hartford Daily Courant*, September 19, 1864.

63 "To Whom It May Concern," *Hartford Times*, August 19, 1864; *Hartford Times*, September 24, 1864. See also "Another Word with Candid Republicans," *Hartford Times*, September 17, 1864, in which the paper once again pointed out what it viewed as Lincoln's hypocrisy regarding abolition.

64 "The Difference," *New Haven Register*, September 8, 1864. See also, "The Difference," *New Haven Register*, September 7, 1864.

65 "Lincoln vs. Sherman," *New Haven Register*, September 16, 1864; "Negro Catchers of White Men," *New Haven Register*, September 20, 1864.

66 "How Many More Years of War!" *Hartford Times*, October, 20 1864; "Lincoln vs. Sherman," *New Haven Register*, September 16, 1864.

67 Lane, *A Political History of Connecticut during the Civil War*, 288.

68 "A Republic or a Monarchy," *Hartford Times*, November 7, 1864: "Elect GEORGE B. MCCLELLAN, and the days of Peace, tranquility, prosperity, and happiness will dawn their glorious light upon our country. The war will stop, the good old Union will be restored, and, God be praised, Liberty and the Constitution will be again triumphant and the most glorious jubilee that ever rejoiced the heart of man will burst forth upon this people, redeemed, disenthralled and standing up in all the splendid attributes of a Heaven-inspired manhood."

69 "Close Up the Campaign of 1864," *New Haven Register*, November 7, 1864.

70 "The Flag Raising," *Hartford Daily Courant*, October 8, 1864.

71 "GRAND TORCHLIGHT PROCESSION!" *Hartford Daily Courant*, October 22, 1864.

72 "A General Jubilee," *Hartford Daily Courant*, October 21, 1864. For more on the radical Republican movement in Connecticut against Lincoln, see Lane, *A Political History of Connecticut during the Civil War*, 277–80.

73 "The Presidential Question — Shall We Have an Insurrection at the North?" *Hartford Daily Courant*, September 6, 1864; McPherson, *Battle Cry of Freedom*, 781; Hines, *Civil War Volunteer Sons of Connecticut*, 104, 112, 139.

74 "Victory," *Hartford Evening Press*, November 9, 1864.

75 By 1864, nineteen states had passed legislation allowing soldiers to vote in the field. In New York and Connecticut, these votes provided the margin for Lincoln's victory. See McPherson, *Battle Cry of Freedom*, 804–5; 1818 Constitution of the State of Connecticut, art. 3, sect. 5, http://www.sots.ct.gov/sots/cwp/view.asp?a=3188&q=392280. See also Josiah Henry Benton, *Voting in the Field: A Forgotten Chapter of the Civil War* (Boston: privately printed,

1915), 175. Connecticut election results were 44,693 for Lincoln and 42,288 for McClellan (Connecticut Election Results, http://www.uselectionatlas.org/RESULTS/state.php?year=1864&off=0&elect=0&fips=9&f=0).

76 "The Old Flag Still Waves!" *Hartford Daily Courant*, November 8, 1864. See also "A Bright Day," *Hartford Evening Press*, November 8, 1864.

77 William A. Buckingham to Abraham Lincoln, November 17, 1864, Abraham Lincoln Papers; "A PROCLAMATION, William A. Buckingham," *Hartford Daily Courant*, November 24, 1864. See also Nehemiah D. Sperry to Abraham Lincoln, November 8, 1864, Abraham Lincoln Papers. "Signs of the End," *Hartford Daily Courant*, November 12, 1864.

78 "The Presidential Election; Lincoln Elected," *Hartford Times*, November 9, 1864; "The Election," *New Haven Register*, November 9, 1864. See also "The Election, The State," *New Haven Register*, November 9, 1864; "The Result," *New Haven Register*, November 11, 1864.

79 Abraham Lincoln, "Annual Message to Congress," December 6, 1864, in *The Collected Works of Abraham Lincoln*, ed. Roy P. Basler (New Brunswick, N.J.: Rutgers University Press, 1953), 8:149–15. See also "The President's Message," *Hartford Evening Press*, December 7, 1864; "The President's Message," *Hartford Daily Courant*, December 7, 1864; "The President's Message," *Hartford Times*, December 7, 1864.

80 Lincoln, "Proclamation Calling for 300,000 Volunteers," December 19, 1864, in *The Collected Works of Abraham Lincoln*, 8:171–72; quoted in William Tecumseh Sherman, *Memoirs of General W. T. Sherman*, ed. with an introduction and notes by Michael Fellman (New York: Penguin, 2000), 592.

81 Croffut and Morris, *The Military and Civil History of Connecticut during the War of 1861–1865*, 767. See also Niven, *Connecticut for the Union*, 259.

82 "Jubilate!" *Hartford Evening Press*, February 1, 1865; "The Constitutional Amendment," *Hartford Daily Courant*, February 2, 1865. See also McPherson, *Battle Cry of Freedom*, 839.

83 "Amendment to the Constitution," *Hartford Times*, February 1, 1865; "The Abolition Amendment," *New Haven Register*, February 4, 1864; "How the Constitutional Amendment was Carried," *Hartford Times*, February 28, 1865; See also "The Amendment," *Hartford Times*, February 2, 1865; "Amendment to the Constitution," *New Haven Register*, February 2, 1865.

84 "Inferiority of the Negro Race," *Hartford Times*, March 1, 1865.

85 Lucas, *Dear Mother from Your Dutiful Son*, 355, 384–85.

86 Lucas, *Dear Mother from Your Dutiful Son*, 359, 360–61, 363; McPherson, *Battle Cry of Freedom*, 821.

87 Hines, *Civil War Volunteer Sons of Connecticut*, 262.

88 Quoted in McPherson, *Battle Cry of Freedom*, 846.

89 "GLORIOUS NEWS!" *Hartford Daily Courant*, April 10, 1865.

90 "THE NATION MOURNS," *Hartford Daily Courant*, April 15, 1865; "The Assassination of the President," *Hartford Daily Courant*, April 17, 1865. See also "AWFUL CALAMITY; TERRIBLE LOSS TO THE NATION! PRESIDENT LINCOLN ASSASSINATED! ATTEMPT TO ASSASSINATE SECRETARY SEWARD! He Still Lives. THE ASSASSIN ESCAPES! FULL PARTICULARS," *Hartford Daily Courant*, April 15, 1865.

91 Ernest B. Barker, *Fred and Jennie: A Civil War Love Story*, with letters edited by Ernest B. Barker, assisted by Anthony J. Barker (Goshen, Conn.: Purple Door Gallery, 2002), 134–35.

92 Justus M. Silliman, *A New Canaan Private in the Civil War: Letters of Justus M. Silliman, 17th Connecticut Volunteers*, ed. Edward Marcus (New Canaan, Conn.: New Canaan Historical Society, 1984), 101–2.

93 Charles J. Hoadly to William A. Buckingham, April 15, 1865, RG 005, Governor William A. Buckingham, Connecticut State Library, Hartford, Connecticut; "THE NATION MOURNS," *Hartford Daily Courant*, April 15, 1865. "Monument to Abraham Lincoln," *Hartford Daily Courant*, April 25, 1865. There were also attempts to make Connecticut a stop on the journey of the Lincoln funeral train, which stopped in several locations on its way from Washington, D.C., to Springfield, Illinois. See Scott D. Trostel, *The Lincoln Funeral Train: The Final Journey and National Funeral for Abraham Lincoln* (Fletcher, Ohio: Camtech Publishing, 2002).

94 "Results of Copperhead Teachings," *Hartford Daily Courant*, April 17, 1865; "Funeral of Abraham Lincoln," *Hartford Daily Courant*, April 20, 1865.

95 "ASSASSINATION OF THE PRESIDENT, A National Calamity!" *Hartford Times*, April 15, 1865. The *Courant* reported that those Democrats who did utter harsh words about Lincoln's death were treated roughly ("Results of Copperhead Teachings" and "Sympathizers with Assassination Roughly Handled," April 17, 1865).

96 [Fiske], *Mr. Dunn Browne's Experiences in the Army*, 366.

97 "A Grand Review. A Magnificent Display of Veterans. All Branches of the Service Represented. Fine Marching Enthusiasm," *Hartford Daily Courant*, May 24, 1865; Niven, *Connecticut for the Union*, 261–62.

98 The earliest source for figures on Connecticut soldiers is Croffut and Morris, *The Military and Civil History of Connecticut during the War of 1861–1865*, 800, which states that 54,882 soldiers served. Another work, *A Compendium of the War of Rebellion, comp. and arranged from official records of the Federal and Confederate armies, reports of the Adjutant Generals of the several states, the Army registers, and other reliable documents and sources*, by Frederick H. Dyer (Cedar Rapids, Iowa: Dyer, 1908), has become an indispensable source on the history of regiments throughout the nation. Dyer adjusts Connecticut figures to the higher 55,864. Several websites make

his work available: "The Civil War Archive," http://www.civilwararchive .com/unionct.htm; "The Civil War Homepage," http://www.civil-war.net/ searchstates.asp?searchstates=Connecticut. Population figures and calcula- tions are based on the Eighth Census, 1860, Population of the United States, State of Connecticut, 36–41, http://www2.census.gov/prod2/decennial/ documents/1860a-04.pdf. Most recently, Hines, *Civil War Volunteer Sons of Connecticut*, xii–xiii, states that 39,395 men actually served in Connecticut regiments, and 43,837 enlisted.

Chapter 6. Survival's Memory, 1865-1965

Most inscriptions on civil war monuments were carved using only uppercase letters. To make this text more readable, this format has not been retained here.

1 Jefferson Davis, *The Rise and Fall of the Confederate Government* (New York: Appleton, 1881); Alexander H. Stevens, *A Constitutional View of the Late War Between the States* (Philadelphia: National Publishing, 1870); Charles Dew, *Apostles of Disunion: Southern Secession Commissioners and the Causes of the Civil War* (Charlottesville: University Press of Virginia, 2001); Garry W. Gallagher and Alan T. Nolan, eds., *The Myth of the Lost Cause and Civil War History* (Indianapolis: Indiana University Press, 2000).

2 David W. Blight, *Race and Reunion: The Civil War in American Memory* (Cambridge, Mass.: Harvard University Press, 2002); Chandra Manning, *What This Cruel War Was Over: Soldiers, Slavery, and the Civil War* (New York: Knopf, 2007); Earl Hess, *Liberty, Virtue, and Progress: Northerners and Their War for the Union* (New York: Fordham University Press, 1997).

3 Blight, *Race and Reunion*, 3.

4 Drew Gilpin Faust, *This Republic of Suffering: Death and the American Civil War* (New York: Knopf, 2009).

5 David F. Ransom, "Civil War Monuments of Connecticut," *Connecticut His- torical Society Bulletin* 58, nos. 1–4 (1993) and 59, nos. 1–4, (1994).

6 *History of Battle Flag Day* (Hartford, Conn.: Lockwood and Merritt, 1879). Most Connecticut Civil War regimental and unit flags were given to the Con- necticut adjutant general's office at the close of the war. They were stored in the state armory and released for the Battle Flag parade.

7 For the background of Connecticut's 1818 constitution and the 1846 attempt to amend it, see chapter 1. It is not entirely clear when the 1864 amendment was proposed. For its 1865 announcement, see "Connecticut Legislature," *Hartford Daily Courant*, May 4, 1865.

8 Buckingham won the 1865 election with 42,374 votes to Seymour's 31,349. This was his largest gubernatorial election victory. See *The Connecticut Register: Being an Official State Calendar of Public Officers and Institution*

(Hartford, Conn.: Brown and Parsons, 1859–66), p. 18. *Message of His Excellency, Governor of Connecticut, to the Legislature of the State, May Session, 1865* (Hartford, Conn.: A. N. Clark, 1865), 9.

9 *Message of His Excellency, Governor of Connecticut, to the Legislature of the State, May Session, 1865*, 16.

10 *Hartford Times*, February 23, 1865.

11 "'Inferiority' of the Negro Race," *Hartford Daily Courant*, February 28, 1865; "Nigger on the Brain," *Hartford Daily Courant*, March 3, 1865. See also "The Republican Party vs. the Times and the Democratic Party," *Hartford Daily Courant*, March 9, 1865: "What the republican party proposes to do, is to give the negro the same political rights the whites enjoy, and then let him take his chances in finding his social level, and learn him to understand that his interests are identical with our own in the politics of the country."

12 "Negro Suffrage," *Hartford Daily Courant*, May 24, 1865.

13 Quoted in "Connecticut Legislature," *Hartford Daily Courant*, May 19, 1865. The Supreme Court was ruling on the status of a slave, Dred Scott, who had lived for an extended period of time in a free territory and a free state. Thus the issue before the Court was his freedom, not the citizenship of all blacks.

14 "Connecticut Legislature," *Hartford Daily Courant*, June 16, 1865. See also "Connecticut Legislature," *Hartford Daily Courant*, June 17, 1865. The House and Senate concurred on this legislation, the former voting on the 15th and the latter on the 16th.

15 Quoted in "Connecticut Legislature," *Hartford Daily Courant*, June 28, 1865. When the 1865 decision was published, the reporter of judicial decisions, John Hooker, inserted a footnote referring to the handling of this issue in the famous Prudence Crandall case, when she was tried for teaching black children. Hooker recalled that Chief Judge Daggett had determined at the trial that free blacks were not citizens, but that the issue was not formally decided at that time by the state Supreme Court since it decided the case on a technicality. His note confirmed that the panel of judges that heard and decided the Crandall case in 1834 included Daggett and Judges Williams, Bissell, and Church. Minutes of the judges' discussion of the case, found in Bissell's papers following his death, indicated that the issue of the citizenship of free blacks had been discussed among the judges at length, and that while Daggett continued to hold the opinion he had stated in the trial—that free blacks were not citizens—all the other judges involved in the 1834 case either believed or were inclined to believe the contrary. In addition, the note refers to a letter written by Williams to Bissell in 1857, in which he indicated that some people had misconstrued the court's decision in the Crandall case to say that free blacks were not citizens, when in fact the issue was not formally decided then. Williams's letter states: "According to my recollection . . . , all

of us differed from the Chief Justice so far as we expressed an opinion, but we gave no definite opinion and concluded to dispose of the case on other grounds. . . . For myself I must say that I did not then doubt, nor since have doubted, that our respected friend was wrong in his charge to the jury." I am indebted to James Brown for this information. For sources, see 32 Conn. 565, Reporter's Note; Wesley W. Horton, "Hosmer to Peters to Daggett," *Connecticut Bar Journal* 73, no. 4 (1999): 275–96.

16 Quoted in "Connecticut Legislature," *Hartford Daily Courant*, May 19, 1865.

17 "Negro Suffrage," *Hartford Daily Courant*, May 24, 1865.

18 "Connecticut Legislature," *Hartford Daily Courant*, May 25, 1865.

19 "Connecticut Legislature," *Hartford Daily Courant*, May 25, 1865, The legislative report notes the laughter caused by portions of Barnum's speech.

20 "Negro Suffrage. Speech of John A. Douglas, Esq., in the House of Representatives," *Hartford Daily Courant*, May 26, 1865.

21 "How Is It?" *Hartford Times*, June 20, 1865.

22 "Negro Suffrage. Speech of John A. Douglas, Esq., in the House of Representatives," *Hartford Daily Courant*, May 26, 1865.

23 "Speech of Judge Munson, In the Connecticut Legislature, May 25th, 1865, on the Question of Negro Suffrage," *Hartford Times*, June 8, 1865.

24 "Speech of Judge Munson, In the Connecticut Legislature, May 25th, 1865, on the Question of Negro Suffrage," *Hartford Times*, June 8, 1865; "Judge Munson's Speech," *Hartford Times*, June 8, 1865.

25 "The Constitutional Amendment," *Hartford Times*, May 24, 1865; "Negro Suffrage," *Hartford Times*, May 26, 1865. In delivering the majority opinion, Justice Henry Brown argued in 1896 that "legislation is powerless to eradicate racial instincts or to abolish distinctions based upon physical differences, and the attempt to do so can only result in accentuating the difficulties of the present situation. If the civil and political rights of both races be equal one cannot be inferior to the other civilly or politically. If one race be inferior to the other socially, the Constitution of the United States cannot put them upon the same plane."

26 "Connecticut Legislature," *Hartford Daily Courant*, May 26, 1865. See also "Justice to the Negro," *Hartford Daily Courant*, May 26, 1865.

27 "Connecticut Legislature," *Hartford Daily Courant*, June 1, 1865. The *Courant* announced that the Senate vote "will give the black man who can read, the rights and privileges of citizenship which are his due. Now let the people, when the question is submitted to them, ratify the action of the legislature, and thereby do justice to a much abused race" ("The Suffrage Question," June 1, 1865).

28 There is a rich and important history in the many arguments surrounding the amendment, and the discussion in this chapter is by no means intended

to be an exhaustive study. More research is needed, although some work has been done. See Joanna Cowden, "Civil War and Reconstruction Politics in Connecticut, 1863–1868," (Ph.D. diss., University of Connecticut, 1975); Jane M. Reynolds, "Connecticut's Black Suffrage Referendum: A Crucial Test of Republican Policy," (senior thesis, Trinity College, 1992). For additional arguments in the General Assembly, see a sixteen-page pamphlet that contained excerpts of various speeches ("Voices from Connecticut for Impartial Suffrage" [1865]). For additional newspaper arguments on the matter, see the following articles from the *Hartford Daily Courant* in 1865: "The October Election," September 15; "Should the Colored Men Vote?" September 27; "Under Which King?" September 30; "The Hartford Times and Negro Suffrage," September 27.

29 Leslie H. Fishel Jr., "Northern Prejudice and Negro Suffrage 1865–1870," *Journal of Negro History* 39, no. 1 (January 1954): 8–26.

30 "The Question of Negro Suffrage," *New York Times*, September 12, 1865.

31 Quoted in Fishel, "Northern Prejudice and Negro Suffrage 1865–1870," 11–12.

32 "Prejudice," *Hartford Times*, August 17, 1865.

33 See the following articles in the *Hartford Times* in 1865: "Negro Suffrage in Connecticut," September 15; "The Harford Evening Press on Negro Suffrage," September 21; "Negro Suffrage—Cowardly Dodging!" September 23; "Did Negroes Ever Vote?" September 23; "Progress, Blackways," September 26; "Get Rid of the Negro," September 26; "Move On-Step Onward!" September 26; "The Negro 'Must' Vote," September 28; "The Destructives," September 28; "The Courant's New Negro Correspondent," September 29; "Colorado—Negro Suffrage Defeated!" September 29; "One Word to the Hartford Courant," September 29; "The Negro Conflict," September 29; "The Negroes," September 29.

34 "To Citizens of all Parties," *Hartford Times*, September 29, 1865; "Citizens of Hartford," *Hartford Times*, October 2, 1865. See also "The Negro Conflict," "The Negroes," "The Constitution," "The Destructives," *Hartford Times*, September 29, 1865.

35 "The Election Yesterday," *Hartford Daily Courant*, October 3, 1865; "The Election," *Hartford Post*, October 3, 1865; "The Election," *Hartford Daily Courant*, October 4, 1865.

36 "CONNECTICUT—THE RESULT. A White Man's State in New England," *Hartford Times*, October 3, 1865. For other articles in the *Hartford Times* in 1865, see "NEGRO SUFFRAGE DEFEATED BY 6,500!" October 4; "Connecticut—Importance of Its Vote," October 6; "A Full Vote," October 7; "Connecticut," October 10; "Connecticut—Official," November 8.

37 *Hartford Daily Courant*, October 4, 1865.

38 The final vote was 27,217 votes in favor and 33,489 votes against the amendment, for a margin of 6,272. For a discussion of the town elections and an account of the vote, see Cowden, "Civil War and Reconstruction Politics in Connecticut, 1863–1868."

39 "The Connecticut Election," *New York Times*, October 4, 1865.

40 "The Connecticut Election," *New York Times*, October 4, 1865.

41 "The Connecticut Election," *New York Times*, October 4, 1865.

42 William Lloyd Garrison, "An Evil Decision," *Liberator*, October 13, 1865. There is no doubt that the black community was engaged in fighting for voting rights, as they had in every previous push for civic rights. I have not yet found evidence of such involvement in this case, however. Amos Beman and James Pennington had left the state by this time, though other black leaders remained who could have taken part.

43 Considering the 1865 vote not to amend the Connecticut constitution and extend suffrage to blacks, William C. Fowler speculated that in ratifying the Fifteenth Amendment, the Connecticut General Assembly may have been misrepresenting the opinion of the majority of Connecticut voters (*Local Law In Massachusetts and Connecticut: Historically Considered; and The Historical Status of the Negro in Connecticut* [Albany, N.Y.: Joel Munsell, 1872], 145). The 1876 amendment to the Connecticut Constitution, Article 23, stated that Article 8 of the amendments to the constitution be amended by erasing the word "white" from the first line. See 1818 Constitution of the State of Connecticut, art. 23, http://www.sots.ct.gov/sots/cwp/view.asp ?a=3188&q=392280.

44 Frederick A. Lucas, *Dear Mother from Your Dutiful Son: Civil War Letters, September 22, 1862 to August 18, 1865, Written by Frederick A. Lucas to His Mother*, ed. Ernest Barker (Goshen, Conn.: Purple Door Gallery, 2003), 202.

45 I am indebted to the excellent work of Jaclyn Levesque, a graduate student at Central Connecticut State University, who researched and wrote a paper on the history of the Kensington monument. See also Joseph Nathan Kane, *Famous First Facts: A Record of First Happenings, Discoveries and Inventions in the United States* (New York: H. W. Wilson, 1950), 294; "Kensington Scene of Patriotic Celebration in Memory of Martyred Soldiers and Unveiling of Old Monument," *New Britain Daily Herald*, July 26, 1913; "The Town of Kensington," *Connecticut Magazine* 6 (1900): 405; Ransom, "Civil War Monuments of Connecticut." "Monument Dedication in Kensington," *Hartford Daily Courant*, July 29, 1863, listed the names of the six soldiers and where they died: James L. Bailey (Cedar Ridge), Leverett H. Gladding (Fredericksburg), John L. Kent (Antietam), Henry F. Allen (between Charleston and Savannah), Birdsey J. Beckley and George W. Horton (both

in a New Orleans hospital). The causes of death ranged from killed in action to diseases.

46 "Monument Dedication in Kensington," *Hartford Daily Courant*, July 29, 1863.

47 Bristol's monument was erected January 20, 1866; North Branford's, April 12, 1866; Cheshire's, July 1866; Northfield's, September 1866. All information about the monuments is taken from Ransom, "Civil War Monuments of Connecticut."

48 Ransom, "Civil War Monuments of Connecticut."

49 I am not going to attempt to provide an individual reference for each quote used regarding the monuments. Ransom's study is available at the Connecticut Historical Society and provides a complete, alphabetical listing of each town and their monuments. Thus, unless otherwise cited, all information concerning the monuments comes from Ransom, "Civil War Monuments of Connecticut." Only three monuments erected in the nineteenth century used the name "Civil War": Ledyard George T. Meech Plaque, circa the 1870s; North Haven Memorial Town Hall, 1886; and Windsor Locks Memorial Hall, 1891, and even in those cases, I have doubts as to the use of the name. The date of the Ledyard plaque is uncertain, as is the actual placing of the plaques at the North Haven site. The Windsor Locks memorial may be the first to use the name. Roughly ten twentieth-century monuments referred to the conflict as the "Civil War," beginning with Thompson's Soldier's Monument, in 1902.

50 There are a few monuments that note soldiers connected to the 29th and/ or designate soldiers as "colored." The Smith Gateway at Union Cemetery in Niantic (East Lyme) lists soldiers' names followed by symbols, one of which means "colored," as explained at the bottom of the plaques. On the Weatogue Soldiers' Monument in Simsbury, seven of the 194 names are identified as from "Colored Regiments." The Soldier's Monument in East Hartford also designates some names with "(col'd)."

51 "Completing the Arch," *Hartford Courant*, August 8, 1891; "Last Statue Placed in Position," *Hartford Courant*, May 23, 1893; David F. Ransom, *George Keller, Architect* (Hartford, Conn.: Stowe-Day Foundation, 1978). I am indebted to Amanda Roy, a graduate student at Central Connecticut State University, for her excellent paper "From Triumph to Traffic: Hartford's Soldiers and Sailors Memorial Arch."

52 Ransom, "Civil War Monuments of Connecticut," provides an excellent description of this monument.

53 "Monument to honor 'colored regiment' of Civil War," *New Haven Register*, September 9, 2009; "Colored Regiment Monument Previewed," *New Haven Independent*, August 29, 2008.

54 There are also a number of monuments dedicated to specific regiments.

55 The other fiftieth-anniversary monuments were: New Milford's 1912 Lincoln Herm; Putnam's 1912 Soldiers' Monument; Plainville's 1913 Defenders of the Flag; Griswold's 1913 Soldiers' Monument; and New Haven's 1915 Soldiers' Memorial Gateway.

56 These quotes obviously cannot be accurately displayed as they are on the monument itself, given that they appear on different sides and the spacing varies.

57 Ernest F. Faehtz, comp., *The National Memorial Day: A Record of Ceremonies over the Graves of the Union Soldiers, May 29 and 30, 1869* (Washington: Headquarters of the Grand Army of the Republic, 1870), 5.

58 "Decoration Day," *Hartford Courant*, May 28, 1868; "The Soldiers' Graves," *Hartford Times*, May 29, 1868. I am indebted to Emily Gifford, a graduate student at Central Connecticut State University, for her paper "From Decoration Day to the Centennial Commission: Modes of Civil War Commemoration in Connecticut, 1868–1965."

59 I am indebted to Todd Jones, a graduate student at Central Connecticut State University, for his paper "Patriot, Soldier, Statesman: General Joseph R. Hawley and Civil War Commemoration in Connecticut During the Late 19th Century." This discussion of Hawley is derived from Mr. Jones's work. In the 1866 election, Hawley received 43,888 votes to James English's 43,433 (*The Connecticut Register*, 18). See also Joseph R. Hawley, *Major General Joseph R. Hawley, Soldier and Editor (1826–1905), Civil War Military Letters*, ed. Alfred D. Putnam (Hartford, Conn.: Connecticut Civil War Centennial Commission, 1964), 3–5; Ellsworth S. Grant, *The Miracle of Connecticut* (Hartford, Conn: Connecticut Historical Society, c. 1992), 103–6; "Our Greatest Soldier," *Hartford Scrapbook Vol. 13*, Hartford History Center, Hartford Public Library, Hartford, Conn.; "Biography of Hawley," in the papers of Joseph R. Hawley, Biographical Sketches, 1875–December 2, 1899, and undated, Container 35, Reel 20, Connecticut State Library, Hartford, Connecticut.

60 "Senator Hawley" (reprinted from *New York Mail and Express*), *Hartford Courant*, September 30, 1886. See also "What the State and the Country Thought of General Joseph R. Hawley" (reprinted from *Springfield Republican*), *Hartford Courant*, March 21, 1905.

61 "The Memorial Arch," *Hartford Courant*, September 18, 1886; See also Connecticut Army and Navy Club, *Reports Nos. 1–17, 1879–1895*, "Report from 1891," Connecticut State Library, Hartford, Connecticut, 11; Hawley, "Speech on Connecticut History, 1890s," the papers of Joseph R. Hawley, Speeches and Statements, 1880–October 1, 1894, Container 32, Reel 19; "Manchester's Dead Heroes," *Hartford Courant*, August 19, 1890.

62 Quoted in "Honors to the Dead! The Monument Unveiled!'" *Greenwich Graphic*, October 25, 1890; quoted in "Honor to the Heroes, Dedication of the Soldiers' Monument at Mystic Bridge," *Day* (New London), June 14, 1883. See also "The Memorial Arch," *Hartford Courant*, September 18, 1886.

63 Hawley, "Dedication of the Soldiers' Monument, Springfield, Mass., Sept. 28th, 1885," the papers of Joseph R. Hawley, Speeches and Statements, September 28 1886–July 26, 1896, Container 32, Reel 19.

64 "Battle Flag Parade, at Hartford, Wednesday, September 17, 1879," 1879, Broadsides Collection, Connecticut Historical Society, Hartford, Conn.; *History of Battle Flag Day, September 17, 1879* (Hartford, Conn.: Lockwood and Merritt, 1879), 57–58; "The Veterans' Day!" *Hartford Courant*, September 18, 1879.

65 Frances Clarke, "'Honorable Scars': Northern Amputees and the Meaning of Civil War Injuries," in *Union Soldiers and the Northern Home Front: Wartime Experiences and Postwar Adjustments*, ed. Paul A. Cimbala and Randall M. Miller (New York: Fordham University Press, 2002), 361–94; "Notice Relating to Artificial Limbs," *New York Times*, July 27, 1870. For a wider understanding of Connecticut veterans' issues, I am indebted to Mark Stepsis, "The Grand Army of the Republic and the Drive for Connecticut Veterans Benefits," paper presented at the Connecticut at War Conference, Hartford, Connecticut, the Association for the Study of Connecticut History, November 5, 2008.

66 "Classified," *Hartford Courant*, July 26, 1870; "Classified," *Hartford Courant*, October 1, 1887; *Hartford Courant*, August 29, 1870.

67 See Eric Dean, *Shook over Hell: Post-Traumatic Stress; Vietnam, and the Civil War* (Cambridge, Mass.: Harvard University Press, 1997). See also Larry Logue and Michael Barton, *The Civil War Veteran: A Historical Reader* (New York: New York University Press, 2006); Judith Anderson, "The Haunted Mind of the Civil War Veteran," in *Years of Change and Suffering: Modern Perspectives on Civil War Medicine*, ed. James M. Schmidt and Guy R. Hasegawa (Roseville, Minn.: Edinborough, 2009); Dennis W. Brandt, *Pathway to Hell: A Tragedy of the American Civil War* (Lehigh, Penn.: Lehigh University Press, 2008); Jeffrey McClurken, *Take Care of the Living: Reconstructing Confederate Veteran Families in Virginia* (Charlottesville: University of Virginia Press, 2009).

68 The work on Connecticut soldiers suffering from post-traumatic stress disorder was begun by Michael Sturges, a graduate student at Central Connecticut State University. His excellent paper "A Study of the Psychological Costs of the Civil War on Connecticut" sparked the push for access to patient records at Connecticut Valley Hospital. For more on this subject, see Mat-

thew Warshauer, Complainant, against Commissioner, State of Connecticut, Department of Mental Health and Addiction Services; and State of Connecticut, Department of Mental Health & Addiction Services, Docket #FIC 2009–200, Connecticut Freedom of Information Commission, hearing date July 29, 2009. See also Jesse Leavenworth, "Researchers Want Access to Civil War Veterans' Health Records," *Hartford Courant*, June 1, 2009; Jesse Leavenworth, "Researchers Gain Access to Mental Health Records of Civil War Veterans," *Hartford Courant*, February 27, 2010; Thomas B. Scheffey, "A Legal Skirmish over Civil War Records," *Connecticut Law Tribune*, April 26, 2010.

69   The individual papers for these men are in the records of Fitch's Home, series 400–599, RG 73 box 81, Connecticut State Library.

70   "FIFTY YEARS SINCE THE FIRING ON SUMTER; STATE G.A.R. WILL CELEBRATE WITH CAMPFIRE, National Commander and Governor Baldwin Will Speak," *Hartford Courant*, April 7, 1911.

71   "Editorial," *Hartford Courant*, April 12, 1911; "Veteran Commits Suicide," *Hartford Courant*, April 21, 1911. See also "GRAND ARMY STATE ENCAMPMENT HERE; CAMPIRE AT FOOT GUARD HALL THIS EVENING, Orders to Various Organizations Which Will Take Part, PRIVATE SESSIONS OF GRAND ARMY AT UNITY HALL," *Hartford Courant*, April 12, 1911; "VETERANS MEET IN ANNUAL REUNIONS; Evening Exercises at Foot Guard Hall Follow Street Parade; GOVERNOR BALDWIN AND OTHER SPEAKERS; Reminiscences of the War," *Hartford Courant*, April 13, 1911; "UNION VETERANS HOLD REUNION; PRISONERS OF WAR ASSOCIATION MEETING; Ranks Have Been Greatly Thinned by Death Since Last Year," *Hartford Courant*, April 15, 1911.

72   "Appropriation for Gettysburg Trip," *Hartford Courant*, February 14, 1913; "$10,000 to Go to Gettysburg," *Hartford Courant*, March 20, 1913. "Blue and Gray Camp as Friends at Gettysburg," *Hartford Courant*, July 1, 1913. See also "Blue and Gray to Meet at Gettysburg; Each to Welcome Other Back to Battleground," *Hartford Courant*, May 16, 1913.

73   "Wilson Speaks at Gettysburg," *Hartford Courant*, July 5, 1913. See also "ANTIETAM FOUGHT FIFTY YEARS AGO; The Part Connecticut Had in the Conflict, Eighth, Eleventh, Fourteenth and Sixteenth Engaged. What the State Has Done in Their Honor," *Hartford Courant*, September 17, 1912; "LOOKING BACKWARDS HALF A CENTURY; Eleventh C.V. Veterans Recall Civil War Days. Old Soldiers Observe Anniversary of Battle of Antietam," *Hartford Courant*, September 18, 1912; "VETERANS CELEBRATE BATTLE OF ANTIETAM," *Hartford Courant*, September 18, 1912; "Mammoth Camp for 70,000 at Gettysburg," *Hartford Courant*, January 23, 1913.

74   "Berlin Proud of its Monument," *Hartford Courant*, February 10, 1913;

"Kensington Ready for Celebration of Soldiers' Monument Semi-Centenary," *Hartford Courant*, July 2, 1913.

75 "At Kensington Today," *Hartford Courant*, July 26, 1913. See also "Hundreds to Honor Civil War Heroes," *Hartford Courant*, July 26, 1913 "Patriotism Reigns at Semi-Centenary," *Hartford Courant*, July 28, 1913; "McLean Speaks at Kensington," *Hartford Courant*, July 28, 1913.

76 "McLean Speaks at Kensington," *Hartford Courant*, July 28, 1913.

77 "McLean Speaks at Kensington," *Hartford Courant*, July 28, 1913.

78 Blight, *Race and Reunion*, 4.

79 Robert J. Cook, *Troubled Commemoration: The American Civil War Centennial, 1961–1965* (Baton Rouge: Louisiana State University Press, 2007).

80 Charles Poore, "Books of the Times," *New York Times*, April 26, 1962. Poore was reviewing Edmund Wilson, *Patriotic Gore: Studies in the Literature of the American Civil War* (New York: Oxford University Press, 1962).

81 I am indebted to Carolyn Ivanoff, a Civil War enthusiast and the housemaster at Shelton Intermediate School, for these intriguing insights.

82 "Six Appointed to State Group on Civil War," *Hartford Courant*, August 27, 1959; Civil War Centennial Commission, RG 52, Box 1, Connecticut State Library.

83 "The Connecticut Civil War Centennial: A Manual for Its Observance in the Towns and Cities of the State of Connecticut" (Hartford, Conn.: Connecticut Civil War Centennial Commission, 1960), 7.

84 E. P. Leddy, draft of the centennial manual, Civil War Centennial Commission, RG 52, Box 1, Connecticut State Library.

85 James I. Robertson Jr. to Albert Putnam, January 4, 1962, Civil War Centennial Commission, RG 52, Box 1, Connecticut State Library.

86 John Niven, *Connecticut for the Union: The Role of the State in the Civil War* (New Haven, Conn.: Yale University Press, 1965). See the Connecticut State Library's collection of pamphlets published in Hartford, Conn., by the Connecticut Civil War Centennial Commission, including: Robert J. Jurgen and Allen Keller, *Major General John Sedgwick, U.S. Volunteers (1813–64)*; Joseph R. Hawley, *Major General Joseph R. Hawley, Soldier and Editor (1826–1905), Civil War Military Letters*, ed. Alfred D. Putnam; Allen Keller, *Andrew Hull Foote, Gunboat Commodore (1806–1863)*; William J. Finan, *Major General Alfred Howe Terry (1827–1890): Hero of Fort Fisher*; J. Doyle De Witt, *Lincoln in Hartford*; Stanley B. Weld, *Connecticut Physicians in the Civil War*.

87 Egbert White to Marcie M. Richards, July 4, 1962 (Richards was executive assistant to Robert C. Sales, the state librarian; the commission had an office at the State Library), Civil War Centennial Commission. The box also contains the program for the Emancipation Proclamation ceremony.

88 Quoted in Charles Morse, "Dempsey Urged to Name Negroes to Commission," *Hartford Courant*, February 2, 1963.

89 Robert Maule, "The People's Forum: Let Negroes Pick Their Own Leaders," *Hartford Courant*, February 8, 1963.

90 "Dempsey Names 8 to Civil War Centennial Group," *Hartford Courant*, September 28, 1963. Those appointed were: Allen A. Sharp of Groton; Lavius Robinson of Putnam; Harold J. Bingham of New Britain; William J. Massie of New Haven; Esther B. Lindquist of Guilford; Daniel I. Fletcher of Hartford; John E. Rogers of Manchester; and Thomas J. Caldwell of Rocky Hill. The names are also listed in the Civil War Centennial Commission, RG 52, Box 3, Connecticut State Library. "I. Fletcher Dies; Ex-Housing Official," *Hartford Courant*, November 12, 1975, includes a picture of Fletcher. It is unclear how many of the other appointees were black.

91 Robert Penn Warren, *The Legacy of the Civil War: Meditations on the Centennial* (New York: Random House, 1961), 3, 4.

92 Warren, *The Legacy of the Civil War*, 7, 60–63, 75. David Donald, "When the Smoke of Battle Cleared, an Ideal Had Been Born," *New York Times*, May 14, 1961. See also Charles Poore, "Books of the Times," *New York Times*, April 27, 1961.

93 "EX-GOVERNORS TOUCEY AND SEYMOUR," *Hartford Times*, April 29, 1865. For information on their removal, see chapter 2, and "It will Stand," *Hartford Daily Courant*, October 19, 1861; "Toucey and Seymour," *Hartford Daily Courant*, October 29, 1861; "CONNECTICUT DISGRACED," *Hartford Times*, October 16, 1861; William A. Croffut and John M. Morris, *The Military and Civil History of Connecticut during the War of 1861–1865* (New York: Ledyard Bill, 1869), 136.

94 Warren, *The Legacy of the Civil War*, 107.

Epilogue

1 Thomas Friedman, "Finishing Our Work," *New York Times*, November 4, 2008.

2 The historian David Blight made exactly this point in "Marking the Civil War Sesquicentennial: Will We Do Better This Time?" (*Chronicle of Higher Education*, May 9, 2009).

3 Edward T. Linenthal, "Epilogue: Reflections," in *Slavery and Public History: The Tough Stuff of American Memory*, ed. James Oliver Horton and Lois E. Horton (New York: New Press, 2006), 213.

4 Quoted in "House Resolution Apologizes for Slavery," UPI.com, July 29, 2008 (http://www.upi.com/Top_News/2008/07/29/House-resolution-apologizes-for-slavery/UPI-84171217375080).

5 Quoted in Greg Vadala and Edward Epstein, "Senate Adopts Slavery Apology

Resolution," *CQ Politics News*, June 18, 2009 (http://www.cqpolitics.com/wmspage.cfm?parm1=5&docID=news-000003147458).

6 For a number of reactions, see Desiree Evans, "Congress' Slavery Apology Draws Mixed Reactions," *Facing South*, August 1, 2008 (http://southernstudies.org/2008/08/house-of-representatives-slavery.html). For more a formal study, see Melissa Nobles, *The Politics of Official Apologies* (New York: Cambridge University Press, 2008). Before the apologies were passed by Congress, they had been debated for some time, and a number of scholars had weighed in on the subject. See, for example, Ira Berlin, "American Slavery in History and Memory and the Search for Social Justice," *Journal of American History* 90, no. 4 (March 2004): 1251–68; Eric K. Yamamoto, Susan K. Serrano, and Michelle Natividad Rodriguez, "American Racial Justice on Trial—Again: African American Reparations, Human Rights, and the War on Terror," *Michigan Law Review* 101, no. 5 (March 2003): 1269–1337; Robert R. Weyeneth, "The Power of Apology and the Process of Historical Reconciliation," *Public Historian* 23, no. 3 (Summer 2001): 9–38. A great number of less scholarly opinions are scattered over the Internet.

7 Chris Matthews, "Senate Passes Resolution Apologizing for Slavery," *Hardball with Chris Matthews*, June 19, 2009 (http://mediamatters.org/mmtv/200906190030).

8 Connecticut General Assembly, House Joint Resolution No. 1, January Session, 2009, "Resolution Expressing the Profound Regret of the Connecticut General Assembly for the History of Wrongs Inflicted upon Black Citizens by Means of Slavery, Exploitation and Legalized Racial Segregation, and Calling on All Citizens to Take Part in Acts of Racial Reconciliation" (http://www.cga.ct.gov/2009/TOB/H/2009HJ-00001-R01-HB.htm). The other states are Alabama, Virginia, North Carolina, New Jersey, Maryland, and Florida. For a variety of rather cranky reactions, see comments at "Formal Apology for Connecticut's History of Slavery Passes House," AmericanRenaissance .com (http://www.amren.com/mtnews/archives/2009/06/formal_apology .php).

9 Blight, "Marking the Civil War Sesquicentennial."

10 "Statement of Governor Bob McDonnell," Virginia.gov, April 7, 2010 (http://www.governor.virginia.gov/news/viewRelease.cfm?id=111. See also Anita Kumar and Rosalind S. Helderman, "McDonnell's Confederate History Month Proclamation Irks Civil Rights Leaders," *Washington Post*, April 7, 2010. McDonnell's two Democratic predecessors had refused to issue similar proclamations of Confederate History Month.

11 Walton Brown-Foster to Matthew Warshauer, June 13, 2009. My response read:

Hi Walton,

Thanks very much for your email. I had a meeting with the Freedom Trail Commission about two weeks ago and they did express dismay over what you mention below. I tried to explain that this project had begun in a rather piecemeal way, that people and organizations have been added to the committee as it has continued and that all are welcome. More organizations join as they learn about the project or some members have the opportunity to make contacts. That was the very reason I went to the Freedom Trail Commission meeting.

I did mention this project to you last semester and we traded emails.

Thanks,
Matt

FURTHER READING AND RESEARCH

A huge amount of material related to Connecticut's experience during the Civil War is available. Much of this is cited in the endnotes of this book. The purpose of this section is not to repeat those notes, but to offer those interested in further reading a few suggestions on where to start, and to suggest additional topics that need more research.

Certainly the best source to begin with is William A. Croffut and John M. Morris's *The Military and Civil History of Connecticut during the War of 1861–65* (New York: Ledyard Bill, 1869). Published just a few years after the war, it offers hundreds of pages of detailed information that can be found nowhere else. Although long out of print, it is available online via Google Books, can be downloaded in pdf format, and is searchable by key word. It is a remarkable resource that can be read from the comfort and privacy of one's own computer. Similarly important is John Niven's *Connecticut for the Union: The Role of the State in the Civil War* (New Haven, Conn.: Yale University Press, 1965), published as part of the centennial commemoration. The first broad history of Connecticut and the Civil War since Croffut and Morris's work, Niven's book offers a detailed look into the state's experience, though it is at times challenging to read given its rather haphazard chronology. Still, there is much to be gleaned from this important work. Unfortunately, it is no longer in print and can only be accessed through libraries.

Histories of Connecticut regiments abound. Most of these were published within a decade or two of the war and written by members of the regiment. Not only are many available online through Google Books, but the Kessinger Publishing Company has been producing reprints of these histories. A simple Amazon.com search will unearth many works related to particular regiments. To gain a very good, encyclopedic approach to understanding Connecticut regiments — when they were formed, where they fought, and their casualty figures — and similar information about particular towns throughout the state, Blaikie Hines's *Civil War Volunteer Sons of Connecticut* (Thomaston, Conn.: American Patriot, 2002) is indispensable. The more personal stories of particular Connecticut soldiers are also readily available. Samuel Fiske's *Mr. Dunn Browne's Experiences in the Army* (Boston: Nichols and Noyes, 1866) is available as a 1998 reprint, edited by Stephen W. Sears, and is also available via Google Books. Fred Lucas's letters are available in two books: Frederick A. Lucas, *Dear Mother from Your Dutiful Son: Civil War Letters, September 22, 1862 to August 18, 1865, Written by Frederick A. Lucas to His Mother*, edited by Ernest Barker (Goshen, Conn.: Purple Door Gallery, 2003); and Ernest B. Barker, *Fred and Jennie: A Civil War Love Story*, with letters edited by Ernest B. Barker, assisted by Anthony J. Barker (Goshen, Conn.: Purple Door Gallery, 2002). John William De Forest's account of his military service was originally published as essays and then as a book: *A Volunteer's Adventures: A Union Captain's Record of the Civil War*, edited, with notes, by James H. Croushore (New Haven, Conn.: Yale University Press, 1946). It has been republished (Hamden, Conn.: Archon Books, 1970) and is readily available. Indeed, it is the availability of these works and the incredible stories they tell that influenced my decision to use these soldiers' particular stories. These works are not the only Connecticut soldiers' stories available, however. For example, the incredible set of letters by Captain Andrew Upson can be obtained online through the Web site of the Barnes Museum in Southington, Connecticut (http://barnesmuseum .wordpress.com).

Any number of the specific topics discussed in this book can be delved into in far greater detail. For politics, J. Robert Lane's *A Political History of Connecticut During the Civil War* (Washington: Catholic University of America Press, 1941) though dated and out of print, is an important resource. For dissent within the state, an important source is Joanna D. Cowden, "The Politics of Dissent: Civil War Democrats in Connecticut," *New England Quarterly* 56, no. 4 (December 1983): 538–54. For abolition and its opponents, see David Menschel, "Abolition without Deliverance: The Law of Connecticut Slavery 1784–1848," *Yale Law Journal* 111, no. 1 (October 2001): 191–94; John J. O'Connell, "The Abolitionist Movement in Connecticut, 1830–1850" (master's thesis, Trinity College, 1971); Lawrence Bruser, "Political Antislavery in Connecticut, 1844–1858," (Ph.D. dissertation, Columbia University, 1974). For black abolitionists see, David E. Swift, *Black Prophets of Justice: Activist Clergy before the Civil War* (Baton Rouge: Louisiana State University Press, 1989).

All of these topics, and more, need further research. The economics of how Connecticut paid for its war effort, politics within the state, its difficulties with the draft, the problems of dissent in varying regions of the state, its naval contributions — all are important areas that require additional study. Some of these are explored in the spring 2011 issue of the journal *Connecticut History*, and others are discussed in essays published in the spring 2011 issue of *Connecticut Explored*. Still, more research needs to be done. This is particularly true of abolition within Connecticut, especially the story of black abolitionists and the larger story of black residents during the war. It is a topic that I was able to touch upon only briefly in this much wider history of Connecticut and the Civil War. Such information is not always easy to find, but it is out there if one is willing to dig. I look forward to the day when an author is able to tell the story of African Americans throughout the antebellum and Civil War periods in one well-articulated work.

There is also a great deal that can be learned outside of books and articles. As this book is published, Connecticut is beginning the commemoration of the 150th anniversary of the Civil War. Museums, historical societies, and libraries throughout the state are offering exhibits, books talks, lectures, symposiums, art presentations, reenactments, encampments, and many other events to highlight the important history of this nation-changing event that we call the Civil War. A master calendar of these events can be found at www.ccsu.edu/civilwar. It is hoped that this book will open one window through which readers can gain a level of insight into the war, one that will spark further interest in this great and troubling history.

INDEX

Numbers in *italics* indicate figures.

abatis, 148

abolition: distinguished from emancipation, 95, 175–76; linked to the draft, 131; message of, newspapers' debates about, 68–69

abolitionism: Democrats' response to, 94–95; development of movement for, 18–22; dispute over, 93; serving to reduce the Confederacy's ability to fight, 94

abolitionists: pushing for national emancipation and equal rights for blacks, 24–28; violence against, 22–24

abolition societies, 10, 228–29n13

Act for the Defense of Liberty in This State (1854), 37

Adams, Charles Francis, Jr., 120–21

"Advice to South Carolina" (poem), 56

aid societies, 90. *See also* soldiers' aid societies

Albemarle Sound, 73

American Colonization Society, 18, 233n43

Amistad case, 1, 25–26

amnesty proclamation, 270–71n109

Anaconda Plan, 65–67, 72, 77, 141

Andersonville Boy statue (Hartford, CT), 199

Andersonville Prison, 141–42, 199

Andrew, John, 132

anniversaries, celebrations of, 177–78

anti-abolition movement, development of, 18–19, 22–24

antislavery societies, 11, 19–20

Arlington Cemetery, 189

arms industry, 64, 118–19. *See also individual companies*

Army Corps (U.S.): 9th, 110–11; 11th, 122, 123; 12th, 122

Army of the Gulf, 145

Army of the James, 145

Army of Northern Virginia, 80

Army of the Potomac, 64, 80, 120–23, 138, 145–46, 148, 150

Army of Virginia, 145

Arnold, John, 53

Atlanta (GA), 150, 158

Babcock, James, 38, 45

Bacon, Elijah W., 265n76

Bacon, Leonard, 19, 33

Baldwin, Raymond, 210, 211

Baldwin, Roger, 243n26

Baldwin, Sherman, 26

Baldwin, Simeon, 24

Banks, Nathaniel, 80, 81, 124, 125, 145

Banning, John, 199

Banning and Rowe Monument (East Hartland, CT), 199

Barber, Sophronia, 63

Barbour, Henry H., 108

Barnum, P. T., 60, 61, 180–81, 246n59

Battell, Robins, 243n26

Batterson, James G., 172, 176–77, 192, 198

battle of Antietam, 82–88, 92–93

battle of Bull Run (first), 41, 57–59, 61, 70

battle of Bull Run (second), 82

battle of Cedar Mountain, 81–82

battle of Chancellorsville, 121–23

battle of Chickamauga, 136
battle fatigue, 208–10
Battle Flag Day, 177, 208
battle of Gettysburg, 125–30
battle of Wilson's Creek, 67
Beaufort (SC), 150
Beauregard, P. G. T., 57, 58, 145
Beckwith, Josiah G., 91, 243n43
Bell, John, 47
Beman, Amos G., 19–20, 24, 26–28, 95, 103, 283n42
Beman, Leverett, 28
Benham, H. W., 75, 77
black regiment, called for, in Connecticut, 134–35
Black Republicans, 38
black rights, movement for, 11–12
blacks: participation in the Civil War, opposition to, 3–4; violence against, 23–24; voting rights of, 25, 26–28, 176, 178–88. *See also* free blacks
black troops, 79, 104–5, 132–35, 154
Blake, Edward, 81
Blakeslee, Benjamin, 84
Blight, David, 175, 189, 213, 223
Blinn, Jarvis, 86, 92
blockade strategy. *See* Anaconda Plan
Booth, John Wilkes, 169
bounties, 63, 248n
Bragg, Braxton, 136
Branford (CT), monument in, 196
Breckinridge, John C., 47
Bridgeport (CT), monument in, 198
Briggs, James, 43
Bristol (CT), monument in, 191–92
Britain, interest of, in the war, 82
Brooks, Preston, 29, 37–38
Brooks/Sumner beating, 29, 37–38
Brown, George, 171
Brown, Henry, 281n25
Brown, John, 1, 38, 119
Brown, Joseph, 27
Brown v. the Board of Education, 213–14
Browne, Dunn. *See* Fiske, Samuel

Bruser, Lawrence, 34
Buckingham, William A., 6, 37, *42*; annual message of, to the General Assembly, 53–54, 45–46, 115; assuring Connecticut's loyalty to the union, 51; calling for arrest of traitors, 61; calling for reinforcements (1863), 136; calling for volunteers at outset of war, 53; congratulating Lincoln after the 1864 election, 165; election of, as governor, 43–45; funding the first regiments, 53; instituting a draft, 90, 131; on granting blacks the right to vote, 178; on slavery and the Constitution, 94; reelection bids, 102–3, 107–8, 113, 142–43; sending Lincoln resolution supporting him, 99–100; sending representatives to peace conference (1861), 50–51; supporting constitutional amendment to end slavery, 157–58; views of, on slavery and secession, 46, 49; writing to Lincoln about the 1864 state election results, 143–44; writing to Lincoln about the preliminary Emancipation Proclamation, 96–97
Buford, John, 125
Bull Run syndrome, 65
Burnham, Hiram, 58
Burnham, John, 92
Burnside, Ambrose, 72, 73, 88–89, 120
Burnside's Bridge, 83
Burr, Alfred, 238n88, 239n103
Bushnell, Horace, 61
Butler, Andrew, 37
Butler, Benjamin, 68, 77, 145

Cadwell, Charles, 66–67
Cahill, Thomas, 78
Camp, Henry Ward, 74, 95
Camp Parapet (LA), 78
Canton (CT), monument in, 199
Carr, David, 61, 246n57

Cedar Creek (VA), 159
centennial commemorations, 213–15, 218
Chapman, George, 81
Charleston (SC), 75, 134
Charter Oak, 24
Chatfield, John, 77
Cheshire (CT), monument in, 191, 193–94
Chester Station (VA), 145
Chicago Platform, 161
"Christmas Eve" (Nast), *99*
civil rights movement, 213–14
Civil War: beginning of, 51; death toll from, 5; expected to be brief, 41; healing from, desire for, 175; local preparations for, 55–56; meaning of, changing and under dispute, 174–75; medical and psychological reminders of, 208–9; timing of, related to party system, 32
Clay, Henry, 28
Cleveland, Chauncey, 243n26
Cohen, Steven, 222
Cold Harbor (VA), 146, 148–50
Collins & Co., 119
colonization, 2–3, 18, 34
"Colored Schools Broken Up, In the Five States" (woodcut print), *21*
Colt, Samuel, 54, 64
Colt firearms company, 49, 90, 118, *119*, 152
commemoration, as focus of postwar years, 176–77
Compromise of 1850, 29, 33–34
Confederacy, coming military defeat of, 166
Connecticut: amendment proposed in, to grant blacks the right to vote, 176, 178–88; apologizing for slavery, 222–23; approving gradual emancipation plan (1784), 11–12; arms industry in, 49, 118–19, 152; banning further importation of slaves (1774), 11; black participation in regiments of, 135–36; businesses in, transacting with the South, 49–50; combating Democratic resurgence in, 102–3; contribution of, to the slave trade, 9–10; division of, in the 1864 presidential election, 165; gubernatorial races in, 43–45, 102–3, 106–15, 142–43; having higher incident of mob violence against abolitionists than other N.E. states, 23; industry in, 6, 64, 65, 119–20, 152–53, 220; losing patience with the South, 34–36; only New England state to bar all blacks from voting, 178; opposition in, to the war, 6; percentage of fighting-age men participating in war, 5; political divisions in, during the war, 6–7; position of, on slavery, 1–3; practice of slavery in, 9, 10–11, 26; racism in, 2–4, 26; residents of, not advocating black civic equality, 176; Republicans in General Assembly, venting anger toward Democrats, 63–64; response to Lincoln's assassination, 171–72; response to South Carolina's secession, 48–49; soldiers from, fighting in every major engagement, 5–6; support in, for the war, 6; viewpoints in, regarding the Missouri Compromise, 16–17
Connecticut Anti-Slavery Society, 19, 24
Connecticut Arms Company, 118
Connecticut Civil War Centennial Commission, 214–16
Connecticut Civil War Commemoration Committee, 223
Connecticut Colonization Society, 18
Connecticut Freedom Trail Commission, 223
Connecticut Hospital for the Insane, 209, 210
Connecticut Liberty Party, 30

Connecticut for the Union (Niven), 4, 215

Connecticut Valley Hospital, 209

Connecticut Volunteer Infantry (CVI), 53. *See also* regiments

contraband, slaves treated as, 68, 78–79, 94

Converse, Joseph, 74, 83–84

Cook, Robert, 214

Copperheads, 98, 108, *109*, 110, 143

Copperhilt, Daniel, 209

Corbit, George W., 92

Corliss, George W., 81

Cornish, Virgil, 90

cotton gin, invention of, 13

cotton industry, effect of, on slavery, 13–14

Cowan, Sarah S., 117

Crandall, Prudence, 1, 2, 20–22

Crane, Gilbert R., 92

Crittenden, John Jordan, 50

Crittenden Compromise, 50

croakers, 270n106

Croffut, William A., 80, 81, 141–42, 148, 166

CSS *Virginia*, 79

Curtis, Holbrook, 33

Danbury (CT), monument in, 199

Davis, Jefferson, 124, 132, 153, 174

Day, Thomas, 3, 39–40

Declaration of Independence, debate over intent of, in granting equality among the races, 182

Decoration Day, 177, 206, 218

De Forest, John William, 78–79, 115–16, 124–25, 133, 159–60, 219, 220

Democratic Party: accusing Republicans of rigging the 1863 election, 113–15; convention of (1860), 47; in the 1864 presidential election, 161–66; revitalized by Emancipation Proclamation, 98, 101, 103–4; split of, 29, 30, 31–32, 47, 93–94, 161–62; state convention (1863), 107–8; supporting Compromise of 1850, 34; working to gain political control in Connecticut (1862–1863), 98

Democrats: anger toward, paired with joy of victory, 130–31; attacks on blacks increasing after passage of the Thirteenth Amendment, 168; disputing emancipation's legality and efficacy, 167–68; focusing on Lincoln as abolitionist, 153–54; issues for, in 1864, 140; losing in 1864 elections, 143–44; new vulgarity among, 154–55; opposing the war, 54–55; questioning the accounts of black troops, 134

Dempsey, John, 216

de Quincey, Thomas, 116

Derby (CT), monument in, 198

desertion, 169

Dewitt, J. Doyle, 214

Dickinson, Anna, 113

District of Columbia, emancipation in, 94–95

Douglas, John, 181–83

Douglas, Stephen A., 34–35, 46, 47

Douglass, Frederick, 96, 132

draft, inefficiency of, 131

draft riots (1863), 130–31

Drake, Albert, 73, 74

Dred Scott decision, 29, 38, 47, 179–80, 280n13

Drewry's Bluff (VA), 145

du Pont, Samuel, 66

Dwight, Timothy, 91

Eagle Manufacturing Company, 64

Early, Jubal, 150–51, 158–59

East Hartford (CT), monument in, 196

East Hartland (CT), monument in, 199

Easton, Hosea, 28

Eaton, William H., 107–8, 143

Eaton, William W., 3–4, 134

educational institutions, as focus of Connecticut abolitionists, 20–22

Edwards, Henry W., 24
Eli Whitney arms company, 90, 118
Ellis, Theodore, 126
Ellsworth, P. W., 91
Ellsworth, William, 136–37
Elm City Bank (New Haven), 53
Elmer, Samuel E., 91
emancipation: distinguished from
    abolition, 3, 95, 175–76; moral
    imperatives of, 167; reasons for,
    95–96; viewed as reward enough,
    188
"Emancipation" (Nast), 102
Emancipation Proclamation, 101,
    213; Davis's response to, 132; free
    blacks' response to, 103; linked
    with the draft, 132; Republican
    press's response to, 105–6; response
    to, in Connecticut, 103–5; response
    to preliminary version of, 97–98;
    support for, 3
English, James, 207
Enrollment Act (1863), 130–32
Era of Good Feelings, 15
Essig, James, 228n29n13
Europe, conflict in, 14
E. Whitney's Improved Firearms, 120.
    See also Eli Whitney arms company
exemptions from service, 90–91,
    253n43

Fairfield County Bank (Norwalk), 53
Farmington (CT), monument in,
    196–98
Farragut, David, 78, 79, 80
fatigue, related to the war, 151–53
Faust, Drew Gilpin, 176
federal government, inability of,
    to cope with needs of the war,
    89–92
Federalist Party, disappearance of, 15
Fifteenth Amendment, 188, 212–13
"First Cotton-gin, The" (Sheppard), 13
Fisher's Hill (VA), 159
Fiske, Samuel, 85, 86, 87, 89, 111, 116,

122–23, 128, 130–31, 138, 142, 144,
    146, 172, 219, 267n90
Fitch's Home, 209, 210
Fletcher, Daniel I., 216
Foner, Eric, 236n70
Foote, Andrew, 194, 215
Foote, Samuel, 16
Forsyth, John, 49
Fort Beauregard (LA), 65, 74
Fort Donelson (TN), 78
Fort Fisher (NC), 166
Fort Hale (CT), 50
Fort Pulaski (GA), 74–75, 76
Fort Sumter (SC), 51, 134
Fort Wagner (SC), 133–34
Fort Walker (SC), 65, 66, 74
Foster, Lafayette S., 38–39, 191
Founding Fathers, viewing slavery as a
    necessity, 9–10
Fourteenth Amendment, 212
Fowler, Chauncey, 161–62
Fowler, William C., 283n43
France, interest of, in the war, 82
Fredericksburg (VA), 89
free blacks: control of, 11–12; growing
    community of, 12; responding to
    Emancipation Proclamation, 103
free labor system, 30, 93
Free Soil beliefs, 3, 17
Free Soil Party, 29, 30–31
Frémont, John C., 67
Friedman, Thomas, 221
fugitive slave laws, 12, 25, 33–34, 37
Fundamental Orders, 207
funerals, following Antietam, 92–93

Gardner, Franklin, 124
Garrison, William Lloyd, 2, 19, 22,
    104, 113, 188
Gaulladet, Thomas Hopkins,
    231–32n32
General Hospital Society, 92
George Greenman & Company, 65
Gettysburg (PA), 101. See also Battle of
    Gettysburg

Gettysburg Address, 189, 196
Gillette, Francis, 36–37
Glenn, Russell, 266n79
glorious cause, identifying, 93–94
Goodrich, Loren, 128
Grand Army of the Republic, 206
Granger, Arthur, 24
Grant, Ulysses S., 78, 79, 123–24,
    125; accepting Lee's surrender,
    169; appointed commander of the
    Military Division of Mississippi,
    136; instructions for the
    Shenandoah Valley, 158–59; losses
    of, at Cold Harbor, 149; strategy of,
    139, 145–46
Grant, Ellsworth, S., 207
Grasso, Ella, 215
"Great Alibi," 216–17
Greeley, Horace, 153
Greene, Lloyd, 103
Griswold (CT), monument in, 285n55
Grosner, William, 185
Guilford (CT), monument in, 196

habeas corpus, Lincoln's suspension
    of, 98–99
Hammond, James Henry, 14
Harkin, Tom, 221–22
Harrison, Henry, 180
Hartford (CT), monuments in, 198,
    199–201
Hartford Civil War Roundtable, 214
Hartford Convention, 14–15, 108
Hartford Courant, inconsistent views
    of, 105–6
Hartford Sanitary Association, 151
Hartford Soldiers' Aid Society, 90,
    117–18, 129–30
Hawley, Joseph R., 68, 76, 77, 141, 164,
    206–8, 215
Hay, John, 153
Hayes, Rutherford B., 213
Hazard, Augustus, 49
Hazard Powder Company, 49
healing, focus on, 217

Henry arms company, 152
Herrick, James, 209–10
Higginson, Thomas Wentworth, 132
Hill, A. P., 125
Hill, Isaac, 136
Hilliard, Charles B., 189
Hilton Head Island (SC), 67, 75, 77
Hincks, William B., 265–66n76
Hines, Blaikie, 244n32
Hirst, Benjamin, 87, 113
Hitchcock, Edwin, 76–77
Hoadly, Charles J., 171
Hoke, Robert, 141
Holcomb, Milo A., 1, 46–47
Hooker, John, 280n15
Hooker, Joseph, 120–21, 125, 136
Hooker, Thomas, 207
Hooten, Thomas, 76
hospitals, lack of, 92
Hotchkiss & Sons, 64, 119, 121
Howard, Mark, 60, 260n38
Hubbard, George A., 87, 246n57
Hunt (English naturalist), 154

immigration, as important issue for
    Northerners, 33
"I'm not to blame for being white, sir!"
    (drawing), 155
interracial sex, 184
Irish immigrants, service of, 77–78.
    See also regiments, 9th CVI

Jackson, Andrew, 41, 196
Jackson, Stonewall, 80, 81
Jefferson, Thomas, 17
Jewett, Pliny, 92
Jocelyn, Simeon, 19, 20, 23, 24
John Benson Marker, 198
Judson, Andrew, 2, 21

Kansas-Nebraska Act of 1854, 29,
    34–36
Keller, George, 198
Kellogg, Elisha, 117, 148
Kellogg, Robert H., 142

Index

Kensington (CT), monument at, 189–91, 211
Kibbe & Co. advertisement, *48*
Kimberly, Dennis, 20
Kingsbury, Thomas H. C., 83–84
Knight, Jonathan, 92
Knight U.S. Army General Hospital, 92, 151, 199
Know-Nothing Party, 29, 32, 33, 37
Ku Klux Klan, 213

Ladies' Aid societies, 62–63
Lanman, James, 16
Latimer, Francis, 271n3
Lebanon (CT), memorial in, to five wars, 199
Lee, Robert E., 80, 82, 88, 141; army of, as focus of the Army of the Potomac, 145–46; at Gettysburg, 125, 130; at Chancellorsville, 121–22; losses of, at Cold Harbor, 149; refusing to send reinforcements to Vicksburg, 124; resourcefulness of, 139; surrendering at Appomattox Courthouse, 169
Legacy of the Civil War, The: Meditations on the Centennial (Warren), 216–17
letters home, 5–6
Libby Prison, 123
Liberator, The, 19, 20
Liberia, 18
Liberty Party, 29, 30, 40
Lincoln, Abraham, 194, 195; amnesty proclamation of, 270–71n109; announcing preliminary Emancipation Proclamation, 72, 96; annual message to Congress (1864), 166; appointing Meade as commander of the Army of the Potomac, 125; assassination of, 169–71; calling for additional troops (1863), 136; campaigning for Buckingham, 43–45; dismayed

after Gettysburg, 130; election of (1860), 47; encouraging border states to enact gradual emancipation plans, 94; focused on winning the war (1863), 137–38; issuing calls for soldiers following Bull Run, 62; nomination of, for president, 46; on 1864 elections, 156; on military strategy, 144; pragmatic approach of, regarding slavery, 95–97; recruiting additional troops (1864), 166; removing Frémont from his command, 67; removing McClellan from the Army of the Potomac, 88; resisting making the war about slavery, 68; responding to rumors of peace (1864), 153; responding to the Battle of Chancellorsville, 122; responding to victory at Vicksburg, 124; securing financial help for Republicans in 1863 election, 115; signing the Emancipation Proclamation, 101; sitting in Davis's study after fall of Richmond, 169; suspending habeas corpus, 98–99; upholding Butler's contraband policy, 68; using war powers, 97, 101, 154–55; winning the 1864 election, 165
Litchfield (CT), monument in, 199
Longstreet, James, 126, 144
Loomis, James C., 93
Lost Cause, myth of, 175
Lucas, Fred, 112, 116, 117, 130, 133, 142, 147, 148, 152, 160, 161, 168–70, 189, 219–20, 268n95
Lusk, William, 77
Lyon, Nathaniel, 67
Lyons, James, 119

Maddox, Joseph, 27
Madison (CT), memorial hall in, 199
malaria, 78
Mallory, Charles Henry, 50

Mallory, Stephen, 50
Mallory shipyard, 65
Manassas. *See* Bull Run
Mansfield, Joseph K. F., 74
Marye's Heights, 89
Matthews, Chris, 222
Maule, Robert, 216
Maxson, Fish & Company, 65
Mayer, Nathan, 117
McClellan, George, 64–65, 79, 80,
   88; accepting the Democratic
   presidential nomination, 161;
   replaced as commander, 120;
   running against Lincoln, 140
McCurdy, Charles K., 243n26
McDonnell, Bob, 223
McDowell, Irvin, 57
McLean, George P., 211–12, 213
McPherson, James, 65, 82, 122, 124,
   149–50, 151, 169
Meade, George Gordon, 125, 130, 145
Mechanics Bank (New Haven), 53
Melish, Joanne Pope, 11, 22
Memorial Day, 177. *See* Decoration Day
memorials, 195–96. *See also*
   monuments
mental illness, 208–10
Mexican War, 29, 30
Mississippi River, canal dug at
   Vicksburg, 80–81
*Miss Ravenel's Conversion from
   Secession to Loyalty* (De Forest),
   220
Missouri Compromise, 15–17, 28, 35,
   38, 230n23
Mitchell, Henry, 134
monuments, 7–8, 176–77, 189–206,
   218
Moore, Nelson Augustus, 189
Morehead, Charles, 50, 68
Morris, John M., 80, 81, 141–42, 148,
   166
Morse, Nathan, 59, 60
Mothers' Soldiers' Monument (Union,
   CT), 199

Mowry, 64
Munson, Harris, 183
Mystic shipbuilding companies, 65

Napoleonic wars, 14
National Association for the
   Advancement of Colored People,
   Connecticut Chapter, 223–24
National Civil War Centennial
   Commission, 214, 215
nativism, 32
naval warfare, 79
Negro Fourth of July, 103
New Berne (NC), 73–74, 141
New Britain (CT), monument in,
   203–6
New England Brigade, 77
New Haven (CT): black college
   planned for, 20, 22; monuments in,
   198, 285n55
New London (CT), monument in, 203
New Milford (CT), monument in,
   285n55
New Orleans (LA), 78
Newton, Alexander, 136
Niagara Falls, rumors of peace
   conferences at, 153
Niven, John, 4, 89, 215
Norfolk (VA), 79
North Branford (CT), monument in,
   191, 193, *195*
North Carolina Expedition force,
   72–74
Northern nationalism, 176
Northfield (CT), monument in, 191,
   194–95
Northwest Ordinance, 12
Norwich Arms Company, 119
Nullification Crisis, 41

O'Brien, Lawrence, 81
Obama, Barack, 177, 221
Old Lyme (CT), memorial hall in, 199
Olmstead, Charles, 74, 75
Olustee (FL), 141

Opequon (VA), 159, 160
Oregon Territory, boundary dispute
    over, 28–30
"Our Women and the War" (Homer),
    118
Oviate, George A., 60

Palmer, Andrew, 55
Pamlico Sound, 65, 72
Panic of 1819, 230n24
Pardee, Benjamin S., 72–73, 134
Parrot guns, 74
party system: containing the problem
    of slavery, 32; cracks in, 31–32;
    fueling racial animosity, 28–30
Patent Fire-arms Manufacturing
    Company, 64
peace, rumors of (1864), 153
peace conference (1861), Connecticut
    represented at, 50–51
Peace Democrats, 93
peace flags, 55, 60–61, 245n42
peace movement, 41; effects on, of Bull
    Run, 59, 61; interruption of, 61
Pemberton, John, 124
Peninsula Campaign, 79–80
Pennington, James, 19–20, 27, 28, 103,
    283n42
personal liberty law, 37
Petersburg (VA), 149–50, 169
Petersburg Express monument
    (Hartford, CT), 199–201
Pettingill, A. A., 59–60
Phelps, Amos A., 22
Phelps & Crow, advertisement for, 64
Pickett, George Edward, 126
Pierce, Franklin, 43
Pinney, A. Searle, 216
Plainville (CT), monuments in, 196,
    285n55
Plessy v. Ferguson, 176, 214
Plymouth (NC), 141
Pocotaligo (SC), 77
Polk, James K., 28
popular sovereignty, 47

Port Hudson (LA), 124–25
Port Royal (SC), 65–66
post-traumatic stress disorder, 208–10
Pratt, George, 179–80
Pratt, James T., 243n26
presidential elections: 1860, 41, 47;
    1864, 140, 156, 161–66; 1876, 213
Prigg v. Pennsylvania, 25
Putnam, Albert, 214
Putnam (CT), monuments in, 285n55

race, as part of the larger context of the
    war, 132
racism: Connecticut known for,
    2; Democrats' use of, 104, 138,
    140, 154, 179; entrenched in
    Connecticut, 4, 26, 27; growing
    along with abolition, 22, 217;
    precluding concept of justice, 175
Ransom, David, 195–96
Raymond, Henry J., 156, 158
Raymond, Stephen, 59
rebel flag, meaning of, 174
reconciliation, focus on, 217
reconstruction, 136–37, 213
reenlistments, 142
regiments: 1st Connecticut Heavy
    Artillery, 54, 75, 201; 1st
    Connecticut Volunteer Cavalry, 62;
    1st Connecticut Volunteer Light
    Batteries Artillery, 62; 1st CVI
    (Connecticut Volunteer Infantry),
    53, 61–62, 68, 207, 245n48; 1st
    Squadron Connecticut Volunteer
    Cavalry, 62; 2nd Connecticut Light
    Artillery, 126; 2nd Connecticut
    Volunteer Light Batteries Artillery,
    62; 2nd CVI, 53, 57, 58–59,
    245n48; 2nd Heavy Artillery, 110,
    116, 147, 148, 159, 160; 2nd Light
    Artillery, 264n70; 2nd Maine, 58;
    3rd Connecticut Volunteer Light
    Batteries Artillery, 62; 3rd CVI,
    53, 57, 59, 245n48; 4th CVI (see
    1st Connecticut Heavy Artillery);

5th CVI, 54, 65, 81,, 74, 75, 77, 122, 126, 150, 158, 173, 264n70; 6th Connecticut, 134, 145, 150, 165, 166; 7th CVI, 62, 66, 74, 75, 77, 116, 134, 141, 145, 150, 165, 166, 207, 268n95; 8th CVI, 62, 65, 72–74, 83, 84–85, 142, 145, 147, 148; 9th CVI, 62, 77, 78, 80–81, 110–11, 159; 9th New York, 73; 10th CVI, 62, 65, 72–74, 145, 165; 11th CVI, 62, 72–74, 83, 84, 142, 145, 147, 148, 150; 12th CVI, 62, 78, 110–11, 124, 142, 159, 173; 13th CVI, 78, 110–11, 124, 142, 159, 160; 14th Connecticut, 113, 122, 123, 126–28, 146, 147, 148, 173, 265–66n76, 83, 85–87, 89; 16th Connecticut, 83, 84, 87, 141–42; 17th Connecticut, 116, 122, 123, 126, 264–65n70; 19th CVI (*see* 2nd Heavy Artillery); 20th CVI, 109–10, 122, 123, 126, 150, 173, 265n; 21st CVI, 145, 150, 147, 148; 22nd Connecticut, 111; 23rd Connecticut, 78, 110–11; 24th Connecticut, 78, 110–11, 124; 25th Connecticut, 110–11; 25th Massachusetts, 73; 26th Connecticut, 78, 110–11, 124; 27th Connecticut, 89, 122, 123, 126, 265n; 28th Connecticut, 78, 110–11, 124; 29th Connecticut Colored, 5, 8, 135–36, 150, 169, 199; 30th Connecticut Colored, 5, 135–36, 150; 31st U.S. Colored Infantry, 150; 31st United States Colored Infantry, 135; 33rd Virginia, 58; 54th Massachusetts, 132, 133–34; 132nd Pennsylvania, 123; sending resolutions to state newspapers during 1863 election, 109–10; varied duties of and conditions for, 115–16

Reitemeyer, John R., 214
Relyea, William H., 84, 271n3
Republican Party: principal issues of (late 1850s), 38–40; rise of, 29, 32–33; state convention (1863), 107; success of, in 1858 election, 37–38

Republicans: amnesia of, regarding the war's causes, 106, 137; denying interest in black rights, 38–39; going to extremes to deny charge of abolitionism, 39–40; inconsistent views among, 156, 158; issues for, in 1864, 140; openly embracing an end to slavery, 156–58; planning for presidential election of 1860, 46; responding to *Dred Scott* decision, 39; responsibility of, for defeating black voting rights amendment, 187–88; taking control in Connecticut, 43; winning in 1864 elections, 143–44; worried about attacks after the 1864 election, 165

Ribicoff, Abraham, 214
Rice, John, 157
Richards, Leonard, 22–23
Richmond (VA), 79, 80, 88–89, 169
Ripley, James, 64
Roanoke Island (NC), 73
Roberts, W. W., 92
Robertson, James I., Jr., 215
Rogers, John E., 216
Root, David, 236n70
Rosecrans, William, 136
Rowe, Rodolphous, 199
Ruffin, Edwin, 78
Russell, Charles, 73

sacrifice, 7–8
Sailor's and Soldier's Memorial Arch (Hartford, CT), 177, 198, *200*, *201*, 207
Sanford, Oliver, 75, 145
Savage Arms Company (Savage Fire Arms), 64, 118
Schnabel, Ellis B., 246n58
Scott, Winfield, 65
secession, 7, 14n, 41, 47–49, 50, 54

secession flag, 55, 245n42

Secessionville, 76

Second American Party System, 17

Sedgewick, 215

segregation, 176, 213

semicentennial remembrances, 210–12, 218

sesquicentennial, importance of, 223

Seven Days Battles, 80

Seward, William H., 90, 106

Sexton, Henry, 63

Seymour, Origen S., 143

Seymour, Thomas H., 6, 7, 34, 43–45, 47, 55, 63, 93, 102–3, 107–8, 143, 217

Sharp's Rifle Company, 49, 64, 90, 118, 127

Shaw, Robert Gould, 133

Shenandoah Valley (VA), 80, 158–60

Sheppard, William L., 13

Sheridan, Philip, 158–59

Sherman, Thomas, 66

Sherman, William Tecumseh, 136, 150, 158, 161, 166

Shiloh (TN), 78

shipbuilders, 65

Sigel, Franz, 145

Silliman, Justus, 100, 129, 170–71, 268n95

Slave Power, 29, 32–33, 35–38, 93, 167

slavery: as cause of war, 93; avoiding discussion of, 4, 17–18, 22, 24; avoiding the politics of, 17–18; criticism of, as form of sectional politics, 15; end of, in Connecticut, 26; first post-Constitution conflict over, 15–16; growing animosity over the issue of, 18–21; Lincoln's speeches on, in Connecticut gubernatorial race, 44–45; malaise in thinking about, among Northerners, 69–70; outlawing of, after independence, 10; Republicans openly embracing

an end to, 156–58; settlements regarding, responses in Connecticut, 50–51; significance of, continuing to generate discussion, 221–22; U.S. government apologizing for, 221–22; westward expansion of, 3, 15–17

slaves: problems with, arising after attack on Fort Sumter, 68; treated as contraband, 68, 78–79, 94

Smith, Gerrit, 234n52

Smith, Truman, 35

soldiers: letters from, brought into 1863 election, 107–13; voting from the field, 165

soldiers' aid societies, 6, 90, 91, 102, 151, 220. *See also* Hartford Soldiers' Aid Society

soldier's heart, 208–10

Soldiers' Monument (Waterbury, CT), 198–99

South, commitment of, to slavery, 12

South Carolina, secession of, 41, 47–49

Southern nationalism, 174

Southern states, secession of, 49

Southern sympathizers, presence of, in Connecticut, 59–60

South Mountain (MD), 87–88

Southwest Ordinance, 12

Spencer rifles, 141

Spotsylvania (VA), 146

Sprague, Ellen M., 117

Stanley, Sidney, 151

Staples, Horace, 49

states' rights, 174

Stedman, Griffin A., 148, 199–201

Stevens, Alexander, 174

Stevens, Henry, 128–29

Stevens, James, 16

St. John's Bluff (FL), 77

Stone, G. W. Smith, 203

Stone, Henry, 81

Stowe, Harriett Beecher, 1, 33

Stratford (CT), monument in, 196

Stuart, Jeb, 80

substitutes, hiring of, for the draft, 130–32, 133, 142
Sumner, Charles, 29, 37–38, 69, 155, 185

Talcott, Samuel L., 92
Tallmadge, James, 15
Taney, Roger, 38, 103, 179
Terry, Alfred H., 53, 58, 62, 166
Terry, Harriet, 62
Texas, annexation of, 28, 29, 31, 33
textile industry, 13
Thames Bank (Norwich), 53
Thirteenth Amendment, 155, 166–68
Thomaston (CT), monument in, *197*
three-fifths clause, 12, 14–15
Tilden, Samuel, 213
Totten, Joseph, 74
Toucey, Isaac, 36, 63, 217
"Treasure of Virtue," 217
Treat, Amos, 243n26
Treaty of Guadalupe Hidalgo, 33
trench warfare, 124–25
troops: financing and payment of, 63; training of, 54
Troubled Commemoration: The American Civil War Centennial, 1961–1965 (Cook), 214
Trowbridge, Caleb, 210
Trumbull, Lyman, 45
Tuller, Isaac, 63
Twining, Alexander, 119
Tybee Island (GA), 75
Tyler, Daniel, 53, 57
Tyler, W. S., 146
typhoid fever, 78

Uncle Tom's Cabin (Stowe), 33
underground railroad, 1
Union: preservation of, as glorious cause, 93; sanctity of, 7
Union (CT), monument in, 199
units, 31st Colored Federal, 5
Upson, Andrew, 76
U.S. Constitution: protecting slavery, 12, 36, 103, 106; support of, 94; three-fifths clause, 14. *See also individual amendments*
U.S. Sanitary Commission, 90, 102
USS *Monitor*, 79

Van Buren, Martin, 28, 29, 30
Van Deursen, William, 133
Van Dusen, Albert E., 240–41n1
Vicksburg (MS), 80–81, 101, 123–24

Wade, Edward, 128
Wadhams, Jennie, 219–20
Wadhams, Martin, 63
Wainwright, Jonathon Mayhew, 18
Walkley, Stephen, 66, 67, 75, 268n95
war, memory of, 174
War Democrats, 93
War of 1812, 14
Warren, Robert Penn, 214, 216–17, 218
Washington, Augustus, 30–31
Washington (NC), 141
Washington, D.C., victorious Union Army marching through, 173
Waterbury (CT), monument in, 198–99, *202*, *203*
Watertown (CT), monument in, 196
Weatherby, Charles, 69–70
Webster, Noah, 24
Weed, Thurlow, 115
Weld, Charles, 198
Welles, Gideon, 3, 39, 96, 115
Wesleyan University, Memorial Chapel, 199
western theater, 67, 80–81. *See also individual battles in Western theatre*
West Hartford (CT), monument in, 199
westward expansion, battle over, 28–30
Whig Party, 29, 31–32, 34, 36, 37
White, Egbert, 215
white men, rights of, 93
Whitney, Eli, 13, 49
Wide Awakes, 45

Wilderness campaign, 146
William Muir arms company, 118–19
Wilmot, David, 30
Wilmot Proviso, 29, 30, 31
Wilson, Woodrow, 211
Windsor Locks (CT), memorial hall
   in, 199
Winsted (CT), monument in, 196, 199
Wolcott, Oliver, 16

Wolcott Congregational Church,
   234n52
women, role of, 6
Wood, Fernando, 45
Woolsey, Theodore D., 91
Wright, Dexter R., 134

Yale University, 50, 201–3
Yorktown (VA), 79

Garnet Books

Early Connecticut Silver, 1700–1840
  by Peter Bohan and
  Philip Hammerslough
  Introduction and Notes by
  Erin Eisenbarth

The Connecticut River:
A Photographic Journey through
the Heart of New England
  by Al Braden

Connecticut's Fife & Drum Tradition
  by James Clark

The Old Leather Man: Historical
Accounts of a Connecticut and
New York Legend
  by Daniel DeLuca

Dr. Mel's Connecticut Climate Book
  by Dr. Mel Goldstein

Westover School: Giving Girls
a Place of Their Own
  by Laurie Lisle

Crowbar Governor: The Life and
Times of Morgan Gardner Bulkeley
  by Kevin Murphy

Water for Hartford:
The Story of the Hartford Water
Works and the Metropolitan
District Commission
  by Kevin Murphy

Henry Austin: In Every Variety
of Architectural Style
  by James F. O'Gorman

Making Freedom: The Extraordinary
Life of Venture Smith
  by Chandler B. Saint and
  George Krimsky

Welcome to Wesleyan:
Campus Buildings
  by Leslie Starr

Connecticut in the American
Civil War: Slavery, Sacrifice,
and Survival
  by Matthew Warshauer

Stories in Stone: How Geology
Influenced Connecticut History
and Culture
  by Jelle Zeilinga de Boer

About the Author

Matthew Warshauer is a professor of history at Central Connecticut State University. He is the editor of the scholarly journal *Connecticut History* and the author of *Andrew Jackson and the Politics of Martial Law: Nationalism, Civil Liberties, and Partisanship* (2006) and *Andrew Jackson in Context* (2009). He is also the chairperson of the Connecticut Civil War Commemoration Committee, and co-chair of the Connecticut Civil War Commemoration Commission.

About The Driftless Connecticut Series

The Driftless Connecticut Series is a publication award program established in 2010 to recognize excellent books with a Connecticut focus or written by a Connecticut author. To be eligible, the book must have a Connecticut topic or setting or an author must have been born in Connecticut or have been a legal resident of Connecticut for at least three years.

The Driftless Connecticut Series is funded by the Beatrice Fox Auerbach Foundation Fund at the Hartford Foundation for Public Giving. For more information and a complete list of books in The Driftless Connecticut Series, please visit us online at http://www.wesleyan.edu/wespress/driftless.